THE EDITORIALS OF
HENRY WATTERSON

COMPILED WITH
AN INTRODUCTION AND NOTES

BY

ARTHUR KROCK

259

NEW YORK
GEORGE H. DORAN COMPANY

*With Respect and Affection, this Book is Dedicated
to the Gentle but Firm Wielder of the Only Blue
Pencil that Marse Henry Ever Suffered to Change
His "Copy":*

Mrs. REBECCA EWING WATTERSON

CONTENTS

PAGE

INTRODUCTION 13

EARLY WRITINGS
RECONSTRUCTION 17-19
THE SOUTH AT CHRISTMAS, 1868, 1869 19-26
THE FRANCO-PRUSSIAN WAR, A PREVIEW OF 1914 . 26-28
THE TREATY OF FRANKFORT 28-30

POLITICAL CAMPAIGNS, 1872-1916

1872:
THE GREELEY CAMPAIGN : THREE EDITORIALS . 33-41

1876:
GRANT SCANDALS : THE LAUNCHING OF TILDEN . 41-49
TIMEO OHIO 49-50
GREENBACKISM 50-53
THE PEACEFUL ARMY OF 100,000 53-56
"GRANT THE VOLUPTUARY" 56-57

1880:
AN ATTACK ON GARFIELD 57-59

1884:
FAREWELL TO TILDEN 59-62
"A TARIFF FOR REVENUE ONLY" 62-63

1888:
A POET IN POLITICS ; AND CIVIL SERVICE REFORM 63-69

1892:
"THROUGH A SLAUGHTER-HOUSE INTO AN OPEN
GRAVE"; THE ARGUMENT FOR CARLISLE VS.
CLEVELAND AND HILL 69-74

1896:
"NO COMPROMISE WITH DISHONOR"; THE LONG-
DISTANCE FIGHT AGAINST BRYAN 75-87

1900:
WITH BRYAN AGAIN 87-92

1904:

                                          PAGE

AGAINST BRYAN AGAIN 92-100
THE BATTLE FOR PARKER AND THE FIRST
FAINT OUTLINES OF THE MAN ON HORSE-
BACK 100-102

1908:

"A MESS OF POTTAGE AND A MAN OF STRAW" 103-108
"THE MONEY DEVIL," AND A NEW ESTIMATE
AND ENDORSEMENT OF BRYAN 108-118

1910-1912:

THE HOUSE VICTORY IN SIGHT 118-121
MARSE HENRY ACCEPTS WILSON AT BALTIMORE 121-123

1916:

A SKIRMISH IN THE INEVITABLE WAR WITH
THE KAISER; A SECOND FIGHT FOR WILSON 123-127
ON POLITICS IN GENERAL: THE EDITOR WRES-
TLES WITH SUGGESTIONS THAT HE RUN
FOR OFFICE AND DEAL IN PATRONAGE . 127-133

PERSONALITIES

ROOSEVELT:

THE VISION OF CASSANDRA, AND POSTSCRIP-
TUM WRITTEN FOUR YEARS LATER . . 137-147
THE COLONEL'S MANIFEST DESTINY . . . 147-154
THE BALLINGER CASE 155-160
THE THIRD TERM MENACE 160-161
THE ONE-MAN POWER 162-164
"HE WILL NEVER COME BACK" ⎫
ROOSEVELT AND OUR NEUTRALITY ⎬ . . . 164-170
IN FAVOR OF SENDING THE COLONEL AND HIS
DIVISION TO FRANCE 170-172

WILSON:

AN ACCOUNT OF THE INCIDENT AT THE MAN-
HATTAN CLUB 172-179
AFTER THE VICTORY IN 1912 179-183
A CALL IN 1918 TO STAND BY THE HEAD OF
THE REPUBLIC 183-186

LINCOLN:

TWO ESSAYS 186-206

CONTENTS

BLIND TOM: PAGE
   MR. WATTERSON ON MUSIC 207-209

BRYAN:
   THE INEVITABLE BREAK WITH WILSON FORE-
      SHADOWED 210-212
THE THACKERAY-DICKENS ARGUMENT:
   TWO BLOWS FOR THE AUTHOR OF "VANITY
     FAIR," AND WHY THE BOOK IS NOT IMMORAL 212-219
CARRIE NATION: HER DEATH 219
JEFFERSON DAVIS: THE LAST FLAP OF THE
   BLOODY SHIRT 219-223
ZACHARY TAYLOR: THEY NAME THE LOUISVILLE
   CAMP FOR HIM 223-225

PROFESSIONAL

THE FAMOUS BET WITH THE *World* THAT TAFT
   AND ROOSEVELT WOULD BREAK—VERY CONFI-
   DENT UNDER THE GOLDEN DOME—VICTORY
   FOR MARSE HENRY, BUT NO DINNER EVER
   EATEN 229-239
THE EDITOR INTERVIEWS HIMSELF 239-245
THE FORTIETH BIRTHDAY OF THE *Courier-
   Journal* 245-250
ON PERSONAL JOURNALISM 251-260
SOME ODD VIEWS ON NEWS CENSORSHIP IN WAR-
   TIME 260-263

ESSAYS AND TRAVELS

WHAT THE EDITOR THOUGHT ABOUT FOREIGN
   RELATIONS IN 1896: VENEZUELA, LEAGUES
   AND JINGOES; A MUZZLE FOR AMERICAN AM-
   BASSADORS 267-271
MEMORIES OF NAPOLEON AND JOSEPHINE AT
   MALMAISON 272-276
CAN CUBA GOVERN HERSELF? A 1909 ANXIETY . 276-282
GAMBLING AND REAL SPORT AT MONTE CARLO . 282-289

MISCELLANEOUS

A RESTRAINED PAEAN ON THE SPANISH WAR . 293-295
THE CANAL, THE FORTY THIEVES, THE HAY-
   PAUNCEFOTE TREATY AND PANAMAN MAT-
   TERS IN GENERAL: TWO ARTICLES . . . 296-304

LOOKING DOWN ON WALL STREET, STEEL-ETCH-
ING MR. MORGAN AND GLEEFULLY FOLLOWING
THE STANLEY INVESTIGATION : TWO ARTICLES   304-312
SOME POLITICAL ADVICE TO NEGROES   .   .   .   312-315
FOR CONFIRMING JUSTICE BRANDEIS   .   .   .   315-317
THE SEMI-CENTENNIAL OF GETTYSBURG   .   .   317-323
SEVERAL ARTICLES URGING THE ABANDONMENT
OF THE MONROE DOCTRINE TO IMPROVE
LATIN-AMERICAN RELATIONS AND TO AVOID
TROUBLE WITH EUROPE, 1913-1914   .   .   .   323-346
MARSE HENRY'S PROOF THAT MARLOWE WROTE
THE PLAYS OF SHAKESPEARE, HIS THOUSAND-
DOLLAR FEATURE STORY   346-358
WOMAN'S SUFFRAGE AND PROHIBITION, HIS
MAJOR TWENTIETH CENTURY THEMES, IN-
TRODUCING "CRAZY JANES, SILLY SALLIES
AND RED-NOSED ANGELS"   358-373

"WAR OF THE KAISERS"

"TO HELL WITH THE HOHENZOLLERNS AND THE
HAPSBURGS" UTTERED AND DEFENDED   .   .   377-378
IS CHRISTENDOM A CHRISTIAN, OR THE DEPRES-
SION OF THE WAR   379-387
THE LUSITANIA MURDERS, AND A PLAN TO PRE-
VENT SUCH ATROCITIES THEREAFTER : THREE
ARTICLES   387-401
THE TEUTONIC INSANITY AS PROVED BY THE
EXECUTION OF EDITH CAVELL   401-405
A LOVED THEME : THE IRISH IN BATTLE   .   .   .   405-409
"TO HELL WITH THEM" AGAIN, AND DOWN
WITH PEACE TALK, JANUARY, 1917   .   .   .   409-411
ON BRYAN AND PEACE, TWO DAYS BEFORE THE
WAR MESSAGE IN APRIL, 1917   412-415
CELEBRATING THE UNITED STATES' ENTRANCE
INTO WAR, THE EDITOR UNSUSPECTINGLY
WINS THE PULITZER PRIZE : TWO EDITORIALS   415-421
AGAINST NEGOTIATING WITH WILHELM OR THE
JUNKERS WHEN THEY SEEK PEACE   .   .   .   422-425
MARSE HENRY OBSERVES ARMISTICE DAY, 1918 .   425-426
THE LEAGUE OF NATIONS, BY THE EDITOR
EMERITUS   426-430
THE EDITOR EMERITUS RETIRES, 1919   .   .   .   430

THE EDITORIALS OF
HENRY WATTERSON

INTRODUCTION 259

It was as an editorial writer that Henry Watterson attracted and influenced three generations of Americans. As an orator and statesman he was famous, and as a conversationalist he was renowned. But that product of his which for over fifty years was poured into a newspaper column was his best work, and the most notable examples of that work are sought to be preserved in this volume.

Mr. Watterson did not believe that any editorial writing could be of interest many days after its publication. Its effectiveness arose from its currency and from its manner of presentation, he said. The first element dying practically at birth, the second could not preserve the life of the editorial. He knew, of course, that he was a perosnage; and many public triumphs had made him conscious that his editorial style captured the general admiration. He was aware that thousands of persons of literary discrimination had preserved certain of his writings. He had watched some of his phrases dart back and forth through the press until they became part of the American language. And yet he could not believe that any collection of newspaper writings could be invested with the strength of permanency.

"To the newspaper drudge," he once wrote in a discussion of personal journalism, "the futility of all newspaper writing must often edge its way into his tired fancy. The best of it seems so quickly swallowed by the ocean of currency, like waves upon the beach, each day succeeding the other to efface its existence. Words, words; even thoughts, thoughts, what does it matter?"

And yet he had not been a day in retirement, in 1919, before the American public began to refute his theory. From every part of the country persons of all ages and conditions began to inquire whether his editorials would be cast in permanent mold. Many of these interrogators recited lists of favorite writings; nearly all of them asserted that yellowing and crumbling newspaper clippings, bearing some words by Watterson, were their precious possessions. One correspondent had a copy of the newspaper from which first, as Athene from the head of Zeus, had sprung "the Star-eyed Goddess of Tariff Reform." Another had clipped and, confident of greatness, retained the first editorial the young publisher had scribbled in 1868 when he became one of the partners in the *Courier-Journal*.

He began to admit that he was "thinking of that book"; but about that time came a fresher occupation for his pen and

13

script for his purse in writing his reminiscences for the *Saturday Evening Post*. He had steadfastly rejected all suggestion of an autobiography, but I obtained for him a generous tender from the periodical for serial rights, and another from the George H. Doran Company for book rights, and he yielded. "My name's Crummy and I wants money," said he, drawing on the nursery rhymes of the forties, and promptly set to work on "Marse Henry, An Autobiography," which was published in 1919 and 1920.

Consequently the book of editorials languished. The difficulty lay in the labor. His secretary, G. E. Johnson, had kept a scrap-book dating from 1908, but for forty years preceding many of Mr. Watterson's most celebrated writings had been appearing daily. The editor had neither the inclination nor the physical strength to mine that Himalayan range of files; and the health of the faithful secretary was failing.

While the obstacle remained unsurmounted, Mr. Watterson died. This was towards the end of December, 1921. And then, emerging from the mass of personal and press tributes to his memory, there reappeared the wraith of the request of 1919 for a collection of the newspaper writings of the most famous of American editors. Since that time the request has become insistent. The result is this volume.

As Washington correspondent, managing editor and general news and editorial manager of the *Courier-Journal*, I had worked under Mr. Watterson's eye and enjoyed his kindliest favor. In many places and various atmospheres I had been his fascinated companion. He had expressed the wish that I be his "literary executor." The death of his secretary had removed the person most competent to perform this part of that task, and so it appears under my hand. The complete files of the *Courier-Journal* as well as a mass of the editor's papers, have been carefully read, and the selections have been made on these bases: the effect of the editorial on its objective; the individuality of its style; the historical importance of its topic; and its literary quality. All needed verification has been made, and the writings hereafter published are all from Mr. Watterson's pen.

In the great mass of newspaper writing, many an editor is praised or blamed for the work of a subordinate. During his long career, Mr. Watterson wrote actually millions of editorial words, and his associates wrote several times that many. But what follows is clearly marked as his own. All doubtful articles were rejected. The bulk of the labor of going through the files was performed with fidelity and intelligence by the compiler's secretary, Miss M. N. Dumas, and without her efforts this book could not have appeared.

The reader will find revivified in these writings the events of a half century of world history. He will see occasions restored; he will behold the conflict and hear the din of political campaigns that once divided the nation. The memory of forgotten wars will return to him, and at the brilliant touch of a dead hand the heroes of three generations will walk in procession before him. It is fifty years in mortmain.

The man who wrote them has been called the last of the great editorial writers. He knew the emptiness of such a statement. There will be no Deucalion of that race until newspapers have ceased to exist. More accurately, Mr. Watterson was the last of the great editors, for the reason that he was the last of those editors who wrote with the power of ownership. A hired journalism, however zealous, however loyal, however entrusted, however brilliant, cannot be great because it speaks through the mist of subordination. Mr. Watterson had substantial ownership in the *Courier-Journal*. By a delegation of authority he was the arbiter of the editorial policy and of the news initiative. While he often consulted with his associate, Mr. Haldeman, and after his death with Mr. Haldeman's sons, the responsibility rested with him. In the many instances on a newspaper when quick decision must be reached, Mr. Watterson shaped his course with utter confidence that his associates would approve and stand behind him. That strengthened his wrist and energized his pen. From that fortunate circumstance came much of his effectiveness and renown. Even history and geography favored him: for Louisville lay on the border and his service began in the period of reconstruction.

The time will not soon come again when a man of Mr. Watterson's newspaper talent and editorial genius will find himself in so ideal a situation. But when it does, there will be another great editor.

Throughout these articles there runs a rhythmic quality of diction which explains much of this journalist's hold upon his audience. In his youth he had been carefully educated as a pianist, but poor eyesight and an injured hand had closed that career for him. The measures pent up in his finger-tips somehow escaped into his writing, and, especially when he was composing in an invocational strain, his paragraphs become strophes and his sentences scan. From this harmonic impulse came many of the phrases with which he sublimated public issues; and his oratorical gift was intimately associated with his musical feeling. Voltaire would have disdained, as Macaulay would have admired, the Watterson style; but, whatever its place in literature, it wrought greatly with a nation.

A. K.

Note of Explanation

In all the articles which follow, Mr. Watterson's methods of capitalization and punctuation have been retained by the compiler.

EARLY WRITINGS

EARLY WRITINGS

RECONSTRUCTION

When the *Courier-Journal* began its life, the South was in the grasp of Northern troops and carpetbaggers. In Mr. Watterson's opinion, the first obstacles to a successful re-Union were these, and he set out along two courses to dispose of them. One was a systematic effort to bring the Southern people to a true appreciation of the greatness and benevolence of Abraham Lincoln and an understanding of the miseries wrought upon the South by his murder; and all of his writings, from 1868 forward, were full of Lincolniana. The other course was to convince the Government at Washington that the South should be released from military rule, and he pounded away on this point until, in 1877, after the Tilden-Hayes decision, the troops were recalled. Then the South disposed of its own carpet-bagger and negro legislator problems.

Of the carpetbagger, who is the subject of the following editorial, published November 9, 1868, when the *Courier-Journal* was one day old, Mr. Watterson wrote:

"His interest, if he gets an office by aid of the military or the machinery of reconstruction, is to keep up the idea for the necessity of reconstruction, and the necessity for troops in order to keep his office. He therefore . . . makes himself as odious to the native population as possible. . . . The more kicks he gets, the higher he will bounce."

Later in his editorial career, Mr. Watterson polished his phrases longer, but he at this period was writing in haste and at a high temperature. Hence the bumpy construction. The editorial, complete, follows:

Carpet-Baggery and Peace

(November 9, 1868)

What the South wants above all things is just what General Grant says let us have, and that is peace. But there is often a very great disparity between the desires of one party and the expressions of another party, though the expressions be never so

17

strong in the same direction as the desires. In order to get at the truth we must look a little into motives. The surface of things is but too seldom genuine. Trace a man to the den of his interest and you have him. Track an idea up to the fountain head of policy and you have it. Thus Grant, who enters the Executive office with almost dictatorial powers, may cry out, "Let us have peace" and the disasters of the South, which are well-nigh heart-breaking, may cry out "Let us have peace," and yet we may have no peace.

When we say we may have no peace, we do not mean to say we may have war. Not at all. On the contrary, we think there is less likelihood of a war on this continent now than there has been. But there is a state which is not a state of war that is not a state of peace. It is a sort of purgatorial camping ground which lies between the two conditions, partaking of the suspense of the one, and the lassitude of the other. Such is the situation at the South. Carpet-baggery has taken possession of the country, and carpet-baggery is an unmitigated curse and swindle. The Northern people ought to be ashamed of it. The Republican party ought to blush for it. Reputable newspapers everywhere should expose it. The Radicals call it liberty, and, indeed, it may be a new-fashioned sort of liberty. But it has a marvelous likeness to the old-fashioned sort of pillage which was represented by the Goths and Vandals and other classic carpet-baggers who figure in polite and barbaric literature.

General Grant says "Let us have peace." The necessities of the South say "Let us have peace." Why should we not have peace?

The answer is simple. In order that a roving class may prey on a stable people, the Republican party has deprived the whole South of its liberties. The foundations of society are reversed. Power is taken out of the hands of the responsible by force and lodged in the hands of the irresponsible. It is not the interest of the rulers thus fabricated to administer the government justly. It is to their interest to administer it unjustly. Their tenure rests on force. This force relies upon the presumption of a perturbed and dangerous condition of society. Remove the supposition and the plea for force falls to the ground. Remove the force and the carpet-bagger has nothing else to stand on. He is without means or merit. He is merely a strolling statesman and patriot who goes about with his pack of loyalty strapped to his back like a peddler, only he has nothing to sell and expects to fill and not to empty his pack. His interest, if he gets an office by aid of the military or the machinery of reconstruction, is to keep up the idea for the necessity of reconstruction and the necessity for troops in order to keep his office. He, therefore, uses only harsh language, engages in the manufacture of harsh laws, and strives to make himself as odious to the native population as possible. He wants to aggravate them. He wants them to kick him. He has taken the chances and risks of fortune through a course of self-abasement, and the more kicks he gets, like a football, the higher he will bounce.

There can be no peace as long as the carpet-bagger reigns in Dixie. There can be no peace as long as the North allows itself to look on the South either as a quasi-belligerent, or as a conquered province. That is not the road to peace. There must be a mutual spirit of forgiveness. There must be a reciprocal spirit of charity. Government is intended to bless and not to injure mankind. Republican government is designed to be liberal and tolerant, resting on the consent of the governed. The Union professes to be equal. The people claim to be just. Alas, for the pretensions of us all! Are we just to each other? Are we reasonable in our practice? We do not differ in our theory. Grant says, "Let us have peace." The North echoes, "Let us have peace." The South, from the depths of its distress, cries out "Let us have peace."

"Words, words, words."

There is nothing tangible in all this. It does not mean business. It does not mean peace. The way to peace is through justice. The first step to justice is toleration. The question ought not to be a party question. It is higher than that. It is deeper. It is purer. It is nobler. It is dearer. It is a question of social existence. The carpet-bagger is a nuisance. Carpet-baggery is a swindle. If General Grant really means what he says, let him abolish both, and, if his party be sincere, let it confirm his act. The people of the South ought to have their hands untied. The military ought to be withdrawn from every state. The Freedmen's Bureau ought to be split up for Christmas fires. Then we should have peace and Union sure enough.

THE SOUTH AT CHRISTMAS

1868 and 1869

In this essay on the state of the Southern people at Christmas, 1869, the young editor's evident purpose was to assuage the pangs of war recollection, to plead the Southern cause and to set his readers to reflecting upon the blessings which would return to them. It is interesting, further, to those who, noting the moist and warm winters along the Mason and Dixon

line during the last few years, contend that the old-fashioned
season of snow and ice used to be annually recurrent in the
Ohio Valley.

This Christmas essay, joined to a discussion of the state
of public affairs, is companion to a second Christmas
editorial which follows it. The date of the second was 1869,
and in that article Mr. Watterson's aim was solely literary.
As an example of the Victorian journalistic style, once so
popular and now discarded, it has many points of interest:

Kentucky

(December 25, 1868)

A little after mid-day on the 25th of December, 1778, a group
of ten or a dozen pioneers in buckskin knee-breeches and linsey-
woolsey hunting-shirts gathered around a log heap in front of
a cabin, which, from a high cliff, overlooked the frozen bed and
snowy banks of the Kentucky River. It was very bleak and cold.
The sun had not shone out since the second day of the month.
The streams were everywhere choked with ice. The very springs
were inaccessible, and game was scarce and powder scarcer still.
Foremost among the little knot of woodsmen were Daniel Boone
and James Harrod; and they had met, as they declared, to offer up
their prayers to God on behalf of the "brave men and patriots"
who were "fighting the battles of freedom beyond the mountains." They knelt down and prayed accordingly; they sang a
hymn; they adopted what they called a resolution; and then, having affirmed devotion to the cause of the colonies against the
Crown, they dispersed, each going his several ways, but all inspired by the same good purpose and free-born spirit.

In those days there were negro slaves in Massachusetts. There
were none in Kentucky. But the laws of commerce and of climate
had their way. The Massachusetts slaveholders found that negro
labor was not profitable among them. They, therefore, sold
their slaves into the South and invested the money in that which
was profitable. No one blames them. They did what they thought
was best and what they had undoubted right to do. The times
were not so "civilized" nor so "progressive" as they have since
become. Doubtless if Massachusetts had the matter to reconsider
and go over again, she would free all of her slaves, vote each
family a homestead, build for each a snug cottage and, having
comfortably stowed the poor dears away in cosy homes, kindle for
each a blazing fire, put a kettle on it and thrust into the kettle a
Christmas turkey, amid whose steaming odors the songs of
Whittier and of freedom would ascend to heaven!

Time sped on. There was a deal of trouble for many and
many a year; and wars with the savages; and wars with Britain;
and wars with Mexico, and tariff wars and what not. But the
country went on growing and prospering until it was so big and
prosperous that it forgot its early vows and its early struggles
and its early lessons. More's the pity! It forgot them all, and
it fell together by the ears and no man can say that it did not
demonstrate to the full its boasted fighting capacity. Somebody,
however, had to get the better of the shindy; and the muscle and
the numbers were with the North, and the North came out winner.
It won not only the practical item which it contended for, but in
the scuffle it got several trifles which it had not at first expected;
so that, the arms of the combatants being laid aside, the spectacle
that was presented to the world was curious to see—slavery
gone; secession abandoned; the Union in condition for immediate restoration; and peace hovering, like a goddess crowned
with olive-leaves, about the threshold of every home in the
land.

We do not propose to review what followed. Kentucky was
not one of the seceding States. She stood true to the principles which were enunciated in those memorable resolutions at
which it is common to hear men sneer. Whatever may be said
of those resolutions, they embody a just and true spirit, and mean
nothing which is base, or sordid, or narrow, or slavish, or mean.
Kentucky's head was with the Union and her heart was with the
South; for it is the nature of a generous and manly people to
sympathize with the weak in its struggles with the strong. The
war closed. Kentucky alone of the free States that were left
in the Union was true to herself and to the professions with which
the war was begun. She proscribed no one. She gave welcome
to all. Today she is prosperous, peaceful, happy. The laws are
better enforced in Kentucky than in Indiana. There is less crime
in Kentucky than in Ohio. Tennessee is poor. Missouri is poor.
Both are the victims of despotic power running roughshod over
the liberties and disregarding the private rights of the people. In
Kentucky there is no partisan militia. In Kentucky there are
no franchise laws. In Kentucky there are no threats of confisca-
tion. Public opinion is the only arbiter of public questions, and
every man is allowed to hold office who obtains votes enough.
As in Massachusetts, public opinion is very much one way. There
the people are Republicans for the most part; vote the Republican ticket; decline to vote for Democratic candidates or Democratic measures and are, we dare say, conscientious. Here it
is exactly reversed. We are, for the most part, Democrats; we
vote the Democratic ticket; we decline to vote for Republican
candidates and measures; we are perfectly honest and think we

have a right, as free citizens of a free republic, to decide for ourselves.

For so doing and so thinking we are denounced as traitors to our country and a despotism is sought to be placed over us by those who claim that we ought to be forced to vote for Republican candidates and Republican measures, and who declare that if we do not, we are guilty of rebellion and should be punished therefor.

This was not the spirit of Boone and his companions, who prayed God to bless Massachusetts on Christmas day, 1778. It was not the spirit of the Kentuckians who fought the battles of the country from King's Mountain to the City of Mexico. It is a new-born spirit; the spirit of rapine and war, not of liberty and peace. That the people of Kentucky should regard it with detestation is reasonable and natural. That they should cling the more tenaciously to their original fastening as the pressure from without becomes more violent is also reasonable and natural. But they are not intolerant nor inhospitable, but kind, generous, peaceful, enterprising, progressive; faithful to the past; liberal with the present; hopeful of the future. The snows of nearly a hundred years have come and gone since the Christmas of 1778. Many a change has come also over the land. The canebrakes are all gone. The old pioneers are all gone. Their graves are deep-sunken under the ploughshare, and are hid beneath the clover blooms. But the hardy manhood; the warm, impulsive love of freedom; the honest hatred of persecution; the keen sympathy with the weak and suffering, all these noble sentiments that honored the lives of the fathers remain and are illustrated by the children in the unanimity with which they resist the despotism set up over their brothers at the South. Remove this despotism, and we may divide on a thousand issues; but as long as it continues we are one in opposing it as unnecessary, tyrannical, and cruel.

A Gush of Christmas

(December 25, 1869)

Aside from the touching contrasts which it places most palpably before the sense of the great mass of human beings who live and eat turkey in civilized countries and answer to catechisms and worship one ever-living God, the Christmas period—the one, sole universal holiday which is recognized among Christian people —furnishes a suitable as well as beautiful occasion for reviewing our past actions and overlooking the conduct of our friends, neighbors and enemies, in a not uncharitable spirit of serious, reflective criticism. It is impossible to be very harsh of heart as we sit

before the glowing Christmas fire or moralize beneath the happy
shadows of the flaming Christmas tree. The seasonable cold
without and the comfortable warmth within, joined to that blessed
spiritual communion that makes the whole world kin for a day
at least, impress the hardest natures, and light and chasten millions of faces that are not wont to be kind or genial. Albeit
most of us are given to gushing at Christmas, let us hope and
believe that the gush is honest, and, be it never so transitory, that
it will surely come again next Christmas, and all our lives, as
regularly as the twenty-fifth of December. So, we may be proud
of it as an heirloom in the family, which we array just once in
a year.

None of us, in truth, no, not the least of us, can look back
and be very proud of all we have said and done the last twelve
months; the little peccadillos and the large neglects, which speckle
and spot the blotter of our lives; the unworthy thoughts and hasty
words we cannot forget, but would give worlds to recall; the
petty sins and weaknesses to which human affections and earthly
vanities are exposed. But, bless God, we may each of us promise to amend, and, if the performance go not a foot's length
beyond, we are, at any rate, none the worse for it.

We often hear it said that sentiment is nothing more than a
species of maudlin self-flattery; but be sure this is a cynical view
of it. Whenever we sentimentalize we plow up the moral soil
within us. We may, indeed, plant no seed there. What then?
The soil is still soft and warm, and ready to bear good fruit, if
we will only sow and reap as God gives us grace and knowledge
to do. And so, commending self-inspection at all times which
are favorable—such as dozing under a sleepy sermon or dreaming
to orchestral or other satisfying music—the admonition comes
with special fitness at Christmas, when nature and tradition join
hands in mysterious benediction over the elements, and the ever-
green wreaths and whitening blossoms crown the kindest and
best-loved, most familiar household saint.

What if the good wife at the fireside permits her sentimental
memories to run away with that matronly discretion which bids
her fancies stay at home and look after the children—why, bless
you!—she will have her little romance—to be sure—and haven't
you had yours? On this point men are all brutes; and they refuse
to suffer the intrusion of the thought, much less the image of, as
Mr. Toodles has it, "that other man," or—in better Congressional
phrase—"my honorable predecessor." Of course we, in our short-
hair and divinity, have nothing on our conscience—oh, no! It
has been all work and scarce any play with us. We occupy
the great arm-chair at the edge of the rug—young ones noisy
around about us—a kind soul, busy and weary with making every-

body comfortable except herself—and we see no faces in the fire
—no shadows come down to us in little fairy boats that ride upon
the waves of tobacco smoke—no voices sing in the kettle and
call out of the flames—and it isn't a striped frock and a summer
evening under greenwood trees, and eyes—(Madame's, there, are
black, you see)—eyes that were as blue as—No, oh, no. The men
are so matter-of-fact. Reminiscences of this nature belong exclusively to women and story books; and he who has made his
fortune in pork and grain does not turn back into the lanes nor
wander in imagination along the brooks from which all his money
—in the original leaf and suckling—sprang; not he! But, if
he should? Ah, that is quite different indeed, and perhaps it
would not make him very much the worse—ha? There's a deal
of what we call sentiment, and sneer at, in this wicked, cross old
world of ours, and hot whisky has an uncommon tendency to draw
it out, as a corkscrew draws out the aroma of the liquor, from
the most unpromising jug. Given a corner in winter, a tumbler
of punch, a blazing heap of coals or faggots, and there is no knowing where a man's—a very selfish, cold, morose, literal man's—
reflections will lead him, nor how much of the shell of worldliness,
of wisdom, of glum cynicism, will open, disclosing the human
kernel within—decayed perhaps, but easily reached and touched
—not thoroughly rotten for God's uses. There was probably never
a romantic situation—never a romantic passion—never a romantic
episode "told in story or done in rhyme" which had not its exact
counterpart in actual life. The power of the novelist is this. We
know that history is a great falsehood. But we read in fiction
every day that which has arisen in our hearts or come within
the circle of our observance; so that, in spite of masculine disdain, the novel is a part of our existence. The good man smokes
his pipe. The good wife stirs about the house like a ladle in a
bowl of frothing egg-nogg. Down come the shadows. Silently
the flakes choke up the crevices. And there is never a roof which
does not shelter some little drama, more or less tragic or pathetic,
if we could but know it; if the dusky mists would open and blab
—as they some day will—their secrets, and when perchance it
may be said of all the couples on earth, as was said of David and
of Jonathan, "in death they were not divided." Wherefore it is
wisdom to look to these winter fancies and Christmas sentimen-
talisms as well as to material things, such as turkey and cham-
pagne. The very bird that hops on the window-sill may be a
sprite or goblin. The very cricket on the hearth may be a ghost.
But they are not dangerous. Not at all. You may stake your
life on it, their presence makes no one the harder or colder. It
is when they cease to visit us that we need be most afraid. The
poet did not mean to give out a sad or maudlin idea, but a truth

drawn from the heart of the truest and purest nature, when he wrote—

> 'Tis better to have loved and lost
> Than never to have loved at all.

Albeit there are wags, sturdy and jovial and full of Christmas beer and things, who will declare it to be better to have loved and lost a great many times over, as doubtless they believe from their personal experience, and will stand by it to the end of their days.

Be these things as they may, here is a blessing to Christmas and to all who enjoy it and celebrate it in the spirit of the gentle, kindly and peaceful teachings of Christ! Bless it for what it is, and for what it brings to us! Bless it as a poem and bless it as a reality! Bless it for its many-colored, happy suggestions, for its olden associations, for the dear, the loved, the chastening, and the softening memories which it summons out of a world that is bygone only for a season, and will come again as certainly and as blessedly as this blessed season, its spiritual *avant courier!* Through the glow which spreads over our inner life as we look out upon the day and the objects it discloses; as we look into ways that have been; as we look into faces that were; as we see hands stretched to us from shadowy depths, and feel strong grasps of love and tenderness meet our own, and kisses, pure and trusting, fall upon our lips, the tears may come indeed and blind us.

> The walks we have ta'en without tiring,
> The songs that together we've sung,
> The jest to whose ruddy inspiring,
> Our mingling of laughter hath rung,
> E'en trifles like these become precious,
> Embalm'd in the mem'ry of years,
> And the smiles and the joys so remembered,
> How often they waken our tears.

But they are happy, ennobling, purifying tears, and bless Christmas for them with all its other blessings! Bless it to our homes and firesides and little ones! Bless it to the poor, and to the sorrowing, to the halt, the lame and the blind! And as we bless it for the pictures it brings us of those things that are passed away, so shall we bless it for those things which it promises us, for stores of future wealth and plenty. The heart re-opens. The desires of life regerminate. Out of the fallows which time plows up within us, out of the seams and scars of afflictions suffered and wretchedness nobly borne, spring up fresh violets. Bless God for them and Christmas, which is their ministering angel; and as we gather close about the chimney, we shall none of us forget to bless the good Saint Nicholas, to whom be thanks and praises and blessings, so long as there is a peg in the mantel-board and a stocking to be hung, so long as there are little hearts to be glad and to glorify the morning that glorifies the Christmas year!

THE FRANCO-PRUSSIAN WAR

A Preview of 1914

While the common newspaper comment in the United States touching Prussia's defeat of France in 1870 ascribed ambitions for European ascendency to Bismarck's government, Mr. Watterson, when he wrote the following editorial in September, 1870, saw a little farther than the most of his colleagues. This sentence seems unusually prescient: "Prussia, which is now the leading power in Europe, may reasonably be suspected of all ambition which belongs to recent and sudden elevation in the scale of nations." His citation of Napoleon's mock claim to England by France "as an island off our coast," in derision of the German claim to Alsace, represents an attitude which the editor maintained all his life and which stirred him to the cause of the Allies in 1914.

And in a second editorial on the Franco-Prussian Treaty of Frankfort, which he wrote in June, 1871, he went deeper into the probabilities so thoroughly realized in our own generation. "The ransom demanded by a triumphant highwayman from his fettered captive," said Mr. Watterson of the Treaty of Frankfort, and concluded: "This treaty will only serve to increase the hatred existing between the two nations. Henceforth it will be the mission, the sole purpose, of France, to take revenge for her humiliation."

The Peace Prospect

(September 20, 1870)

Louis Napoleon, late Emperor of the French, stowed snugly away in a German inland village and the Prussian troops before the walls of Paris, Count Bismarck grants—"grants" is the word —"an interview to Jules Favre." This may imply, we hope it does imply, peace, as it certainly implies a wonderful political revolution, and in considering the outlook we must consider the diplomatic antecedents no less than the relations of the powers immediately and indirectly involved.

Prussia, which is now the leading power in Europe, may reasonably be suspected of all ambition which belongs to recent and sudden elevation in the scale of nations. A hundred years ago it was hardly recognized among Christian communities; was distant, isolated. This distant isolation has had its influence on the character of the people and on the policy of the government. The diplomatic system of Europe was formed on the traditions of the old empire, which was a central power for enforcing its obligations on the several communities which were ruled by the sceptre of Charlemagne. Austria and France have always professed a respect for treaties and a desire to be ruled by the old traditions of diplomacy. They have both, indeed, sought good repute as professing to be the powers that, wielding the remaining influence of the great empire, have to enforce conformity to the rules of diplomacy on the part of smaller powers. There were three competitors for the empire—Austria, France and Spain. Spain dropped from the list, and Austria gained the prize, not so much because she was the most powerful as because she was the least dangerous competitor. Still France, though unsuccessful in gaining the empire, preserved a decorous respect for the rules of diplomacy which it was the duty of the empire to enforce. She may have done so as a clergyman who is looking out for a bishopric, or a lawyer ambitious of a seat on the bench, assumes dignity and decorum. The reign of Napoleon was an exception to everything; but if we watch the form taken by the permanent expansion of France, we shall see that no other State enlarged itself in a more legitimate, feudal and diplomatic shape—by the lapse of fiefs and intermarriages. Its two great conquering monarchs, Louis XIV and Napoleon, did nothing for French aggrandizement. The Bourbon king made but a trifling perceptible addition to the French territory, and the other made none. Prussia, on the other hand, has taken whatever she could take and keep. Her policy has ever been that attributed to Rob Roy by Wordsworth. Hence Prussia, and at the same time Russia, have by their neighbors been called the robber powers of Europe. Prussia went into the present war to overthrow Napoleon. Now the representative of a new popular government succeeds in obtaining only an informal meeting; and assurances are reiterated that Count Bismarck will only treat on terms which imply conquest and secure reprisal. He must have Alsace at least, *because it is German*, "because," as he says, "Alsace naturally belongs to Germany." This seems to all plain and honest dealing to be the merest pretext.

The arguments about what naturally belongs to a State were thoroughly put in caricature by Napoleon, when he said that Britain naturally belonged to France. What was she? "Merely an island off the French coast." People are talking of Prussia naturally annexing Alsace because the people there speak German. That territory did once belong to Germany, yet it happened that to no part of its territories has the French Government enjoyed a better title. It was an appendage of the House of Hapsburg, inconveniently distant from their other domains, and at the treaty of Munster, in 1648, they sold it to France for three millions of livres, cash down. At all events, if France is to lose Alsace, Prussia has no other title to hold that territory but the title of conquest. From any other source she would have as good a claim on the English principality of Wales or the British Channel Islands. And yet, tracing back the policy of Prussia a century, no one can doubt the end of the negotiations, if they are really begun, and as the other European powers seem disposed to hold off, Bismarck may do as he sees fit and demand almost all he wants.

The Humiliating Treaty

(June 8, 1871)

The official document of the treaty concluded at Frankfort by the German and French Peace Commissioners shows that this agreement between the two countries—if we can so call a treaty forced upon one of the contracting parties by the might of the other—is even more unfavorable for France than we had supposed it would be from the information transmitted to us by the Atlantic cable. It is a startling illustration of the fact of how mere brutal force still prevails over humanity and justice. At no time during the whole history of France has such a humiliating treaty been imposed upon her people—humiliating, not only in its chief conditions and stipulations, but also in its minor details and in the phraseology in which the different articles have been framed. It is not the contract of two nations willing to put an end to bloody strife and to settle their differences in an amicable manner, but the haughty statement of terms imposed by a proud conqueror upon a conquered and helpless foe—the ransom demanded by a triumphant highwayman from his fettered captive.

The stipulations of the peace preliminaries have not only not been moderated, but they have been made harsher. The time given to the French to raise the money demanded by the Germans has been decreased, and the money has to be paid all in gold or in the best bank notes of Europe. The first five hundred millions of francs must be paid in thirty days after the ratification of the treaty of peace and the establishment of order in Paris; another thousand millions during the course of the year, and another installment of five hundred millions on the first of May, 1872. The three remaining milliards will have to be paid with interest at five percent.

on the 2d of May, 1874. This arrangement gives the French but three years in which to raise the money, instead of five.

Nor do the Germans, as had been agreed upon, propose to evacuate the Parisian forts and the surrounding departments after the first five hundred thousand francs of the indemnity have been paid. All those parts of the peace preliminaries which fixed a certain line of demarkation for the German troops in France have been wiped out of the treaty, and in their stead there has been inserted an article which places it entirely at the discretion of the German Government to occupy France as long as it pleases. During those three years an immense German army will remain in France at the expense of the French Government, and if the sums which that government has agreed to furnish for its support are not promptly paid in, the German Government has the right to levy taxes, not only in the occupied districts of France, but in all other parts of that country. In order to carry out the monstrous privilege given to them by this outrageous article, the Germans must necessarily have possession of all France, and complete control of all its civil institutions.

The cable that brought us the news that Jules Favre had stoutly declined to conclude a treaty of commerce between France and Germany stated that the immense sums required by France for the next few years would compel them to raise money by high tariff rates. This sounds well enough, but the treaty itself tells a widely different tale. It is true no treaty of commerce was concluded between the two nations, but instead of it a provision was included in the treaty which insures to the Germans the same commercial privileges in France as to the inhabitants of the larger countries of Europe which are most favored in this regard by France, that is to say, England, Russia, Austria, Belgium, the Netherlands and Switzerland. This is as advantageous to Germany as a treaty would have been. But it is not all, for during the next six months all the products of Alsatia and Lorraine are allowed to enter France duty free, but no reciprocal concession is made to France.

Bismarck had good reason to be satisfied, and he hardly did justice to the matter when in the sarcastic speech in which he announced the treaty to the German Reichsrath, he remarked that Germany could not have decently asked more from France. It is hard to imagine how Frenchmen could force themselves to sign such a document, but the explanation which the German Chancellor gives of the manner in which he forced the French commissioners to sign the humiliating treaty goes far in throwing light on his peculiar diplomacy. "If we had not arrived at this arrangement," he said, "the German army would have occupied Paris, either by coming to an understanding with the Commune or by using force." This implies that Bismarck had doubtless secretly negotiated with the rebels of Paris, and thus by intimidations obtained the submission of the regular government of Versailles to the humiliating treaty. If this should prove true, it would add another and still heavier guilt to the terrible list of crimes committed by the Paris Commune.

This treaty of peace will only serve to increase the hatred existing between the two nations. Henceforth it will be the mission, the sole purpose, of France, to take revenge for her humiliation.

POLITICAL CAMPAIGNS, 1872-1916

POLITICAL CAMPAIGNS, 1872-1916

THE SECOND ELECTION OF GRANT

1872

The young editor's first adventures .n national politics were in the campaign of 1872. In his autobiography he has given a great deal of space to the narration of how, with Halstead, Bowles and Horace White, he formed the "Quadrilateral" of journalists at the Liberal Republican convention of that year in Cincinnati with the hope of nominating a Northern man other than Horace Greeley, Mr. Watterson's purpose being to urge the Democrats then to endorse the Liberal Republican candidate and thereby "get the South out of irons" if their candidate won. The plan went through with the exception that Greeley, instead of Trumbull or Adams, was the Cincinnati nominee.

The three editorials which follow were written in the period between the nomination of Greeley, at Cincinnati, and the election of Grant. The first article is a double argument: part one, addressed to the South from a standpoint of sectional interest; and part two, addressed to the Democratic party at large from a standpoint of party interest. The second editorial as a contemporary study of Greeley has unusual value; and in the third article Mr. Watterson, impatient with Southerners like Toombs, of Georgia, who opposed supporting any Republican for any purpose, first reveals, so far as this volume is concerned, his dashing ability to carry the war to the enemy.

What Ought the Democracy to Do?

(May 17, 1872)

The New York *World* asks that somebody will tell it "what the Democratic party will gain, besides a share of the Federal offices, by indorsing Mr. Greeley?" The task is not a difficult one. Like the *World* we expect to abide by the decision of the Democracy at Baltimore, arrived at after full consultation, and

33

with all the lights before them. That decision we are quite sure will be to support the nominee of the Cincinnati Convention. In the meantime, as a free interchange of views and opinions among Democrats is eminently proper, we take pleasure in giving our New York contemporary the coveted information.

Should Horace Greeley be elected President of the United States by the co-operation of the Democracy, we shall have an honest and faithful administration. That will be a great gain alike to the Democratic party and the country. Nobody doubts Greeley's honesty; nobody believes that he would deliberately countenance or connive at official rascalities of any kind. With his inauguration nepotism would come to an end. He has no worthless relatives to place in fat offices, and, if he had a thousand, it would be all the same. In his appointments he would select men whom he believed qualified. It is not to be denied that Mr. Greeley is sometimes a little too credulous, and it may be that now and then he would be imposed on by designing people. But if that should occur nothing is more certain than that the culprit would have to walk the plank the moment any irregularity came to light. Under an administration with Horace Greeley at its head there would be no Leets and Stockings extorting money from the people months after the exposure of their crimes; no custom-house vampires like Casey retained up to the very eve of another Presidential election; no notoriously infamous persons like Consul-General Butler suffered to go on unmolested, dishonoring and degrading the American name abroad. With Greeley as President we should have no Seneca sandstone jobs, no Santo Domingo speculations, no Government officials enriching themselves and their families at the public expense. With all his eccentricities and imperfections we should have a Chief Magistrate who would attend to his duties—a Chief Magistrate that would spend his summers at Washington instead of at Long Branch, and whose attention would not be occupied, to the neglect of public business, with bull pups and fast horses, Partagas cigars and old Bourbon.

From the election of Mr. Greeley universal amnesty would result, for with that event a most salutary change in the constitution of Congress would necessarily take place. That would surely be a gain to the Democratic party and the country. The *World,* we are sorry to see, underrates the importance of this measure. If it were better acquainted with Southern affairs we are persuaded it would not talk so flippantly as it does of "the few elderly men at the South that are alone to be benefited by amnesty." Seven years have passed since the war terminated, and peace has not yet been restored to the South. The obvious reason is that Grant and his partisans, in the language of the Cincinnati platform, "keep alive the passions and resentments of the late civil war, that they may use them for their private ends." Universal amnesty is a necessity for the pacification of the section and the restoration of prosperity at the South. Will it be no gain if the nominee of the Cincinnati Convention, standing on the Cincinnati platform, succeeds over Grant, with his proscription, his Ku Klux laws, his suspension of the writ of habeas corpus, and his carpet-bag policy? No one can question that Greeley, if elected, would adhere faithfully to the principles enunciated at Cincinnati. Whatever his former views, he was honest in them, and he is sincere and earnest now. He will not go back on his present principles.

The election of Greeley over Grant would gain for the Democratic party, because it would gain for the country, reform in the civil service.

The election of Greeley over Grant would establish the supremacy of civil authority, and the country would no longer be cursed by the domination of a military ring.

The triumph of Greeley over Grant would be an emphatic recognition of the principle that the power of the Federal Government is limited by the Constitution and that the proper guarantee of local interests is found in State legislation. Would this be no gain for the Democratic party? The progress made of late years in the direction of centralization and consolidation has been fearful. The election of Mr. Greeley, standing as he does on the Cincinnati platform, would put an end to this progress, and reinaugurate the time-honored policy of the Democratic party and of the Constitution.

Democrats would of course prefer a Democrat for the Presidency; but that, we regret to say, is wholly out of the question; and our New York contemporary must see that it is so. The question for Democrats to decide is, then, Shall we prefer a straight ticket that is sure to be beaten to the establishment in the conduct of the government of some of the most vital and fundamental principles of our party? The *World* will pardon us for saying that its present position is at once extraordinary and inconsistent. If that paper had been in the past one of the few hidebound Bourbonistic journals that still linger in the land, its course would be easily accounted for. But, on the contrary, it has usually been liberal and intelligent in its views, and capable of grasping the reality. The position it now occupies is wholly abnormal to it. It would be just the thing for the impracticables that harp continuously on the resolutions of '98, and utterly refuse to recognize the de facto binding effect of reconstruction laws or Constitutional amendments, but it is not the thing for the *World*. To throw away the certain prospect of the realization of Demo-

cratic principle for a technicality and a sentimental abstraction
would be the veriest midsummer madness.

The Democratic party has everything to gain, and nothing
to lose, by the indorsement and support of the Cincinnati nomination. If Greeley is successful, as must be the case and as the
World virtually concedes will be the case should he receive the
Democratic support, the Republican party will be in a hopeless
minority, and the Democratic party, as the most numerous and
potent organization, will necessarily succeed it. We have much
reason for the conclusion that the result of the Liberal movement
in Missouri would be nationalized.[1] It is not in contemplation
by any Democrats to give up the party organization. On the
contrary that organization will be maintained in every State, and
as early as November we shall have an earnest of what is coming
in an increased Congressional representation. Even in the event
of Greeley's defeat the position of the Democratic party would
be greatly improved, for, then, our organization being still intact,
the dissensions in the Republican party would be past reconciling.

While it is quite apparent that the New York *World* does not
now appreciate the importance, nay, the absolute necessity, of
defeating Grant and the Radical party in the approaching contest,
we have every confidence that it will yet do good service for the
candidate it condemns. The success of that candidate will not
only inure to the great gain of the Democratic party, but it
involves the continuance of Republican institutions and the
restoration and perpetuity of constitutional government. When
the Democracy finally determine at Baltimore on the course for
the party to pursue, if not before, the *World* will fall into line
and fight side by side with the *Courier-Journal* against the Grant
party.

Greeley and Schurz

(July 3, 1872)

Much is said of Horace Greeley's personal unfitness for the
Presidency. We, ourselves, remembering his peculiarities, have
felt, and have expressed, the force of the suggestion. But, after
all, may we not make a common psychological mistake, and attach
too much importance to the outside of the man?

Mr. Greeley is an odd, exceptional person. He is now sixty
years of age. His hair is as white as silver. But the bloom of a
lad of sixteen is in his cheek. He has the compressed and collected strength of a life devoted to useful pursuits, to study, to
exercise, to charity, to drudging, to intellectual work and physical

[1] The Democrats swallowed the Liberals in that state.

work, to perfect sobriety and regularity. His mind, like his body, is vigorous and live. He is a prodigious talker, writer and farmer. He does everything with a vim. He could engage in a wrestling match with Schurz, who is a lithe and active man, with a fair show of success. He can out-talk Charles Sumner, whose tongue is equal to a mill-wheel. He can ride with John Breckinridge, who has been known to keep the saddle three or four days on a stretch. He hews trees, plows, and—in short—does the work of half a dozen ordinary men. In appearance Mr. Greeley is farm-like. Those who have seen Harvey Eads can form an idea of Horace Greeley—neat, old fashioned, somewhat queer, but pleasing—a figure in whom Walter Scott would have delighted.

There never was a more perfect antithesis than that raised up by the Creator in Carl Schurz and Horace Greeley; and yet, striking as the contrast is, there are strong points of similitude. Schurz may be fairly ticketed as the Hero of Civilization, the Cavalier, so to say, of our nineteenth century culture, with all of the inspiration and none of the vices of the Ruperts and the Sidneys,—the most brilliant, natural representative of the morality of American political life, which we hold to be the leader and progenitor of all modern political philosophy, to be found anywhere occupying an active place in public affairs. If Schurz depended upon his talents as a politician for success he would be a failure. He has succeeded in spite of his simplicity as a contriver and because of his extraordinary power as a leader. His is immeasurably the best intellect that has appeared in this country since the death of Calhoun, whom he resembles in many points, but whom he surpasses in breadth of culture and knowledge of the world. Calhoun had a superb understanding, but he was provincial. Schurz has a superb understanding, and is a nationalist. Schurz really unites to the patriotism of Webster—without Webster's shortcomings—the logical mind and purity of character which made Calhoun so powerful in spite of Calhoun's limited horizon. In fine, Schurz is the leader—earnest, straightforward, brave, unpretentious, reliable, large-headed and large-hearted—whom the South has been looking for during years of floundering about among such execrable cattle as Toombs and Stephens and other political shams.

Greeley, on the other hand, is a sentimental ascetic—a product of that Scotch-Irish creativeness which has peopled our history and our literature with oddity and with power; a strong man; a moral man; a shrewd man, abounding in mother wit, intuitive perceptions, self-will—a natural, honest demagogue in the original and complimentary sense, when the demagogue was the true representative of the people. Horace Greeley reflects the mediocre average of the American sentiment more accurately than any living man, and this will account for the rallying of the people against the politicians.

It is a good sign. Put Greeley in the White House; make Carl Schurz Secretary of State, and what more do you want? Or put Greeley in the White House and leave Carl Schurz in the Senate, backed by the young impulse of the country, and you have an ideal placement of public affairs full of promise.

May it not be, to come back to our mutton, which, in Mr. Greeley's case, is no sheep, that we are falling into the error of ascribing to Mr. Greeley's personal oddities, which, after all, are most amiable and admirable, too much weight, and, by so doing, missing his real, intellectual characteristics? He is the best-posted politician in America. He has for thirty years administered a great daily newspaper—a mimic Government within itself— with extraordinary practical success. He is a model, practical farmer, and makes his model farm yield him a handsome revenue. In all his worldly gear he is a success. Mr. Buchanan made us a very bad President. Yet Mr. Buchanan was an educated public man; a pattern statesman; as perfect a piece of political marble as Charles Francis Adams; having served as a Senator, as a member of a cabinet, as a foreign ambassador. May not Mr. Greeley—who is not our ideal of what a President ought to be in his outer man—prove a contradiction to all our worldly notions?

Well, well, well. We mean to take our chance of him, anyhow. He is an able man. He is an honest man. He is a good man. He may be cranky—he may be curious, according to our preconception. Who knows? We do know that Grant is an iron-hearted, wooden-headed nutmeg, warranted to kill; we know that he is obstinate and parsimonious; we know that he is a good fellow to his friends, with a bad faculty for choosing a bad set of friends, and a bad fellow to his enemies, who are of our best people. So, feeling towards Horace Greeley downright affection, not unmingled with the fear of the boy that didn't know what confounded notion the old man might take in his head, only he was sure "the old man would neither lie nor steal," we take Horace Greeley, and that hopefully, with a distinct and uncontrollable belief that he will give us a cabinet unsurpassed in our political annals, and an administration which will contradict all the fears of those who reason not by Horace Greeley's inner self, but draw their inferences from his outward and visible man, which—to say truth—is merely that of a simple, cleanly, country gentleman.

One thing is certain. The rank old partyism of by-gone times receives the deepest of gashes from the ascendancy of that Liberalism which, defying antecedents and prejudices, takes Horace

Greeley as its sign and leader. The South cares nothing about party titles and records. It looks to its own emancipation—moral not less than legal. It seeks relief. It seeks association. It seeks *principles,* not men or measures, as the foundation of its future fabric. It goes back to Jefferson—a thorough liberal and reformer—and takes its new departure from the founder of our Democracy. Be we not too critical about minor points, about dead issues. Let us look upward and forward!

Thersites as a Comedian

(July 3, 1872)

Toombs, of Georgia, talks very like a madman, only he is not a madman. He belongs to the melodramatic school of politicians, who are miserable if they are not tearing the passion of the period to tatters. Burly, brilliant, insolent, swaggering, audacious, he personifies the actor, who, denied the legitimate stage on account of his shocking ribaldry, betakes himself to the regions of that Bohemia which, in politics not less than in literature, is full of vicious inspirations and hopeless misdirection. He will read what we say of him with pleasure because it adds to his notoriety. All that he asks in this world is, no matter how, to be kept before the foot-lights.

To be sure, Mr. Toombs has a certain power, limited indeed and applicable to a class that is passing away. Edwin Forrest, who was once a famous tragedian, can still startle the cock-loft. There is power in brazen impudence and abundant lungs; in a big belly; in coarse invective. Mr. Toombs has this sort of power. It is the power of the mountebank who will roar you an' the groundlings shall cry "let him roar again." But it appeals to no intelligent, considerate or feeling set of people; it promises nothing but a destructiveness out of which Mr. Toombs will be pretty sure to profit, for he is, strange to say, a thrifty man, who, in spite of his political excesses, takes uncommon care of himself. But he is the very worst counsellor of others.

We, in the South, need moral emancipation no less than political enfranchisement. It is hard for us to overcome the prejudices of the old system and to adapt ourselves to the exigencies of the new epoch; and yet this is the lesson we must impress upon our children if we expect them to be prosperous and happy. No wise man can desire to load the next generation with more of the burdens of the present generation than fairly belong to it. This is what the Bourbons are trying to do. This is Mr. Toombs' cue and keynote. Moss-grown themselves, the dismal dupes whom he trifles with are trying to transfer their moss to the backs of their younglings, and to continue, in an endless circle of discontent, the passions of bygone social and political conflicts.

In the Liberal movement we see a reaction against this bad tendency. The thrifty, adaptable genius of the American character halts before the bonfires which civil feud would keep perpetually burning in honor of the God of Hate, and it says: "Hold up a bit! Let us play no post-mortem games here! We have had our bellyful of fighting. Suppose we try the other tack." Thus the liberalism of peace organizes itself against the ultraism of war, and, massing on Horace Greeley, proposes to elect him President of the United States.

Suppose he may not realize our best ideal of the marble-image that ought to be set up in the White House, what of that? Is it quite clear that we are correct in our conception of the place or the man? May not we have made a mistake either in our estimate of Horace Greeley's peculiarities, or in our notion of what constitutes a good President? He is able, honest and kind-hearted. Everybody admits that much. Well, why should such excellent qualities in the individual be such bad qualities, as his enemies say they are, when applied to Horace Greeley in a Presidential connection? We propose to take our chance. We believe Horace Greeley is going to be the next President of the United States, and we believe he will make us a chief magistrate worthy of the "better days of the Republic." In President-making, as in marrying, one must e'en take some risks.

In any event the bare candidacy of Horace Greeley is an element of good. It can not be said that he was a copperhead. It can not be said that our preference for him over Grant is treason to the State. They *will* say that we take him as a tool. But *our* enthusiasm and *his* power—each in its way—contradict the statement. Mr. Greeley is at once a solvent and a nationalizer. He cuts deeply into the two old fossil party organisms. He gives the young life of the country a chance, and the canvass we shall make for him will go far to liberalize and emancipate us, to make us sensible of that which we need most pressingly and most sorely, to elevate us, to bring us into national rapport.

The South wants to be restored to its rightful place in the Union. Mere legal enfranchisement is but a mechanical contrivance. It would come of itself. Grant would toss us that bone. What we should strive for is *moral enfranchisement*, along with emancipation from domestic errors derived from the misfortunes of our fathers, and this can only be obtained by a new "cut, shuffle and deal" *all* around, so fusing and recasting the political elements that the devil himself will not be able to tell t'other from which; a general wiping out and beginning

again, wherein each of us shall have a fresh start and an equal
chance.

What we really need in the South, above all else—what is
embraced in moral enfranchisement—is identity with things national. As matters have stood the last seven years, we have been
denied that cordial and practical relationship with our Government which is the spring of real patriotism—the source and
resource of good administration. This was inevitable. The
Radical party is a war party; its inspirations are derived from its
military record; and it is its nature to smell treason in the Southern air, and to dread rebellions in the Southern heart. Its view
has been, not unnaturally, jaundiced. The hearty support which
the South is giving to Horace Greeley is an unequivocal answer
to the eccentric arguments of the party of hate. Mr. Morton is
no better than Mr. Toombs; and the two use the same appliances.
The country is sick of too much Morton and too much Toombs;
of too much bombast and venom. We need to be rid of both.
As far as the South is concerned, it can be truly said that we
detest Toombs even more than we detest Morton. The fighting
Confederate element, in particular, regards Toombs with disgust.
He will never receive the vote of an honest, right-thinking Southern man. He and his friend Stephens are the worst enemies the
South ever had, being at once unwise, selfish, conceited, cold-
hearted, ready at any moment to sacrifice us all to their over-
weening vanity, spleen and lust for notoriety. All we ask of
them is that they will go at once to Grant, that they will leave us
forever. They are simply despicable in the last degree; and it
is useless for them to hang on any longer where they are, unless,
by so doing, they can secure better terms of the Administration
than they could by openly supporting it. We want them to understand that there can be no truce or reconciliation between us. We
merely ask them, in candor, to leave us.

The young manhood of the South has its own destiny to work
out. It seeks to rid itself of the burden imposed by such men as
Toombs and Stephens. The burden is great, but the opportunity
is noble; and, by the blessing of God, we shall, bearing the cross,
yet wear the crown.

TILDEN AND THE AFTERMATH

1876-1877

The four editorials which follow represent the period when
    Mr. Watterson was more interested in the personalities
    and causes of current politics than at any other time in his

career. All of them relate to the Presidential campaign of 1876. What accomplishments the editor had hoped for from Abraham Lincoln in reuniting the sections he at this period envisioned in Samuel J. Tilden, Governor of New York. No other figure in American politics during the more than fifty years of Mr. Watterson's personal and editorial activity commanded as much of his respect, admiration and affection.

In the first of the editorials in this group the editor took for his theme the scandals of the Grant Administration. With this besom he sought to clear the obstacles from the path of the Democratic party. His life-long hatreds of self-consciousness of social position and of "personal government" appear strongly in this article, as does this saber cut at General Grant's policy: "An affair of horses and dogs supplemented by the companionship of congenial spirits."

Having exploded his bomb under the Republican edifice, the editor one month later brought forward his materials for the nomination of Mr. Tilden. At this time Mr. Watterson was thirty-six years old. Later, when Mr. Cleveland and Mr. Wilson were elected to the Presidency by his party, his enthusiasms for men had waned. In this editorial he warned the South that it must forsake Greenbackism and Sectionalism if it would be restored. This article was of the greatest importance at the time of its publication. It was everywhere republished and discussed. Today it would be difficult to think of the emanation of any newspaper in America so potent in a National sense. Mr. Watterson, apparently conscious of revolving as a buffer between the Northern and Southern wings of his party, adopted in this writing a conciliatory tone, and, to assure politicians that he was not singing for his supper, he remarked: "Neither office nor patronage is in our line of business."

The third article of this group was written with two purposes: to warn Kentucky Democrats of the efforts of the Ohio Greenbackers to capture the delegates of the Blue Grass state from Tilden, and to stick a few pins in a rival newspaper, *The Cincinnati Enquirer*. Nor did the editor hesitate to make a few unkind personal allusions.

So long ago was the Greenback agitation in this country that the fourth editorial of the 1876 group means little to the modern reader. Yet in 1876, as in 1896, the fight was sound money against inflation, and Tilden was the sound money man. Therefore, Mr. Watterson sought to plant his candidate's feet firmly on the inevitable financial platform. The Greenbackers proceeded on the theory of the fabled housewife who believed she had money in the bank as long as she had checks in her check-book. This fantasy soon vanished 'from American affairs, but for some years it required such opposition as the fourth editorial of this series undertook to provide.

The Fruit of Personal Government

(March 3, 1876)

The miserable tidings which are brought us from Washington by telegraph this morning were sufficiently foreshadowed by our special dispatches yesterday. Nay, the charges against the Secretary of War which have been at length verified by an investigating committee were published in the *Courier-Journal* some time ago with considerable detail; so that those who take note of such matters are not altogether astounded by the revelations of the present moment. Mr. Belknap's discomfiture has indeed been regarded as a question of time by those who have had any personal knowledge of his public and private conduct. He was a small man in a great place; he had an ambitious wife. The dénouement brought round by the Committee on Expenditures in the War Department presents a spectacle as old as Personal Government: the retainer betraying his trust; the betrayer in turn betrayed; exposure and ruin bringing with them not merely the overthrow of Vanity Fair, with its dismal crowd of meannesses and mortifications, but the disgrace of the Public Service. In one aspect it makes a man blush for his country, in another for his kind.

When General Grant came into office he announced that he should have no policy that was not dictated by the people. If he meant anything by this, which is doubtful, he thought that it sounded well and might prove peradventure a pretext or recourse in extremity. Now as the people rarely give themselves up en masse to the making of administrative policies, and, in a country such as ours, are likely to be so divided on momentous questions as to defy fixed conclusions in the minds of persons even more penetrating than the President, that functionary was speedily thrown back upon the slender experience of his civil career, and was forced to evolve a policy out of his inner consciousness. This necessarily took its form from the objects familiar to the soldier's life. It was, therefore, not long in becoming purely an affair of horses and dogs supplemented by the companionship of spirits congenial to the enjoyment of these luxuries. The result produced Tom Murphy in New York, a jovial blade, who bled freely, both for his master and his country, and Borie in Philadelphia, whose patriotism was equally luminous, and Alex. Shepherd at

Washington, who knew the mysteries of plumbing. General
Grant made up his Cabinet with the same loose disregard of consequences and ceremonies which he applied to his cronyships.
There was Ackerman appointed Attorney General for no better
reason than that he had been refused entertainment at a Georgia
hotel. Then came Williams, who had been serviceable as a
Senator, and whose wife happened to be in high favor at the
White House—he was not only made Attorney General, but,
having notoriously failed in the Department of Justice, was actually elevated to be Chief Justice, and would at this moment, but
for the intervention of his own party, outrank such jurists as
Davis, Clifford and Strong. Is it wonderful that, under such a
system, Richardson had to step down and out of the Treasury,
barely escaping a criminal prosecution; that Delano, blackened
all over, was dragged from the Interior Department a degraded
man; and finally that the President's most confidential friend and
closest official connection escaped the doors of a penitentiary
through the technology of law and the interposition of his betters?
This is but a brief recital of a few years of Personal Government.
It is assumed that General Grant has not participated in the corruption of his favorites. In that event what must be thought of
him as a judge of men? He sends Schenck to England and keeps
him there when his appearance in public is a reproach and scandal.
He has no idea of remanding Babcock to his military duty in the
army. He was so fond of Boss Shepherd after the Republicans
themselves broke up his District Ring that he sent in his name for
confirmation as chief of the new Ring. Indeed, he sticks to his
friends; but what must be believed of his friends? Either that in
choosing them he has shown very poor judgment or has had very
bad luck. And yet this man seeks a third term and thinks that
an emergency may arise by which he alone of all his fellow-
citizens may be qualified to pilot the ship of state.

The case of General Belknap has a special and particular
interest for the people of Central Kentucky. His first wife and
his last went hence, and both were famous belles. If the secretary's official malpractice does not antedate his marriage two
years ago he is to be deeply commiserated. Much can be said for
a weak man who has to support the honors of a great place and the
extravagances of an ambitious woman. The victim of this unhappy combination was in no sense equal to its demands. The
duties of a chief clerkship in one of the Bureaus of the Department over which he presided would have fully taxed his competency. He was prepared for the elevated station to which
favoritism had assigned him by the experiences of neither public
nor private life. He was a nobody called to the front for a purpose by a friend. He had not the fortune to support the grandeur

of office nor sustain the fashionable whims of a single season in an expensive capital. He had not a great name, achieved by long, arduous and honorable service, to care for. Stealing seemed to be the order of the day. It was going on all around him. Neglect of duty was the example set in the most shameful ways by his Chief and Creator. Better men than himself were constantly misusing public trusts; why should not he? Almost in sight of the War Department might be seen the palaces of men grown rich in the Government service, and yet walking among their fellows unscathed and unscorned. Precedents in plenty were furnished by the common usage; and there was the Temptress not merely to stimulate his passions and to instigate his vices, but actually to participate in his crimes. The man is to be pitied as much as blamed. The President is responsible for his fate. His wife is merely an executioner chosen by a Providence which seems to link woman with all the great tragedies as well as all the great blessings of life, to carry out and fulfill the worldly no less than the moral law, that pride shall receive its accustomed fall; that those who soar too high in the air must soon or late come down; that it is best to be honest, to pay our just debts, and to live on what we have, not on what we may steal. *Ecce signum?* The gayest house in Washington gone to tatters. The handsomest woman in the capital, surpassed by none as a leader of *ton*, blighted forever. A gorgeous dinner-table turned upside down. No more flashes of merriment and wit around that board. Even the flunkeys are gone now, and those that were not flunkeys —who pretended to be friends, running about from house to house making, exchanging and retailing scandal to still further blacken the reputation of these already ruined people. They lived splendidly. But what of that? We now know how. They gave delightful entertainments. But what of that? Any pretty woman can flourish who is indifferent as to next day. Their dinners were unexceptionable. But what of that? It is easy to give dinners on other people's money, and no man's hospitality is to be remembered who has furnished a reason why it may not be referred to with a show of self-complaisance and honor. So the Belknaps will go, bag and baggage, the pretty woman along with the secretary, who will be lucky if he escapes the penitentiary.

It is really a mournful recital and one not to be dwelt upon. No patriotic American can wish to see his country disgraced through one of its Cabinet officers even to wreak a partisan judgment. We were disgraced enough at Vienna. But if that was not enough, God knows the cup has been filled to overflowing in London. Now, to cap the climax of that sense of irresponsibility which comes after long political tenure, the Republican party presents us as a final trophy of its domination this Secretary of

War, this poor Belknap, fished out of his original obscurity to disgrace the whole of us, and to make us hang our heads in every part of the world.

Tilden for President

(April 25, 1876)

We publish this morning a carefully-prepared biographic sketch of the Democratic governor of New York. If it were not our opinion that Governor Tilden is the best hope the Democrats have of beating the Republicans, we should still make this publication. We should make it as an act of justice. It is enough to dishearten well-informed people to hear Southern men, born and bred in the faith, turn upon this life-long, courageous and able Democratic statesman the phials of an unjustified, unreasoning and fatal wrath. Because he is from New York—the one great State in the North which his genius has saved us, and without which we cannot elect a President—and because he has refused to follow the semi-civilized gods of finance, who have set up their impotent ragged idols in the West—he is discredited by those who, of all men, should recognize in him the representative of the principle and policy by which the South can hope to regain her upright posture.

The South has had many misfortunes and much misleading the last quarter of a century. For ten years before the war, for four years whilst the war lasted, and during ten years since the war, it has been the victim of its sentimentality. It has never been able to pick itself up, to sit itself down, and in a cool, business-like way, to consider its real situation. Those who have stood out against its prejudices have been too often suspected and denounced. Yet, steadily, the counsel of those who have incurred its displeasure has prevailed against the clamor of its hotheads. These have come to grief from year to year, passing away into oblivion and obscurity.

Shall there never be an end or at least a truce to the power of ignorance and noise? Shall faction always divide and weaken those whose unity is their sole salvation? Are we united only in our passions, never in our judgments? Is it forever to be that he who seeks to point us a way out of our ruin is to point us blind-alleys, circles and ruts, or else none at all, under penalty of accusation and distrust?

The South is today a bankrupt. What has made it so? Maladministration. How shall we escape this? By administrative reform. Even if the Rag Baby had any power, it could not help us. But it has no power. It is a dead baby, a very dead and a very dirty rag baby. It enjoyed a spasm of fitful life last fall, and gave up the little ghost it had forever. There never was any chance for it. With Grant in the White House, and a Republican majority in the Senate, it could perfect no measure of financial relief. It could put not one additional greenback dollar into any man's pocket. It was a device to destroy whom it pretended to save, and those who were lured by it failed to consider that—though they should be never so right in their opinions—the time was unpropitious for the realization of their scheme. The South, which took no stock in it, should loathe its memory. We tried it in the Confederacy under the idea that it would pay our debts. It paid nothing. By and by it had not credit enough to buy a bushel of beans for a bushel of dollars. If its plans were practicable now—which they are not and never have been—the result would be precisely what we experienced, a universal breakdown and bankruptcy, tenfold worse than the existing business depression.

The South's avenue of escape, its highway to relief, is reform in the General Government, in our State government, and in municipal government. Reform—close, well-directed and unsparing reform, making money here and saving money there, will alone reduce the taxes under which we are blighted and enable us to accumulate enough to repair the waste places, to pay our debts, and to start once more fairly with the world. Behold how we are governed and see the source of our distress! Where our money is not stolen by thieves, it is squandered by incapables. For years it has been with us first a lot of cheats in office, and then a lot of politicians, capable of lip-service chiefly. Above all things, and first of all, we need to introduce to the public business some of the painstaking, trained and frugal habits which mark the conduct of successful private business. We need less speaking and more work, fewer heated appeals and a fuller stock of information. Far be it from us to stigmatize honest feeling of any sort, or to disparage the honorable sensibilities which disaster and proscription have swelled and quickened in the Southern heart. But passion, however justified, is rarely a safe guide; whilst vociferation, the offshoot of sentimental folly, is, when employed by a minority, the most misleading of public vices. The spirit of unrest in the South should be calmed into a spirit of hope based upon something more substantial than dreams of bygone glory. The South can never exert the kind of influence it once exerted in American politics. Every time it ranges itself upon the lines from which it has been driven, its allies in the North and West will experience defeat at the hands of a sectionalism combined and organized against us. For the present at least all sectional calculations must be made to our disadvantage.

The South can not unite with the West, which bad party management on the part of the Democrats has Radicalized. Indiana is the only Western state which we hold and can retain, and we should lose Indiana if the sectional question should come into ascendency. The States which we can carry are New York, New Jersey and Connecticut, California, Oregon and Nevada, and we can only carry these with a nominee who is neither wild nor equivocal in his financial opinions. The issue is not one of sections, but of definite strength, calculable in detail, State by State. This strength is all that is left the Democratic party, and unless the party considers it dispassionately, and decides its course upon it, we shall be defeated in the election.

We do not say that Governor Tilden is the only Democrat who can be elected; but we do say that he can best gather together the elements of success we have named and utilize them. He beat Governor Dix for governor of New York by a majority of 50,000 votes, though Governor Dix was and is the most popular Republican in the State, and had made the most efficient executive. Again, last year, when the Democrats were divided, losing 30,000 or 40,000 votes in the four great cities by reason of local causes, it was Governor Tilden's personal strength and his genius as an organizer which again saved us the State. He is still governor of New York, still the favorite of the States upon which we must rely for success, and we urge that his nomination would give us an assurance which no sophistry can displace. The South should simply seek the strongest man. It should try to enforce no special crotchet of its own. It should go to St. Louis resolved to see things as they are in the North, our political battle-ground, and to act in accordance thereto.

As a contribution to the current stock of information under this head, we produce the antecedents of Governor Tilden. He is, as will be seen, and he always has been, like his law-partner, Charles O'Connor, a doctrinaire Democrat of the school of Thomas Jefferson. He is a man of unimpeached private character and of conceded ability and courage. He is the one Democratic Reformer of the period, when Reform is the hope, as it is the cue, of thoughtful men everywhere. In spite of Democratic thieves, who have made alliance with the Republicans, he has held New York firmly, proceeding with the trained skill of a practical statesman to readjust the home fabric upon honest and scientific principles. It is this resolute spirit and this veteran skill which we need in the General Government, and, by example, in all our state and municipal governments. The election of Governor Tilden to the presidency would give it to us, and it would also give a guarantee of frugal and upright administration to the large non-partisan classes in the North, a guarantee which the Democratic party needs to give, which is indispensable to its future, and which is realized in the person of no other Democratic statesman with so much precision and force.

These are reasons, and they may be ill-founded; but, if they are so, we should be glad to have their weak points specified. We sincerely wish to see the Democratic Party triumph, and we wish to see it triumph upon sound principles. The Republican Party is sectional, proscriptive and corrupt. It would keep the South in a perpetual state of disquiet in order that it may keep the passions and fears of the North alive. This is ruinous to us as a policy, but it is full of a dangerous power, and needs to be met with all possible wisdom and prudence on our part. We submit that we have treated the question as its magnitude deserves; and, if we are in error, the error is not venial. It is not of supreme importance to us who occupies the White House. Neither office nor patronage is in our line of business. But in our poor way we would do what we can toward the end sought by the better elements of both political parties, realizable only in a change of parties, and the election of a fit Democrat. The purification of the public service is to be reached by reforms, set on foot by a reformer who joins to fixed opinions the experience to know how and the courage to do. Governor Tilden has shown himself the man for the work, and he has that sort of strength which is essential to the first act in the drama—Success at the Ballot Box.

A Word or Two Edgewise

(May 24, 1876)

The *Cincinnati Enquirer* continues to appeal to Kentucky. It wants Kentucky to attach itself to Ohio by a system of political links stretching across the Ohio River like the bridges which connect Covington and Newport with Cincinnati, the control, the perquisites and the tollage all to be on the Ohio side. Its excess of love for Kentucky is plaintive, and, for a wonder, it has nothing to say about mortgages, lottery swindles and poker sharps.

We fear that we shall have to throw a wet shawl over the *Enquirer's* ardor. It swears that it loves Kentucky, but WE'LL swear that Kentucky does not love it. Like the unhappy swain in Olivia's ballad, it—

> ". . . grieves for friendship unreturned,
> And unregarded love."

We know very well that, if it suits the caprice of this strumpet, to change the sex if not the metaphor, she will turn about and abuse us as furiously and as vulgarly as ever.

So much for the *Enquirer*. We have other words for Ohio and Ohio's favorite son.

It would be strange if Gov. Allen had no friends in Kentucky. He has lived alongside of us for forty years. During the great part of that time he has been conspicuously in public life, and he came to the front after a period of obscuration which vitalized and idealized his character in the popular fancy. It is true that his financial opinions involve a renunciation of his entire antecedent record; but it is equally true that thousands of men, pressed by hard times and seeking relief, see, or think they see, an outlet in the platform—contradictory, tessellated, curious as it is—on which he stands. We shall not quarrel with him, or it, or those who regard him and his theories with favor. But we ask thinking Democrats in all seriousness whether it is quite safe to look to Ohio just now for political guidance and deliverance? Torn by internal dissension, can we rely on Ohio? Even if, by some mysterious circumstance, Ohio is to come round all right at last, can we take the risk of tacking Kentucky to the tail of the Ohio kite? For years Ohio has been the Democratic *bête noir*. It may be Ohio's misfortune, not Ohio's fault, but Democratic misleading and disaster have come plenteously thence. Kentuckians may love Ohio much, but they love Kentucky more; and no true Kentuckian will care to get his opinions at second hand, or take them from lips that are used to reviling Kentuckians and sneering at Kentucky. At present Ohio is a Democratic apple of discord. Good Democrats everywhere regret the fact; but it is no fault of theirs. Nor will they utter any reproaches. It is the law of self-preservation, not the rule of hate, which bids us give Ohio a wide berth. When Ohio has come again to the front smiling and united, when she has put aside the scowl which now darkens her visage and ceased to threaten, then, and not till then, can she take up the baton of command.

In the meantime the Democratic party will try to disentangle itself from the embarrassments of Ohio's making, as best it may. It can not afford to throw itself away on Ohio. That is the long and the short of it.

Financial Bugaboos

(May 24, 1876)

As to the finances, a deal of humbugging nonsense is talked nowadays. It is fashionable to discuss the finances and every man thinks he must be a financier. There are as many financial sects in America as there are parties in Spain. We have the Inflationados and the Contractadissimos. These are subdivided into the Greenbackers and the Hardmoneyites. In turn, bloated bond-holders are to be found who don't mind a small infusion of rags, whilst here and there an advocate of paper and plenty of it may be coaxed into taking a bit of silver for his shinplaster. There's the Resumptionist who wants to take a back somersault into a gold basin. There's the ninety-day Resumptionist. There's the Resumptionist who thinks the Radical resumption act a swindle. The three are met by Mr. Toombs' old Georgia friend, who wanted to "stamp as much money as folks could spend," and, being asked how it was to be redeemed, replied, "that's just what I'm coming to; I'm ag'in redemption." Even the Ohio platform says, "no forced inflation; no forced contraction," which both sides can endorse.

Seriously, is not this child's play? All of us can not be educated political economists, capable of nice, hair-splitting distinctions. For our part the sum of our financial knowledge has not materially increased since the day we bought a ginger cake for five cents, traded it for a ten-cent watermelon, and sold the watermelon on credit to a black boy, who afterward repudiated the debt. Ever since we have had a prejudice, as it were, against repudiation. We believe in paying our private debts, when we have the money, and are in favor of paying the national debt, provided the money is not to come out of our pocket. Every man should hold the public honor near his own.

Is there a sane man in this country who believes that we can resume in '79? That which is wanted is a financial policy at once honest and stable, giving a guarantee of ultimate resumption. The Democratic party is not responsible for the currency which is. But if it comes into power it will be responsible for the national well-being and honor, and it must plant itself upon ground sufficiently solid to maintain the public credit. But this is no time for details. Nor are details fit subjects for the heated discussion of tumultuous assemblies. No man would be willing to trust his private business to a convention of excited friends. Why should we drag the public business through the like ordeal? The details of the Democratic scheme of finance which shall be finally adopted will need to pass many tests, be subjected to much deliberation, and must realize not merely a liberal and enlightened spirit of concession, but that cool, painstaking care which prudent and thrifty men bestow upon the most delicate and important transactions. At last and at best it is sure to disappoint some of us, for, seeing the differences that exist, all of us can not hope to get precisely what we wish.

As matters stand we can not perfect or carry out any scheme of our own. The whole question will have to be relegated to the future, and ought to be relegated to the Congressional districts. Assuredly it is unwise in us to wrangle over it on the heels of a presidential contest in which the question is not so much what sort of money shall we use as what sort of government shall we have. We want to beat the Radicals first, and settle the finances afterward. In cooking a rabbit, the first principle is to catch the rabbit. The Democrats can do nothing until they get the power, and they ought not to bind themselves too tightly in advance. The example of Ohio, torn by feuds which may lose us the state for a dozen years to come, should be a warning to Kentucky, and, indeed, to all the States, to beware of premature and causeless wrangle. We have seen what use personal ambition can make of the money-devil in the Holman-Landers fight, which may cost us Indiana. Here in Kentucky we are fairly united. We mean to be just and honest as to general principles. We differ only as to details. Is it not best to bottle up our differences, such as they are, until we can uncork them to some better purpose than the fomentation of private broil? We have enough on our hands to meet and defeat the Republicans who, united by their corruptions and by the danger menacing their tenure of power, hope to see us split upon this issue. If the split is to come, let it; but sufficient unto the day is the evil thereof; and, as we can make nothing except capital for the Republicans by splitting NOW, why suppose we just postpone the scrimmage among ourselves until we have overcome the common enemy? Nay, let us even hope for better things. There may be no split at all. An amount of misconception exists, and there has been some misrepresentation. When we come to understand ourselves, and, as custodians of the Government, when we fully realize the problem with which we have to deal, each sect may, and doubtless will, grow more conservative. Moderation is certainly our cue today, as it is our interest and duty. We have a gigantic battle before us, and if, as reasonable men, we have any expectation of winning it, we must bear and forbear.

Profoundly convinced of the need of reform in all our governments, national, state and municipal—holding that prosperity can only return to the people by lessening the expenses of government—holding that a thorough change of parties is essential to this end—we have not allowed ourselves to be drawn into entangling controversies upon financial topics. In a general way we have maintained the sound-money traditions of the party in which we were reared. In a particular way we have reprobated the supreme folly of those visionary politicians in Ohio who trumped up this disturbing question last fall to divide us, to unite the Republicans, to defeat Allen and destroy Thurman. Evil enough has come out of Nazareth for one political season. We call a truce to passion which, no matter how reasonable, is out of time and out of order.

The people seek lighter taxes. These are to be obtained only by
cheaper government. This can only come with a change of
parties, since no party in power was ever known to reform itself.
Let us, therefore, hoist the poor man's flag of administrative
reform and economic government, send the philosophers to the
rear, wrap the ensign of the Republic around the man of our
choice, whoever he is, and give the enemies of the Constitution
and the authors of our adversity—those who have employed the
twin vices of proscription and corruption to drive the iron into
our souls and to produce hard times—the very best fight we can.
Nobody doubts that we can whip one another. But that is not
the spirit with which we should enter upon this great conflict of
principles and ideas. On the contrary, each, using the words of
the poet of fraternity and peace, should say to each—

> "You can not chain the eagle,
> And you dare not harm the dove;
> But every gate you bar to hate
> Will open wide to love."

The "Hayes Conspiracy" was what Mr. Watterson and millions of his fellow citizens considered the certification of
the Republican candidate in 1877. Never, except in 1861,
was there so much likelihood as then that Americans would
take up arms against one another. At Mr. Tilden's request,
the Louisville editor had agreed to serve out an unexpired
term in Congress for the purpose of acting as the Democratic
candidate's personal representative. From Washington he
sent flaming editorial dispatches to his newspaper, of which
the following, published in the *Courier-Journal*, January 8,
1877, was the most famous.

It was this article which was responsible for the report
around the United States that Henry Watterson proposed
to lead an army of a hundred thousand men into Washington
to prevent the certification of Hayes. While in this writing
the editor counsels peace, there is a good deal of belligerency
in his suggestion of massing the protestants in Washington.
And what alarmed the Federal government most was the
injunction to the Democrats of Kentucky to "provide for the
presence of at least ten thousand unarmed Kentuckians" in
Washington a month later.

The Political Situation

(Correspondence of the *Courier-Journal*, Ebbitt House, Washington, January 5, 1877)

Congress reassembles, after ten days of useless junketing, to find the situation precisely what it was when it took its recess, and, indeed, very much as it was the first day of the session. Thus far nothing has been developed at Washington except the ways and means by which the leaders of the Republican conspiracy expect to count Tilden out and Hayes in. The election of Tilden, the existence of the conspiracy and the names of the conspirators are known today no better than they were a month ago. The President, the Secretary of the Interior and the Secretary of War, Senators Morton and Sherman and the general of the army ambrace the list in full. How they are to partition the Government out among themselves after they have usurped it belongs to the category of details which it is not worth our while just now to attempt to fathom. Their organization and purpose are clear. It is unlikely that the conspiracy reaches farther among the leading Republicans. The persons indicated have constituted themselves into a close corporation. They think that, with the army at their command, they can, by a bold, defiant and lawless policy, bring the Senate to their heels, and compel the people to choose between them and civil war. Hayes is a mere incident; men like Logan and Taft [2] simple tools. Much encouragement has been given the hopes of the conspirators by the pliancy of these, but still more by the seeming apathy of the country, which, in the vain hope that Congress would strike out a lead, has waited upon the non-acting Democrats. Meanwhile, the Democrats, unused to the responsibilities of power, have hesitated, and not without reason; whilst the Eastern press, representing the wealthier classes, has added its influence to the prevailing irresolution. The truth is that Congress is merely a reflector. It is not a breeder of ideas. Time was, before modern appliances had given the people the opportunity to commune promptly among themselves, when men looked to Washington for advisement. Now Washington looks to the country. The chief argument offered in favor of adjourning over the holidays was embraced by the suggestion that members would come back refreshed and reinvigorated by contact with their constituents.

The people must act for themselves. Without their support the House of Representatives is powerless. A corporal's guard may disperse it. The arrest of half a dozen of its members

---

[2] The reference is to Alphonso Taft, father of William H. Taft.

would demoralize it. Anything, everything is possible to those who oppose themselves to the conspirators. But unless the people act there will be no need of violence on the part of the conspirators. They will proceed without regard to precedents or facts with their plan to put the defeated candidate for president in the White House, leave Congress to pursue its policy of impotent protest, and, having weathered the 5th of March, say with complacency to such as question, "What are you going to do about it?"

Is there no peaceful remedy? I think there is. There is the right of petition, which, adequately presented and urged, becomes a power. The Democrats do not include civil war in the list of their resources. Civil war is not a red-tape affair. It does not come in the regulation way. Nor is it likely to happen ever until all the peaceful methods for the redress of grievances have been exhausted. The Democratic party plants itself upon the law and the facts. It declares that the vote of no State shall be counted without the consent of both houses of Congress. No State vote has ever been or ought to be. Since the foundation of the Government to the present time, including the evidence furnished by the Republican leaders themselves, all authority sustains this position. On it the Democratic party plants itself, and means to stand until it is driven off at the point of the bayonet. It is for our people to determine, therefore, whether this shall be done. If they will rise in their might, and, exercising the peaceful right of petition, will memorialize the Senate to do its duty, to do that which every Republican member of the Senate is committed to, and will send a hundred thousand petitioners to Washington on the 14th of February to present the memorial in person, there will be no usurpation and no civil war. The conspirators will be thwarted. There will be Republicans enough in the Senate to defeat them, and we shall have the presidential result settled by well-established constitutional methods. Otherwise, those Republican senators who wish to do right, seeing that the country is going to submit, will submit too, and we shall drift into a new era of popular discontent, the end of which no man can see.

The convention called to assemble in Louisville on the 18th should consider these things. There is little complexity whatever in the situation. All that I have written here may be relied upon with absolute assurance. It is no pleasure to write such things; but they should be written simply and distinctly. If the convention wishes to do something, let it take ground firmly, not noisily, for the joint right of the two houses, fortified as it is by all precedent; and, having thus memorialized the Senate, let it provide for the presence of at least ten thousand unarmed Kentuckians in this city on the coming 14th of February. Less than this will be of no avail. So much, supplemented as it will be by other

States, will secure through civil agencies the peaceful settlement of the most dangerous issue that ever menaced the existence of a free government.

H. W.

The Tilden-Hayes controversy rested bitterly upon the soul of Mr. Tilden's chief apostle. Therefore, in perusing the attached highly uncomplimentary discussion of the character of the great Union leader, the modern reader need not regard it as a fixed opinion. Mr. Watterson, like all of those who must write in the heat of the moment, said harsher things than he intended. While he undoubtedly meant the bulk of the subjoined, he would have been shocked if, in 1923, he could have read his reference to General Grant as a "voluptuary."

General Grant's Future

(March 30, 1877)

General Grant said the other day in his two minutes' speech to the Cincinnati business men, "I shall now be a better fellow than I was six months ago."

Considering how great the room for improvement is, the ex-President's observation will not be violent or striking. This, however, in a public sense; for the real weakness in Gen. Grant's character has been his liking for good fellows and his desire to be regarded by them as a good fellow. Being out of employment he may pursue his bent, and there is small doubt that he will be credited with all the character for good fellowship which his heart may crave. He has a turn for horses, bull pups and tobacco; is fond of a glass of grog and a game of cards; and, in short, like Will Wimble, is extremely well versed in various little handicrafts of an idle man. It is said, after his visit to his old friends in the West, he will go to Europe to stay two or three years. Unless he becomes enamored of the English turf and is lucky in falling in with a congenial party of sportsmen, he will hardly spend the half of three years abroad. After the novelty of travel has worn off, there will be little to amuse the General outside his peculiar tastes, and these he can gratify very much better in the United States. The sour wine of France is a poor substitute for American strong drinks. The frivolous amusements of Paris are meant for people of a sensuous, æsthetic turn, not for solid men who seek the substantial. A drive in the Bois, a dinner at Valfour's, an evening at the opera—the routine of every-day life in the French capital—grows humdrum and monotonous. There is some rough sport to be had in St. Petersburg and Berlin, and a ramble over Italy is not without its amusement. But General Grant is an indolent man as well as a pleasure-seeker, and the fatigue, no less than the monotony, will bore him. They say he is not over-fond of Sartoris, and, if this be true, he will hardly pass much of his time in the company of that buxom youth, although Sartoris is hand-and-glove with the people about Tattersall's, and has it in his power to make the stay of his father-in-law agreeable enough. Nevertheless, it is presumable that the ex-President will grow sick of continental sightseeing and weary of English provinciality, and that presently he will come home to stay.

But what will he do? Where will he go? There is no place for him in the army. No place has been provided for our ex-President anywhere. Is he really a poor man, and will he need a pension? These are pertinent questions. On the whole, General Grant's future is not encouraging. The Democrats will never forgive him. The Republicans have always secretly disliked, when they have not feared, him. He is too old to make another career. The rumor that he is meditating a stock farm in the Bluegrass country is perhaps not without foundation. It is the best thing he can do. There is no country in the world where a voluptuary can get as much pleasure and profit out of so little work as in the Bluegrass country. All the fellows up there hunt, fish and play mumble-the-peg. The thoroughbreds are abundant. The cattle likewise. General Grant has only to buy him four or five hundred acres of land and a hammock, to swing out the rest of his days in plenty and peace. Personally, he will be made welcome. He shall have free passes over all our railroads. He shall be elected a life-member of our Jockey Club. In his old age he might go to the Legislature, and, when he dies, we'll bury him with all the honors of war by the side of his Mexican comrades, who lie in the cemetery at Frankfort.

THE CAMPAIGN OF GARFIELD

1880

As late as 1880 all those who had participated in the Hayes-Tilden affair were anathema among the Democrats. This explains the bitterness of the following editorial, the only one selected for this volume relating to the dull campaign of 1880. Disappointed in obtaining the renomination of Mr. Tilden, Mr. Watterson had deferred to the decision of those who selected General Hancock to cope with General Garfield, but his heart was with Tilden and the campaign was based upon one of his early national phrases, "Turn the rascals out."

To a generation which remembers of General Garfield the tradition of kindliness and culture and cherishes his memory as one who lost his life by assassination, this attack during the pre-election campaign of 1880, linking General Garfield with the Tilden affair, will light up some forgotten passages in American political history. In his autobiography, Mr. Watterson forgot and forgave much of this sort of controversy.

Judge Black on Fraud

(July 5, 1880)

It was on the 27th of February, 1877. The Electoral Commission had reached the South Carolina case when Mr. Shellabarger, who knew from the first that it had been determined by the eight to declare Hayes elected President in defiance of the Constitution and common decency, arose and stated that his side did not want to waste any more time in arguing cases and they would "submit the case without argument." They knew from the beginning that, having packed the jury, they were sure of the verdict.

Garfield sat there. He was a party to the steal. He, with his brother Judases, was anxious for the mockery to be over. He had determined with his brother Judases that, for the occasion, they would be extreme State rights men, and affirm that, however fraudulent might be the certificate coming from a State; however odorous of fraud it might be, it must not be questioned after it reached Washington. By this means alone could they seat the defeated candidate for the Presidency. Garfield was a party to this fraud. He knew it to be a damnable crime, and yet his partisan greed made him willing to share the responsibility with other murderers of popular liberty.

There was another man present at that session of the Electoral Commission. We refer to Judge Black, of Pennsylvania. Three years before, Judge Black had written a letter to James A. Garfield, who is a prominent member of the church to which Judge Black belongs, seeking to exculpate him from the charges of guilty connection with the Credit Mobilier business. Judge Black had not read the report of the Poland Committee when he wrote that letter, and was not acquainted with the scope of the investigation. He had reason, shortly after, to believe that he had given a certificate of character to the wrong man. Garfield sat before him on the Electoral Commission. Judge Black had read the purpose of the eight from the start. He read the guilty deed in Garfield's eyes, as though it had already been performed, and when the tricky Shellabarger proposed to submit the case without argument, the intention of the Republican buccaneers was apparent to any man. It was then that Judge Black uttered a most memorable speech, which made the conspirators tremble before him. He alluded to the "horrible calamity with which the country is threatened; a President, deriving his title from a shameless swindle, not merely of fraud, but a fraud detected and exposed." He then rose to heights of defiance and flung this at the conspirators:

"You do not think it any wrong that a nation should be cheated by false election returns. On the contrary, it is rather a blessing which heaven has sent us in this strange disguise. When the omnipotent lie shall be throned and sceptered and crowned you think we ought all of us to fall down and worship it as the hope of our political salvation."

That "omnipotent lie" was throned and Garfield fell down and worshiped it, offering incense along with such ruffians as J. Madison Wells and his fellow-burglars with whom Garfield had held criminal intercourse in New Orleans. That "omnipotent lie" Garfield worships today. He is stamped with the impress of the seal of that beast, and he has been chosen as the leader of the party which stands convicted before Heaven, angels and men of the most infamous political crime of the century.

DAYS OF PHRASEMAKING

1884

In the spring of 1884 it being obvious that Mr. Tilden would not if he could further be considered for Presidential honors, Mr. Watterson affectionately bade the great man farewell. The editorial which follows is the last article written by the editor which dealt with Mr. Tilden in a contemporary mood. Its spirit, its literary quality and the fact that it bounded a period in American politics are responsible for its inclusion in this volume.

This is the first occasion when Mr. Watterson groped for that famous phrase which several years later was to be the most widely quoted political expression in American history. Discussing the condition of Mr. Tilden's health as a deterrent to those who would have thrust him into the leadership in 1884, his friend the editor referred to the possible death of the Sage of Greystone during the campaign, saying that the Democrats might only "follow the glory of triumph to an open grave." That this expression captured the editorial fancy is certain, for, in the campaign of 1892, he declared that the nomination of Cleveland would mean the progress of the Democrats "through a slaughter house into an open grave."

The Sage of Greystone

(April 28, 1884)

The undiminished vitality and overshadowing pre-eminence of Mr. Tilden contradict the adage that a prophet is not without honor save in his own country. All parties testify—the one by its assaults, long-sustained and never-flagging; the other by its confidence and admiration—to the universal homage which this great philosopher and patriot has inspired in the bosom of his countrymen; and whether the transactions of the current political year come too late to render actual justice to him or not, there is in the spontaneity of the call upon the old statesman to emerge from the seclusion of his declining years, and to draw, if need be, even the robes of death about him, that before he passes hence forever he may lead once more the hosts of freedom and reform, a poetic justice rarely achieved in the world.

It is not that Mr. Tilden is too old, nor yet too ill, to accept the leadership thus sought to be thrust upon him, and by none so noisily as by those who withheld it four years ago. He is intellectually the same man he was in 1880. But they who know him best and love him most feel, and he feels himself, that the length of his days is conditioned upon complete repose, and that he has not the strength to stand the wear and tear of a great national struggle. It would be but a poor consolation to the mass and body of Democrats, who are right at heart, if their rash, and not wholly unselfish, enthusiasm should prevail, only to enable them to follow the glory of triumph to an open grave, or perchance to encounter the yet greater calamity of finding a living movement turned, before its time, into a funeral.

It has been to avert the chance of such a contingency that Mr. Tilden has spoken as decisively as one may speak who has not had the occasion to make any formal, public utterance. As far back as two years ago he signified to those about him his purpose not again to be a candidate. Since then he has received unmistakable assurances that, if he would accept the nomination, no one would enter the lists against him. This induced him to be more explicit in the expression of his resolution and to give it a wider circle, and he has never changed his mind or his word, as far as anyone has reason to know or believe.

The average American is unable to imagine how his neighbor can be sincere in declining office. He may trust his friend with his purse, his razor, or even his wife and feel entirely safe. But let his friend in an unguarded moment, insinuate that, after all, the sweets of home and the sweat of honest toil, and the good will of men, and fair standing for integrity and veracity are better than swinging upon the see-saw of popular favor and sucking the sugar-candy of public preferment, that moment will he suspect him. Hence when a man says he doesn't want to be President, or go as a delegate, or what not, it is straightway surmised that he does; and if he puts his wish into reading, writing or arithmetic, the word goes out that he can't. Mr. Tilden has not escaped this insidious, though not very malign, predisposition of his fellow citizens. In spite of the circumstance that he was never an aspirant or seeker after place, no sooner did he get a taste of one than it was assumed that he was poisoned by it, and ever since, without any evidence whatever, or rhyme or reason, everything that has happened, and many things that never happened at all, have been construed to mean that he was intriguing and conspiring, and losing sleep to outwit somebody. Even those who could not keep his name off their pens for twenty-four consecutive hours charged him with being the author of their own malignant and foolish lucubrations. All the while our genial old sage was tending his flocks, and feeding his goats, and trailing his vines at Greystone, or secretly plotting a wainscot, or deeply designing an alcove in Gramercy Park; nor yet without a corner for his friends, and a pretty sharp lookout for his enemies, either!

Well, it has come to this at last—as everything seems to come to us—a little late. That the politicians of the party see, what the people saw four years ago, that Mr. Tilden is the universal choice. He himself has but to say the word, and that ends it. The National Convention will come together only to confirm it.

The question, however, is one of the very greatest moment. The whole future of the party may hinge upon it. Nothing should be done in the dark, hastily, or without advisement. The various State conventions can readily express their preference for the Old Ticket. Long before the 8th of July these preferences can be officially known to Mr. Tilden. He can then with propriety, and in advance of the meeting of the National Convention, and in time to allow Democrats opportunity to consider the situation if he declines, give his decision to the country. It should not be, and we are sure it will not be, left to the last moment, if, meanwhile, the action of the party is as conclusive as his will be. The people can not afford to have a matter so vital left to the haphazards of an excited and tumultuous assembly, or the dexterous manipulation of managers who happen to be prepared and in possession of the organization and the machine.

Let the States speak out resolutely and with resonance. If

the old ticket is to be nominated, the fact should be known in time to avert easily conjecturable disaster. If it can not be, by reason of Mr. Tilden's refusal to take the helm, that should be known. The very suggestion of taking some other nominee than Mr. Hendricks for Vice President—which would be fatal—illustrates, if everything else did not, the need of deliberation and consultation.

The Eighties were the years of rich phrase-making for the Louisville editor. It was in this period that the "Star-Eyed Goddess of Tariff Reform" was grouped with "A Tariff for Revenue Only," as the twin slogans of Democracy. Mr. Watterson especially used them in the campaign of 1884, as the following article demonstrates. In that year he wrote the national platform, as he also did in 1876 and 1888, and they redound with his favorite phrases.

The Star-Eyed Goddess

(April 29, 1884)

Returns from the counties come rolling in as clear and sweet as the waves of an inland sea. The Democrats of Kentucky have but one word to send to the Democrats of the Union. That word is "Courage."

Victories are not won by cowards, nor party advantages gained by dodging issues. In politics, at least, the complacent philosophy that

"He who fights and runs away
May live to fight another day,"

is replete with vicious and misleading counsels. If eternal vigilance be the price of liberty, incessant battle is the price of power. We shall never drive out the entrenched Republicans with blank cartridges. Our guns must be loaded, not with negations, but with shot and shell. If we have convictions, we must stand by them and fight for them; if we are a party, and not a reminiscence or a reflection, we must have a policy and assert it.

Kentucky stands as a stone wall in the center of the Democratic line of battle. We see only the enemy in front of us. Above us floats the free heart's hope and the free-home's flag —the ensign of fair and free government—bearing the motto: "Honesty, Economy, Equality and A Tariff for Revenue Only!" And what do we propose?

We propose just taxation. We propose that the blessings of Government, like the dews of Heaven, shall fall upon all alike. The tariff is a tax. As enacted by the Republicans it is paid by the poor. We propose that it shall be paid by the rich no less than the poor, each according to his means. We propose that not a cent of it shall go to enrich individuals, but that every cent of it shall go to the public Treasury, and that no more of it shall be collected than is needed by that Treasury. Millions, if need be, for defense; not a penny for tribute.

This is the monster that affrights the hardened soul of bounty-fed avarice. It is the dread specter that stands at the door of as wicked and as heartless a monopoly as ever wrung blood and tears from the needy and the weak, the widow and the orphan. It is the inexorable spirit of Justice which says to a blind and brutal system of rapine, born of the cruel necessities of war and kept alive by the sharp and venal forces of corruption, "Choose for your executioner, Me or the Mob!"

Democrats, everywhere, gather about this star-eyed Goddess of Reform, and fear not, for Truth is mighty and will prevail.

THE HARRISON CAMPAIGN

1888

The following political editorials in this book have many points of value to the student of political history and for those interested in Mr. Watterson and in American journalism. They were both published in the *Courier-Journal* on the same date, January 10, 1888, and it is probable, such was his capacity for labor, that he wrote them one after the other, at a sitting.

The first editorial reprinted here gives to the modern reader an unusual picture of James Russell Lowell as a politician. So fevered was the campaign of 1888, in which the Republicans were seeking desperately to recapture the Federal Government, that the editor lumped Mr. Lowell with all other Republicans and envisioned him simply as a party man. Nor did he scruple to quote from the "Biglow Papers" to confound Mr. Blaine with an attack from the Ambassador to St. James', the author of the Harvard "Commemoration Ode."

The second editorial of this day was on a favorite Watterson theme: bureaucracy, as exemplified by Civil Service. The editor sincerely had no patience with the Republican slogan of 1888 which later has become a general political attitude. He approved the effect, if not the language, of General Jackson's "To the victor belong the spoils." In this editorial Mr. Watterson made his stock arguments against Civil Service Reform with some prescience of the overloaded Government departments of today. As a rejoinder this editorial was milder than his wont, but that was probably because he liked George William Curtis and because he was engaged in a rather ticklish enterprise in defending what was called the Spoils System.

Lowell and Blaine

(January 10, 1888)

The attentions of the New York *Tribune* are just now divided between Mr. Lowell and Mr. Lamar. There is some kind of politics in this, we suppose, but we can not find it. The Republican party needs, as we see it, to strengthen itself in both sections of the country. It is in the opposition and must, in order to change the administration, concentrate all the elements of opposition and direct them against a united Democracy.

The attitude of the *Tribune* toward Mr. Lamar is the attitude of the Republican party toward the South, and, taken in connection with Mr. Chandler's electoral bill, it makes impossible any Republican gains in the South during the next campaign.

Equally impolitic is the *Tribune's* attitude toward Mr. Lowell and the element in the Republican party which he represents. For Mr. Lowell, judged by all the tests of the past, is a Republican with a Republican record which will match very well with the record of the *Tribune* itself. The extent of the dissatisfaction among the Republicans is well measured by the recent speech by Mr. Lowell. In 1884 these dissatisfied Republicans voted for Cleveland against Blaine, on grounds largely personal. They voted against Mr. Blaine because they did know him, and for Mr. Cleveland because he was an unknown quantity in national politics. From the standpoint of Mr. Lowell this vote was an experiment; it bound these dissatisfied Republicans to nothing for the future.

Now the situation has changed. The choice this year will not be to such an extent personal; the issue will be one that is definite and practical. This issue will be represented by Mr. Cleveland and by Mr. Blaine, with this difference, that in the past four years the untried man in national politics has developed wonderful sagacity; he approaches important questions in a spirit that is broad and national rather than partisan, and confronts his opponents with a courage that is a new element in political contests. On the other hand the representative of the reactionary element is the defeated candidate of 1884. In these three years he has made only two notable utterances. The first came immediately on his defeat. It was the expression of disappointed ambition; it was in bad temper; it was narrow, bitter and partisan to an extent that surprised his friends and shocked the public.

The second utterance was his Paris manifesto. which is reactionary to a marked degree; a shock to the intelligence of the country, and an appeal to class cupidity. In neither of these addresses is there anything to attract the alienated Republicans to Mr. Blaine.

The address of Mr. Lowell is evidence of this fact. It shows that in 1888 the Democratic issue will be what the Democratic nominee did in 1888. Instead of recognizing this situation and attempting to alter it the *Tribune* proceeds as if the task was hopeless and the only consolation left is in abusing the bigoted Mugwumps and the traitorous Democrats.

In order to further fan the flame of this hatred the *Courier-Journal* refers the *Tribune* to deliverances by Mr. Lowell even more personal and obnoxious than those contained in his recent Boston address. We find for instance the following lines in the "Biglow Papers," and they apply with peculiar aptness to Mr. Blaine as the Republican candidate in 1888:

> "Some candidates air dead an' gone, and some hez been defeated,
> Which 'mounts to pooty much the same; fer it's been proved repeated
> A batch o' bread that haint riz once ain't goin' to rise agin,
> An' it's jest money throwed away to put the emptins in.
> But thet's what folks wun't never larn; they dunno how to go,
> Arter you want their room, no more'n a bullet-headed beau;
> There's ollers chaps a-hangin' roun' that can't see peatime's past,
> Mis'ble as roosters in a rain, heads down and tails half-mast;
> It ain't disgraceful bein' beat, when a holl nation doos it
> For chance is like an amberill—it don't take twice to lose it."

This is a low, vulgar fling at a most unfortunate knight. The language is coarse, the spelling is irregular, the truths are blunt and homely, the comparisons are particularly odious. It is disgraceful to compare a distinguished American statesman with headquarters in Paris and hindquarters in the Tall Tower, to "a batch o' bread that hain't riz once," or to a bullet-headed beau who does not know his room is wanted, to a chap who does not know when peatime's past, or last and worst, to "roosters in the rain, with heads down and tails half-mast."

It may be urged that Mr. Lowell wrote these lines in 1861, and long before he supposed Mr. Blaine would be twice a candidate for the Presidency, but this excuse will not avail. A poet is a seer, and if Mr. Lowell did not intend that these lines should apply to Mr. Blaine he should not have written them.

We feel after reading them that the animosity of the *Tribune* is fully justified. They account for the abuse of Mr. Lowell in-

dulged in by the *Tribune,* for which the Boston address alone did
not suffice. The *Tribune* has our sympathy; we warn it against
taking the fatal leap with Mr. Blaine.

"For chance is like an amberill—it don't take twice to lose it."

The Civil-Service Phantom

(January 10, 1888)

In the recent issue of *Harper's Weekly,* and in the course
of some observations touching the Reform of the Revenue
couched in terms of such appreciation and compliment as to
make it a kind of churlishness to question them, we find the
following:

"Mr. Watterson has been a reluctant supporter of the President,
   although he has anticipated Mr. Cleveland's nomination, and
   has announced his adhesion to him as the probable Democratic candidate. His feeling has been largely determined by
   the President's views of civil service reform, which Mr.
   Watterson regards as an aristocratic and British and un-
   American device. This view is so shallow that it seriously
   affects the estimate of the value of his judgment upon other
   questions of reform in administration."

We have no disposition to complain of this, which possesses
at least the merit of candor. But we take it for granted that
the Editor of *Harper's Weekly* is incapable of a purpose to mis-
represent the opinions of anybody. In the passage above quoted,
however, he does, in point of fact, misapprehend and mistake
those of the editor of the *Courier-Journal.* If the objections
which the latter felt it a duty to set against the civil service orders of the President in the Stone-Benton cases, and to the civil
service chapter of the second annual message of the President
to Congress, rested on no other grounds than those suggested by
Mr. Curtis, they would, indeed, deserve to be described as "shallow." The truth is otherwise.

The platform resolution of the last convention of the Democrats of Kentucky, whose spirit and tenor have been adopted by
nearly if not by all of the Democratic State conventions which
have since assembled, reads thus:

"We favor honest civil service reform; by which we mean the
   enforcement of the faithful performance by persons appointed to office of all public duties intrusted to them, and to
   this end, as well as to the maintenance of the spirit of our

representative form of government, we demand the strictest measure of personal and party responsibility, and are opposed to the substitution, in room of this, of life tenure, a civil pension list, and all other appendages of a bureaucratic system foreign to the genius of our institutions and people."

This was meant as a protest against the revolution of our entire official system threatened by the extreme lengths to which the President seemed resolved to carry a tentative act of Congress, embracing, by its provisions, only a certain class of subordinate appointments. It is an assertion of the principle of party responsibility for the honest and efficient administration of the public service according to and contemplated by the representative character of our Government. It no wise affirms the doctrine that to the victors belong the spoils in the sense that cleanliness and fitness may be disregarded in the selection of public servants by the party in power. It simply invests that party with its full accountability for the results of its tenure of power.

Free government is referable largely to public sentiment, forcing upon those who are charged with its conduct its own virtues, or vices. Good administration is good administrators. Great abuses are possible to systems, admirable in themselves, but hedged about by prescription and fastened by red tape. The President, spurred on by a well-intentioned purpose to stamp out admitted partisan excesses and to give the people more of business and less of politics in the practical working of their official fabric, was going at a gallop toward the complete overthrow of the representative feature of our constitutional organism, and, in doing this, was assuming a right of dictation unauthorized by that instrument and using language to officials not embraced by the Civil-service Act which better became an overseer to field-hands than a Chief Magistrate to citizens invested equally with himself by the responsibilities of untrammeled public station.

To this the *Courier-Journal* made strenuous opposition; but at no time did it advocate the repeal of the civil service statute. On the contrary, we would give that act its fair trial in the character of the experiment which it was admitted to be when Congress enacted it. Undoubtedly, among those covered by its provisions, there should be as great a separation from partisan machinery as is consistent with individual liberty.

The editor of the *Courier-Journal* was in early life a civil servant in the Land Office at Washington, and is personally familiar with the operations of both the old and the new system. He prefers the new. The under-clerks should be protected against the insecurity of mere favoritism and the demands of political blackmail. State party organizations, in the National Capital, which are only devices for the exploitations of noisy zealots and the extortion of money from timid starvelings, should be discouraged, if not suppressed outright, by the President, and the heads of the departments "going home to vote," another and a fruitful scheme of fraud, should be disallowed. The active participation of officials in elections is not, per se, a good thing. But, after all, it is an abuse which is as like to defeat itself as not; and, be this as it may, as long as we have a free, representative government, it is an abuse inseparable from that form, because to deny the right is to disfranchise the citizen whenever he takes office.

The true course is the middle course, resting upon the intelligence and patriotism of those intrusted with power, and the enlightened interest of the representatives of party organizations, who should be given the largest latitude of selection in the matter of their subordinates and held on the strictest measures of responsibility for the consequences.

All this may seem very "shallow" to the editor of *Harper's Weekly;* but it embraces the belief of an overwhelming majority of Americans of both parties, and, not alone of self-seeking trenchermen and spoils politicians, but of thoughtful, unselfish citizens who love their country and who wish to preserve its free institutions, even at some cost of expert work and of dollars and cents, in their fullest Democratic spirit.

We have set no particular stress upon the "aristocratic" character of life-tenure in office. On this point all that we have said is, that it does establish a class undemocratic in every way. The civil service of England, and the Bureaucracies of Germany and France, are by no means ideal institutions. They no less than the spoils system of America have their abuses. We prefer not to correct our abuses by copying them and their abuses, but to mend our system as it stands. The Civil Service Act, fairly and intelligently administered, ought to produce good results. But its radical application everywhere will merely defeat its purpose. The President's letter to the New York Democrats is its own best commentary upon the civil service "orders" in the Stone-Benton cases and completely vindicates our animadversions. We think that, in that letter, the President was right. His name was being used against his party and its candidates in his own state. It was due to both that he should not allow himself to be so used by the enemy. He is not outlawed from political thinking, nor from freedom of speech, because he is President.

Mr. Curtis is an accomplished and an able man, and we have no reason to question his perfect integrity of purpose, but, in this matter of the Civil Service, he has never been just either to the *Courier-Journal* or its editor.

CLEVELAND OVERTURNS A PROPHECY

1892

In his own book of recollections, Mr. Watterson related as much about his personal and political attitude toward Grover Cleveland as he chose. The distinguished pair did not work well together after 1888, and, when the campaign of 1892 approached, the editor was anxious to prevent the third nomination. In this connection was uttered his famous remark that, were the party to go to New York for a nominee, "we shall walk through a slaughter-house into an open grave." This was uttered in the course of an address (published hereafter) to the Kentucky Democratic convention in May, 1892, and, while it applied equally to David B. Hill and Cleveland, the real target of the attack was the former President and its intended beneficiary was John G. Carlisle, of Kentucky.

A specimen of the editorial argument which, in that year, Mr. Watterson employed in an effort to establish his position is also appended. He always believed that the unforeseen strikes at Homestead defeated Harrison and logic and elected Cleveland.

BEFORE THE CONVENTION

May 26, 1892, addressing the Kentucky State Convention at Louisville, Ky., Mr. Watterson said:

In spite of the cordiality of your welcome, and the glow of good feeling which warms these cold walls and turns this old hall into a flower-garden, I shall hope, and take leave to think, that this is a deliberative body; a deliberative body of Democrats; a deliberative body of Kentuckians; a deliberative body of Kentucky Democrats; for that is the kind of body I am myself! If I have ever said anything about anybody, or anything, that anybody, or anything, objects to, I take it back! If anybody has an opinion about anything that anybody else objects to, I am opposed to that! There is only one thing that I won't do, even to please you: I won't lie to you, or for you. I shall try to tell the truth as I am able to see it; and, if you can't see it, as I see it, may the good Lord still be good to you.

It is not my purpose on this occasion to inflict a speech upon you, or to waste your time and my time in threshing old straw. You know as well as I do that the situation which faces us is a most serious situation. It can not be smeared over with a little goose-grease on the one hand, nor carried by storm on the other hand. It bristles with disagreeable facts, with facts that will down at no man's bidding. It is beset by dangers, by dangers which are both seen and unseen. I beg you to believe that I have tried faithfully, tried like an honest, unselfish man, having some experience in public affairs, to deal with the facts as they are, to compass the dangers as they seem to be—evading no issue and shirking no responsibility—and, at last, I am bound to tell you that all I can make of it is that the long-threatened has come to pass; we are literally and actually between the devil and the deep blue sea, between Scylla and Charybdis, and whichever way we turn, to whatever point of the compass we steer our bark, the weather thickens, and the prospect becomes more and more uncertain.

To me there is but one comfort in sight—though it is a very great comfort indeed—and that is that our political adversary, our friends the enemy, are as bad off as we are ourselves. Yes, there is another comfort; a comfort which I derive from the wisdom of a philosopher native and to the manner born. It was a saying of old Governor Charles Scott, the Indiana fighter, that "when things are bad, they are hard to mend; but when they get damned bad, they just cut loose and mend themselves." Gentlemen, you can make your own application. This is your affair, and whatever you finally conclude to do, that I shall support with all my heart.

In the meantime, I ask you as reasonable men and as good Democrats to consider the case as it is, calmly and justly, without prejudice or favor, or any interest except the vindication of truth and right, as embodied, and alone attainable, in the triumph of Democratic principles and policies, and the election of a Democratic President.

That is my only objective point. I have no other. To attain it, I would make any sacrifice short of the surrender of conviction and honor. Happily, I am required to make none; for I am personally concerned in no man's fortunes, and have not the least pride of opinion to set against the will of my party when it has been deliberately formed and decisively proclaimed.

I think that there is something more than a good fighting chance to nominate a National Democratic ticket which can be elected next November. But I can not believe that such a ticket is to be found where faction reigns among Democrats. On the contrary, it seems to me that we shall need the solid and hearty co-operation of all our forces to carry any of the States which are usually described as debatable and which are indispensable to the election of a Democratic President. For this reason, and because of none other, I have urged, and I do urge, the wisdom of the very greatest moderation and caution; and, particularly with respect to those predilections which represent not harmony, but dissension; not unity, but division; not peace, but war. I am the enemy of no Democratic aspirant; nor the friend of any to the point of placing his personality, and my preference, before the party welfare. Certainly some men may take better candidates than some other men. I would by no means leave men entirely out of the account. But ideas, issues, policies are above and beyond all else and no man is a good Democrat who is unwilling to stand by these when the party interest requires it.

In one of the great states of the Union—in the greatest of all the states—a state which ordinarily ought to be safely Democratic, and whose electoral vote is absolutely essential to Democratic success, I am able to see nothing but chaos. If you can see anything else you have better eyes than mine. But, to me, it seems that if we go there for a nominee we shall walk through a slaughter-house into an open grave.

I may be mistaken; but, according to all human experience, according to the precedents which control the political action of all parties, the very statement of the case ought to be conclusive, for it is axiomatic. We do not gather grapes from thistles, nor pluck the flower of love from brands blazing with the fires of hate and strife. If I am asked for my witnesses, I point to the conflicting testimony of both sides to the controversy; though you, fellow-Democrats, should need no such evidence. The controversy itself is enough.

But at least in this place, I will entertain no gloomy forebodings. My hope is that the darkest hour is just before the dawn; and that out of much confusion and many counsels, good will come. There is a destiny that has presided over the life of Democracy; which has hovered above us as a star during the long watches of the night; which has enwrapped us as a garment through the toilsome journey of the weary day; and, which, please God, shall continue with us to an end that shall not go down in sorrow and disgrace.

My friends, I have not come here to tire your patience, or to tax your temper, or even to seem to tell you what to do. I want nothing for myself. All that I am, all that I have been, all that I could be in the public life of the country, is but the emanation of your confidence and support; and I am ready to lay it all at your feet, so that the cause of good government be advanced and the glory and honor of the dear old Commonwealth are fulfilled, through a Democracy unterrified and undefiled.

The Square Deal

(February 23, 1892)

Now that the Democrats of New York have spoken, through the regular and lawful channels appointed for party expression, and the Honorable David Bennett Hill is formally presented to his fellow-Democrats of the United States as the choice of the Democrats of the Empire State for President, the question before the country becomes one of ayes and noes; for whoever secures this nomination must beat Mr. Hill.

Whatever else we do, let us not mistake the issue. It is squarely before us. Mr. Cleveland is no longer a possibility. His selection as the Democratic standard-bearer, if such a thing were, under the circumstances, conceivable, would be, on the part of the National Democracy, an act of deliberate suicide. He could not be elected; and we are so sure of his own good sense, as well as of his dignity of character, that we have no idea that he will allow his name to go before the National Democratic Convention. To do so would be to submit himself to four months of wrangle, ruinous to his party and most hurtful to himself, dragging his great name and career through an embittered, and a more or less indecent, controversy, with certain defeat, in the event of his nomination by the convention, at the polls. We shall need the consolidation of all our forces to elect a Democratic President next November; and we can afford to take no man who has to fight his way through a line of hostile Democratic camps before he could get a place to fight the Republicans.

The Democrats of the Union should meet the act of the New York Democrats in setting Mr. Cleveland aside, officially, as it were, and advancing Mr. Hill to the party leadership—for this is the meaning of the work done yesterday at Albany—with all possible consideration. We must treat it fairly. It is not the part of wisdom, nor is it just or prudent, to fly into a passion about it; to assail its authors and to abuse its subjects. They are all Democrats. It is a legitimate movement. Many as may be the reasons for respecting those Democrats who protest against it, they represent a minority, according to the record; and party discipline, indispensable to results, can not be maintained if the will of the majority, ascertained by constitutional methods, is not accepted as the law. Much as we owe the Mugwumps, so-called, and greatly as we may desire and need their continued alliance and co-operation, they are not, and do not claim to be, Democrats, and we can not regard their wishes as paramount, or look to their opinions first and foremost in selecting a National Democratic ticket. Before all else, our duty, as Democrats, is to ourselves and to one another.

In this spirit let us say that, whilst we are fully impressed by the array which Mr. Hill has behind him, and whilst we thoroughly understand the logic of the argument which urges his nomination with so much plausibility and force, we can not for the life of us see how, even upon the propositions in practical politics which are put forward so cogently in his behalf, he does not stand except in less degree on the same footing with Mr. Cleveland.

The followers of the ex-President must see, as Mr. Cleveland must see himself, that his election is not possible in the face of the stubborn opposition to Mr. Hill and his friends. But how much more probable is Mr. Hill's election in the face not merely of the wide-spread disappointment caused by the subordination of a popular favorite, but of an Independent ticket which his nomination will surely force into the field? There are Democrats, of course, who will scout this suggestion. But an organized movement, led by clever and clean men, conjuring in the name of potent issues and amply provided with the sinews of war, is not to be despised. It will appeal to great bodies of people, particularly to great numbers of young voters, losing us every doubtful State; even assuming that Mr. Hill can carry New York, which his nomination would by no means guarantee, because it is certain that he will encounter, as a candidate for President, obstacles and an opposition he has never had to encounter as a candidate for Governor.

It does seem to us that, leaving out all other considerations, the nomination of Mr. Hill would be a great risk in purely practical politics. But, in our judgment, there are, back of any questions of practical politics that may be involved, considerations of far-reaching, and at the same time, of present and pressing importance. These embrace all that is animating and inspiring in the public life of America on the side of our manhood and our convictions, on the side of fair play, both to leaders and ideas, and, above all, to that great Democratic sentiment of popular sovereignty, as opposed to the mere machinery of organization which, outside of the State of New York, has a lodgment in every Democratic heart.

Mr. Hill does not represent this ideal so dear to the Democracy of the West and South. Mr. Cleveland does. Without saying a word at the expense of the one, or to extol the other, this is a simple fact. Nor can Mr. Hill escape its consequences as long as he appears as the rival of Mr. Cleveland, and the residuary of the benefits of a disadvantage inflicted upon Mr. Cleveland.

There are thousands of Democrats who, recognizing the hopelessness of the case, may consent to the loss of Mr. Cleveland. But they will not accept Mr. Hill. The transition is too abrupt, the wrench is too violent. The disaster of 1888, however wrongfully ascribed to Mr. Hill, rankles in many a Democratic memory. If nominated for President, Mr. Hill would carry it through the canvass as a wound upon his sword-arm, which would certainly impair his fencing, if it did not, in the end, prove fatal to his candidacy.

His nomination can only be reached after a long contest, and then only by the agency of resolute and expert organization; and, when it has been so reached, will he not have much weakened, if he has not exhausted, himself?

There is not time between now and the day of election to educate the mass and body of Democrats out of their preference for Mr. Cleveland and into an acceptance of Mr. Hill as his successor in the party leadership. They feel already that they have been cheated out of Mr. Cleveland by the political managers. They may rally to one who has had no part nor lot in this. But, no matter how the work is accomplished in the coming State Conventions, and in the National Convention, they will not rally to the man who stands accused of having done it all, and that for his own, selfish purposes.

That all this does injustice to Mr. Hill we know as well as anybody. It is his misfortune, not his fault. But in politics, personal mischance counts for quite as much as personal shortcoming. It is hard lines to Mr. Cleveland that he is not as strong at home as he is elsewhere. Because of this, he must stand aside. Mr. Hill is strong in New York; but he is weak everywhere else, and this is as serious a disability to him as that which disqualifies Mr. Cleveland.

Individualities are nothing in great movements unless they are attended by great qualities that rise out of these movements, or are requisite to them. The political world is very exacting and very just. It recognizes in its real leaders both inspiration and equipment, and blindly follow such; but the least of its leaders must be available, and the hand which has proved itself so puissant in destroying Mr. Cleveland we fear has paralyzed itself.

To the nomination, therefore, put forward by the Democrats of the Empire State, we must respectfully, and for the reasons given, vote no; and we offer, as a substitute, the Hon. John Griffin Carlisle, of Kentucky; next in succession to Grover Cleveland, as leader and embodiment of the great issue of Revenue Reform, and in eminence of abilities, in public services and in personal integrity altogether worthy to wear his mantle and entirely large enough to fill it.

THE CRITICAL BATTLE OF FREE SILVER

1896

The fight of the *Courier-Journal* against William Jennings Bryan in 1896 was not conducted by Mr. Watterson. After the nomination in Chicago he thrilled political circles by sending from Switzerland to his partner, Mr. W. N. Haldeman, the famous cablegram, "No compromise with dishonor"; and several times in the course of the campaign he wrote long political articles from abroad. It was Mr. Haldeman and his associates who engaged in the bitter activities which carried Kentucky for McKinley and lost the *Courier-Journal* much of its circulation and prestige among Southern Democrats. At that time Mr. Watterson had expected to retire from active journalism and was supervising the education of his children abroad. But so serious was the financial effect of the *Courier-Journal's* bolt of Bryan and support of Palmer and Buckner that Mr. Watterson returned to his desk and the next four years of his life and those of his partner were the busiest and most anxious in their careers. By 1900 the disaffection caused by the *Courier-Journal's* 1896 position was thoroughly balanced by its support of Bryan in that year, and not again did a Republican Presidential candidate carry Kentucky.

It should not be assumed from the foregoing that Mr. Watterson was not completely, in spirit and in principle, allied with his partner, Mr. Haldeman, in the anti-Free Silver fight of 1896. While it lacked the active magic of his pen, the editorial course had his heartiest approbation. To the partners, and particularly to Mr. Haldeman, the financial programme of Mr. Bryan meant ruin and misery in the United States, and they were entirely willing to lose their property —which they almost did—in an effort to prevent the election of the Democratic candidate. Twelve years later, in 1908, the editor, supporting Bryan for a second time in the *Courier-Journal,* declared that he and his associates had "made a mistake in 1896 in thinking that the currency was in danger" and remarked that Mr. Bryan was too amiable to put a Government in peril. When Mr. Watterson wrote this Mr. Haldeman had been dead six years, and it is the only indication in any of his writings that his mind had ever suffered a change with respect to the serious intention of Mr. Bryan to apply the Free Silver principle to the currency.

Mr. Watterson had rejoiced over the nomination of

Parker in 1904 and in 1907 he attempted by a curious device to head off the third Bryan movement. He announced that he had a "Dark Horse who was the Democratic governor of a northern state, was tall and eloquent and wore a mustache." Except for the mustache this description fitted Governor John A. Johnson, of Minnesota, who, the editor later admitted, was his dark horse. He added that he had put in the mustache merely to make it more difficult to discover the identity of his candidate. Nothing came of this effort, however. With Mr. Bryan and Mr. Watterson it continued a case of off-again and on-again, and the last record in these writings touching the gentleman from Nebraska is a fervent prayer of thanksgiving that he had resigned as Secretary of State.

Subjoined will be found the notable cablegram which started the 1896 fight; and a representative article on the situation which Mr. Watterson sent from abroad.

Watterson to the Democracy

(Published in the *Courier-Journal*)

Geneva, Switzerland, July 13, 1896, via French Cable—
    Walter N. Haldeman, President *Courier-Journal* Co.,
    Louisville, Ky.
    Another ticket our only hope. No compromise with dishonor. Stand firm.

HENRY WATTERSON

The Democratic Crisis

(*October 9, 1896*)

I

The issues of the presidential election are at length fully set before the people of the United States. Three presidential tickets draw upon themselves the interest of voters. If the voters do not decide for the best it will not be for any lack of advisement; for has not this been a campaign of education?

In Europe where Democracy has no friends it is freely predicted that the great Republic of North America is about to go the way of the little Republics of South America, a victim to revolutionary schemes and ambitious leaders. Here the currency question cuts no figure except among the resident or traveling Americans. The European banker would welcome a free-silver act of Congress for the simple reason that it would confuse exchanges and make him business. Whatever happens to others he would get his profit. The average European cares nothing about it either way; but being, as a rule, hostile to the United States it flatters his vanity, whilst bolstering his prejudice, to think that agrarianism, as he calls Republicanism, is about to bring forth fiscal anarchy, and, along with it, the beginning of the end of Democracy.

Could anything be sadder or furnish matter for deeper reflection than the spectacle of the simple, honest farmer of the West and South, wanting to do right, loving his country and eager for accurate information, yet told by men he is used to believing that the money kings of Europe have fastened the gold standard on America, and that, if the people of the United States do not rise in self-defense and declare a policy of their own, the creditor class will wipe out the debtor class and all of us become mere vassals of monarchy under the style and title of Plutocracy?

II

As it approaches the end of the most opulent of its centuries, the world is passing through a period of economic transition. Mechanical contrivance, based upon the discovery of things hitherto unknown and unapplied, has worked a revolution in the art of construction and production; time and space have been bridged by human agencies operating as a kind of Providence in the simplest affairs of life; and questions have arisen thence which baffle the wit of the wisest. Nowhere has society wholly adjusted itself to the changed and changing conditions; and he who thinks he has found a solution of their problems—an answer to the riddle of the ages encompassed by the genius of modern invention—must entertain a most optimistic view of his own powers of divination. We are at best, and the best of us, mere atoms in the hands of God. But if He who, creating man and placing him upon the earth for some all-wise purpose, denied him omniscience, He yet endowed him with certain faculties by the use of which he may from time to time ascertain the exact point he has reached upon the line of his travel and tell the time of day, and otherwise distinguish between right and wrong in the material, as in the moral, journey from the cradle to the grave.

There is no nation in Christendom which has not to consider questions of the gravest moment, peculiar to itself. In the United States, blessed as we have been and as we are, it would be strange if we should be exempt from the common lot of man. One of the candidates for President in this campaign has put himself to the pains of denying that it is the purpose either of himself, or those who support him, to enter upon a reconstruction of human society, though, if he will forgive my saying so, that would seem to be both the promise and the reason for his being, since, if he be sincere, it can have none other. A second candidate would content himself with reconstructing the Tariff, and leaving all else where it is. Assuredly, three matters of prime importance press upon the immediate attention of the people; and although each of these embodies an issue separate and distinct, they bear more or less a relation one to the other. They may be grouped under these several heads:

First—The integrity of the nation; its credit at home and abroad, laid chiefly and first of all, in orderly Government holding a just balance between liberty and law.

Second—The system of taxation; Federal, State and municipal; the principle of public revenue, and of revenue only, dominating the whole, with the attendant requisition of honesty and economy in the expenditure of the taxes thus collected.

Third—The money of the country, expressed in gold and silver, and paper convertible into coin on demand, its purchase power and its stability assured to the people everywhere, at all times and under all circumstances.

III

The buttress of liberty is order. The bell-tower of order is the law. Both liberty and order are assailed by the platform of the Chicago convention.

To that extent, and in that regard, it was distinctly a concession to the exactions of Governor Altgeld and Senator Tillman.

Those Democrats who affect to disapprove the platform, yet support the ticket upon the point of party regularity and discipline, are mightily displeased by any references to those gentlemen. They repudiate both of them with more or less impatience and acrimony. Even the Chicago convention whilst adopting their extreme views hastened to turn the cold shoulder upon them. Since the adjournment of the convention it has been the aim of the managers of Mr. Bryan's campaign to keep them in the background. But, if Governor Altgeld and Senator Tillman had never lived, the ideas which they represent, fully embraced by the movement which Mr. Bryan represents, would remain an inseparable objection to it, and to all concerned in it.

Mr. Bryan is careful to reiterate and to reiterate that he stands on the platform. He indorses it word for word, and letter for letter. His protestations are superfluous. The speech which gained him the nomination was enough. It fully committed him to any extremes the platform might advance, and, in the event of his election, to any excesses to which the pretended friends of the discontented operative could be the more easily led by the ring which these professional politicians, each with some office to guard or to get, imagined they had inserted in the nose of either.

Fatal error! The people are never so credulous as they sometimes seem to be. There is always a reserve which does not show upon the surface; and the gentlemen who planned to capture the title and effects of the Democratic party, and, with these as an asset, to organize a new party, reckoned without a due regard to this popular reserve boon of intelligence and virtue. The charlatan, always blatant and aggressive, is led to mistake the outcry of his fellow charlatans for the voice of mankind. To the last moment he remains unconscious of the silent many, who think and do, making no sign; and except for whom politics would be an easy trade. In this election they will show themselves in unprecedented force—wise, brave, temperate men—who can not be lured from their duty by the specious sophisms of a plan of campaign which would substitute exclamation for oratory and clamor for economic truth, who can not be driven away from the polls by appeals to party loyalty, or personal abuse and threats of violence.

We are nearing the beginning of the end, not of Democracy, but of Populism, to which the Chicago convention surrendered when it nominated Mr. Bryan, a representative Populist, and placed him on a platform dictated by Governor Altgeld and Senator Tillman, and framed to meet the exigencies of the forthcoming Populist convention at St. Louis.

IV

The familiar example of misrepresentation in this presidential campaign—the never-failing source and resource of the advocates of the free coinage of silver under the present, and every and all conditions—is the claim that they learned their lesson from the present Secretary of the Treasury.

As the intellectual head of the sound money party in the United States, no less than the first fiscal officer of the Government, this gentleman naturally draws the fire of the opposition. He is a man of commanding talents and unassailable integrity. He has not encountered good fortune in the circumstances attending his administration of the Treasury Department; but it is not easy to specify what he might have done other than what he has done. But the silver advocates, forgetting their debt to Mr. Bland, of Missouri, and Mr. Jones, of Nevada, insist that they learned their lesson from Mr. Carlisle. Now, what was this lesson and when, how and where did they learn it?

Twenty years ago everybody in the United States was for silver. Nobody was against it. Not to be a bimetallist was not to be a

humanity might claim his allegiance. To reconstruct the S
Court under the pretext of reforming it would become an
istration measure of the first importance; and, in case of a
tion of the outbreaks of two years ago, the arm of the
Government must not be stretched out for the protection of
property, even its own life and its own property. The p
which Mr. Bryan heralds so loudly and proclaims so defian
not in specific terms condemn the President of the United
nor extol the Governor of Illinois; but, in effect, this pa
plank declares that in asserting the power of the Govern
maintaining the public peace Mr. Cleveland was wrong, and
practical encouragement which Governor Altgeld gave the
he was right.

The purpose of those who, inspired by Governor Altg
Senator Tillman, made the platform was to catch what t
"the labor vote," under the impression that every man who
for day wages is an anarchist. The spirit underlying the
agrarian. It is not Democracy. It is not Republicanism
simply the arraying of class against class, appealing to the
passions and the densest ignorance for its justification.

No government on earth could stand on such a principle
an open invitation to lawlessness. Once admitted, it coul
appease the appetite of the ever-existent turbulent elem
society. By its leave, and under pretense of Mr. Bryan's
of humanity" behind it, we should soon have in place
Plutocracy which—in one and the same breath—it crea
proposes to remove, a mobocracy, leveling all men and all th
suit the varying moods of each succession of firebrands.
Governor Altgeld and Senator Tillman might find it hard
up with the procession; and one trembles to think what wo
come of Mr. Bryan if, invested with even a momentary sens
sponsibility, he should, in the interest of society and the
happen to consult the primitive law of self-preservation, ar
his hand against a chaos provoked and precipitated by hin

The scheme, as outlined by the Chicago platform, thoug
last degree sinister, is happily chimerical. The visionary m
begat it—too self-willed and short-sighted to recognize ther
and one another as the merest architects of ruin—will surel
if they do not bitterly repent, their perversity. It was laid
fancy that a majority of the people of the United States
equal to self-government. It was nurtured by the conceit t
needy and the poor naturally take to quack nostrums, ar
liberal advertising and loud protestation will effect the same
in the game of politics that they do in the sale of patent me
It was matured and launched in the belief that the time ha
when, under pressure of hard times, the overtaxed farm

Christian; and I suspect that most bimetallists knew quite as little about bimetallism as many Christians know about Christianity. To speak plain truth, none of us, not even Mr. Sherman or Mr. Carlisle, had the faintest conception of the question as it now presents itself. How could they? The great silver mines, since opened, were unknown. The difference between gold and silver was but a fraction. The coinage question had always been left to experts. Mr. Jefferson had laid down the doctrine that we must ascertain the market value of gold and silver and regulate the ratio thereto. It was not a matter for political science to worry about. It was simply an affair of commerce and arithmetic. It required the advent of such masters in finance as Mr. Bland, of Missouri, and Messrs. Jones and Stewart, of Nevada, and such political philosophers as Mr. Bryan and Mr. Watson and Mr. Sewall, and such statesmen as Gov. Altgeld and Senator Tillman to turn Thomas Jefferson down and to proclaim that all the wrongs of which the human family—especially in the United States—complains are directly traceable to a something which they vaguely but boisterously describe as "the demonetization of silver."

As a matter of fact, silver is not demonetized. It not only freely circulates, is as good as gold, and is legal tender for all debts, but there is fifty times more of it in circulation than had been coined by our mints during the Nineteenth Century before this dread act of 1873. If that act was an injury it has been amply avenged. But, in 1878, Mr. Carlisle, like everybody else the friend then, as he is now of silver, declared that the greatest hurt that could come to mankind would be its elimination from the coinage of Christendom. Allowing for some pardonable rhetorical exaggeration, that is not wholly a bad proposition even now, with silver down to little more than half its value then. Mr. Carlisle has small reason to be ashamed of his utterance. But what was true in 1878 was less true in 1883, and what was true, or seemed to be true in 1886, is wholly false in 1896. Nothing remains stationary—not even silver. Information with intelligent people does not remain stationary; and Mr. Carlisle, like every other intelligent man, knows a great deal more about the money question today than he, or anybody else, knew twenty years ago, or ten years ago.

The free-silver organs are making much ado over an editorial which is alleged to have appeared in the *Courier-Journal* the 10th of August, 1886. Having passed that year in Europe, I never saw or heard of this editorial until its reproduction in the present campaign. It may, or may not, be genuine. But, assuming that it is, what does it prove? Either that whoever wrote it was mistaken when he wrote it, or else, if he was not mistaken, his conclusions do not apply to existing conditions. One thing I can aver, that neither the *Courier-Journal* nor its editor ever favored fiat money, or gave their assent to a depreciated currency. During the greenback controversy, when fiat money and a depreciated currency were an issue, the paper, and its editor, stood almost alone in the West and South in opposition to that form of repudiation, and in support of the integrity of the nation.

To favor silver as long as there seemed to be a chance to arrest its downward progress was one thing. To favor its use as money along with gold, and supported by the Government, every silver dollar as good as a gold one, is one thing. To drop the governmental responsibility whilst retaining the Government's stamp—to detach silver from gold and to turn it loose on its own hook, as it were—to force fifty cents' worth of silver for one hundred cents' worth of debt—is quite another thing.

The attempt to save silver by legislation was certainly a mistake, but it was an honest error of judgment, arising out of friendly ignorance. But the silver zealots attempt to make this friendship a cause of added offense. They would punish one man more for having tried to help silver than ninety and nine who were always its enemies. If I believed a free-silver act of Congress would restore the lost parity between gold and silver, and bring silver back to the ratio of 15 or 16 to 1, I would be for it. But I believe no such thing. On the contrary, I feel assured that the effect of such an act would be to drive out gold, to put the country on a monometallic basis, preparatory to a flood of irredeemable paper currency, with the certain result of public discredit and private disaster.

Against so desperate a financial adventure the Democrats who have nominated Palmer and Buckner set themselves resolutely and they stand on impregnable ground. They stand for the honor of the nation among the nations of the earth, and for the moral being of commercial society. They are in line with the best thought of the best countries; and they have the experience of mankind, the warnings of history and the teaching of the fathers of Democracy in support of their plea for sound money and good faith. In General Palmer and General Buckner they give hostages to the confidence of the people. What have these two noble and rugged old heroes to gain by the brave fight they are making if it be not the honor and glory of rescuing their country and their party from imminent and real peril? I know them both and I know them well. Braver soldiers never drew blade in battle, purer patriots never offered counsel in civil affairs. Before their sturdy personality, other candidates are dwarfed. In the Senate and in the field, as administrators and as statesmen, and, above all, as private citizens, they have always commanded the affection and respect of their own people. Those who knew them best loved them most. The character of the movement of which they have been made the leaders protects them against the accusation of self-seeking. Their age is a guarantee of their disinterested sincerity. When such men offer themselves as sacrifices upon the altar of principle and duty, it may well give pause to the inconsiderate among their old comrades-in-arms and associates in Democracy. They at least can not be charged with selling themselves for a price, or with being ignorant of Democratic gospel, or saddled with any purpose other than that which is set forth in the admirable platform on which the Indianapolis convention placed them. If they be false, then there is no such thing as truth among men. If they be not Democrats, then there are no Democrats. He must indeed be a poor sort of Democrat who prefers Bryan and Sewall, or Bryan and Watson, piebald platform and all, to such men and such a platform.

v

In concluding this letter I would like to address a few serious words to those Democrats who seem to be unable to vote according to what they consider their party duty, without visiting opprobrium and hurling epithets upon those Democrats who, admonished by their conscience, are unable to take that view of the situation. It is a poor cause that needs abuse to sustain it. So much is a truism; but shall we never have done with the senselessness, to say nothing about the indecency and the injustice, of crimination and recrimination, the political mountebank's immemorial stock-in-trade? To call names is to accuse one's self; but, by the suppression or distortion of facts, to seek a dishonest advantage, or, for the same purpose, to tell lies outright, is to put an affront upon the people, which, soon or late, the people will resent. In the long run truth always wins. It is a melancholy part of the plan of human existence, an illustration of the irony of fate, that the victory so often comes too late to rescue merit from needless sacrifice, or even to soothe the last moments of expiring martyrdom.

That Mr. Bryan will be beaten seems as certain as any event which has not yet come to pass. One may confidently predict this without setting up for a prophet. When he is beaten, does anyone suppose that the gentlemen responsible for the ill-starred movement, of which, in a spasm of hysteria, the Chicago convention made him leader, will be trusted to recognize the Democratic party; or that the party may be reorganized on the lines laid down by a platform stultifying axiomatic principles of Democratic truth?

This platform was framed to meet the approval of the Populists. Mr. Bryan was nominated because he is a Populist. Those who are prepared to quit the Democratic party and join the Populist party, with Mr. Bryan at their head, can do so and will do so.

Their present course is logical. Their future is assured. But what about those Democrats who are not so prepared, who are not Populists either in head or heart, and who support Mr. Bryan on the plea of party discipline—where will they be? The lines laid down at Indianapolis are the only lines on which the Democratic party can be reorganized. If the party is to have a hereafter it must be the representative of the platform of principles on which General Palmer and General Buckner stand; because that platform is Democratic doctrine pure and simple, drawn directly from the well of Democracy, unterrified and undefiled.

But why should any right-thinking Democrat put forth the plea of party discipline in support of the vote he proposes to give a Populist candidate on a Populist platform? Does what happened at Chicago go for nothing? Does what happened at Indianapolis go for nothing? Is the attitude of the National Democratic Administration to be accounted as nothing? But, above all, is the future of the country and the Democratic party nothing? The fewer votes Mr. Bryan gets the easier will be the reorganization of the Democratic party. The more he gets the harder it will be. Bryanism is Populism; and we may be sure that after Mr. Bryan is defeated we shall have no further claim from him—or from anybody else—that he is a Democrat.

I am one of those who believe that the Democratic party was not born to die except with the death of republican government. It is inherent to our constitutional system, and essential to the wholesome existence of that system. That it has, on important occasions, failed of its duty to the State and fallen short of the requirements of the hour, merely proves that its leaders were unequal, not that the principle of its being was at fault. In spite of the mistakes of its leaders, and in spite of grievous perversity and misadventure, the party has survived disasters enough to destroy half a dozen parties. As long as free institutions built upon recorded law need a firm, enlightened defender—a defender alike against the encroachments of organized rapacity and the excesses of popular sentiment—the Democratic party, as directed and inspired by Jefferson, will stand between those institutions and every assailant, even as it is standing now between the country and the two extremes of rampant paternalism, one led by Mr. McKinley and the other by Mr. Bryan, which seek to engulf it.

As far as the paternal theory of Government is concerned the Bryan platform is equally objectionable with the McKinley platform, the Bryan candidacy with the McKinley candidacy. The two platforms differ in degree, not in kind. The two candidates agree in theory to differ on its application. Except for the Indianapolis platform and ticket the people would have to choose between radical paternalism masquerading as a Democrat and radical pa-

ternalism, open and undisguised, pressing the pretensions of
radical Republicanism. The triumph of either is bad enough; but,
in the case of Mr. McKinley, we are promised at least immunity
from tampering with the money and credit of the nation, whilst in
the case of Mr. Bryan we embark our all in a leaky boat upon a
shoreless sea; and set sail in quest of adventures. We have tried
McKinleyism, and odious as it is, we know what it is. Bryanism
we have only taken in broken doses, as in Colorado and South
Carolina, and, tested by these homeopathic experiments, we may
well draw back aghast before the thought of applying it, allopathi-
cally, to the General Government.

I will not say that every Democrat who casts his vote for Mr.
Bryan will have reason to regret, or to be ashamed of that vote.
Each of us must proceed according to his lights. For me, I shall
never blame any Democrat for what may have been said or done
in this campaign. But I do think that with such a platform as
that adopted at Indianapolis, and such a ticket as Palmer and
Buckner—the election of McKinley being a certainty—there is
scant reason for any real Democrat to throw away his vote on a
platform which is not Democracy, and a candidate who is not a
Democrat. The safe course is the brave course; and in the end
to all who are Democrats we must come back to the old beliefs,
and start afresh from where we left off in 1892.

I am loath to speak about myself. But, five thousand miles
away from home, an ocean rolling between, shall one not be for-
given the vanity, dwelling in the hope that there may be friends
who have not forgotten, as there are enemies who have despitefully
used, him?

In an autobiographic memorandum written in 1860, Abraham
Lincoln said, referring to the years between 1849 and 1854, "I
was losing interest in politics when the repeal of the Missouri
Compromise aroused me again." I confess that, with the failure
of the victory of 1892 to record itself in the results it promised,
and with selfish greed and embittered faction rising like a noisome
tide, or vapor, all about me, I felt very much as Mr. Lincoln says
he felt.

There are times when, hopeless of doing a public good, a man
has the right to consider his private interest, and the interests of
those who have claims upon him. Thus it has been quite two years
since I bore any part in political transactions. During nearly all
of this time I have been outside of Kentucky. I came abroad
to avoid nothing, to escape nothing; but in obedience to domestic
plans long made, and to professional advantages I had no right
to disregard. It was my desire never again to trouble myself, or
anybody else, about politics; and to leave to younger hands the re-

sponsibility and details of my own particular business. I thought I had earned my right of discharge—the more so since I occupied no official place, deserted no post of duty and had never asked anything of the people, or my party, for such services as I had rendered.

The action of the Chicago convention changed all this. I did not believe it possible that the party leaders who happened to be in the saddle were grown so mad. I could not foresee that recklessness and heresy would be able at a single bound to clear such a distance separating truth and falsehood. Between the impending folly of the Democrats and the clever but unscrupulous opportunism of the Republicans, it seems to me that conscientious and thoughtful men would, before they could interpose effectual action, wait yet a little longer to give an opportunity to those honest men who had a realizing sense of the havoc being wrought by the professional politicians. I was mistaken. I underrated the capacity of the senatorial cabal for blundering. I miscalculated the amount of Populistic alloy which had gotten mixed up in the pure gold of Democracy. The scandalous circumstances attending the Chicago proceeding, the shameless abandonment of Democratic truth in the platform there adopted and the grotesque character of the ticket nominated, left me no alternative as a true Democrat and an honest man; and, having in this way been drawn back into a certain relation to a political warfare which has never had any personal attractions to me, I am back to stay, and, on my return to Kentucky, shall consider myself enlisted for the war. I have no explanations to make or apologies to offer, and, ready to take all the blows it may please Heaven to send, please God they shall be returned with interest, if the power in me lies.

There is but one hope for the country, but one for the Democratic party, and that hope lies imbedded in the principles unfolded by the Indianapolis platform and represented by the candidacy of Palmer and Buckner. If we are to have a free country, it is only a question of time when those principles will prevail in its government. If we are to have a great party it must after the election be mustered on the line therein laid down. But better before than after; and, invoking the faith of the fathers and the memories of the past, I entreat Democrats everywhere, but particularly the Democrats of Kentucky and the South, to withdraw themselves out from the body of this death, and to stand with me upon the sunlit heights of truth; truth for the sake of the honor of the country and the glory of the flag sought by these madmen to be desecrated in the sight of foreign nations; truth for the sake of the moral character and well-being of the people menaced by this rash essay in political debauchery; and last, not least, truth for the sake of that constitutional party which, though misled by reckless leaders and rent by factions, is still capable of good works for conservative government and popular liberty.

H. W.

Geneva, October 1, 1896.

WITH BRYAN AGAIN

1900

"No compromise with dishonor," scrupulously adhered to by the *Courier-Journal* in supporting the Gold Democrats in 1896, had almost wrecked the property of Mr. Watterson and Mr. Haldeman. Their newspapers were literally proscribed and physically burned. Threats were made against their printing plants. The four years which followed 1896 were the most difficult in the history of the famous newspaper institution; and it required all the business sagacity of the one and the editorial genius of the other to keep the ship afloat.

An opportunity of political rehabilitation arose in 1899, however, and the *Courier-Journal* strongly supported Senator Goebel for the Kentucky governorship; following this with adherence to Mr. Bryan in 1900. The accompanying editorial by the editor reveals him at the unpleasant task of swallowing the Free Silverite of 1896. He conceived as the issue against Mr. McKinley the hold of the "Money Devil" and the "Trusts" on the administration through Senator Hanna. He was not in sympathy with the cry of anti-imperialism, then so strong in the Democratic party, and he realized that only a miracle could elect Mr. Bryan. But Mr. Watterson entered the fight with a will and soon was declaring (as below) that the trust evil was a greater peril than Free Silver and that the re-election of Mr. McKinley meant the end of the Republic as founded.

The Paramount Issue

(October 1, 1900)

I

At this stage of a great National Campaign, it seems relevant and proper that a newspaper, like the *Courier-Journal*, should take a reckoning of the political situation with the purpose of boxing the compass, as the saying is, and if not of actually squaring the account, at least of giving reasons for the faith it goes by; the reasons that move and control it; to the end that the simplest and least instructed among its readers may be able to answer with clearness and intelligence when anybody asks them why they read it; for the *Courier-Journal* has always been one with its readers; it has taken them into its confidence; it has no secrets from them; and though it holds the professional politician somewhat lightly, and has but scant respect for the party platforms, it is answerable to those whom it has the right to call its friends.

In 1896 there was precipitated upon the people a signal and a real crisis. It greatly simplified and curtailed the freedom of action and choice among thoughtful, patriotic citizens. Owing to circumstances very plain to see, but not necessary to recall, the conservative elements of the Democratic party went to the rear, and the radical elements came to the front. The currency was in imminent peril. The public order was menaced. The public credit was involved. The country did not want McKinley. But it was afraid of Bryan. It finally took McKinley as a choice of evils.

Four years have come and gone. They have carried the usual changes with them. They have brought new questions upon the scene, and along with these have raised up new duties. They have considerably modified the older issues. There need be no more fear of a Mexicanization of the currency than there is of the reestablishment of African slavery. He who thinks so is either the dupe of his own fancies, or else a credulous listener to partisan harangues. The two actual and present dangers that beset the country arise out of the proposed disposition of the foreign territories come under our control as a consequence of the war with Spain and the domestic circumstance of so strengthening the hands of the party in power, and of fostering and centralizing the organized forces existing through its favor, as will lift it out of reach of the people and make its ultimate dispossession difficult, if not impossible, as the result of the pressure of public opinion and by the agency of a free and peaceful ballot.

On these accounts, the *Courier-Journal,* seeing no cause for alarm upon the vanishing lines of 1896, accepts Mr. Bryan, in spite of many differences of opinion, in preference to Mr. McKinley, and the considerations which have moved us have prevailed with the great body of the more conservative Democrats led by men like Olney and Cockran and Wilson.[3] If Mr. Bryan were the same man he was in 1896, we should prefer him to Mr. McKinley, because he would be powerless to carry out any of the vagaries by which he then seemed to be bound. But he is not the same man. He has had four years of experience—a great matter

[3] The "Wilson" mentioned above is, of course, William L. Wilson.

at this time of life. The conditions back of him and about him are wholly changed. Both his added years and the increased sense of responsibility arising out of them and out of his larger perspective —especially the elevating and broadening force of his larger following—give to his candidacy a character it lacked before.

He is admittedly an honest man, a clean man, and a man of ability and courage. His election will call a halt upon that rampant partyism which, if it be not checked, will presently so intrench itself in power as to defy ejection. Mr. McKinley may be all that Mr. Bryan is, and more, but Mr. McKinley is the creature of his environment. He is the representative of a ring of officeholders, who rely upon the organized money interests of the preferred classes—the aggregations of vast wealth—to keep them in power, and who, intrusted with four years more of power, expect to construct out of Cuba, Porto Rico and the Philippines such a political and money-making machine as will for at least another generation make them masters of the situation at home and abroad. This is even a greater peril to the country than was Free Silver at Sixteen to One four years ago, and, as a consequence, conservative men of all classes, who are not hidebound to party, are breaking away from the Republicans and acting with the Democrats.

II

The *Courier-Journal* has always stood for sound money against the various forms of depreciated money, from irredeemable greenbacks to free silver, which have from time to time assailed it. It approves the Gold Standard. Whatever the rights or the wrongs of the Crime of 1873, they are past remedy. The vast gold output may yet restore the lost parity between silver and gold. Whether it does or not, the commercial world has adjusted itself to the present conditions and they are here to stay.

For ten years after the War of Secession one could now and then hear some abstraction relating to the institution of African Slavery. There were men who thought the Thirteenth and Fifteenth amendments, if not void, were yet voidable. As a matter of fact, slavery died with the Confederacy. It died the death. Nothing could resuscitate it. So with Free Silver at the ratio of 16 to 1, or any other ratio. As a disturbing element it is dead. As a political issue it is dead. It died with the defeat of the powerful coalition of 1896. It can no more come again than the ghost of our once blatant "rights in the Territories" can revisit the glimpses of the moon. Though men may cling to it and platforms may proclaim it—sometimes on account of pride of opinion and sometimes through sheer perversity—the fifty cent dollar has had its day. If another foray should be made upon the currency, it will take some other shape.   Hence on monetary lines it costs the *Courier-Journal* nothing to support Mr. Bryan.   His platform we discounted long ago.

The *Courier-Journal* is an Expansionist.   It is entirely wedded to the greatness and the glory, the prowess and the renown of the country.   It would behold it first among the Nations of the earth.   It has seen the Union grow from a huddle of petty sovereignties fringing the Atlantic seaboard, until, taking in its strong arms the body of the mid-continent, it stands a World Power, whose word must be respected from the Bosphorus to the Gulf of China, yet still, thank God, a Republic both in fact and in name. We would keep it so.   We would save it from the perdition that came to Carthage, Greece and Rome.   Hence without reserve we oppose the re-election of Mr. McKinley.

That Mr. McKinley is a good and patriotic man needs no averment from us.   That he has in his mind and heart some scheme of "benevolent assimilation" feasible as he sees it and wholly sincere we do not doubt.   But, after all, the President is only one man.   He is but the creature of his surrounding.   That surrounding is an admirably organized and a most potential political Trust.

Its aims are predatory.   Its Chiefs are callous.   To retain possession of the Government by corrupting the election and then to do with the country what it pleases is the objective point to which, with wondrous activity and address, it immediately devotes itself.   Its forces are deployed with the regularity of an army. Its muniments of war are collected as by the inexorable hand of the tax-gatherer.   Upon every part of the field political its dispositions have been made by veteran leaders, skilled in the arts of party warfare; a redoubt here; a rifle pit there; and, back of all, the inexhaustible resources of the other Trusts which it is its business and mission to perpetuate along with itself.

To meet this gigantic array are the undisciplined and unpanoplied masses of the people, the raw militia, so to say, of political life, ill-clad and ill-equipped, with an eloquent and dashing leader in the person of Mr. Bryan to inspire them, but, as far as the organized engineries of battle go, a species of monster without a head.

The encounter is most unequal.   But by no means hopeless. History abounds with examples showing how the race is not always to the swift, nor the battle to the strong, from days of David and Goliath to those of

> "the old Continentals
> In their ragged regimentals."

There is a reserve power in the people.   There is a mysterious strength in Trust. It cannot be that we are yet grown so weak and rotten that the Government may be bought for a price and that all that was fought for and won upon fields of death and glory from Yorktown to Appomattox shall be dissipated upon one final debauch of the Money Devil under the ministrations of such a man as Mark Hanna?

III

We are an Expansionist. But we would expand on Jeffersonian, not on Cæsaristic lines. We are an Expansionist. But we would have the Constitution to follow the flag. We are an Expansionist. We rejoice in the knowledge that at last the scattered and discordant Confederacy, the uncertain and for a time dismembered Union, the belittled and despised Republic is a World Power, known, honored, respected of all men. We would have its word go forth to the Nations a trumpet blast. But not of mere militarism. Not carrying a message of desolation and war. Not echoing the bellicose tyranny of England, nor the bloodthirsty vengeance of Germany, merely a poor second in the jarring concert of Feudalism and Vandalism. But we would have the word go forth as Washington spoke it, as Jefferson signed it, and as Lincoln sealed it with his blood. Even as Moses lifted up the Serpent in the Wilderness would we lift up the Spirit of Liberty, of Republican liberty, saying to mankind: "Here are life and hope and room for all!"

The party of Mammon, the party of Unrighteousness, the party of Reconstruction, with the Money Devil in the person of Mark Hanna at its head, and every villainy in the land hanging about its shoulders, or clinging to its skirts, can never accomplish this.

That it should pretend to do it is a saturnine farce, equally shameless and grotesque. Its Trust-breeding Tariff forbids it. Its Franchise-breeding system of legislative puts and calls forbids it. The ghosts of its carpet-baggers rise, grim specters on the scene, to point first at the stricken South and then at Cuba and Porto Rico already rife with scandal and spoliation, the Philippines waiting their turn and still to be heard from; whilst the very angels in heaven cry out against the desecration. We want the word, when it goes forth, to be a clean word, not an unclean word, a true word, not a false word. If we may not preserve in all its simplicity the bucolic Republic of Washington and Franklin, let us at least maintain its integrity. Let us not at one and the same time lose both the shadow of their benign influence and the substance of the noble fabric they left us, substituting in room of the reign of law, the rule of money; in room of the old aristocracy of titles, a new aristocracy of shekels; of which some future historian shall write as a great historian has written of the period immediately preceding the decline and fall of the Republic of Rome.

We yet believe in self-government. We still have faith in the intelligence and virtue of the people. Mr. Hoar, considering his re-election to the Senate, may go from us, but Mr. Boutwell, considering only his country, comes to us; Mr. Bryan may not be Mr. Tilden. Since he has no barrel, it is quite sure he is not; but Mr. Tilden was abused quite as much as Mr. Bryan has been, and all that is being said against Mr. Bryan was said against Mr. Jefferson. One thing is certain, Mr. Bryan is four years older than he was four years ago. He must have learned much during his interval of growing and his many migrations. At his worst, he is better than any representative of the Mark Hanna Combine. At his best, he may turn out another Lincoln. Who shall say?

And so it is that the *Courier-Journal* supports Mr. Bryan and opposes Mr. McKinley. Mr. Bryan we do not know at all; Mr. McKinley we believe to be much better than the men who are running him. That which is final and conclusive with us is the "paramount issue." That issue is, shall the people recover possession of their government whilst they may, or shall they wait until four years more of Trustism and Militarism so entrench the present custodians of power in their places that they can safely resist attack and defy the people, holding on until division in their own ranks and rank corruption oust them, but too late to save the Constitution of the Fathers, the moral integrity of the Republic and the character of the people? The organized Democratic party is something of a shorn lamb. If the great body of the people, disregarding past political differences, do not come to its rescue it cannot win, but, if it loses, good-bye to all the Republics and Republicans have held sacred and dear.

THE GOLD DEMOCRATS' LAST STAND

1904

The autobiography is almost silent on the campaign of 1904 during which the editor wrote with as much vehemence and frequency as at any time in his career. He had done his best to prevent the third successive nomination of Mr. Bryan, and in the first of the appended articles he reviewed his reasons for that course and warned the St. Louis convention against the Nebraskan Democrat with all the vigor of his pen. Kentucky in that year was for Bryan, which complicated the editor's task; but, when Parker had been successfully nominated, and the "gold telegram" from the candidate to Sheehan had settled the money question in that campaign, Mr. Watterson, as the second and third editorials subjoined reveal, went to work as he had not since 1876. Opposition was his forte. It was in this campaign that he began his line of reasoning to prove that Theodore Roosevelt not only inherited the Republican party's endorsement of "trustism and the money devil," but was an imperial menace in himself.

Mr. Bryan's Latest

(June 23, 1904)

Mr. Bryan's latest performance is rather more curious and amusing than significant. One would suppose that a party leader, with any sense of dignity, having set his own house in order, would leave the houses of his friends to take care of themselves. But this is not the way of Mr. Bryan. Not content with the action of Nebraska, he is no sooner through with the business that detained him at Omaha than he hies away to New York, hires a hall, assembles a rabble, and assails the organized Democracy of the Empire State, like any Republican or Populist, or other enemy; though no one has impeached the regularity or the orthodoxy of the New York Democracy, whilst their preference for President, Judge Alton Brooks Parker, is an eminent and lifelong Democrat, who supported Mr. Bryan both in 1896 and in 1900.

There can be no mistaking the meaning of such demonstrations. They ought to make it plain to Democrats everywhere that Mr. Bryan means mischief and only mischief. He goes to St. Louis to stir up strife. Hair-splitting, which is rarely considerate and only efficacious when fighting is the word, becomes a crime when friends—particularly when party associates—seek, after a period of internal conflict, to bury their dissensions and to get together on some basis of rational agreement.

The differences of 1896 turned on Free Silver. All other differences might have been adjusted. In 1900, the acute state passed, Free Silver no longer a menace to sound money and the public credit, many Democrats supported the National Ticket, who, in the former year, had opposed it. Today the very suggestion of Free Silver is ridiculous.

It ought to be abominable, because it not only cost us two Presidential elections and the loss of both Houses of Congress, but involved us in eight years of embittered and ruinous controversy. Out of this we got nothing but disaster and discredit. If ever a political issue was dishonored by results, Free Silver has been. Not the Alien and Sedition laws were more damaging to the old Federalists than this figment of Greenbackism, this fantasy of folly, has been to us. Upon the highways of thought, in the arenas of intellectual combat, he would seriously invoke so much as the spirit of that bogus, yet defunct, divinity, would be laughed at. It is not only dead, but it lies in a neglected grave, having wrecked the reputations and hopes of all who made it the god of their idolatry.

Mr. Bryan perfectly understands that "Free Silver at the ratio of 16 to 1" are no longer words to conjure with. So he has cast aside his auriferous cross and his oracular crown, to find some new fire-brand with which to stir up the excitable and unthinking. He finds what he wants in the silence of Judge Parker. This at least is Golden, and Mr. Bryan hates Gold. It is Golden, and he thinks it will inspire hatred in others.

It happens that David Bennett Hill is a friend of Judge Parker. Mr. Bryan hates David Bennett Hill. It happens that Mr. August Belmont is a friend of Judge Parker. Mr. Belmont happens to be a banker. Mr. Bryan hates banks and bankers; that is to say, he pretends that he does. All bankers, according to the Nebraskan, either live in Wall street or do business along that enterprising Cul-de-Sac; and, in this way, he identifies the New York Democrats with Wall Street; through Wall Street he gets at Belmont, Hill and Parker, and, finally, at Plutocracy; and Plutocracy is the varmint, that is, the ostensible varmint, Mr. Bryan affects to be laying for.

Thus the thusness. Says Mr. Bryan,—having Hill aand Belmont and Parker and all the rest of the Eastern Democrats in mind—says he—

> "Now, whether he kill Cassio,
> Or Cassio him, or each do kill the other,
> Every way makes my gain . . .
> . . . if Cassio do remain,
> He hath a daily beauty in his life,
> That makes me ugly."

The "daily beauty" in Judge Parker's life that makes Mr. Bryan "ugly"—yea, that makes Mr. Bryan sick—is Judge Parker's silence.

In short, and in fine, the sum and substance of it is this, that, seeing in Judge Parker the strongest symbol of a reunited Democracy—seeing in him a possible nominee and the head of a probably successful Democratic ticket—Mr. Bryan makes him the object of particular attack; singles him out from among those he has blacklisted for an extra coat of tar; and will appear at St. Louis expecting to get in the entering wedge of his predetermined work of discord and ruin under the ribs of the eminent New Yorker whose only offense seems to be that he voted for Mr. Bryan both in 1896 and in 1900, and that, being Chief Justice of the Supreme Court of the Empire State, he resolutely, chastely and wisely refused to step down from that lofty pedestal into the bull-ring of self-seeking contention and become a party to a vulgar babble of tongues, the loudest of which is that of Mr. Bryan himself!

Nothing more disreputable has ever come about in American politics. If one could credit Mr. Bryan with the least sincerity; if he had any tangible objective point, or reasonable alternative; if he could even trump up a decent pretext! Nothing of the kind shows either above or below the surface of Mr. Bryan's surpassing folly, malevolence and disloyalty.

It can no longer be doubted that what Mr. Bryan aims at is a divided Democracy. What he seeks is the defeat of its ticket. Where he has failed he has resolved that none other shall win. That Judge Parker was faithful among the faithless is nothing to him. That Judge Parker is a lifelong Democrat is nothing. If another stood in Judge Parker's shoes, that other would invite Mr. Bryan's resentment. Hill is but as a red rag to a mad bull, Belmont is but a figure-of-speech. Hearst is the only wear—quite a good-enough Morgan up to the assembling of the Convention—with a brickbat for the party and a butcher knife for its ticket after it.

Happy indeed are those who are out of politics; yet manhood is still manhood; honor is still honor; and truth is still truth. How different all this might have been. Mr. Bryan might have gone into the St. Louis Convention a very angel of light. He might have appeared there amid its cheeriest applause. He had only to be just, to be true to the spirit he has so often invoked, to show himself a large-hearted, magnanimous man, seeking the general good. He could have made himself a tower of strength. It was not in him. One who could wrangle with a widow over her husband's estate, who could accept diplomatic favors from the Republican Administration, who could pay his way abroad writing letters to the Yellow Journals and at home make common cause with the Hearst Circus—yet orate the while about the ideal in public life and morals—must carry to the end the twin distaffs of pharisaism and malignity, recalling the glum figure of the dog-in-the-manger who could neither eat himself, nor would permit any others to eat.

But Mr. Bryan will find before the end of the chapter that he has both overestimated his powers and overreached himself. He may make a scene in the Convention; nothing more. If he bolts, his bolt will lose the Democrats no State that they have and help them gain some States that they need. Mr. Bryan may go on making money. He may keep himself alive as an agitator. But the day of his power to wreck and ruin the Unterrified and Undefiled Democracy of these United States is over!

Unterrified and Undefiled

(July 10, 1904)

I: THE NOMINEE

It reads Parker and ——.[4]

In the case of Judge Parker the expected has happened. In all ways the eminent New Yorker embodies the requirements of the place, the needs of both the party and the time. If we cannot elect him, we could elect no one.

It is our belief that we can and that we shall elect him. The antithesis of all that Theodore Roosevelt is—in character, temperament and political conviction—a jurist and a statesman—a man of the people, yet learned in the law—he presents the voters of the United States the opportunity to change the administration of the Nation's affairs without any wrenching of its machinery; to transfer their Government from the custody of self-glorifying righteousness, with its pharisaic pretensions and bogus heroes, to the hands of plain, practical men, who will consider the facts of the country, ascertain where the syndication of its public business has left us, and turn over a new leaf in the horn-book of political debits and credits. If they avail themselves of the opportunity— as we think they are sure to do—then all will be well. If they fail to do so, then good-bye to the chance this side of some convulsion against which even Rooseveltism cannot provide.

The dignity with which Judge Parker has carried himself through a long and trying ordeal emphasizes as it attests his claim to the confidence of his fellow-citizens. His silence has been truly golden. It gives guarantee at once of the sense of propriety and of the power of resistance. It means self-respect, stability, judgment. It assures us in the candidate those qualities which the country could most wish to have in its President.

There was no need for the Chief Justice of the Supreme Court of the Empire State to step down from his lofty pedestal into the bull-ring of candidates. He could have uttered no word that would not have been misconstrued and misrepresented. He stood where he stood—a Democrat—a life-long Democrat—who learned his lesson of Tilden—a disciple of Jefferson and a follower of Jackson, what more could any thinking, believing Democrat desire? It was this wise reserve, this prudent decorum, as much as any other circumstance, that separated Judge Parker from the riff-raff of the self-seeking and commended him to patriotic Democrats

---

[4] Mr. Davis, of West Virginia, had not yet been nominated for Vice-President: hence the blank.

as one to be trusted, to be accepted, to be nominated, to be confidently, enthusiastically supported. The convention made no mistake. Who cannot vote for Alton Brooks Parker is no Democrat.

II: THE PLATFORM

Let us say at once that we long ago ceased to set much store by party platforms. As the cynic observed of ghosts, we have seen too many of them to believe in them. They have been mainly springes to catch wood-cock.

In 1852, it was the Whigs who refused to affirm the Compromise Measures of 1850, to lose the election. The Democrats came to the scratch beautifully, won hands down, and, hardly warm in power, they proceeded, in the Kansas-Nebraska Act, to rip them up the back and down the middle. In 1892, the Democrats in National Convention took the trouble to throw out a semi-protectionist Tariff plank reported by the Platform Committee and to adopt one of their own, specific in its terms and requirements. Mr. Cleveland first threatened to nullify this in his letter of acceptance. Dissuaded from doing so by the assurance of what would happen to him in case he did, he weakly gave a kind of grunt as his assent. But, when he got back in the White House, he sent it away back and bade it sit down—which, perforce, it had to do—and when, eighteen months later, he recalled it, the authors of its being would not have recognized it in the Wilson Bill.

In a rough-and-tumble way, our method of choosing our candidates for President and Vice-President gets at the average intelligence, or folly, of a party. The National Convention is a picturesque affair. It abounds with noise and color, keeps the party spirit alive, stirs up the animals, and, sometimes, escapes without breaking something which has afterward to be mended. It affords a quadrennial outing to the old-timers and furnishes by-orators and off-statesmen a chance to disport themselves. Many a man has come home from a National Convention, where he has been "mentioned," to claim a more substantial reward for his enterprise and "services." Some reputations have been made in National Conventions; some fortunes, likewise; as witness Polk and Pierce, Garfield and Harrison, who were not seriously thought of as nominees in advance of the event.

As for the platforms they have been almost as whimsical as the nominees. Half a dozen patriots are contending for the honor of having put the Gold plank in the Republican platform of 1896, when, in point of fact, it was the merest toss-up. The Free Silver plank in the Democratic platform of 1900, was carried in Committee by a single vote and that cast by a plump little nigger from Honolulu. Even then the sane leaders of the party doubted it.

Hence, and naturally too, it has come to pass that the people look rather to the candidate than the platform.

To be sure—to address ourselves to the immediate situation—it would have been better for the General Committee to let the gold-plank of the Sub-Committee stand. Since the matter came up at all—though the wisdom of bringing it up may be questioned—nothing was to be gained by striking it out. If the purpose was to flatter the Free Silver men it was superfluous; because there is no Free Silver man of sense, or judgment, who does not know that the paramount issue of 1896 is as dead as the institution of African Slavery. If it was to placate Mr. Bryan, that was to reward a man for planning infinite mischief, whose influence and following cannot assure us one solitary State in the Electoral College. But, we are free to say that, as an unflinching and undoubting advocate of Sound Money, who has given proof of fidelity and tenacity, we are not disturbed in the least by the circumstance either of its omission, or its adoption; and we cannot but regard Judge Parker's telegram to Mr. Sheehan on this point, while altogether honorable and courageous, as superfluous—as the convention itself regarded it.

Every contention made by us the last eight years has been vindicated by events. There is no longer any danger of the degradation of the money standard. Two months hence, when we get into the thick of the fighting, nobody will be thinking about the currency. The result will turn on other issues. The character of Judge Parker, to say nothing about the proceedings and the complexion of the body which nominated him, will give a sufficient guarantee of enlightened conservatism to thinking people.

So it is in the matter of the Tariff. After the experience we had with Mr. Cleveland, who, even among the extremest of Revenue Reformers, wants to go back to the radical declaration of 1892 for a present starting point?

In 1892, we had had four campaigns of education, beginning with the demand for "a Tariff for Revenue Only," in the platform of 1876. We had had the Tariff Commission fiasco. We had had the Carlisle-Randall contest, ending in a complete victory for Tariff Reform. We had the Cleveland message of 1887, which Democrats believed to be honest and to which they rallied as to a shibboleth. The defeat in 1888 bore no relation to this message, and, in 1892, mistakenly conceiving Mr. Cleveland both a sincere and a courageous man, the party placed him upon what it believed to be his own platform. He denied this. His immediate followers denied it. When, upon it, he swept the country, he paid no regard to it; though then, if ever, we held a commission from the people to go on and do our duty as we had promised to do. The very memory is enough to make the heart sick.

The whole course of the Wilson Bill is a story of tergiversation and surrender, the lines laid down and the defeat prepared by Mr. Cleveland himself.

To a soldier of the Old Guard of Tariff Reform who fought in all the Tariff battles, finally to fall at a Waterloo led by not even a genuine Napoleon, very little promise—so it be true—will now suffice. The country has to be educated all over again. A new generation has come upon the scene. Other leaders than the recreant Cleveland are at the front. That walking arsenal of voluminous and exact information, David A. Wells, is dead. His lieutenants, if any now survive, are scattered. We have had ten additional years of more or less prosperous rapacity under a thieving Tariff. What more can a true believer in a sound economic system expect—seeing the evil wrought by false professions—than that the party lay down the simple, the axiomatic proposition that the Government has no right, constitutionally or equitably, to levy a dollar of taxation except for its own support, that every dollar in excess of this is robbery under the forms of law, and that, if we get the power, we shall proceed to revise the Tariff so as ultimately, not precipitately, to reduce it to a revenue basis?

The time for a radical revision of the Tariff was 1893. We had promised it. The country was prepared for it. There had been fifteen years of discussion, during which the Tariff-for-Revenue-only men had driven Protectionism from one stronghold to another until they had swept away every barricade and had planted, as they thought, the flag of a thorough and lasting Reform upon the White House. When Mr. Cleveland, disobeying the mandate of the men who had elected him, put himself between them and their triumph, he set the clock back a quarter of a century. In short, to Mr. Cleveland, more than to any other human agency, do we owe the present Tariff, with its impositions and exactions, to say nothing about a certain apathy touching the Tariff, the result partly of reaction following disaster and partly of popular ignorance. Unequal to the situation, Mr. Cleveland let the golden moment slip. The young men of the party, with Williams at their head, will have to do the work all over again. They began the retracing of the party footsteps, and rightly enough, very nearly where we began twenty-eight years ago.

Take it as a whole, the Platform suits us. It might be shorter. But, it is sound. It rings no doubtful note. Whatever may be lacking, the candidate can supply. So, clear the decks for action and let every Democrat go to work to elect the ticket. There are only three questions for the people to answer. Shall Absolutism, at home and abroad, reign triumphant? Shall Corruption go unchallenged? Shall the Robber Tariff stand?

*   *   *

Thus much for the Ticket and the Platform. What of the outlook? The *Courier-Journal* will go into action under the sincere belief that we have at least an even show-down as to the array of forces and much the best of it as to the debate. We look to a great campaign and a Democratic victory.

Judge Parker will carry New York. New York will carry New Jersey and Connecticut. The South will carry itself. If Tom Taggart does not carry Indiana we'll hang him. Then there is Wisconsin—where is Vilas? What is the matter with "Dave" Rose and "Ed" Wall, and that delightfully delightful bad boy's delightful father, George Wilbur Peck? Across the Missouri, Colorado, Montana and Utah; over on the Pacific—! Don't everybody speak at once!

Elect the ticket! You bet we'll elect the ticket! Face to the foe—eyes on the target. Every Democrat in his place. No mouthing and no monkey business. No nonsense about either '73 or '96. Fools to the rear. Braves to the front! March.

He of the Big Stick

(October 11, 1904)

The Republican organs affect to be mightily amused by the attitude of the *Courier-Journal* toward the pending campaign, the portents of the political situation and the personality of the President.

"You went on about General Grant," they exclaim, "just as you are going on about Theodore Roosevelt; yet none of the things you prophesied came to pass!"

General Grant did not get the Third Term which his friends arranged for him to get and which was foreshadowed by the Force Bill of 1875. That Bill was beaten because certain Republicans, with Mr. Blaine at their head, dared not put such power in General Grant's hands. Although the Republicans stole the Presidency two years later it came to them so handicapped that they were obliged to get down from the high horse they had been riding and hedge a little. One of the last acts of General Grant, before he went out of office, was to withdraw the troops from the South. The carpetbag Governments could not stand without troops. So Hayes let the carpetbaggers go.

In 1885 Cleveland came in. The course of party absolutism was arrested. It was again held up by the election of 1892. Although nothing was accomplished by either of the Cleveland Administrations other than a transfer of the patronage from one party to the other, they were beneficent interludes to the single-party idea. They signalized the power of the people to change the poltical complexion of their Government by the ordinary process of election. They served warning upon the Republicans that they did not own the earth. They were illustrations of the Democratic principle. If the Force Bill had passed? If General Grant had got a Third Term? If there had continued an unbroken line of Republican Presidents? What then?

In the trial of forces immediately before us the people have the opportunity to make a third exhibition of the same kind. If they avail themselves of the opportunity we shall have four years at least of tranquillity at home and abroad. We shall take a look at the books, stop the leaks, suspend the autocracy having its source in the White House and resting on a clique of Gray Wolves in the Senate and on the Speaker and his Committee on Rules in the House, revitalize both Parliamentary Government and the Reign of Law, and thus checking the tendencies of absolutism, we shall preserve the even tenor of our way, achieving such practical Reforms as may from time to time seem to be wise and fit.

We need a man in the Chief Magistracy who is a Magistrate, and not a Mountebank. We need a just and sensible man, not a theorizing experimentalist. In every respect Judge Parker realizes the Magistrate. In every respect Theodore Roosevelt embodies the Mountebank.

Immoderate in everything, the Republican organs distort the reasonable plea of conservative men against the retention of such a man as Theodore Roosevelt at the head of affairs into a prediction of crowns and scepters and dungeons and the like, refusing to discuss the issues of the campaign on their merits, or to allow any criticism of their idol. We specify his disregard of the law. "Oh," they say, "you called him a pirate." We trace his sinister character through his writings. "But," they say, "you called him a pirate." We show the dangers of party absolutism, the selfish tyranny of personal ambition, the menace of foreign complication and domestic corruption incident to a dynasty encrusted in power and illustrated by examples, some of them startling in character, and the chorus repeats, "but you called him a pirate."

Because Theodore Roosevelt is a man of good moral character, well-born and well-educated, the men around him, his official servants, and their newspaper organs, assume for him every excellence. They forget that there are other vices than those of drunkenness, lechery and profanity. A man may be a decorous man, yet a mean and brutal man; he may wear the cloak of religion, yet be rapacious, cruel and unclean. Some of the most worthy men in domestic life have shown themselves most grasping and vicious in their relations to the State. May a man not be decent and selfish? May he not be decorous and dangerous?

We judge Mr. Roosevelt by his writing and his official conduct. His writing shows us a self-confident, supercilious iconoclast. The vengeful spirit which led him first to wrong and then to insult an old man like Jefferson Davis shows through every printed page of his voluminous productivity. It is not alone that his judgment is faulty, but that his spirit is niggardly. He claims everything for himself, gives nothing, allows nothing, to anybody else. He assails whole classes as well as individual men. Yet his composition is equally inconsistent and illogical. He began a Free Trader, to end a High Protectionist. He built himself up as a Civil Service Reformer, to end the most shameless spoilsman. Do these things mean nothing? How can any upright, thoughtful American respect or admire such a man?

But, his conduct in office has been both brutal and reckless. Why do not some of his organs defend his treatment of Miles? Why are they so persistently silent as to his treatment of Dewey and Schley?

The Panama business was a villainy from start to finish. Why do not some of the newspapers which are abusing us defend it? Forty millions taken from the Treasury to be given to a syndicate of Parisian Stock Gamblers. Ten millions more to a group of stool-pigeons on the Isthmus set up by these Stock Gamblers. A solemn treaty trampled under foot. War levied on a weak Nation by Executive order. The whole beastly swindle as transparent as the day; horrible, infamous; and the man who has put this disgrace upon us, can do no wrong!

Yet, this man is working his Presidential campaign from the White House, which he has converted into a Robber Castle, collecting tribute from the great corporations through Cortelyou, his man-of-all-work, having brought them first to subjection through the Detective System of the Department of Commerce.

Nothing so shameful and shameless has ever been known in American politics; but its author—the man who is to get the usufruct—is above all law, is a law unto himself, and can do no wrong.

He must be elected because he is good.

We must let well enough alone.

The people are not saying much. They are just thinking. Maybe, the 9th of November, the man with the "big stick" will waken up to find it but a broken reed.

A REAL FIGHT FOR BRYAN

1908

"A Mess of Pottage and a Man of Straw" was the first Watterson phrase after the campaign of 1896 which attracted the attention of the country. It referred to William Howard Taft and grew out of the attempt of Theodore Roosevelt to re-create his Secretary of War in his own image. Mr. Watterson threw himself so earnestly into the campaign of 1908 that Josephus Daniels even induced him to act as a sort of honorary publicity chairman at Democratic headquarters in Chicago.

The first following editorial is written in a style which would bring despair to college professors and indulges in more capital letters than in any other Watterson article in the files. When he was engaged in political exhortation the editor was inclined to set great store by capitals. They multiplied with the fervor of his purpose. The dynastic idea of the Taft nomination in 1908 was repellent to Mr. Watterson, and he also believed that what he boldly called "The Money Devil" purposed to annex the Government. These feelings are responsible for the unrepressed style in the group of three subjoined.

In the second article the editor paid his respects specifically to that "Money Devil" (which later, under the name of the Money Trust, was to be the subject of a Democratic Congressional investigation pursued by Samuel Untermeyer). On the ground that the great financial interests were about to purchase another election for the Republican party, Mr. Watterson, in his joint capacity as citizen and Democratic campaign official, appealed to the "plain people" for campaign funds.

The third of these 1908 editorials is the most valuable from a historical and journalistic standpoint, and is notable also for a valuable retrospect of the campaign of 1876. Bryan's bitter antagonist of 1896 saw in him then "an amiable doctrinaire of Jeffersonian tendencies" and prayerfully derived some hope from him. The editor revealed a genuine fear of the possible succession of the Vice Presidential candidate, James S. Sherman, who, however, died a few days before the 1912 election and never was nearer White House incumbency than the Senate chamber.

A Mess of Pottage and a Man of Straw

(June 20, 1908)

Upon a Platform of Imposture, largely constructed out of timbers stolen from Mr. Bryan's back-yard, the Republican Party has set a Man-of-Straw—a very portly and pleasing Man-of-Straw—and has said to the voters, "Behold in William Howard Taft the counterfeit-presentment of Theodore Roosevelt."

The answer which the voters are likely to make in November may be found in the First Chapter of the Horn-Book of Common Sense, which translated from the original Vulgate into Modern English reads, "The Voice is Roosevelt's Voice, but the Hands are the hands of Rockefeller."

Thus, after many centuries we have the recurrence of a famous passage of Holy Writ made political and brought to date, in the last instance, as in the first, a great fraud and a mess of pottage, playing the leading parts.

At length the Republican Party has had to disguise itself as a Populist, and to join in the cry of "Stop, thief," in order to escape the consequences of its own acts.

We mean no disrespect to the Secretary of War. He is a gentleman of noble character, an official of signal service and merit, a citizen of unblemished reputation. He was a typical Republican of the school of Sherman, Garfield and McKinley until he began to temporize with Roosevelt and got the Presidential bee in his bonnet.

James Schoolcraft Sherman, chosen as his running mate, is like unto him, a gentleman of high character, of high connections, and a man of straw. He is a New York Congressman and the President of a New York Trust Company. There is plenty of ruffle to his shirt, just as, considering Mr. Taft's ruffle, there is too much ruffle to the whole Ticket. Mr. Sherman will be depended on to see that every Corporation in and about Wall Street does its duty. The After-Thought, however, will cut little figure in the campaign. Everything will center in, and eddy about, Mr. Roosevelt's designated successor and heir-apparent, the Secretary of War.

The Platform on which they have placed Judge Taft contradicts his rulings as a Judge on the bench. His Party in Congress has falsified his attitude toward our Insular dependencies. He is put forward as the star performer of an enterprising and spectacular Manager who has succeeded in adapting rag-time music to the serious business of the State and in turning the Government of the country into Comic Opera, the White House his Theatre and the Federal Officials his scene shifters, Civil Service Reform, though sadly torn and tarnished, the fantastic drop curtain relied upon to conceal, but not concealing, the mechanism of the stage-carpenters and the meaning of the stage-setting.

For the second time in its history Militant Republicanism goes to the country without conviction and without enthusiasm. In 1884 the Candidate was the handicap. In 1908 the handicap is the Issue. That Issue as defined by Mr. Roosevelt and accepted by Mr. Bryan, as originally defined by Mr. Bryan and accepted by Mr. Roosevelt, is the Encroachments of Predatory Wealth.

The People will question themselves and one another, they will ask the Politicians why, if Bryan means it and Roosevelt means it, there should be any need of the turmoil and outlay of a Presidential campaign; why the two Parties should not equally divide the offices and share the expense; Bryan to have the first four years in the White House as guarantee of good faith, with Taft a sure Bond to follow, thus not only restoring to the Government the lost poise and balance of parties, but giving hostage to the many against the depredations of the few.

As the Republicans frame the Situation somebody is to be fooled mightily. Who is it likeliest to be, Rockefeller and Company, who will provide the sinews of war, or the Masses of the People, who are expected to provide the votes? What is the sum of it, whichever way we take, or consider it.

We are promised a change of Policies. Of which Policies— the Policies of the Republican President, or the Policies of the Republican Congress? The Republican party cannot be true to the one without repudiating the other. It cannot at one and the same time keep step with Roosevelt, the Radical, and Cannon, the Standpatter; with Tariff Reform and the Gospel of Protection; with the Trust of the East and the Farmers of the West; with the People and the System. In one word, Republicanism for all its arts and resources cannot serve both God and Mammon.

When the Republican Congress refused to enact a Law of Publicity, under whose operation blackmail could no longer be levied upon any interest by the Managers of either organization, it proclaimed the purpose of the Republicans to lay tribute upon the Corporations and to fry the fat out of the Manufacturers; again to sell the Foreign Embassies to the Millionaires and promise no real interference to the Trust Magnates, as a return for the Means of corrupting the ballot-box and buying the election.

Is it possible that they look for a hidden letter of Mr. Taft, prematurely exploded, to make denial of this? Is it possible that they rely upon certain glittering generalities of the President adroitly kept out of sight and mind at the crucial moment to help them deny it? By a vote of eight to one they struck the ideal of their Platform. They have no hope of carrying the country by a free Vote and a fair count; of winning the election except by purchase, and all that is meant by the Populistic crazy-quilt they have patched together at Chicago is a screen behind which they may work the familiar devices of Hanna and Cortelyou.

This is the banquet to which the voters of the United States are invited to sit down and partake by the official dispensers of canned goods and cold storage who got up the menu at Chicago apparently without fear of the Pure Food Law, or the uplifted hand of the Ananias Club.

They promised us Tariff Reform. They actually promise us Tariff Reform! Tariff Reform! Good Lord—

> "The Devil was sick, the Devil a Monk would be!
> The Devil got well—"

and he said: "Ain't I the slickest?" Tariff Reform, the fat fried out of the Manufacturers as thick as butter from New York to San Francisco, greasing every door-post and smearing each cross-road between! Tariff Reform! The Robber Barons putting up the money and bossing the job! Why, that were just like Currency Reform, with Old He-Goat, High Finance Aldrich, Papa-in-law Rockefeller behind him, superintending both the Senate and the House! Where, oh, where are Ali Baba and the Forty Thieves? Where are Satan and his Christian Endeavor Society; Falstaff and his Woman's Christian Temperance Union; Friar Tuck and his Sunday School class; Robin Hood and his Bill of Rights; in short, where are Cousin Sereno Payne and his Ways and Means Committee and Uncle Joe Cannon and his Rules Committee? As well set Richard III to draft a new Decalogue, or Munchausen to indite an apostrophe to Truth, as expect these to amend the Dingley schedules.

Neither shall we have any more Government by Injunction, the Taft Judicial Opinions to the contrary notwithstanding. Our Infant Industries at length rich and prosperous, most of them having attained their allotted three-score-and-ten, no longer need Protection; but they dearly love the American laboring man, and just as the Tariff shall be revised purely in his interest, that is to "insure him steady work and high wages"—which, on the faith-cure principle, though the empty pail stare him and his starving children in the face, he is bound to know is only a figment of his fancy—shall the rules of Court procedure be revised to conform to the demand of the Democrats, twelve years old now, so that no matter what he says or does, he shall never again go to jail. Think of the debt the Working Man owes, not to Mr. Bryan, who began it and has fought for it straight since 1896, but to Mr.

Roosevelt, who took the word out of Mr. Bryan's mouth and has brought the Republican Party to a death-bed repentance. All hail the Dignity of Labor!

The rich shall be made richer still—for the business of the country must not be disturbed—prosperity is the keynote of Republicanism—prosperity and a mess of pottage—the old flag and an appropriation—but the poor man shall share the riches of the rich man—for, is it not written in the Book of Morgan that the Steel Trust is the Hope of Man, and has not Rockefeller himself proclaimed that he is but an accountant for his countrymen, lying awake and walking the floor and cutting coupons whilst they sleep? Is not Carnegie a good Republican? Is not Harriman a good Republican? Who made the Steel Trust; the Tobacco Trust; the Whiskey Trust; the Sugar Trust; the Standard Oil Trust—the foundation-stones of American liberty and prosperity —except the Republican Party; Aldrich leading the Senate, Cannon leading the House, the People compelled to pay for the dance, millions to the rich, only toil and taxes to all others.

We have an impression that the argument will be found somewhere threadbare. Hearing it for the thousandth time, the Working man will think at least two or three times before he answers— will think of his forty years in the wilderness with the wild-beasts of Plutocracy—tempted of the Devil and High Tariff and High Finance—the Angels of Democracy alone to offer him words of cheer, which too often he most mistakenly rejected—and, thinking on these things, he will say to Mr. Taft's General Manager and Advance Agent when he comes round telling him of all the Republican Party has done and is going to do for him—"Mr. Hitchcock, let me recall you a passage of Scripture out of the Gospel According to Saint Luke," and then, turning to the ivth Chapter of that Apostle, he will read as follows:

5. *And the devil, taking him up into an high mountain, shew'd him all the kingdoms of the world in a moment of time.*

6. *And the devil said unto him, all this power will I give thee, and the glory of them.*

7. *If thou therefore wilt worship me, all shall be thine.*

8. *And Jesus answered and said unto him, get thee behind me, Satan!*

"So, I say unto you, Mr. Hitchcock"—thus will the American Working Man conclude, "because you have fooled me these many moons, and I now know not only that you can do nothing you say you will do, but you don't even mean to do it. The Republican Party can fool me no longer, Mr. Hitchcock. I shall vote for Bryan."

We mourn for Taft. He is too good a man to be sacrificed in the shambles of spoils by spoilsmen. Alone upon his character, his service and his merit, he might have claimed the first place in the Nation's gift and had his claim allowed; as heir-at-law, never; as the beneficiary of machine methods, never.

Theodore Roosevelt is a popular man. Even the Democrats love him for his good intentions and for the enemies he has made. They will follow him into his retirement with affectionate salutations and deep respect. They will not accept a designated successor, and the dynastic principle, at his hands.

The Republicans go to their doom. The blood of the victims of the Big Stick and the Steam Roller sticks in their throats as they cheer; their cheering has the death rattle. Grand old Republican Party! It was a Hoss in its day. But its living sins have found it out; the ghosts of half-forgotten sins come back to haunt it. Majestic fabric of departed glory!! even as the turgid Burrows and the frigid Lodge reviewed its history; its stand for freedom; its fight for Union; the tramp, tramp, tramp of the boys in blue; the sacrifices of the mothers in Israel; the descent from the heights of Pisgah down, down, down into the plains of Moab, the shade of Lincoln at the elbow of each might have been heard to whisper—"I don't want to interrupt you, friend Burrows, but don't forget to put in something about the complete abandonment of my plan of Reconstruction and the scheme to Mexicanize the Government by the impeachment of Andrew Johnson for trying in good faith to carry it out," and, "Just a moment, friend Lodge, but whilst you are about it, you ought to say something about the Rape of the Presidency in 1876, and its purchase in 1896, in 1900 and in 1904. I could never stand for a Republican Party so faithless to its own integrity and the Republic."

And now, boys, one and all, on for Denver!

To the Plain People of the United States and Especially of Kentucky

(August 1, 1908)

I

After the Franco-Prussian War, when the Germans, led by Bismarck and Von Moltke, had extinguished the little Napoleon and made a desolation of France, crushing their thief-ridden Bureaucracy of the Third Empire like an eggshell,—when, set on by the lust of conquest and the memory of two centuries of invasion and rapine, they had girdled Paris by an unbroken and exultant line of camp-fires, shouting "Die Wacht am Rhein," and had proclaimed their Kaiser and a United Fatherland from the

great Hall of the Grand Monarque at Versailles—there was but
one other thing left to complete the degradation and humiliation
of the brave and gay, but degenerate, scions of Condé, Turenne
and Napoleon, and that was the imposition of a Tribute.

From the Man of Blood and Iron mercy was not to be looked
for. The sum Bismarck named appalled the more generous sensibilities of the Nations. Nor was the soil of the vanquished Gaul
to be rid of the hated Teuton until every franc was paid. It was
stupendous and it was cruel, but—so argued the relentless Chancellor—it was just. Then a strange thing came to pass, at once
a disclosure and an exhibition of patriotism, as exhilarating as it
was pathetic. There seemed to issue from the bowels of the earth
a voice crying, "The people of France—none others—shall pay
the Tribute." No bond-dealing sharks, nor foreign Shylocks—
just the French People should pay the Tribute. They came, these
children of the Loire and the Garonne, of the Rhone, the Saone
and the Seine—these "little Savoyards" of the vineyards and the
farms, to pay the Tribute! It was hard, but it was heroic. It
thrilled all hearts. It brought tears to every eye. Outside the
Bank of France, two blocks down the Rue St. Honoré, the line,
largely of old women, and old men, in blue blouses and white
kerchiefs, extended from day to day until they had paid the
Tribute; franc by franc; mark by mark; every sou, every pfennig
of it; the poor, plain people of France; disgraced by an upstart
Adventurer, having not a drop of Napoleonic blood in his veins;
plundered by the vile creatures of his bastard half-brother, the
Duc de Morny, King of the Bourse and Chief of the pasteboard
Commissariat; devastated by Civil War and foreign invasion;
yet, still Frenchmen; descendants of the Frenchmen who had laid
the very Palatinate in waste and levied an impost, not of dollars,
but of blood and ashes, from the Rhine to the sea many and
many a time.

Vive la France! Vive la Republique! Vive Thiers et
Gambetta!

II

Longer than Louis Napoleon ruled in France has a Money
Devil, equally unsparing, ruled in the United States. Greater than
the spoliations of the King of the Bourse have been the spoliations
of the Gamblers of the Stock Markets. High Tariff begot High
Finance; but a party that begot both has, for forty years fattened,
and is now notoriously proposing still to fatten, upon the iniqui-
tous proceeds of its own creations, whilst pretending to denounce
them.

Every abuse stigmatized by Theodore Roosevelt is of Republican origination. Accepting him as a true prophet, how shall

honest and thoughtful men accept the organization made at Chicago and professing to be his devotee? The familiar picture of the extended ear of corn and the hidden halter is perfectly reproduced by the ample figure and genial presence of Taft in the foreground, leaning lovingly on the Roosevelt arm, with Sherman —the incarnation of all that is sinister in high finance and discreditable in party warfare—standing just behind them, ready to spring blackmail and to scatter promises in exchange for money in amount sufficient to buy the voters and corrupt the election. The process has grown so familiar that it no longer excites either horror or terror.

To fry the fat out of the manufacturers who are not content with the robbing privileges they get through the Tariff, and who dare to hold back the tribute they owe for their protection; privately to guarantee the Corporations immunity against further molestation, whilst publicly exclaiming against them; bartering friendly legislation and franchise rights for boodle funds; even selling Embassies abroad and rich places at home—too often to yielding nobodies—for the price of a State here and a Congressional District there, constitute but a few of the features of their perfectly organized scheme to syndicate the Government and establish at Washington a Dynasty as personal and exclusive and as unrepublican as if it ruled by right divine and were born to the purple.

The Congress nas ceased to be a deliberative body. The Senate is run by a Steering Committee dominated by Aldrich, the mouthpiece of the Lawless Rich, whom Roosevelt has stigmatized, but not unhorsed. The House, under a stand-pat Speaker, is the servant of a Rules Committee, dominated by Dalzell, the mouthpiece of the Predatory Trusts, exposed by Roosevelt, but retaining all their power for evil. The White House itself has been converted into the Palace of a Sovereign, girt about with all the regal usage of the Courts of Europe and ministering to the pomp of wealth and power, and to the vanity of the newly great; the noble simplicity of Republican ideals gone, yet the grandiose dignity of established order not yet arrived; the President himself an Aristocrat, born and ingrain, another Rienzi preaching a Democracy he neither practices nor believes.

A thousand millions of annual expenditure no longer startles anybody. Republican newspapers and orators talk of millions as if money grew on bushes; as it does to many of them. Fifty years ago we were nicknamed a Nation of Shopkeepers. We have become a Nation of Spendthrifts. Yet half of what we are forced to pay in subsidy through the impositions of the Tariff, and in Graft through the corruptions of the Lobby, would amply support the Government, economically administered.

There is not the smallest promise of Amendment. On the contrary, with shameless effrontery, refusing to pass a Publicity Act of Congress, or even to put a Publicity plank in their Platform, yet in these defaults seeking to bamboozle the people by irresponsible asseverations of integrity and fair intention, the Republican Campaign Managers, Sunny Jim Sherman, the Mark Hanna of the time, at their head, say to the masses of those who hew the wood and draw the water and pay the taxes: "What are you going to do about it?"

"We've got the pull and we've got the votes and we've got the money, too."

This is the situation which the plain people of the United States have to meet upon the threshold of another Presidential election. The Banks are closed against them. Even the Railways are fighting them.

Most of the great Metropolitan newspapers, where not owned outright by aggregations of Capital, are, through a short-sighted and narrow-minded community of interest, belittling their Nominees, misrepresenting their Platform of principles, and blacklisting those who venture to speak the truth.

A National Committee without a Campaign Fund is like a Marching Army without a Commissariat. Where shall the Democrats get a Campaign Fund? Their coffers are empty, as a matter of course. They have no retainers to tax, no offices to sell, no legislation to offer that will command a market price. If the plain people of the United States do not come forward to lift this burthen of poverty from their leaders and supply them with the needful sinews of war—as the plain people of France came forward to pay the German tribute—if they do not go down in their socks for the means of driving out the purse-proud lordlings of High Tariff and of High Finance, as the plain people of France went down into their socks for the means of ridding their land of the invader—then we know not how we shall be able even to open shop, to say nothing about maintaining a militant line of battle. It is true to say that the Democrats can make a dollar go as far as the Republicans can make ten dollars go. But, at the outset, we lack the dollar.

We have placed at the head of our National Ticket a man singularly unfitted to its fiscal requirements—a very Don Quixote de la Mancha in the arts of political dicker—who, if he had possessed the tact and had emulated the foresight of more provident, nor yet dishonest, men, might have today plenty of money without any obligations more binding than those which Harriman mistakenly thought he had of Roosevelt.

Mr. Bryan has been greatly maligned as a money-maker. Suddenly elevated to party leadership, a young man and as poor as a church-mouse, he had to live somehow; to find, somehow, an increased livelihood. Turning to the only pursuit which promised a living adequate to his altered needs and, at the same time, the vitality of the mission to which he proposed to consecrate himself, he did what myriads of as good men before him have done, took to a vocation embracing at once his inclinations and aptitudes; that is, to his pen and his tongue. He started *The Commoner*. It has been reasonably successful. He could have reveled in wealth had he prostituted its columns. He went upon the Platform. He worked like a slave and commanded audiences which, happily, stayed with him. But, there was money to give away as well as to earn; gratuitous service of many kinds to render; and we speak what we know to be the truth when we say that his entire accretions since 1898, when his bark was fairly launched upon its new career, do not exceed one hundred and fifty thousand dollars, and have never reached forty thousand dollars a year; a sum which the average speculator of the Stock Markets would regard with disdain, and which, if Mr. Bryan should die tomorrow, would leave his family a bare competency.

And so, fellow-Democrats and fellow-countrymen, if we are to fire a gun, or even to burst a cap, you are the boys that will have to furnish the wherewithal. Whitney died years ago. There are no Thomas Fortune Ryans or August Belmonts to put up in this campaign. They are against us now. Bryan would make no sign—the Simpleton!—he might at least have winked his eye!—only he didn't—and——! Well, that is all there is to it! Nor can we wait for the singing of the Doxology before we pass the plate! This is your fight—nobody's else. If you want to win it, send a letter containing what you are able to give and addressed to "The National Democratic Campaign Fund, care of the *Courier-Journal*, Louisville, Kentucky," and the amount, big or little—ten dollars, five dollars, one dollar, or fifty cents—shall be carefully compiled and duly forwarded to Governor Haskell, the Treasurer of the National Democratic Committee.

We propose to keep a list of all subscribers and subscriptions, and we prefer to make a weekly publication of this. In the event that contributors desire their names omitted, they will kindly say so, and their wish shall be respected; but we hope no good Democrat will be, because none need be, ashamed of the smallest amount; the spontaneous and voluntary tribute of patriotism to country; marking the difference between the Democratic party and the Republican party; the one the party of the unfavored masses, the other of the favored classes; the one asking of its own people the means of their political and business redemption, the other assessing its stipendiaries in corrupt requital for untold advantage and millions of lawless wealth.

The Paramount Issue of the Campaign

(September 6, 1908)

I

Our dual system of parties—the lack of a middle or third party —rob our public life of a needful balance wheel. This is nowise supplied by such side shows as the Prohibitionists and the Socialists. They are too narrow and radical to exert a wholesome influence. They chiefly muddle the campaigns and annoy the managers. Beginning with the Government, popular opinion ranged itself about certain groups of leaders of whom Jefferson and Hamilton stood foremost. Today our political divisions hark back to them.

To the casual eye Roosevelt may seem a popularized Federalist, and Bryan a federalized Populist; but take from the two their academic utterance, and the one remains the embodiment of centralized power, the other the prototype of progressive democracy.

Under the rule and spell of Roosevelt the pendulum has swung too far toward absolutism. It needs to be swung back again unless our Government is to be made the victim of an unconscious but dangerous revolution. Its representative character is being lost by the changed rules of Congress, which becomes more and more the creature of the organized interests. The Senate is largely divided between corporation lawyers and money magnates, either actual or proxy. The House long ago ceased to be a legislative body. At Washington it is not even a play of parties, as the people are given to understand them; but a struggle between Steering Committees and Rules Committees and Administrations for mastery, the people quite lost in the shuffle. Hence it is that I have said, and will continue to iterate and reiterate, that there is but one underlying and paramount question in this campaign, and that is whether the people by their own unaided strength can change their Government against a marching army of Federal office-holders supported by unlimited facilities either wrung from or contributed by the corporations. In other words, is the Money Devil an overmatch for the American voter? Shall the Administration successfully employ upon the country at large the ruthless agencies which were successfully employed upon the Republican party?

All economic issues pale before such an exigency. Mr. Bryan's reviled personality is but an atom. The most hidebound conservative cannot fear him with a Republican Senate already fixed to outlast the next presidential term. Mr. Taft's personality, however attractive, is but an atom, when we reflect that his programme and support is in point of fact but the velvet hand of the old confidence game of High Tariff and High Finance, played upon the American people and American industries by the party of the Standard Oil and Steel and Iron, of the Sugar Trust and the Tobacco Trust, of fraud and force, from the hour when it sought to Mexicanize the Government by the impeachment of a President who had committed no legal wrong, and the setting aside of the verdict of the ballot box by Congressional usurpation, to the hour when it adopted a platform of imposture, placing upon it the pretended counterfeit presentment of Roosevelt, but coupling him with a yoke-mate out of the very jaws of Wall Street.

Flying the flag of Roosevelt the Republican leaders have made their peace with the System. From Rockefeller to Carnegie, from Harriman to Morgan, every chieftain of wealth and predatory wealth, the honest too often making common cause with the dishonest, is well content with Taft and Sherman. They foretoken and imply the old order of special privilege to the few, impositions of every sort to the many; high finance rampant; high tariff, "revised by its friends," rampant; the end of Rooseveltism and agitation for the "good of business"—business only organized capital and licensed monopoly; the same old story, the same old song, the same old crowd slicked over with goose grease from the Roosevelt larder, but meaning four years more of the Rascaldom which Roosevelt has unmasked but not downed; which Roosevelt has exposed, but left intact; which, in spite of Roosevelt and all his works, stands today as impudent and as defiant as ever it stood, a gray wolf lording it over the Senate, a gray wolf lording it over the House, and a gray wolf giving tone and effect to the ticket.

Should any thoughtful Democrat, should any patriotic American, balk of his duty before a lay-out so menacing and obvious?

II

Through the one party power, unchecked by intermediate pressure, which our dual system has imposed, sixty years of scarce broken Republican partyism, great abuses spring into existence; most of the clever rogues get into the winning party and contrive to forge toward the front, and yet everywhere the more cultivated and wealthy classes frown upon agitation because, they tell us, it will "disturb the business of the country."

On this point the Republicans were just as insistent when Mr. Tilden was the Democratic candidate, when Mr. Cleveland was the Democratic candidate, as they are now that Mr. Bryan is the Democratic candidate.

Under Mr. Tilden the Democratic party was reorganized and

revitalized. It put off its bloodstained Sectional apparel and put on National habiliments cut from the Jeffersonian cloth. It had committed hara-kiri in 1860 without quite taking its own life. Mr. Tilden proved a great doctor and restored it to health. Another attempt at suicide during the second Cleveland Administration proved equally abortive; but, taking historic account of these events, the issue of Free Silver seems as far away as the issue of African slavery, and, since Mr. Tilden swept the country in 1876, there is no reason why Mr. Bryan should not sweep it in 1908, and he will sweep it if the Democrats of the East do their duty; because the same array of forces exists now as then.

To realize the truth and force of this one needs only to recur to the story of the fight made by the Democratic party under Mr. Tilden's lead to rescue the masses from the classes, which, during and after the Sectional War, had in the person and through the ministration of the Republican party, taken possession of the whole fabric of society and law. The keynote of that life-giving struggle was reform; the reform of the entire Federal system, debauched in all its parts and branches; reform not written in glittering generalities, but specific and specified; the reform of the public service, dragged through the mire of official delinquency, "the disgrace and censure of a Vice-President"—I quote from the platform prepared under the supervision of Mr. Tilden:—"A late Speaker of the House marketing his rulings as a presiding officer; three Senators profiting secretly by their votes as lawmakers; five chairmen of leading committees of the late House of Representatives exposed in jobbery; a late Secretary of the Treasury forcing balances in the public accounts; a late Attorney General misappropriating public funds; a Secretary of the Navy enriched himself and enriching his friends by a percentage levied off the profits of contractors with his department; an Ambassador to England censured and obliged to fly from a dishonorable speculation; the President's private secretary barely escaping conviction upon trial for guilty complicity in frauds upon the revenue; a Secretary of War impeached for high crimes and misdemeanors."

What an indictment after only fifteen years of domination— yet these were but the beginning of its counts—reform its purpose; the reform of the assumptions and usurpations of a corrupt policy of centralization; the reform of loose financiering methods in the Treasury and wasteful extravagance in the Congress; the reform of the currency, then, as now, out at elbows, intended to betray and cheat the people.

Finally, so ran the rescript of 1876, the conditions almost a duplicate of those that face us now, the reform of the revenue laws, "to the end that capital may be set free from distress and labor be less lightly burdened," in other words, the reform of the tariff, that "masterpiece of injustice, inequality and false pretense," making the rich richer and the poor poorer—father and mother, yea, and wet nurse of the trusts and of trustism, which "prohibits imports that might purchase the products of American labor," I use again the exact language of the Tilden platform, "which has degraded American commerce from the first to an inferior rank on the high seas, has depleted the returns of American agriculture, an industry followed by half our people; which obstructs the process of production, wastes the fruits of labor, promotes fraud, fosters smuggling, enriches dishonest officials and bankrupts honest merchants, and which costs the people five times more than it yields to the Treasury"—

Wherefore—

"We demand that all Customhouse taxation shall be only for revenue."

Every word of this arraignment, and each of its specifications, is as true today as it was thirty-two years ago, with multiplied sins of omission and commission additional thereto, whilst the identical organized interests which are abusing Mr. Bryan so savagely were then as savagely inveighing against Mr. Tilden.

III

Do those that call themselves conservatives imagine that a vote to continue such abuses yet a little longer will stop the agitation of abuses and still the cry for reform?

Take, for example, the Tariff. The New York *Herald* is splicing its editorial page with the inquiry: what can Mr. Bryan do to reform the Tariff with the House and Senate in the hands of the Republicans? Obviously nothing; but does that establish a reason why Tariff reformers should vote to make the House and Senate more Republican, and thus to prolong and fortify anti-reform under the orders of Cannon, Payne and Dalzell, the high protectionist standpatters? This is as illogical as the claim that we shall have good times if Taft is elected and a panic if Bryan is elected. We had a panic last October. We may have another this October. We have panicky times now. Whence came they? The Republicans have been in complete possession of all the departments of the Government for eleven years. Will four years more give us better assurance of amendment than those eleven years have given us?

"Shall the people rule?" says Mr. Bryan. "The people do rule," says Mr. Taft. How much did they rule under the steam roller at Chicago?

A flood of light is thrown upon the matter of popular rulership by the Taft-Foraker reconciliation in Ohio. The issues between Foraker and Taft antedated the Brownsville affair. They were essential in character relating to good government, boss rule in Cincinnati the immediate example. But precisely as the differences between Roosevelt and Wall Street have been adjusted in Taft and Sherman are the differences between Taft and Foraker adjusted upon the give-and-take principle, in each instance the pact expected to carry with it the independent voters and the weak-kneed Republicans, though treacherous to both; because, behind it, stalks the same old dishonest partyism ready to spring when the election is over with no further trouble until four years later when other shifts and resources as occasion requires may be put forth.

Thus it is that the party in power has a tremendous advantage in the deploitation of votes so as to affect results, requiring on the side of the opposition a tidal wave, a very ground swell, to overcome the array of money and machinery and trained skill.

All that is seen today was seen fifty, sixty, seventy years ago in the conflicts between the Whigs and Democrats, ending in a great war after six decades of Democratic ascendancy, due largely to the same material and moral agencies which now prevail over our unequal political combats. It is for patriotic men, for independent, reflecting men, for those men in the East who call themselves Conservative men and to whom I am mainly addressing these letters, to decide whether they will not join their efforts to those of the unorganized and disinterested raw militia of the West and South with the purpose of frustrating the detestable alliance between Perfidy and Partyism, of which Taft is merely the agreeable go-between, Aldrich, Cannon and Dalzell—sponsors for Sunny Jim Sherman—the real leaders. Such combines furnish very good illustrations of how the rule of the people may be and often is set at naught.

I take little stock in campaign shibboleths. They are made to excite and mislead. Neither do I set much store by political heroes. They strut their hour upon the stage. Truth is the star of my idolatry, though usually half-truths are most in evidence. But in this campaign I see on the one side the raw militia, and on the other side the regulars. I see on the one side a party faced at least in the right direction, and on the other side a party faced two ways. I see in Mr. Bryan an amiable doctrinaire of Jeffersonian tendencies. I see in Mr. Taft an amiable opportunist of bloody-shirt Republican antecedents. From Bryan I derive some hope. From Taft none whatever; but in the event of his death from accident, apoplexy or over-exercise, I see in Sherman as President of the United States all that is odious and dangerous in ringism and reaction.

We have a noble system of Government. I would preserve it.

The way to preserve it is to keep it in currents of political thought and action, not to allow it to rust in the grass of the one-party power. Back to the Constitution and punish the rascals is the word; discriminating between the rich and the predatory rich; holding dishonest corporation officers personally to their proper account, not visiting their wrongdoing upon innocent shareholders; the law the arbiter—trial by jury the means of everywhere reaching the ends of justice. Down with the two-faced standard of the spectacular, showing Roosevelt to the West and South, Sunny Jim Sherman to the East, Taft the merest middleman between. Up with the milk white flag of reform, the People's flag which is as unsullied as it was when it waved over Tilden, Cleveland and a united Democracy.

In short and in fine, the way to reform is to turn the rascals out. The way to reform is to punish the rascals. Parties in power never reform themselves. When abuses grow unbearable the only high road to reform leads to a change of party. Good government is the people's rule, not the rule of the steam roller.

THE WILSONIAN ERA

1910-12

A closer view of the inevitable break-up of the Republican party in 1912 is this confident writing of August, 1910, in which the editor recurred to his favorite theme of politics and made two bold prophecies which were realized: one, that the Democrats would certainly capture the house, and the other that they would annex the rest of the Government two years afterward. In this play of his pen, Taft reverted to Buchanan and Roosevelt to Stephen A. Douglas to prove Mr. Watterson's point that history was but repeating itself and the Republican party was to go the way of the Whig.

The nomination of Mr. Wilson at Baltimore was accepted by Mr. Watterson with astonishing ease. His fight had been solely on personal grounds; politically in that year he could hold no company with either Republicans or Bull Moose. And so the article of July, 1912, the second following, is a most graceful engorging of the Democratic choke-pear, and a very earnest support of the nominee of Baltimore. How accurate were Mr. Watterson's prophetic instincts as to public men is again demonstrated in this article: he sees only four states at most not carried by Wilson (there were two) and he wrote confidently on the inevitable rift between the future President and Bryan.

History Repeats Itself

(August 24, 1910)

I

The Republican party, with William Howard Taft in the White House, encounters very much the same conditions that overtook and overwhelmed the old historic Democratic party, with James Buchanan in the White House, fifty years ago.

The rôle played by Stephen A. Douglas then is filled by Theodore Roosevelt now. The Institution of African Slavery, swallowing all other issues, held the center of the stage. The Issue of Predatory Wealth, circling about the Protective Tariff System, has come in the fullness of time to occupy the center of the stage. In many ways the outer aspects and internal qualities of the two are identical.

The former Sectional alignment of North and South has veered round to face East and West. The moral sentiment of the North slowly but surely rose against Slavery. The Democratic party stood for the Constitutional rights of the slaveholder. If the South had been wise it would have marked the rising of the tide against it and have moderated its demands. It would have listened to Douglas. It did not and, as a consequence, the Democratic party was split in twain, and the War of Sections followed.

The beneficiaries of the Protective Tariff System have been pursuing precisely the blind, fatuous course pursued by the slaveholders. Instead of lowering their demands they have gone on increasing them. Scandal after scandal has attended each successive act in the drama of rapacity. The Tariff is a synonym for robbery under the forms of law. High Finance is a byword of shame and reproach. Trustism, like Slavery, has grown to be odious to the better sense of the country.

As the Democratic party was the custodian of the one is the Republican party the custodian of the other. The accretions of Slavery were offensively visible at the South. The North protested. The accumulations of Protection are offensively visible in the East. The West protests. Douglas tried to save the Democratic party, as Roosevelt is trying to save the Republican party.

Parties are the creatures of interests and conditions. The Democrats of the South would not compound with the Democrats of the North to put the institution of African Slavery in commission. Will the Republicans of the East compound with the

Republicans of the West to put the Protective Tariff System in commission?

Taft, an able lawyer and a well-intentioned man, is caught, as Buchanan, an able lawyer and a well-meaning man, was caught, between the upper and nether millstones.

II

The likeness between Taft and Roosevelt and Buchanan and Douglas runs into many incidents as well as along parallel lines, though Roosevelt is not as patient a man as Douglas was, while Taft is much more amiable than Buchanan.

Given the same conditions, parties made up of mortal infirmities do not greatly differ in their character and behavior. They become arrogant by long tenure. They germinate corruption. All the slick rascals get into the party in power if it remains in power long enough. Party spirit holds the loyal, party discipline whips in the timid, the party momentum and resources ride down rough shod the resisting intelligence of the disinterested.

In 1860 Buchanan relied upon the "Old Guard" in Congress for his support, just as Taft has had in 1910 to look to another "Old Guard" for his support. The features of both closely resemble one another. Aldrich makes a good double for John Slidell. For Jesse D. Bright read Joseph G. Cannon.

The Opposition carried the Thirty-sixth Congress, which assembled the first Monday of December, 1859. No sooner had the House fairly organized by the election of William Pennington, of New Jersey, as Speaker, than it raised a committee of investigation, with John Covode, of Pennsylvania, for Chairman. If anybody wants to read a stirring volume of political scandal he will find it in the report of this committee. There is every likelihood that the Democrats will carry the next House. If they do, they will elect Champ Clark Speaker, and then raise a committee of investigation, which will make the corruption of Democracy under Buchanan look cheap by the side of the Republican corruptions under Taft, the difference marked by the amazing growth of everything between those days and these.

Meanwhile, poor Taft being weighted down with Aldrich and Cannon, with Sherman and Ballinger, from whom he cannot disentangle his Administration no matter how hard he tries, Roosevelt is committed to the policy of Uplift, variously identified with Pinchot and Garfield, with Dolliver and Cummins and La Follette, with Bristow and Murdock and Poindexter.

Roosevelt can no more escape the company he keeps than can Taft. Like Sidney Smith's two old women who could never agree because "they argued from opposite premises," the Taft crowd and the Roosevelt crowd can never get together—especially after defeat has overtaken them in the fall elections and crimination and recrimination—as fatal in politics as cholera and yellow fever in physics—begin to tear the party vitals in Congress.

The cry is likely to go up for Roosevelt in 1912 as the only nominee who can save the party. Will Taft quietly submit and lay down his hand? Even if he were willing to do so, would the "Old Guard," the "Standpat Republicans"—the agents and attorneys of the Protective System, with its communities of interest branching out in every direction, commanding unlimited means—permit him; or, in case he persisted, could they not easily find a substitute? The woods are full of straight-out Republicans who might poll the cast-iron party vote even as against Roosevelt.

They may patch up their differences in New York. Sunny Jim may slink away into the hole of the Vice-Presidency and draw the hole in after him. Tim Woodruff may hie away to Europe. Billy Barnes may join the Church, Jimmie the younger, may forget the wrongs done James, the elder Wadsworth, and spend his autumn days amid the blandishments of the Genesee Hunt. But, after it is all over, defeat their portion, there will stand the same old issues and interests, the same old antagonism and passions, the irreconcilable conflict between the professional good and the professional bad, as bitter as ever; Taft, playing baseball on the diamond, Roosevelt playing baseball on the fence, the world, the flesh and the devil unchanged since Buchanan broke with Douglas and historic Democracy was sent to grass in 1860, as historic Republicanism seems destined to be sent to grass in 1912.

Now Let the Battle Go On!

(July 4, 1912)

As Lincoln said in 1858, when beaten by Douglas, "I am too brave to cry and too badly hurt to laugh," may the *Courier-Journal* say touching the result at Baltimore.

There is one thing its readers may be sure of and this is that throughout the long, embittered campaign thus brought to a conclusion it has known no interest except the common interest and consulted no law except the law of truth. There has never been a time when it did not hold itself ready to subordinate private feeling to public exigency. Having its likes and dislikes among men, its preference among aspirants and candidates, it has nailed its flag to the masthead of organized ideas and moral forces, relying upon the virtue and intelligence of the people to do the rest, always, within the sphere of its field of action and duty, yielding to the will of the majority. Having stood faithfully and fearlessly by its convictions, this it does now and proposes to do to the end of the battle before us.

We could wish that the consummation of business of such transcendent importance had been reached without the interposition of the dishonest methods and ruthless spirit tolerated by the convention in Mr. Bryan. It projects into the campaign ahead the single feature that might affect the voting. Governor Wilson was nearer right when four years ago he wanted to get rid of Mr. Bryan than when he mistakenly thought he was buying his support with a few words of complaisance and apology last winter.

Clearly Mr. Bryan overshot his bolt at Baltimore. He had no intention that the trend of events should take the drift it did. Later along the Democratic nominee can hardly fail to feel the discomfort if not the embarrassment of his dictatorial temper, his aggressive, self-assertion and his erring judgment. The quarrel between Bryan and Clark will seem but a battle of love-licks by comparison with the break between Wilson and Bryan when it arrives, as soon or late it is inevitably sure to do. Neither of them is a man for team work, to brook opposition, or take counsel. But Wilson is much the abler of the two.

His nomination is the offspring of a belief among Democrats not merely in his availability but in his representative character. Born in the South, the Democratic Governor of a Northern State, a convert, albeit a new convert, to a line of thought which has taken possession of the popular mind, his leadership which has shown itself omnipotent in the end, seemed irresistible in the beginning. The *Courier-Journal* made no mistake when it recognized his quality and equipment. It abandoned its support of him because of reasons which were solely personal and wholly satisfactory to itself. It gave them to the public equally with candor and disregard of consequences.

It nurses no regrets. It has no retraction to make, nor apology to offer. The ocean of public opinion little recks commotions so trivial among those that cross its deeps. They nowise affect the course or the steering of the ships that pass.

To the *Courier-Journal* it matters little who fill the offices. The business of its life is to ascertain the truth and to print it. It could not be a courtier if it would and it would not be if it could. Wanting nothing for itself, it prefers to hold the politicians who come within its ken to the fullest measure of their accountability, taking each recalcitrant, as it has taken Mr. Bryan, by the throat, and, if not amending him, yet seeking to bring the people to a realizing sense of his delinquency and wrongdoing. Of personal animosity in such matters it has none. Justice between man and man has been and is and will ever be the star of its idolatry.

Of the election of the Baltimore ticket we cannot entertain the shadow of a doubt. Nothing except its identification with Mr. Bryan could hurt it. That it will quickly survive. No party butchered as the Republican party—no candidate discredited as the Republican nominee—can hope to carry the country.

It will not matter much what Roosevelt and the Roosevelt crowd may do. Their purpose will doubtless be to throw the election into the House. That indeed by carrying a few of the Rotten Boroughs of the Far West would be both a menace and a handicap if in the great States of the East and the Central North the Republicans were not so hopelessly divided.

The truth is that Roosevelt has made as great a wreck of Republicanism in 1912 as Yancey made of Democracy in 1860. The Republican party seems to be going to pieces as the Whig party went to pieces in 1852. Wilson and Marshall may come in as Pierce and King came in, four States alone dissenting. It will scarcely be possible for the beaten bosses to cut the throat of the Ticket in New York City, or in Chicago. It will probably carry Massachusetts and Connecticut, Ohio, and Illinois, and all the debatable States.

The *Courier-Journal* did not oppose Governor Wilson because it thought him a weak candidate. It regarded him as a very strong candidate. It opposed him because, from the Democratic point of view and from none other, it held him an undesirable President. Preferring Champ Clark, it would have gladly taken Underwood, not doubting the election of any ticket named by the Baltimore Convention.

With this plain statement, let the battle go on! Sound the bold anthem! The country needs nothing so much as a change of parties. Down with the tattered banner of Taft! Down with the piratical flag of Roosevelt! Up with the ensign of Wilson and Marshall. And if, after they are elected and inducted to office, they don't behave themselves, there's plenty of pitch left over in the pot to do them to a turn!

HUGHES AND THE "KAISER-AMERICANS"

1916

The contest between Wilson and Hughes in 1916 was a preliminary skirmish to the World War, in the view of Mr. Watterson. He made for the Democratic nominee the hardest fight of his life. In Louisville he had been giving and receiving blows from the German-American Alliance; the sinking of the *Lusitania* had convinced him that the Junker Idea must be destroyed in blood; and he turned all his broadsides on Mr. Hughes when that nominee failed to repudiate certain of his supporters. The differences between the editor and the President were put aside in what Mr. Watterson considered a great national crisis, and nowhere in the United States did Mr. Wilson have stronger support than in Kentucky which he carried by an overwhelming majority. "The Kaiser candidate" was what Judge Hughes seemed to the editor. Let others vote for Wilson because "he kept us out of war." Mr. Watterson gave not a thought to such political strategy, and the following editorial is a type of many he penned in the 1916 campaign.

The Paramount Issue

(September 30, 1916)

I

It is easy enough for old-fashioned Democrats who do not personally admire Woodrow Wilson to make a case against him, but when they turn to the Hughes horn of the dilemma, what do they see, and how stands the account?

We do not find it recorded that the fish improved the situation when he leaped from the frying pan into the fire. To begin with, Hughes is a Reactionary. To end with, he is a Sectionalist.

The country might survive either character in the event that he should be elevated to the Presidency. If the taxpayers want to re-ordain the Payne-Aldrich Protective Tariff which robbed the poor still further to enrich the rich, increasing the already high cost of living to all, it is their right, and though the voters of the North want to go back half a century to fight over again the Sectional controversies in order that the Republican party may put a brand upon their fellow-citizens of the South, they can do that too. It is easy to indulge the evil propensities of evil people. Happily they cannot recall the dead days of Reconstruction, nor hoist the Bloody Shirt as a National emblem in place of the star-spangled banner.

The Hughes scheme to do these things is a sure sign of desperation. In any event they are matters we can settle among ourselves and no great or lasting harm done. But to elect a President of the United States in open league with a foreign country—a colony of this foreign country settled among us to proclaim to the world that a foreign ruler holds the balance of parties and political power over us—this at a moment of supreme exigency—is at once to abdicate American sovereignty and to accept the position of an alien dependency.

How any patriotic, self-respecting American can cast his vote for a party and a candidate proposing a contingency so adverse to the standing and influence of our country in the eyes of the world and so humiliating in our own eyes to its dignity and honor, we are unable to conceive.

The facts which are obvious to all men show for themselves. They are of every recurrence. It is not merely that the German influence was seen in the nomination of Hughes at Chicago, nor is it that he has uttered no word to deny that he is pro-German in his opinions and sympathies. This were enough surely to condemn him with patriotic Americans, but in the recent primary elections in New York and New Jersey the bloody hand of the Kaiser Alliance thrust itself into the ballot box and determined the result of two Senatorial contests; and at this moment the newspapers which rejoiced over the destruction of the *Lusitania,* and all the murders of women and children in the Irish Sea, and are whooping up the submarine and Zeppelin assassination of non-combatants, are serving notice upon the American who dares to call his soul his own that the coming seventh of November they will be at the polls in sufficient numbers to kill his vote and the votes of all who vote as he does, insuring the election of Hughes, the Kaiser candidate, and proclaiming to the world that as to the murder-war and all its results and consequences the United States is with Germany.

Is it not time for true Americans to begin to think of the real meaning and portent of all this and in that connection to consider the historic circumstances which have led up to a situation fraught with imminent danger to us as a nation and as a people?

II

in 1848 a wave of freedom passed over central Europe. In France it sent Louis Philippe packing, only to bring in Louis Napoleon. It was not strong enough in Prussia and Hungary to hold its own, but receding before the legions of the right divine of Kings, those who for a time seemed to ride it were carried out to sea and submerged beneath the deeps of Austrian and German despotism.

Many of its leaders sought and found an asylum in America. They were liberty-loving Republicans and Democrats. But in Vienna and Berlin they were branded as traitors and renegades.

Fifty years later, in 1898, a curious change had come over the spirit of the Kaiser court at Potsdam. The scheme of Pan-

Germanic conquest was well on its way. Among other aims it sought a foothold in the western hemisphere. It had intrenched itself in Brazil. It had laid its lines in Venezuela, Colombia and Ecuador. It practically controlled the Dutch and Danish Islands in the Caribbean Sea. It must have a naval base, and it was arranging for this, that finally, when fully prepared, it could turn upon Washington and say: "To hell with your Monroe Doctrine— what are you going to do about it?"

To perfect and carry out plans so ambitious required all the agencies which Prussia could command. A new Teutonic element had sprung up in the United States. The sturdy old German patriots of 1848 were dead. The nouveau riches among their successors were worth cultivation. So Prince Henry was sent over. A host of congenial Kaiser spirits rallied to him. The German-American Alliance, so-called,—a body of Kaiser Reservists—was organized. This through the menace of the German vote was expected to hold Yankee politics and the American politicians whilst Prussia skinned us of our geographic potentialities and commercial opportunities in Central and South America.

The Kaiser was actually about to swoop down upon Portau-Prince when brought to a halt by the initial guns of the opening murder-war in Europe.

Yet, so confident was the Kaiser-German-American Alliance of its strength that it boldly threatened us with civil war if we took sides against Germany, and its leaders and newspapers are now hotly asserting that they possess the voting power to elect a pro-German party candidate President of the United States. If this claim is verified, good-bye to the claim that Americans rule America, for hereafter the Kaiser Alliance will lord it over both our domestic and foreign affairs.

As we have seen in these recent primary elections its chiefs have warrant for their boasts.

*　　*　　*

It was bad enough to have Hughes racing about the country criticizing the Wilson distribution of the patronage. It showed him the candidate of a party which is only out after the offices. It was even worse to see him waving the Bloody Shirt. That showed him a Sectionalist who has learned nothing and forgotten nothing. Much may be allowed a certain Pickwickianism in our party politics. But what shall we think, what shall we say, of a candidate for President of the United States who crooks the pregnant hinges of his knee to the impudent Kaiser Alliance that votes may follow fawning, who dare not open his lips in protest of a policy of frightfulness, who will not utter a word of sympathy for Belgium, for Serbia, for Poland, who silently arrays himself against the French, the English, the Italians and the Greeks engaged in a death struggle with mediæval kingcraft, brutality and wrong? What shall we think and what shall we say of such a candidate? Yea, what shall we think and what shall we say of those Americans among us who are so weak, unreflecting and carried away by party spirit that they forget alike the institutions and the traditions of their native land, their birthright as freemen, their duty as voters, their very integrity as citizens and as men? Truly this is the paramount issue. All other issues can wait. Have we a country, and has our country a sovereignty? That is the question to be decided by this Presidential election. It is up to the people themselves. If they do not sweep Kaiserism and Sectionalism into the dust heap, elevating the Stars and Stripes to the skies, so that the world may see them and know what they mean, we shall be lost indeed!

ON POLITICS IN GENERAL

When he wrote the following derogatory article about office holding as an occupation, Mr. Watterson had just completed his sole brief experience in that business. His term in Congress had expired about sixty days before. Throughout his life the editor maintained the same scorn for office and contended that a newspaper whose editor was placed in the public service became, so far as that service was concerned, a mere gazette. But he engaged so often and so actively in political combat, joining as he did in his own person the dual ability of writer and orator, that every few years his friends attempted to endorse him for office, or his adversaries charged that he was in a receptive mood. This included the Kentucky governorship and senatorship and the Federal Presidency and Vice-Presidency. Nothing more enraged Mr. Watterson than movements of this sort. In the subjoined article, which is selected from many in the same vein, he stated his whole case. It is included also because it marks the transition from the period when visitors to the White House "found the President solitary and alone," and when state office was more sought than Federal; to the crowded executive chambers and Federal departments of today.

It was a favorite remark of the editor that he had no influence with an Administration. He stressed it in the following editorial, and later he did it many times in the days of Cleveland, Wilson and Harding. Yet his endorsement was even sought by an aspirant for a Cabinet office under the incumbent of the White House in 1921.

The Mania for Office

(May 24, 1877)

Office-seeking is always disgusting. There is no occupation which, if diligently followed by a competent person, will not yield better returns than are furnished by the public service. Offices may be filled by anybody—which is perhaps a reason for the indiscriminate application—but few get them. Since the war there has been no change of party in the General Government. Nevertheless the "wild hunt for office," a term bestowed when it implied by comparison merely a duck-chase around a frog-pond, has increased until there is no peace or rest anywhere from the crazy people, male and female who, with horns and hounds, pursue the ignis fatuus, the fox-fire delusion, which draws and guides the lunatics to the capital of their native, and, in this respect at least, their most unhappy country.

Somebody has said that war legislates. That philosopher spoke the naked truth. The President knows it; the members of his Cabinet know it, and the members of Congress know it. Our war legislated with a vengeance, and everybody knows it. It legislated at least forty men into the Senate and not less than one hundred and fifty into the House of Representatives. These men in the good old days of peace would never have reached either branch of Congress. The door of the President's room, before the war, often hung wide open, and the visitor found him solitary and alone. Now, thirty or forty men and women sit in the ante-room daily, waiting for an audience. One wants a foreign mission, and if he can't get that he is willing to accept the position of Consul in the little city of Hoodad. Another is an anxious seeker after a post-office in the interior, and if that is not at his service, he is ready to become a gauger in some big distillery. A third wishes to serve the Government as Secretary of Arizona; and if there be no vacancy to fill in that wild territory, he is patriotic enough to take anything that will pay—and so on to the end of the chapter. Only think of it. The President has to see all these people, listen to what they have to say and send them away as best he can. We come to the Cabinet. The ante-chambers of the Treasury, Interior and Post-office Departments are equally full of people, male and female, in search of clerkships. They are at once told that there are no vacancies. This information does not at all satisfy them. They hang on and hang on—hoping against hope—till their exchequers are nearly exhausted, and then they in no amiable mood return to their homes. Such is the experience of many a man and many a woman. A word in regard to Congressmen. Where he received one letter on business twenty years ago he receives fifty now. These must all be attended to or there is a fuss at home. Depend upon it, his position is no sinecure. The facts we have grouped together are true, and all the parties we have mentioned know it.

The saddest part of this office-hunting mania is its embracement of our feminine population. There is no doubt that our women should have a fair share in the Government. Moreover, there are many functions performed by men which they can fill. But, because a few of them have been favored with office, the mass of them, who seek employment and are dependent upon their own exertions for support, seem to have gone clean daft. They enter into the scrimmage with all the absurdity of men. They have quite as little practical sense as composure, and they become, all of a sudden, as fanatical as the chronic candidate.

We have written thus from sheer necessity. We are receiving daily applications for recommendations to office. A man or woman who thinks we have enough interest with the present Administration to secure the appointment of a gauger has not sense enough to be a dog-pelter. We have signed no petition, made no report, and could not and should not be induced to do so. People who want office must, for the present, go elsewhere. As soon as we are elected President, everybody shall have an office, for then the millennium will have come.

ALMOST PERSUADED

This editorial deals with the one time Satan took Marse Henry to the mountain top and tempted him with office. It is concerned with a disclaimer that, in assenting to the demands of friends that he seek the governorship of Kentucky, the editor wanted the office or did anything actively to seek it. The article is full of colloquialisms which relate to the contest between the Watterson and anti-Watterson factions that sprang up in Kentucky politics after 1896, and is interesting largely because of its admission that the editor was once willing to run for office, which he hated, on a party call.

Mainly Personal

(February 3, 1908)

I see by the papers, as Mr. Dooley is wont to observe, that they are having some trouble at Frankfort over the election of a United States Senator. To me, personally, it matters little who is elected Senator; but, since very free use of my name in that connection is being made outside the State by professional friends and brothers, who are more complimentary than considerate—if I may say so without seeming ungracious—it may not be improper or irrelevant for me to repeat what I have often declared, that if a certificate of election were placed in my hand I would not go to Washington to take the oath of office. If I had wanted that sort of thing I would have sought it thirty years ago, when, as a young man, I stood in the line of succession and all the ways were open to me.

I was born and grew up in the National Capital. I was brought into too close touch with the ups-and-downs, particularly the "downs," of political life to be enamored of it. In point of fact, I knew too familiarly too many poor great men, their servitude, their disappointments and their sorrows. I early resolved that if I ever gained a footing in my chosen profession I would not follow the fatal examples of Greeley, Raymond and Forney, but would pursue my destiny as ever a free man and never a slave wheresoever it might lead me, hewing to the line, leaving the chips to fall as it pleased God and Truth. From that resolution I have never swerved.

The story that I ever wished to be Governor of Kentucky, and was disgruntled that I was not made Governor, is false. That I should nurse any resentment against Governor Beckham on that account is preposterous. The story that I ever sent anybody to him to solicit his support is a lie out of whole cloth.

When it was represented to me that the party could be re-united under my leadership, and that, thus reunited, Kentucky might once more sweep into the National procession at the head and not at the foot of it, I gave a very reluctant and most skeptical consent. It involved many sacrifices, embracing the repose of my declining years, of which I had hoped not to cheat myself, and the surrender of twenty-five thousand of income for five thousand, an exchange I was ill able to afford. But, for the party's sake, I would have done it; yet before doing it I would not have sent, but have gone directly to Governor Beckham, his assent and sympathy being essential to the main purpose.

There was not the least bar to this. Our relations were unreserved and cordial. For three generations his family and my family had been friends. I had stood unswervingly by his nomination for Governor in 1900. I had labored unceasingly for his election. I have in my possession letters from him in which he gratefully declares that if I had been his own father I could not have done a better part by him. Nothing whatever had come between us. With none other aim than the unification of the party, why should I not first of all seek him, the contemporary official head of it?

I surely intended this. But before I had fully made up my mind—there being plenty of time for reflection—the Governor's agents and organs all over the State began to abuse me like a pickpocket. I am not a man to be struck without returning the blow, and my first impulse was to go ahead and give battle where battle was tendered. To this end I was offered an unlimited sum of money—not from any corporation seeking favor, or public service board paying toll—but from two personal friends of vast wealth, having no axes to grind, and moved solely by an affectionate ambition in my behalf.

This brought me to a standstill. I had never in my life touched a dollar I had not earned. I had never passed an unclean dollar, either coming or going. I wanted no office. I stood in no need of any official badge of leadership. What had I to gain at my time of life from such a contest, even with a triumph at the end of it, except trouble? So, an entire year ahead of time, I made my purpose known not to invade the preserves of anybody, or in any wise personally to re-enter the activities of public life, which I had long ago voluntarily abandoned.

This may seem a prolix, but it is a plain, straightforward story, drawn out by the incalculable abuse and misrepresentation of a State press which during forty years has opposed and vilified every effort I have made to establish and keep the party on tenable and high ground.

The Democratic party of Kentucky has been for ten years floundering through the trough of a sea of outrageous fortunes. Some of these have sprung from honest misleading and some from sheer perversity; but most of them may be traced to what has come to be called "practical politics," which, translated into plain English, spells "get there" no matter at whose expense or how. Thus we have seen, and are still seeing, the most startling political anomalies—such as Democratic candidates preaching sumptuary laws—and the strangest political combinations and bed-fellows—such as the heirs-at-law of William Goebel pigging with his very murderers. Conscientious and reflecting Democrats grew each year more and more disgusted, until finally some forty thousand of them stayed away from the polls.

If Democracy is ever to recover possession of the state, is it not time to call a halt upon self-seeking factionalism which plays only a game of heads-I-win, tails-you-lose?

I have no private quarrel whatever with Governor Beckham. I protested against his snap Senatorial Primary. But I stood neutral until the Governor went about the State accusing me of double-dealing, when I gave him the best the shop had in stock and let it go at that. His "come-back" was weak indeed. He "never touched me." If in this present Senatorial business there were none other than personal issues, it would not interest me at all. Even as it is, mine is but a languid interest, because I have very little hope of seeing the party regenerate until its leadership is revitalized, and it will not be revitalized—born again—until some Ignatius Loyola rises from the masses of the people to preach Democracy without money and without price, or any hope of reward other than duty done, Democracy Unterrified and Undefiled.

This our Moses must be a brave man and a true man. He must be a young man, having the courage of his convictions both moral and physical. His feet may be upon the threshold. He may sit in the General Assembly. But wherever he is, and whenever he appears, a great career awaits him, and I, for one, will welcome him.

I believe in party regularity. I have in my time stifled some qualms for the sake of it. Ours is a system of Popular Government based on party representation. But party lines have their limits and to be effectual party discipline must be just. Party leaders must respect public opinion.

The *Courier-Journal* has warned the Democratic leaders in Kentucky time and again of impending danger, still following the flag. It warned them against the Goebel election law. What came of it? It warned them before and after the Music Hall Convention. What came of that? In each instance where they rejected its counsels they came to grief. They have won no victory except with its support. Is this not the literal truth?

Throughout those stormy times it gave all possible proof of its sincerity and disinterestedness. It had everything to lose and nothing to gain by its attempt to stem the torrent of extremism. Why should they doubt it now, when, standing amid the wreck and ruin of the last disastrous battle, it exclaims "how long, oh, Lord, how long?" Is there to be never any redressing of party lines short of extinction, never any change of captains this side of annihilation? Must all men deny what all men know to be true? Must all men assert what all men know to be false—for the sake of party regularity?

The time for revision is now—for a change of base is now—for a politico-military commission, having power to act and equal to its duty in a supreme emergency, is now. Otherwise we shall have in the coming State Convention the same old spectacle of cut-and-dried machinism—blind leaders of the blind at their old stunts, stale and bootless and rank—with the loss of Kentucky's Electoral Vote in the succeeding Presidential Election. Can any thoughtful, upright, sagacious Democrat doubt this, and must I be burned at the stake for saying it?

I assert and I shall defend through all time, my unselfish devotion to the principles of the party in which I was born and reared. I reject that partyism which can see no difference between Jeffersonianism and Quayism. I will not accept the lead of Governor Beckham, and to those who say I have no following I point to forty thousand Democrats who will die before they help to perpetuate Pennsylvania politics in Kentucky.

This is the whole issue and the only issue. I not only want no recognition, or preferment, but I protest against newspaper nominations to office which imply that journalism is not an eminently honorable Department of the Public Service. The journalist who has his weather eye fixed upon office cannot be a disinterested journalist, and disinterestedness is the soul of journalism. Men in their places are the men who stand; not self-seeking aspirants dazzled by the glitter of the footlights of Washington.

Success in public life means preparation as much as success in professional life. No man is born to it. Experience, special training, aptitude, no less than ability and learning and eloquence, lie at the foundation of a career in statesmanship, and whilst all these great qualities might exist in a journalist, they would not necessarily fit the wearer to shine upon the scene of another stage of action. Mr. Greeley, Mr. Raymond and Mr. Forney paid the penalty for the mistake of mixing journalism and officialism with ship-wrecked lives and broken hearts. As I said in the outset, I early made up my mind never to follow in their footsteps.

I am profoundly grateful for the good-will of my professional brethren. But I cannot help feeling a kind of resentment that they should think office a "promotion" and call it a "reward." It is rather a badge of servitude. For all dignities my respect is reverend; for the Army and the Navy for the Senate and the Church; but there is also a dignity in duty done for its own sake, in pride of profession for its own sake; and this dignity cannot be enhanced by any blue-ribbon, or titular distinction.

> "Honor and fame from no condition rise.
> Act well your part—there all the honor lies."

H. W.

Naples-on-the-Gulf
  Lee County, Florida

PERSONALITIES

PERSONALITIES

ROOSEVELT

During the two decades of Mr. Watterson's life in which Theodore Roosevelt moved conspicuously upon the stage of the world, he was to the editor what the head of King Charles the First was to Mr. Dick in "David Copperfield." Somehow, in every political article, Roosevelt wandered about. From 1901 until the time of Colonel Roosevelt's death Mr. Watterson shot at him from every direction: sometimes with cannon, sometimes with poisoned arrows and sometimes with Cupid's darts. He was a great believer in miracles of fortune, and Roosevelt's luck was to him an absorbing topic. The personality of the President, which he knew from association and from long family acquaintance, attracted him as none other, and no editor found better "copy" in Roosevelt.

But it was the "menace of a third term," "the Man on Horseback" and "the Mexicanization of the United States" under a new Diaz which produced the strongest reaction in Mr. Watterson. In the files of the *Courier-Journal* there are literally hundreds of thousands of words on this subject. The compiler of this volume has selected several representative articles about Roosevelt, eliminating only the series of 1907 editorials in which Mr. Watterson set up the question "Is the President crazy?" and proceeded to try to prove a paranoiac cause for third term aspirations. As related in the autobiography, Roosevelt never became affronted at the editor's various methods of seeking to limit his White House tenure, and when the African Colonel died, he and the Kentucky Colonel were close, admiring friends.

The appended group of Rooseveltiana covers a period from 1909 to the end of 1915 and deals in various moods with a number of the public activities of its interesting subject.

The first article published in January, 1908, in the *Cosmopolitan Magazine* and reprinted here by permission, was Mr. Watterson's semi-fictional cut at the third term idea, and evoked much public discussion and a good deal of curiosity on the part of Mr. Roosevelt himself. It purported to be the dream of a "crazed Southern woman that Martha Bulloch's son was to rescue us from the ,mud-sills of the North" by being President during his entire life-time. The autobiography confesses that a statement issued from the White House about the time the magazine appeared, disclaiming further political ambitions for Colonel Roosevelt, "put out of business with a single punch" this figment of Marse Henry's imagination. But events changed the situation, and Mr. Watterson returned to the imperialistic theme many times—as witness the postscriptum.

The second article in this group reveals how, in a contemporary discussion at that period, and especially when descanting on the miracles of luck, the editor invariably found himself wrestling with his favorite topic.

The third editorial is addressed to the once-famous Ballinger case, one principal in which is now dead; the other Governor of Pennsylvania. When it is recalled that this was the knife which slit the Siamese integument between Roosevelt and Taft, it will be realized how farseeing is the appended editorial.

The editorial headed "Whither"—the fourth exhibit in this series—was the beginning of Mr. Watterson's definite attempt to arouse the country to what he called the Third Term Menace. It is a companion piece with the fifth article in which Mr. Roosevelt had become "Boanerges," a character he was to maintain for several years at the end of the editorial pen. The references to incidents at Cairo and Rome, during the return from Africa, relate to the Colonel's criticism of British rule in Egypt, and his enforced choice between the Methodists and the Pope at Rome.

The sixth editorial was published on the next to the last day of the year 1915, and, while it dealt with the then undemonstrable proposition that Roosevelt could come back in 1916, it was but two years ahead of the time when the strongest leaders of the Republican party were preparing to support him for President in 1920. "As God is wise and just," wrote Mr. Watterson, "I do not believe that Theodore Roosevelt will ever come back." But it was the hand of death and not the acts of men which fulfilled the editor's unwitting prophecy.

Quotations from Roosevelt's war attitudes, revealing him far ahead in belligerency of both the President and Mr. Watterson; and the editor's dismissal of Walter Hines Page as a mere "Yankeeized Tar-heel" contribute to the sprightliness of this article.

The concluding article in this Roosevelt series is a warm

endorsement of the Colonel's proposal in 1917 to raise a
division of volunteers for service in France. This was the
enterprise which Woodrow Wilson considered so prayerfully,
hopeful that he could grant the request without damaging
the army morale, and conscious that for whatever reason he
might reject it a burden of public disapproval would fall
upon him. General Pershing finally, for strict military reasons, vetoed the plan. To Mr. Watterson, unacquainted with
the military phase of the problem, it was a good sporting
proposition and appealed intensely to his sentimental side.
His picture of Roosevelt advancing toward Berlin is done in
his brightest colors.

A Midwinter Fantasy

(Reprinted by permission of International Magazine Company
(*Cosmopolitan Magazine*). Copyright 1907)

I

I shall call her Cassandra. During the winter of 1859-60,
and again a year later, no young woman was better known to the
society of the national capital. She was the guest of her aunt, the
wife of an influential senator from one of the Southern states
then upon the brink of secession, and she threw herself into the
passionate extremism of the time with an ardor dissonant not
merely to her beauty and youth but to multiplied accomplishments
in themselves absorbing and far beyond the common.

Being of the party of the Union, I had many a tilt with her,
and we were saved from a breach of friendship only by kindred
artistic sympathies, for we were both devoted to Chopin and
Mendelssohn, and played duos on two pianos, one of which
afforded me at once a retreat and a defense against her rising
anger.

She truly believed secession a Constitutional right, slavery a
divine institution. To her the mud-sills of the North, as she
called them, were an inferior people. Cotton was king, and she
preferred a monarchy to a republic. If there should be any war
at all as a consequence of disunion, which was unlikely, it would
be short-lived. Washington would quickly become the seat of the
Confederate government, the Susquehanna in the East, the Ohio
in the West its northern boundaries, the valley of the Mississippi
—from the Iowa line to the Balize—intact to the South. All
Europe would welcome the New Aristocracy of America into the
firmament of nations.

The last I saw of her she was waving a Palmetto flag defiantly from the window of a lumbering family carriage which rolled away across the Long Bridge toward the blue hills of Virginia, into the misty and bloody dreamland of the doomed South.

II

It was the night after the second day's battle of Chickamauga. Cassandra's betrothed lover commanded an Alabama regiment. He was a gallant and distinguished young officer. News reached army headquarters that he was among the missing, and, in accordance with an agreement, I wired her uncle, then at Dalton, and toward sunset the next evening he and she, with a negro body-servant, reached the front.

We had a long search for the body. At last we found it in a lonely dell, lying face upward to the starlight, as placid as any soldier taking his rest. She made no outcry. Dismounting, she tenderly lifted the dead form in her arms, seemed to utter a prayer to the Almighty, and sank upon the pulseless bosom of all that had been dearest to her on earth.

For a long time it was thought her reason was fading away. But youth and time and travel are great healers. Four years later I met her pursuing her musical studies in Leipzig, reserved, rigid, and prematurely gray. Her family told me that she never referred to the war, never mentioned her lover or her tragedy; from day to day she was serene, sedate, and silent. Ten years later, when she had returned to her home upon the southeast coast of Georgia, under the pretext that her fingers were thumbs she abandoned her piano and addressed her interest to the ancestral library, where there was scarcely a book less than a hundred years old—mostly English editions—and gave herself over to reading mainly historical, her quiet oddities becoming more and more pronounced.

There were those who thought her queer. To me she was simply pathetic. When she died a year ago she left me a great bundle of note-books filled with annotations not a few of which might be described as recondite. She had given much of her later time to economic investigations; but the parts of history which most engaged her were the revolutionary epochs, ancient and modern, the periods of Cæsar and Cromwell and Napoleon leading the rest in fulness of comment and detail. Her remarks were whimsical but, granting her premise, their logic was irresistible.

III

I met Cassandra for the last time three winters ago. There appeared to me less of rigidity. A light shone in her eyes which they had wanted since her girlhood. We went for a stroll about the fine old Southern garden, with its walks of box-elder and mock-orange. At length we sat down on a bench outside a rustic lodge. The moon was shining as bright as day. I was somehow reminded of that September night at Chickamauga, more than forty years agone. She, too, seemed to recall it.

"Well, my friends," she began, "freedom is at last at hand, though I may never live to witness its realization."

What could she mean? I did not dare to ask her. After a pause she proceeded, "The South will get its own and the North be punished for its crimes."

The old, old story. It was useless to reason with such a fatuity. Her mind dwelt in a world of its own apart. So I let it run on like a rivulet through a vista, at its sad, sweet bent. I had never seen her more regal and beautiful—an old woman now very thin and pale, dignity and gentleness in her whole air and manner and in every tone.

"I prayed to God that night," she continued, her voice falling to a whisper, "and God has answered my prayer. The avenger cometh. Let not him that girdeth on its harness boast himself as he that putteth it off. I have been young and now am old; yet have I not seen the righteous forsaken, nor his seed begging bread. It is a long lane that hath no turning. But the crossing of the ways is just beyond, and the dawn is upon us."

"Yes," I ventured, "the South is destined to be richer than ever it was, and if it could be united upon a policy and leaders of its own, its dominancy in the councils of the nation would surely be restored to it."

"And are you, too," she said, with a faint tinge of reproach, "commercialized like the rest? I had hoped otherwise. That cotton will yet be king—yes. That nature and God's will shall be vindicated in the creation of a better system of subjection for these hordes of semibarbarous blacks than our dear but crude old system of African slavery—yes. There must be, will be, pre-ordained hewers of wood and drawers of water. Society must have a fixed substratum. But the Old South, with its high ideals, must not be replaced by a New South with the low ideals of the North, and it will not be, for God has raised up a man to stand between and to forbid and, at the final moment, to rescue his own people from bondage to the mean, ignoble things of which they have been so long the victims, and, I fear, the willing victims. The man is Theodore Roosevelt!"

I was fairly stunned. Theodore Roosevelt, the Federalist—Theodore Roosevelt, the Puritan essayist—Theodore Roosevelt, the Yankee President, who had sat at table with a negro and was even now seeking to force a negro upon the people of Charleston as surveyor of the port—what could this unyielding irreconcilable find of toleration, far less of hope, in Theodore Roosevelt! In the way of an echo I gasped, "Theodore Roosevelt?"

"Yes," she went on with the calm assurance of a Priestess of Isis, "Theodore Roosevelt. In his veins flows the blood of Cæsar and Rienzi, tempered by the blood of Jan De Witt and of Oliver Cromwell. But, what is more to the purpose, within his veins flows the blood of the Bullochs of Georgia. God moves in a mysterious way his wonders to perform. Motherhood is the source of all that is great and glorious in life. I did not know Martha Bulloch—she was ten years before me—but I knew the old admiral, he that fitted out our cruisers and directed our naval operations abroad, and two of the Bulloch girls were my classmates at school. It is the boldest, bravest blood of the unconquered and unconquerable South. Do you know what the admiral did when he found, or rather when he thought, that all was lost? Why, he had in his possession a hundred thousand dollars of Confederate gold—he was in Liverpool, quite out of reach of any jurisdiction—and he surrendered every dollar of it to the United States authorities and went cheerfully to his grave a pauper! That is the kind of people the Bullochs are, and, at last, one of them is in the saddle.

"But Booker Washington and the nigger official for Charleston," I interjected, "and the Mississippi post-office case——"

"Mere subterfuges," she quickly rejoined. "Great men playing for great stakes must do strange things. Sometimes, like us poor women, they have to stoop to conquer. I have watched the career of Theodore Roosevelt as the astrologers of old watched the stars. How could he have swept the country as he has just done if he had not joined to the sagacity and daring of Cæsar, the genius of Napoleon and the profundity of Cromwell? He stood upon a ledge where four vice-presidents before him had failed miserably. Who was to keep him in his place? Himself—only himself. He must secure a nomination of his party, which had no thought of nominating him; and he must secure a campaign fund, with all the great capitalists against him. See how he bent Quay and Platt and Addicks and all the machine men to his purpose—how he taught them practical politics and dominated them. See how he used Cortelyou, first as private secretary and next as secretary of commerce to acquire the inside secrets of the corporations, and then as chairman of the National Committee to force them to disgorge some of their ill-got gains. A coming man, that Cortelyou. They tell me he does Chopin like De Pachmann. That means that he is an artist, has the artistic temperament, and is presumably a gentleman. How those kings of finance must have winced to have him stalk into their dens, an exhibit in one hand and a big stick in the other, deigning not a word, only a look and a nod toward the money-chests! Was not that a stroke of genius?"

"My dear old friend," said I, "if what you say were true, it would make your two heroes a couple of sharpers. One of them, at least, has indignantly denied it."

She looked at me with a kind of maternal compassion. "You will stick to the earth earthy," she said. "There are some lies that are so stupendous and yet so obvious that they become virtues. What is the art of war but to mislead the enemy? What is statesmanship but to deceive the canaille until you are ready to saddle and bridle them, to mount and ride them? Did you never try to catch a wild horse in the meadow with an ear of corn outstretched? Why should Theodore Roosevelt, confident of his powers and seeking empire, be less ingenuous?"

"But," I interposed, "he has declared that he entertains no such purpose, that he regards the new term to which he has been chosen as substantially a second term, that he believes in the third-term tradition; and he has volunteered this declaration, no one impelling him or asking it."

"You talk like a child," she quickly interposed. "They will be taking bonbons away from you next. That is a part of the game. By this very declaration he puts the idea of a third term in the popular mind and in the minds of his friends. Never fear but that it will germinate. What did Cæsar mean when he thrust away the crown? Do you think Napoleon would have been Napoleon if he had intimated the Empire to France before he was ready to spring? They could only get rid of Cromwell feet foremost. Roosevelt has planted the seed. He has given the cue. In good season there will be those who will know how to proceed, not to mention the unthinking herd who were born to gape and bleat and follow where a great man leads."

It was unbelievable, this honorable, self-respecting, high-born woman coolly extolling falsehood and perfidy. She went on:

"It is not for me to say whether Theodore Roosevelt has it quite clear in his heart to avenge his mother's people, but I do know that he is in the White House to stay until death doth render the two asunder. And I believe that, consciously or unconsciously, he is an instrument in the hand of God to make the South a power again. His election—or, rather, his second election—will be yet a greater triumph than the election he has just achieved so gloriously; the foolish tradition once broken down, there need never be another, except as a matter of form, a plebiscite, for in 1912 and 1916 and 1920, if he lives so long, he will have the whole power of the Congress and the army and the navy at his back—yea, and the South, too, heart-sick of democracy and the shams and frauds of shameless, venal politics, naturally preferring a strong, aristocratic government based upon the blood-royal and the purple, and not upon money-getting and vote-buying, where the most successful must be the basest."

She paused for a moment as if to catch her breath, for she was speaking with great earnestness, although in subdued tones, and then proceeded:

"Republican government is a failure. Even you ought to know that. The people are a huddle of sheep meant for the shambles. Look at the rottenness of your political fabric. Look at the rottenness of the omnium gatherum of the nouveaux riches which you call society. Do you think these things bode nothing and can go on forever? They require a strong hand; but it must be the strong hand of a man of genius and a gentleman—a blooded man—and Theodore Roosevelt is that man."

I remained silent, and she continued:

"I was in France just after the Coup d'Etat, and though but a little girl I was old enough to take in what was going on and some of the meaning of it. You may remember that Cousin Mason was the minister. Uncle and aunt had taken me along, and we lived in the thick of it, and though I now know that the little emperor was but a pinchbeck Napoleon—I met him and the empress often at the Tuileries and was twice their guest at Compiegne in '67 and '68, just before the ill-starred Franco-Prussian War—yet did he lift France out of the bourgeoisie of the fat old Citizen King, as they called him, or rather as he called himself under the crafty suggestion of Guizot; and the sheer vulgarity of the Republic, which even the dilettante poetasting of Lamartine and the melodramatic posing of Victor Hugo could not save from ridicule. He did, indeed, just as Theodore Roosevelt will rescue Washington from the crudity and false pretension that now possess it, giving the country the splendors of a real court and the firm puissance of a ruler, such as Louis Napoleon gave to Paris. He wears not yet the purple on his back, only in his heart! With one hand he feeds the cattle with the commonplaces which they best like, while with the other he holds the reins of power to drive the steeds of manifest destiny. We shall have a king—ultimately an emperor—and a rebel king and a rebel emperor, Southern to the marrow of his bones! That is why my youth has come back to me, my friend, for the stars assure me that the cause was not lost, as you thought it, in 1865, and that, in the last equation, it was I who was right, not you, in 1861."

"It may be so," I answered rather in gallantry than in agreement. "We shall see what we shall see, as our old friend, Colonel Benton, used to say."

"No. I shall not live to see it. Nor may you. But this I can see, that the elements are ripe for drastic deeds. You talk of your

Constitution. It is the same rope of sand it always was. It binds nobody. The generation that has grown to manhood since the war knows it not—too busy money-making. The South should hate it, for it carries those dreadful amendments. You were yourself always a muff—belated, as it were—clinging to Bach and Haydn and looking askance upon Schumann and Mendelssohn. Don't you remember how Wagner used to shock you? How you scorned what you called his innovation and his egotism and vanity and self-confidence? Yet, you see now, it was the music of the future! Well Rooseveltism is the music of the future. Your resounding talk about the Constitution is chatter, idle chatter— forgive my plainness of speech; between you and me there can be no offense. It is the same unmeaning echo it was when you thought you were trying to save the Union. Now you call it the Republic. It went out in smoke and flame and spirit long ago. The President has more power than any sovereign on earth. The splendid government your patriots in ruffled shirts and knee breeches affected so much to dread, which was the merest fad of the time, is here. Last winter I was in Washington, and though I did not go about much it was plain that nothing was wanting to a regal court but the name of it. The cabinet members are only the lackeys of the President. He tells them to go and they fly. He bids them come and they kneel. He has but to touch a button and it is done. That is as it should be. The small politicians who label themselves Democrats are but empty bottles on the shelf. The small politicians who label themselves Republicans weakly fancy themselves in power. Theodore Roosevelt will show them all a thing or two when he is ready. You imagine that you are defending the Constitution when you are, as Disraeli once said to Roebuck, only a lone sentry guarding a vacant and dismantled fortress."

"I agree with you," I answered, "that Theodore Roosevelt is a figure of startling possibilities. Already many very notable achievements stand to his credit. I, too, have watched his career from the beginning with interest, having known his family. I recall when he became a member of the little Free Trade Club which a group of young enthusiasts had organized in New York to help us along with the battle for tariff reform and the high hope I had of him as an embryo leader of sound, economic principles, and how I was disappointed when he fell by the way, dropping back into the iron-bound party of protectionism. The wrench shook my belief in his steadfastness. But when, after a successful career as a civil service reformer, he threw his noisy principles out of the window to make terms with Platt and Quay and Addicks, I lost faith in his sincerity as a man of real and deep convictions. At best he is a daring opportunist, impetuous and unheeding, unrestrained by any line of opinions or consistency when his ambition happens to be tempted. He seems to me, indeed, merely a successful moralizer and fantastic showman."

"There you put your finger on the spot," she quickly interposed. "He is an opportunist, and a very clever opportunist. He is a showman—which of the kings of men was not? All great souls must bide their time. They must amuse the herd. But that which strikes you as but the commonplaces of opportunism impresses me as the patient, profound dissimulation of the man of destiny and genius. Revolutions, as the Latin-Americans say, are not made of rose-water. Neither are they hastened by the weather, or hindered by a fall of rain. Like the fruitage of nature, they have their seasons and must be sown and tended long before they can be reaped. At the outset Theodore Roosevelt was but playing with politics—another young Gladstone, or Disraeli. He was seeking a career and making experiments. Nothing much mattered but success. The free-trade boots did not fit him. How did you fare with them after Cleveland put them on his thick legs and stumbling feet? The civil service crutches were well enough to help him walk into some kind of public notice. They were respectable and spectacular. Why should he not throw them out of the window when they were of no further use to him—rather a hindrance? He saw in free trade the merest mirage. So he wasted no time upon it. He knew that civil service reform was a sham and a fraud, but it was the fashion, and he appropriated it as a woman might adopt the mode of the moment, not to outlast the shop-windows. He has crushed the poor old shell you call the Democratic party. He will next make himself master of what remains of the Republican party. Do you think he does not know the value of the goody-goody which he alternates with the gamy-gamy, today an agreeable lay-preacher dealing in the platitudes of the copybooks and the fake idealisms of the women's clubs, tomorrow a daring sportsman, tickling the young idea with his wild adventures, always arresting the public interest and keeping himself in the center of the stage? No deep design beneath it? Why, he is a law unto himself. He creates his own ethical environment. He is the master-builder. Ah, my friend, do not deceive yourself! Remember he is a Bulloch—a Bulloch of Georgia."

She rose and went indoors, leaving me in solitary possession of the garden and the shadows; upon the topmost bough of a neighboring palm a mocking bird was singing in the moonlight; and—the weird-like presence had made its impression in spite of its vagaries—I found myself wondering whether it was a dream, and saying to myself, "if out of the mouths of babes and suck-lings, why not out of the fancy of this crazed old woman of the South!"

Envoy

(Postscriptum—Four Years Later—May, 1912)

At least in the foreboding that she would never live to see it, Cassandra showed herself a true Prophetess. I am not sure that, though it established her case and vindicated her forecast, she would look with equanimity upon her hero's present performance; the swash-buckling, the vociferation and the double-dealing. Though Cassandra had not within her the saving grace of humor, she yet possessed a noble nature and a fine sense of proportion.

Had she lived, the Roosevelt attitude—especially, toward his old friend Taft—must have shocked her. Even she, in spite of her honest hatred of the North, would have drawn back before the Colonel's profound duplicity in the promotion of his Third Term Candidacy, the shameless retraction of voluntary pledges, the still more shameless explanation of what he had meant, and the disingenuous dicker with the seven fetlocked little Governors to get himself in the ring. Her notions of respectability, like her notions of aristocracy, were exact and exacting. The combination of the prizefighter with the prima-donna in her Cæsar could not have escaped her critical attention.

Happily, she died. Had she lived, I think her final words would have been, "He is, after all, little better than a play-actor. He seems to have broken faith with so many persons he might break faith with my hope. He must be insane. I do so want to drag the mudsills of the North still further and deeper through the mire. But I don't want to see a lunatic in the White House— even if he is a Bulloch of Georgia."

H. W.

Queer Politics

I: ON CHANGING ONE'S COAT

(March 30, 1909)

In politics consistency and principle often get curiously mixed. The familiar instance of Gladstone and Disraeli, who actually exchanged places in their party belonging, is sometimes cited to prove the saying that consistency is the bugbear of little minds. Whether it be so depends upon the definition we put upon it. Technical consistency is one thing, idealistic consistency quite another thing. Yet in practical affairs stability becomes a prime virtue, and to be well considered and trusted one may not be too idealistic.

The late Carl Schurz furnished a striking example of the idealist carried too far for effective purpose. With him, it completely dominated the intellectual faculties. He was mentally blind to consequences. But Schurz was alien to our modes of thinking and doing. The last twenty-five years of his life his influence rested rather upon the momentum of the preceding five and twenty and his German constituency, than upon the weight and truth of his counsels, which were in themselves very weighty and very truthful.

It was said of George William Curtis that he lived in a rut of his own fancies. Webster made a Free Trade speech he never could answer when he turned Protectionist. His reason for turning Protectionist, however, was all-sufficient; though not his only change of heart. He was actually for Franklin Pierce in the last great contest between the Whigs and the Democrats. There is good reason for believing that if Mr. Clay had lived to the day of the Presidential election of 1852 he would have voted not for Scott, the Whig nominee, but for Pierce, the Democratic nominee.

In times of convulsion such acts of tergiversation pass unnoted, yet they are more hero-like in quiet times. In the case of Sir Robert Peel it required a world of courage and a wealth of unselfish conviction and fidelity to duty. I doubt whether Hamilton was moved wholly by animosity and rivalry when he held out against Adams and the great body of the Federalists, in favor of Jefferson and in opposition to the dishonest and shortsighted scheme to make Burr the President in 1801.

Truth to say, the multitude rarely look beneath the surface. They see the obvious and superficial, and judge accordingly. If Douglas had lived, he would have stood as Lincoln's mainstay in the Senate and the country. In spite of their blood feud Benton became Jackson's reliance, though Benton fell much out of Democratic fellowship in his latter days, whilst the elder Blair, Jackson's other reliance, may be said to have laid the foundations of Militant Republicanism.

Always to have voted straight, never to have split a ticket, gives testimony rather to a man's strength of prejudice than his strength of character. Nevertheless we live under a Government of public opinion, expressed through party organism to which loyalty is of first account, treason the unforgivable sin, so that he who goes over to the enemy, no matter what his motive or his pretext, takes his life in his hands. Even if he wins he must not be caught napping or out at night. Vide the Seven who stood against the impeachment of Andrew Johnson.

II: A TALE OF TWO HEROES

Assuredly we have seen queer things in politics and have lived through eccentric times. General Sherman urged Mr. Hayes to make General Joseph E. Johnston Secretary of War. Hayes not only wanted to do it, but submitted the proposition to a council of his friends. He did make Judge Key, an old-line Democrat and a Confederate soldier Postmaster General. Cleveland put Gresham at the head of his Cabinet. And here comes Taft with his nerve and his smile to put MacVeagh, the Free Trader, so called, and Dickinson, who "never voted a Republican ticket and never expects to," in two of the foremost places within his gift. Even Knox, his Prime Minister, was but a year ago talking "Back to the Constitution" like a very drab of a Democrat, whilst only a little before that Mr. Bryan was accusing Mr. Roosevelt of stealing his clothes and the cartoonists were picturing Roosevelt and Bryan as the two Dromios.

For my part, I have worn my partyism as my raiment, loose enough for my own comfort. I was a good Union boy in 1861, like thousands of other boys who later along served the Confederacy with loyal devotion. I got what the Protectionists used to call my Free Trade ideas mainly from my good friends Allison and Blaine and John Sherman, who, having "freed the nigger," were "going to free the trade." David A. Wells when I first "consorted" with him, was a Republican. Garfield became along with me in London a member of the Free Trade Cobden Club.

The Liberal movement of 1872 was, in its conception, a Free Trade movement. Horace White, the editor of the *Chicago Tribune,* an out-and-out Republican, had translated Bastiat for us. Joseph Medill, who immediately followed Horace White as editor and owner of *The Tribune,* was a free Trader long before he died, although he could not see his way to breaking his party allegiance, and, when the tariff was at the fore, hobbled along as best he could upon intellectual crutches. George Hoadley, Stanley Matthews, Schurz, the Brinkerhoffs, Lyman Trumbull, David Davis, the Adams contingent, headed by Sam Bowles, Republicans all, were Free Traders, that is, Revenue Reformers of varying degrees.

The nomination of Greeley knocked the calculations of these into a cocked hat. Some of them fell back into line and supported Grant. The Republican party got its second wind, so to say, as to Protectionism. The Democrats found with the coming of Tilden four years later an issue that did not originate in, or carry back to, sectional agitation; though we had a long, hard fight against the elements led by Randall before we made it party law. And now Taft, with Franklin MacVeagh on his right and

Jacob McGavock Dickinson on his left, thinks to take this away from us by the make-believe of a revision, which will eliminate the Tariff from the public mind for a dozen years or so. Go to, Mr. President, go to; the country does, indeed, need the rest cure; but not from Tariff agitation until the duties are reduced to a revenue basis; rather from the ravages of your friend, Theodore Roosevelt's intemperate agitations and strenuous personality.

Meanwhile, between them, Grover and Teddy did a deal of "comboberation," and might be described, as Hans described his wife, as "a hell of a set."

In different ways, and from opposite points of the social and political compass, they came to the Presidency unprepared to meet the multiplied duties and responsibilities of that great office. To this unpreparedness they added certain temperamental disqualifications. The one was not yet forty-eight, the other not yet forty-three years of age. Each was, after his fashion, singularly self-confident.

Mr. Cleveland had been an all-around man about town in Buffalo, filling acceptably the offices of Sheriff and Mayor. By an extraordinary piece of good fortune elevated to the Governorship of New York, the wave which bore him to Albany was still strong enough eighteen months later to bear him to Washington. Mr. Roosevelt had reached his fortieth year without attaining higher rank than that of Assemblyman, Civil Service and Police Commissioner and Assistant Secretary of the Navy. He was regarded by politicians as something of a crank; even by his friends as something of a visionary; overeducated and over-bred for practical affairs, affecting the cowboy among men of letters and the man of letters among cowboys; with rather more of audacity than common sense. Within three years he was rushed through two lucky elections and a tragedy into the White House.

The talents and aptitudes of Mr. Cleveland and Mr. Roosevelt were unalike—the one steady and sturdy; the other impulsive and spectacular, but both of them understood the show business. They also understood the Mugwump character, spirit and power. They well knew how to play to the cant of the time and the humbug of the professional performers. Neither was in reality a devotee of the ideas touching the Civil Service professed and promulgated by the Men Milliners of the East, to whose propaganda they catered, and each of them, when the time of trial came, used the official patronage to reach his ends unsparingly, like a very Jackson or Marcy. But to the point of departure they carried with them the puckered approval if not the hearty support of the self-styled Gentlemen in Politics led by Curtis and Schurz, the Franklin Square people and the *Evening Post* people, and the little group of dilettante publicists about Boston and Baltimore

who made speeches in dress suits on occasional platforms, and
at public dinners, and wrote for the magazines, misconceived, by
the unthinking to be discriminative and superior, since they never
seemed to be pleased. Both Cleveland and Roosevelt came to
despise them; not quite to disregard them, however, until such
Chieftains as Curtis and Schurz had passed from the scene, and
such as Bonaparte had come upon it.

In short, although Mr. Cleveland read, perhaps, too few books,
whilst Mr. Roosevelt read too many, each in his kind took up the
reins of power resolved to do his best for the common weal and
to have his way, seeking to reconstruct the public fabric as nearly
as possible after his own image and to organize, quite apart from
his party, an independent, personal following, all his own.

In this latter at least they measurably succeeded. Not Jefferson, nor Jackson, nor Lincoln was made the center of such adulation as eddied about them. To their idolators all they did and all
they said were wise and good; and though the political fortunes
of the one went down in disaster and defeat, whilst the other
transferred his office triumphantly to a designated successor, their
virtues, real and artificial, retain possession of the stage, leaving
their politics and failures for the future, in case it cares to filch
them out of the rather dark and overcrowded lumber room of
history.

It is still a kind of profanation in the eyes of certain intelligent
people to criticize them. Undertaking to do this the critic subjects himself to the charge of iconoclasm, if not of unworthy
motives. The current writers for the press, proceeding on lines
of least resistance with their daily grind and rarely stopping
to think or to express an opinion of their own—having never
time or inclination to investigate—fall in with the prevailing indifference to truth for truth's sake, when it requires study and
reflection.

Mr. Cleveland has paid his debt to nature. Whether a man
of tact and training could have held the Democrats together and
have won, instead of losing, the Money battle and the Tariff
battle, will always be a question. No one whose opinion is of
value will deny Mr. Cleveland's integrity and good intention. His
lot was cast in troublous times. He did his best. No man can
do more.

III: LUCK IS A FORTUNE

To become the subject of historic controversy, next after successfully identifying one's self with some great cause or principle, is to take a post-obit on the future.

In the case of Theodore Roosevelt there has been, and there
will continue to be, a great deal written from opposing points of

ρ.

view. The extremes of panegyric and invective meet in mortal combat wherever his name appears. Circumstances have signally favored him in this regard. During his passage through a Walpurgis Night of nearly eight years, though he tempted fortune over and over again and had adventures both thrilling and diverse, he encountered no serious mishap. A clever opportunist, he seemed the very child of good fortune; snatched by the gods of human destiny in a playful mood, not from a happy obscurity, as with so many of the world's heroes, but from a succession of fantastic political interludes, and elevated to the heights of power. From the Peace Congress at Portsmouth, where he took desperate chances of failure and ridicule without any justification arising out of the interests of his country, to the naming of his successor in the Chicago convention, which might have been turned to a fatal ending by his own nomination, the giants and dragons— the children might say the Teddy Bears—that have followed his footsteps and run ahead to clear the way, have had the will and the power to see that no serious harm came to him.

To do him justice, he has not been idle, or ineffectual, in caring for himself. His abilities as a practical politician will not be gainsaid, whatever many may think of him either as an actual or dogmatic reformer. With an eye alike to the present and the future, he has surrounded himself with pseudo-literary people, space-writers of varying degrees of irresponsibility, for whose excesses, however, he detached himself betimes by the citation of an apt sobriquet from Bunyan. Not without reason he claims to be a quasi man-of-letters, and quits the Presidency to become an actual Editor, prefacing the change of base by a scheme of publicity universal in reach and unprecedented in character.

He could give James Gordon Bennett lessons in the art of newspaper advertising. He has already shown Joseph Pulitzer and William Randolph Hearst tricks in Yellow Journalism they never dreamed of. Even Mr. Laffan, of the *Sun*, amid the heehaws of his satyrs and the sneering of his cynics, looks on with a kind of dazed perplexity and exclaims: "May the devil admire him."

All the while, and hither and yon, the friendly muckrakers are busy with the effort to prove that Washington was as impulsive and impetuous as Roosevelt. They find in the virulence of certain contemporary newspapers as to Roosevelt an echo of the malignity which assailed the Father of his Country. The thought of a conjunction so inapposite may be dismissed as the flubdub of obsequious flattery, but yet it lays a species of foundation for posthumous sanctification. Fifty years hence, when the socialism faintly foreshadowed by Roosevelt comes to be a living thing, mayhap a vital force, he will be its Jefferson, the Master-singer of the Gospel of Humanity, as Jefferson is the Master-singer of Democracy.

It is true that he has put no malefactor of great wealth in jail. It may be true that his bark has been worse than his bite. But he has left a vast verbal attestation of beliefs and intentions—saved from specified and specialized execration by its volume and irrelevance—which, when the time comes, and the issues sketched in outline arrive upon the scene, will constitute the American Socialists' whole duty of man. The story of the Ananias Club will contribute a sort of whimsical humor to the piece. Its membership, like its griefs, will have been forgotten. A generation is coming on in whose memories Teddy Bear and Teddy Roosevelt will be convertible terms; and what better could a man hope of posterity than to be the hero of its cradle songs?

I had written thus far, in my loose, random, illogical way, when I came by chance upon the following passage in a thoroughly just and thoughtful essay upon Theodore Roosevelt in the current number of *The Bookman*. It is from the pen of Professor Harry Thurston Peck, its Editor, and its appearance here may serve to complete my own train of moralizing:

"Such, when viewed at the moment, appear the two administrations of President Roosevelt. We must, however, take a broader view than this and look, not at the things he has immediately accomplished, but rather at the things which are indirectly to be ascribed to him.

"A century from now his inconsistencies, his errors, his personal defects—all of which seem of such importance in their day—will be remembered only by the curious chronicler of small details. Just enough of them will remain to give color and a certain picturesqueness to the story of the last seven years. The far-sighted observer of political events can already perceive that the name of Theodore Roosevelt will ultimately be linked with a series of social and political movements to which he gave, at times unconsciously, the initial impulse. And this was done almost wholly during his first term of office.

"His extraordinary popularity was the fulcrum upon which the lever of public opinion moved the entire nation. That popularity was at its height during the close of 1904. It might be described in the same words which an American historian has used of President Jackson: 'The people came to believe that he could do no wrong, and that he stood like an angel with a flaming sword guarding their interests against the designs of the politicians.' It gratified him to know that he was hated by the Senate, a body which was held to be the fortress of special privilege and political chicanery. After the ponderous utterances of Cleveland and the bland platitudes of McKinley, the vivid nervous utterances of Roosevelt came like an electric shock. He, the President of the United States, dared to say in plain English the very things which private citizens were saying and had been saying hopelessly for years.

"It put heart into hundreds of thousands who had begun to feel that the power of money was too great for any one to battle with. At once there began a series of exposures directly inspired by Mr. Roosevelt's public speeches. Municipal corruption was uncovered. The life insurance scandals were dragged to light, and the air and sun were let into many dark and noisome places. President Roosevelt himself called this 'muckraking,' and he did so with disapproval. Yet he was actually the first of the muckrakers, and the term ought not to be one of reproach. For, as was remarked at the time, had there not been such quantities of muck, there would have been no necessity for raking it."

Who shall forecast the future? "How can I tell what is going to happen?" Mr. Harriman was quoted the other day as saying to somebody out West: "Has Roosevelt exhausted the years of plenty, leaving Taft to meet the years of famine? Or, must our one-party Government proceed until we are face to face with the one-man power?"

In the antediluvian Democratic party, which after sixty years of almost unbroken tenure was strong enough to make its exit the signal of a bloody war, we had experience of the one. In Roosevelt we have had a touch of the other. How do we like the retrospective in either instance?

Do the masses of mankind discriminate? Can they? Are not the warnings of nature, the lessons of history, the admonitions of wisdom lost upon them by reason of wide separation, divergent local interests, the engineries and resources of prosperous partyisms, with its transcendent advantages, to say nothing of the schemes of able, ambitious leaders? I grew to manhood in the old Democratic camp in the National Capital. The Republicans are doing precisely what we used to do. They duplicate almost every feature. There is even a line of personal identification. That is why I believe occasional changes of party in the General Government are indispensable to the perpetuation of our free institutions.

H. W.

Naples-on-the-Gulf, Florida

A Very Big Cocoanut and Exceeding Sour Milk

(January 11, 1910)

I

The organs of an Administration, already much discredited, and destined yet more to lose the confidence of the country, are seeking to belittle the Pinchot-Ballinger affair as the merest quarrel between two officials.

It might have been so had the President kept hands off. But he has made himself a principal, the principal: Ballinger and Wickersham accessories; Pinchot Attorney General for the people; Shaw, Price and Glavis witnesses for the prosecution; Congress, the lower and immediate trial court. The Nation, being the final Court of Appeals, is so much the friend of the defense that it is yet a question whether a fair trial can be had.

There is Aldrich in the Senate, the most expert of jury-fixers, and Cannon in the House, a Sheriff who knows no relenting; and there may be found rascally Democrats as well as ironclad Republicans to work the will of corruption, backed by the power and resources of a party organism which thinks it has the world in a sling, and that, no matter what its leaders may do, its sins will never find it out, nor the popular vengeance overtake it.

Upon the threshold of a search for truth which the *Courier-Journal* means to pursue to the end, if need be to the bitter end, we wish to draw a distinct line between Taft, the President, and Taft, the individual. Not only do environment and interest color the opinions of us all, but men do collectively what they would not do separately; they do as partisans, even as churchmen, what, if done in any private transaction would, to say the best for it, look exceedingly queer. As between the Secretary of the Interior and the Chief Forester, the President occupied that narrow strip of territory lying betwixt the devil and the deep blue sea. Narrow as this is, however, it was dry land, and he was not bound to diverge either way from the straight line ahead.

The Secretary of the Interior, as other members of the Cabinet—the Secretary of Agriculture among the rest—is a kind of Departmental Head Clerk to the President, high in authority and confidential in character. The Chief Forester is a subordinate under the Secretary of Agriculture. In the present instance all are Republicans. The accusations of Pinchot, the Chief Forester, were not originally directed against Ballinger, the Secretary of the Interior, but against certain specified acts of threatened corruption in the Land Office, a bureau of the Interior Department. The

President could very well have let the facts stand for themselves, and show for themselves, taking sides neither way, in case there was nothing to be concealed and kept from the public view.

But here the milk in the cocoanut sours. Ballinger comes from the diseased quarter. If he got none of the pork, or if he had no guilty knowledge of the criminal destination of some of it, why the row? What was to be hid? Who was to be covered?

Without either rhyme or reason, the President, becoming the partisan of a partisan, misled by the false representations of partisans, influenced by the squabble in Congress and perhaps by the muddle and the misadventure of the Chinese Embassy business, conscious that it had left a bad taste, if not a stench behind it, perpetrated the mistake of confusing public interest with private feeling, thus committing himself and his Administration to a scandal, the like of which the country has never known before, unless a parallel may be found in the Whisky Ring frauds which disgraced and wrecked the second Grant Administration.

General Grant was as innocent as a child, although his own private secretary had been the head center of the Whisky Ring, and wherever this investigation may lead, we believe it will show equally the innocence of Mr. Taft. Yet his official action bears all the earmarks of a particeps criminis. The dismissal of Glavis seemed as warning to other subordinates, whilst removing an important witness. What would be thought of it in an ordinary court of law, preceding, or pending, a trial? The dismissal of Pinchot, however, and along with him of Shaw and Price, who have committed no other offense than that of investigating the statements of Glavis, has every appearance of a purpose and effort to protect the perpetrators of crime, being quasi-confession of crime which can no longer be concealed.

Wickersham, the Attorney General, the law officer of the Administration, makes himself a party to these proceedings. The Administration managers in Congress, led by Aldrich in the Senate and Cannon in the House, are moving heaven and earth to secure a packed committee. Thus, what might have remained a bureau affair becomes a National issue of the first importance. Like the Whisky Ring cases, Credit Mobilier and Pacific Mail, it will, after working destruction to the Administration—perhaps to the Republican party—pass into history as a *cause célèbre*.

Here is the case in a nutshell from the *Chicago Tribune,* a war horse of Republicanism, which cannot be suspected either of disloyalty to the Republican party or of unfriendliness to the Republican President:

"Without inquiring into the technical justice of the discharge of Mr. Pinchot, *The Tribune* must repeat that the country will stand by Pinchot, right or wrong. It does not understand legal technicalities, and it is prepared to accept the President's statement that Mr. Ballinger has acted within the law. But long since the country has been able to distinguish between men who are honest and those who are moved by moral zeal for the preservation of the public interest against private privilege. In that sense *The Tribune* believes that the great majority will disapprove the action of the President in discharging Pinchot, Pinchot who of all men under President Taft represents in the clearest sense the spirit of the Administration of Theodore Roosevelt.

"Whatever Mr. Pinchot's faults may have been, they were faults that the heart of the people must forgive. They were faults not disapproved by Mr. Roosevelt. He is a zealot battling in the public interest with his zeal confirmed by his successful efforts to redeem the public domain from private spoliation.

"There was to be a hearing before a joint committee of the House and Senate to inquire into the charges against Secretary Ballinger and Mr. Pinchot. The President remarks in his letter of dismissal that Pinchot has not heard the defense. Nor has the public seen the Glavis charges. The investigation by the two houses of Congress now will not serve the purpose for which it was intended. The papers must be laid on the table and the case tried before the bar of public opinion in order that it may decide whether the lawyer Wickersham in approving of the action of the lawyer Ballinger was right or whether Pinchot, impelled by the zeal of his cause and acting only on the information vouchsafed to him as regards his side of the case, was right."

II

The attempt of the Administration, its leaders in Congress and its newspapers throughout the country, to whistle down questions of such magnitude and moment will nowise avert the coming storm. The wiser ones among them already realize that it is not going to be the tempest in a teapot which the more foolish are so ready and so eager to forecast it. Ballinger may be little and Pinchot may be less; but when the Attorney General of the United States, the sworn law officer of the people, takes the field, backed by the President of the United States, as in effect the attorney of land-pirates and franchise-grabbers—for that is the real and only issue involved—engaged to stifle the facts and to crush an upright official—the matter of discipline having failed by star-chamber process—the Nation is thrown upon its primal and reserved rights, and perforce, will know the truth on't.

The student of history needs not to be reminded how often great things have hung upon small things in human annals, nor in that connection to have the lines of Burns recalled to him, for most of us know out of our own experience and observation how—

"The best laid schemes of mice and men
  Aft gang agley."

The Affaire of the Diamond Necklace did more to precipitate the French Revolution by the ugly, albeit the false, light it flashed upon the Austrian Woman than any other mishap of the Monarchy and the times. The click of a mouse-trap awakening the sleeping guards and revealing the recumbent assassins saved the life of Catherine of Russia, prolonging her hideous and baleful career. A rain-storm rescued Wellington from annihilation at Waterloo delaying Napoleon many hours and changing the future of Europe.

Coming to our own country, almost to our own period, and certainly to a period within the memory of men still living, it was a sleepy old game of whist at Washington which proved the avant courier of our Sectional War, for, when the Kansas-Nebraska Bill was framed to make a Territory immediately west of Missouri, which David R. Atcheson was to go and organize and bring in as a State—so returning him to the seat in the Senate he had lost—and back to the sleepy old game of whist whose players loved and missed him—nobody dreamed of making the Compromise Settlement of 1850, or repealing the Missouri Compromise of 1820, opening Pandora's box and letting loose again the sectional furies which the country believed to have been laid and locked up forever by the overwhelming popular vote of 1852.

We are not willing to see in the Affaire Pinchot-Ballinger merely the first gun in the inevitable war between Taft and Roosevelt. Even that delves deeper than appears above the surface. It will be, when it arrives, a kind of destiny.

The Protection System is as bound to go as ever the institution of African slavery was bound to go. Theodore Roosevelt, the most astute politician now alive, realizes that, and has for a long time realized it. The Republicans of the West are with him almost to a man. Beveridge and Cummins and Dolliver and Nelson and Bristow, not to mention LaFollette, and all the insurgents of the House—good Republicans every one—know they can long hold none of their States upon any High Protectionist measure such as the Payne-Aldrich Act. Their plan is to quibble and qualify, to pare a little here and a little there, so as to hang on a little longer.

By throwing himself into the arms of Aldrich and Cannon, and the standpatters, Taft commits his Administration to a High Protective System and certain defeat. Roosevelt can alone save the day. Hence is it that, in closing the article from which we have quoted, the *Chicago Tribune* says:

"Over the whole activity at the White House and the Capitol during the last twenty-four hours there has hung the shadow of a great figure. What has been done seems to have been done lest that shadow grow greater or less. The issues are not yet joined, but they are nearer and nearer unto us. The rancor which has been begotten by difference of opinion within the party is assuming a graver aspect than *The Tribune* hoped, and carries with it even more momentous consequences than *The Tribune* foresaw.

" 'Ex Africa, semper aliquid novi.' "

Again, here we have it in a nut-shell. The Republican party is used to looking to Africa; in many a closely contested campaign in the debatable States have the Africans come to its rescue in the nick of time; why not now? What will Theodore Roosevelt say, what will he do, when, his junket over, he returns to his native land? Will he sit supinely down, silent as a poor relation and like Niobe, all tears, by the shipwreck Taft has made? Or will he, putting away the crown, yet accept the command? Aldrich hates him; Cannon hybominates him. Nobody needs to tell him that. Taft has surrendered to these. Pinchot was his well-beloved. Will he tamely submit to the ruthless sacrifice and the new partition?

All things have their seasons and all things in time. We shall see what we shall see. The *Courier-Journal* surveys the field and considers the situation with neither prejudice nor joy. It had hoped for the best from the new President and his Administration. As to the customs, it fought, bled and died for a simple scale of revenue duties long ago. It stands toward the Protective System precisely where Phillips and Garrison stood toward the Institution of African Slavery. Nothing short of a tariff exclusively for public purposes will satisfy it. Every dollar of Protection is subsidy to somebody, and to that extent robbery under the forms of law.

It has small hopes of a Tariff for Revenue Only through Democratic agencies. As to the Reform of the Revenue, the Democratic party went to pot under Cleveland. It again went to pot the last session of Congress. But even as Chase and Hamlin, Hale and Trumbull, original Democrats, were required to form a successful anti-slavery party, so are Cummins and LaFollette, Bristow and Beveridge and Dolliver required to make a triumphant anti-subsidist party.

To that end we should hate to go under the leadership of Theodore Roosevelt, but nobody can foretell what will happen in the public life of America whilst all of us know that politics makes strange bedfellows.

Whither?

(April 8, 1910)

The time has come for the people of the United States to consider Theodore Roosevelt as they have never considered him before; to take him more seriously than they have ever taken him; to realize that he is altogether the most startling figure who has appeared in the world since Napoleon Bonaparte, a circumstance not without significance and portent.

He must be a poor American whose heart does not glow with pride at the unwonted honors bestowed upon this representative of his country and swell with exultant admiration at the splendid way he is carrying himself. It is too late, if it were not personally offensive, to talk about self-exploitation. The incident in Cairo was wholly characteristic. The incident in Rome was thrust on him. In both he showed the Theodore Roosevelt whose brilliant many-sidedness has captivated the universe.

He is pre-eminently a man who fits the word to the act, the act to the word, and does the thing which, however provocative of controversy, redounds to his advantage.

All that has happened in Rome, and more, will be repeated in Berlin, in Paris and in London. No conquering hero was ever made the subject of such demonstrations, each of the foreign capitals, each of the foreign potentates, vying with the other to pay him homage. Yet is he the winner of no victory on land, or sea. What is the meaning of it?

Something must be allowed for a disposition in Europe to be civil to America and Americans. The year in Africa may not be lightly dismissed. It has appealed to world-wide interest and wonder. It displays upon a sufficient field, manhood making good. The "fighting philosopher," the Mayor of Rome describes him. That flatters the vanity of human nature. We rejoice in a man of battle who is a man of thought. Third after Washington and Lincoln, said the Mayor of Rome, Washington the "creator," Lincoln the "consolidator," Roosevelt the "purifier" of the Republic. "We look again to see him at the head of the Republic," said the Mayor of Rome. That is the keynote. And it will continue to be the keynote wherever he goes. Thus he will come back to us the European nominee for President of the United States.

Let no one fancy this an unmeaning, or an idle compliment Taken in connection with what appears to be the hopeless breakdown of the Taft Administration it constitutes an event of the first consequence. With the Waterloo which seems certain to overtake the Republicans in the fall elections, the cry for Roosevelt in 1912 as the only man who can save the party will come up from every side, and it may prove irresistible. Hence the candidacy of Theodore Roosevelt for president in 1912 may be regarded from this time onward as so probable that the people should begin seriously to consider it. If we are to return Theodore Roosevelt to power let there be no mistake about the terms of the new commission which is to be issued to him.

History has agreed that the best of all government is a wise and benevolent despotism. If the Government of the United States under our written Constitution of checks and balances be a failure—as many think it—and if there be needed for its Executive Head a strong man having the courage to take all the bulls of corruption by the horns, and, regardless of obsolete legal restraints to shake the life out of them, then, indeed, Theodore Roosevelt would seem one fitted by temperament, education and training for the work. He is a patriotic American with humanitarian proclivities. He is an incorruptible man. He has shown himself fearless of consequences. If the people are sick and tired of the slow processes of constitutional procedure; if they want in the White House a President who, disregarding the letter of the law, will substitute his own interpretation of its spirit and intention; if they think that the reign of hypocrisy and cant and graft which marks our professional politics may be ended by the absolutism of a ruler who, as Roosevelt himself puts it, "translates his words into deeds," and who, charged with the cleansing of the Augean stables by an election putting the seal of popular approval upon conceded excesses in the use of power and bidding him to go forward and apply the same remedies to a disease otherwise incurable, then Theodore Roosevelt fills the bill to perfection, for he comes directly from the family of the Kings of Men and is a lineal descendant of Cæsar and Cromwell.

Before we get into the acrimonies of party conflict, the *Courier-Journal* asks its contemporaries throughout the country to reflect without passion or levity, and to answer to themselves, amid the blaze of light which casts an aureole about our wandering Ulysses, whether Representative Government in America is a failure, and whether the only cure for the evils which are admitted is the one-man power; because they may be sure that the return of Theodore Roosevelt to power will be so construed by Europe, and that on this account the demonstration of monarchism has its chief significance.

The One-Man Power

(October 12, 1910)

The Boanerges of Republicanism has penetrated far enough into Dixie-land to be so impressed by the popular demonstrations as to exclaim in his own enthusiastic way, "By George, if I thought I could carry a single Southern State I would willingly run for the Presidency," which may be taken as an intimation, or a menace, whichever way the mood of the reader cares to consider it.

Without undertaking any construction, the *Courier-Journal* recurs to the point of view which six months ago it sought to induce its newspaper colleagues to adopt with respect to a proposed reconsideration and review of Theodore Roosevelt, still, as we think, the most extraordinary figure that has appeared in the world since Napoleon Bonaparte.

Much that was said then has been since verified. His semi-regal march through Europe, hailed everywhere to be the next President of the United States, was quickly followed by his return to America, like a real god of battles, instant to take the field as chief of his clan and first in command. Thenceforward he has allowed no grass to grow beneath his feet. His capture of the political machinery and subjugation of his party associates in the Empire State demonstrated his power conclusively and at once. His triumphal tour of the West, followed by his welcomed invasion of the South, come therefore in regular order as equally an object lesson and a warning, because he puts himself forward in the character of a universal regulator, proclaiming, under the disguise of morality and religion, theories of government at war with our established institutions and personal intentions, which need only to be put into action to become high treason.

Believing in the virtue and intelligence of the people, the *Courier-Journal* has never feared that, advised fully and in time, they can be victimized by a popular idol seeking profit for himself in their favor, no matter how unthinking and enthusiastic. Hence, recognizing the gravity of the pretensions of Theodore Roosevelt, and declining to join in personal abuse of him, we have tried to get the public to see the transcendant issue behind him. This is nothing less than the future of the Constitutional System which has cost so much in the building and which ought to be so dear to the hearts of men. Meeting thus far the historic tests, the struggle for existence, the foreign invasion, internecine strife and the disputed succession, can it be possible that it must be wrecked at last in port and upon the visible shallows of hero worship, the people, unseeing and indifferent through their prosperity and vanity, lulled into unconsciousness by the charm of the spectacular and captivated by the lure of a promised millennium?

To our mind it is inconceivable. But that constitutes no reason why we should not discuss it. For now, as ever, eternal vigilance is the price of liberty, and especially of that liberty which is so abundant and seems so secure that many have come to despise it, holding the very name of it in a certain disrepute.

II

The President of the United States has more and greater power than any sovereign in Europe. He is Commander-in-Chief of the Army and Navy. He has the Appointment of the Federal officials at home and abroad. Through the Treasury Department he may control the rise and fall of prices. Through the Department of Commerce he may coerce the corporations; through the Interstate Commission, the railways. He is master of the Secret Service. It is his to forbid an act of Congress to become a law.

In the hands of a strong, ambitious and unscrupulous man, nothing short of armed resistance could stand against such an array of forces, and armed resistance could nowhere organize itself against a President having the foresight to provide against it; able by a word to concentrate troops at any given point; by the touch of a button to order the arrest of the resistant at the furthest ends of the Republic.

There is no tyranny more unreasoning than that of majorities, no despotism so relentless as party despotism. Backed by these, while inventing a pretext, a President of the United States could do with impunity what a Czar of Russia or a Sultan of Turkey would never dare attempt. Thus throughout the ages have absolutism and arbitrary power done their perfect work. All that stands between the people and these is the time-limit set upon the Presidential elections and the Third Term tradition bequeathed us by Washington, which has for a hundred years restricted the individual occupancy of the Presidential Office to eight years.

Lift this time-limit and life-tenure is the logical consequence. Life-tenure means absolutism and arbitrary power. Under the title of President we should have an Autocrat, having already an Imperial Republic under Democratic forms and names.

Nor is there any less reason why we should not find such a ruler in some popular favorite than that England found one in Cromwell and that Mexico actually has one in Diaz, except that we guard the approaches to life-tenure by preserving the Third Term tradition, because the four years' requirement upon the Presidential election, as we have seen in Mexico, raises no bar against life-tenure. The need of one day becomes the exigency of another day, until self-perpetuation is not only easy, but taken for granted by a people accustomed to usurpations of power. At last the revolution is accepted as a matter of course.

The plea that we are not as other Nations, that that which has happened elsewhere could not happen here, is a figment of self-love, heedless of the future and glorying in its ignorance. We may not indeed be as the Mexicans. But the French are as enlightened and as patriotic as we are. They love liberty, as we do not, and have contended for it bravely and continuously ever since the Revolution. They seem to have it at last. But, they had to turn down their Citizen King, the son of Philippe Egalité, proclaimed because a pretended and supposed devotee of freedom, and to survive Louis Napoleon, mistakenly elected President as a harmless figurehead. Down to the very hour when war burst upon a startled country with the firing upon Sumter and the calling of the troops by Lincoln, very few people, North or South, believed that there would be any war.

Can Roosevelt Come Back?

(December 30, 1915)

I

I am beginning to be drawn into the impression, the fancy— I will not say the belief—that Theodore Roosevelt may be the Republican nominee for President. The suggestion ought to seem preposterous. Yet stranger things have happened—the nomination of Horace Greeley by the Democrats, for example—and we live in a land and an era of the paradoxical.

No one who has considered the character, the antecedents and the methods of the ex-President can doubt that he is a candidate. His coquetries with Root and Hughes will certainly not deceive Hughes and Root. The basis of his pretension is the popular support he received in 1912; of his hope the chaos which envelops the Republican situation. The leaders and masses of the party are all at sea.

They know not where to turn, whom to turn to. The deadlock among "favorite sons" is both bewildering and blighting. No single aspirant has any considerable following. None possesses the vote-catching magnetic quality. It were as easy to convert an iceberg into a volcano as Fairbanks, or Burton, the two best of them, into a hero, and, for the matter of that, any of the rest.

There is not even an essential issue clearly dividing party lines. The tariff? Absurd! Economy? Tell it to the marines. The flag? Does anyone imagine that at the psychic (the new name for opportune) moment Wilson will not wrap it around him, march down to the footlights and fire the traditional hosspistols?

Parties which are down and out are never squeamish about principles. There is but one objective point, and that is to win, and to win any old issue will suffice. The professional politician is nothing if not adaptable and complacent. Penrose thinks now that he could never vote for Roosevelt. But all the same, he would. So would the rank and file of those who followed Taft to defeat. With the Money Kings and the Captains of Industry behind him—having forced himself to the front as the embodiment of the opposition to Wilson—Roosevelt can say to the National Republican Convention, "Reject me at your peril."

It will be but a gamble in any event, and the word and the law of the gambler is "take a chance."

II

Projecting one's fancy ahead into the possibilities of the National Republican Convention it is easy to conceive the nomination of Theodore Roosevelt, hard to conceive that of anyone else. On such occasions the dramatic quality is a positive force. Truth to say, it abides in none other.

Talk about Hughes is mainly chatter. If Fate had meant Hughes to be President, Fate would have lifted him bodily from Albany to Washington. Great judges have always proved disappointing candidates. Hughes is no small bunch of an iceberg himself. The faithful, who hew the nominating wood and haul the campaign water, want their "look in" and they can see no promise in the cold, steel-gray eyes "which he doth stare with," not to mention an attending conscience which has shown itself singularly unadjustable.

To meet and beat Wilson the Republicans must have something gamer. They must make a bold, aggressive canvass; the fearsome onset; the imminent, deadly breach; after the manner of those blood-curdling San Juan Hill pictures; the lion-slayer in the jungle; Jack-the-Giant-Killer; Alone in Cuba. Teddy's the boy for that sort of thing, and there is but one Teddy.

The cat is said to have nine lives. The President Emeritus of the Ananias Club has fifty. Many times over he has survived that which has sent a dozen party leaders to their graves. There can be as little doubt about his attitude as his puissance. If the following be not a demand and a programme, what is it? I quote from his latest manifesto:

" 'Stand by the President'—yes, while the President is right; and stand against him when he is wrong. In '56 and '60 the only way to stand by Lincoln was to stand against Pierce and Buchanan—as Lincoln did. If, after the firing on Sumter, Lincoln had immediately in a speech declared that the friends of union might be 'too proud to fight,' and had spent the next four months in exchanging 'firm' diplomatic notes with Jefferson Davis, he would have received the enthusiastic support of the ardent adherents of peace—and we would now have no country.

.   .   .   .

"The Administration has recently devised a new campaign catch phrase 'Safety first.' It certainly expresses their attitude in putting honor and duty in the second place, or rather, in no place at all. Safety first? This is the motto on which in a shipwreck those men act who crowd into the lifeboats ahead of the women and children.

.   .   .   .

"The present Administration has behaved as regards Mexico in a way to make every decent American hang his head with shame. But in this respect it has nearly followed in the footsteps of the previous Administration. What has been done for nearly three years by Mr. Wilson as regards Mexico is only what was done for nearly two years previously by Mr. Taft. Moreover, as regards the outrages and humiliations which we have suffered, thanks to the action of the Administration during the present European War, while of course President Wilson is responsible for our conduct, Mr. Taft has gone out of his way heartily to commend him for his action. Finally, when Mr. Wilson ate his own words— and reluctantly advocated ineffective measures of preparedness—Mr. Taft, after some hesitation between Mr. Bryan and Mr. Wilson, tagged after the latter.

.   .   .   .

"Over a year ago I pointed out that it was the duty of the United States to 'champion the integrity of the neutral rights' of Belgium (which had received the sanction of The Hague conventions to which the United States was a signatory) against the 'lawless conduct' of belligerent Germany.

"At that time the defenders of Mr. Wilson denounced me on the ground that I wished neutrality violated, and wished the United States to ignore its own interests and meddle in something which was, financially speaking, not its own affair. Mr. Wilson himself publicly announced that it was not our duty to champion these neutral rights of Belgium against the lawless conduct of belligerent Germany, but that we should be neutral 'not only in word, but in thought.' Yet now, a year later, Mr. Wilson repudiates his former position and himself expresses exactly my thought and my demand in practically exactly my language. Only—I meant what I said, whereas Mr. Wilson's acts have shown that he did not mean what he said so far as a nation of which he was afraid was concerned.

"The difference is that, having caused this nation to shirk its duty to others and to its own citizens in this country, he now valiantly asserts, against a nation whose representatives have no voting strength and which he believes can with impunity be defied, rights as regards cargoes of merchandise upon which he did not dare to insist when the point at issue was the slaughter of women and children, whereas I ask that we stand up for the wronged and the weak against the strength of evil triumphant, and that, while we defend our property rights, we even more strongly defend the lives of our men and children, and the lives and honor of our women.

"Mr. Wilson, a year later, has finally adopted my principle about preparedness, although he has sought to apply it in a half-hearted and inefficient manner; a year after I denounced peace-at-any-price, he followed suit, quoting the verses of Ezekiel which for months I had been quoting; a year after I had attacked hyphenated Americanism Mr. Wilson followed suit—at least before the Colonial Dames; and now he accepts my doctrine of America's duty to neutral nations, which a year ago he stoutly opposed. But he applies it only as regards American dollars, and only in relation to nations which can be trusted not to be rude. I believe it should be applied as regards American dollars, but even more as regards American lives, and that it should first and most stoutly be asserted as regards the chief and most formidable offenders."

As if to drive this pronunciamento home—to give it pith and moment to the Republican understanding—to show that there are other ways of obtaining "fat" besides frying it out of the manufacturers—the Gary dinner coincides with its publication. Campaign money has not ceased, perhaps will never cease, to play a leading part in American elections. But sometimes it works both ways. Woodrow Wilson derived a positive advantage from the false story, artfully exploited by his managers, that he had indignantly refused the money of a Well-Street magnate. There was in 1884 a gathering of financiers in the interest of Mr. Blaine quite as imposing as that of the Steel King in the interest of Mr. Roosevelt. It did more execution at the breach than at the muzzle and came to be called Belshazzar's Feast.

If Roosevelt be the Republican nominee the Gary dinner will

figure as an issue of the campaign. It will point the moral and adorn the tale of another issue; a very great issue, indeed; the Mexicanization of the Republic and the Diazification of the Presidency; because in the person of Theodore Roosevelt third-termism can only mean life-tenure. If he should ever get back into the White House there will be no getting him out, except feet foremost. With all that is going on in Europe before their eyes will the people of this country deliberately submit themselves to the Man on Horseback? I cannot believe they will.

III

The arraignment of the President by the ex-President, albeit exparte, is not without force. The Democrats will find it uphill work defending the course of the Administration in the matter of Mexico. On the other hand, the European war-game is not played out and the greater issue will swallow and absorb the lesser. It is much too early to indict the chief magistrate upon his parts of speech and to dismiss him as merely a rhetorician.

Woodrow Wilson remains even to his familiars something of an anomaly—a medley of contradiction—whose real character has yet to reveal itself. Seeming to prefer isolation, he has frequently reached out after sympathy; disdaining companionship and counsels, he often revises and sometimes reverses his judgments. He has made many noble utterances and a few frivolous utterances. Barring a brother from official recognition on altogether strained grounds of nepotism, the circumstance that the Secretary of the Treasury is a son-in-law does not appear to have given him concern, though at once an impropriety and a menace. In authority unyielding and even austere, the boy in him—and at that a rather bumptious and heedless boy—has shown him capable of hilarious enjoyment—still as it were the undergraduate.

Since Mr. Bryan God-blessed himself out of the Department of State there has been noticeable improvement in the President's temper and tone. From the first Mr. Bryan was a serious handicap and must have sorely tried the patience of his chief. Mr. Wilson had come to the head of affairs with the bravery and inexperience of the college president—shall I not, without offense, say the schoolmaster?—lacking the long and hard discipline in public life which had better qualified a weaker man. He was distinctively an academician, much taken with the semi-library fad of the uplift adopted by the cheap periodicals when the scurrility of muck-raking had proved commercially unprofitable. Even now he has not wholly rid himself of the disposition to preach to the texts of the "spiritual" and the "ideal," as the space-writers are used to dubbing their bombastic cant. I have never quite for-

given the President for sending one of these sham apostles of
sweetness and light to Mexico when he should have read the riot
act to the Mexicans, and followed it with an army—as he might
have done from Vera Cruz and Tampico—or for wasting the
great English embassy upon a Yankeefied "tar-heel," having
neither personal fitness, political standing, nor party claim, when
he might have paid a debt of honor and gratitude and sent to the
Court of St. James the most representative and highly capable
American of his time. It pains me to say these things. But men
in great place have never had anything but truth from me, and
no man needs more to hear the truth, though bluntly spoken, than
the present occupant of the White House.

These, however, are but personal idiosyncrasies. The President's lack of the noisy popularity attending the self-exploitation
of the magnetic men need not trouble him. From Clay to Bryan,
including Douglas and Blaine, at the supreme moment they met
defeat. There is a destiny, and, whether Woodrow Wilson is to
play a world part in modern affairs, or to pass off the scene the
hero of an interlude, remains to be written. Neither Louis XI
nor Richelieu has come down to us a paragon of the generous and
the charming. When he has finished the chapter, this cold, self-
confident, unloving, but very able, man may with them make a
good historic third in the annals of the heartless in beneficent and
successful statecraft.

Which brings us back to Theodore Roosevelt. In the event
that he be the Republican nominee for President another fatalistic
spectre rises before us. If Fate meant him to come again, why
did not Fate so order and arrange the performance in 1912?

It seems now sure that, when Teddy returned from his tour-
de-force in Africa and his more than Buffalo Bill triumph in
Europe, he had only to sit down quietly at Oyster Bay, to keep
a stiff upper lip and to wait. The Republican disasters were on
the way. They were bound to arrive. Taft, not he, was in for
the bills. The Republicans would have turned to him as their only
savior and a united Republican party could not have been beaten.
But that mysterious power, which has so often interposed in the
darkest hours of tribulation and danger to rescue the American
republic, here put forth its hand to muddle the situation and make
a fool of Theodore Roosevelt, who had had his fling, and to elect
Woodrow Wilson, who was backed to have his fling.

My belief is that the President will be his own successor. As
the *Courier-Journal* has repeatedly said, no one can beat Woodrow Wilson, except Woodrow Wilson; this is by no means to say
that the very earth may not rise on its hind legs and knock the
stuffing out of the best prospects toward the wee sma' hours of
October ten months hence.

It is idle to attempt a forecast of next year's military conditions in Europe. The Allies may be in Berlin. In that event what of the sudden stoppage of their orders on America; the men thrown out of employment; the consequent reaction in every line of business? *Quien sabe!* Do you take me for a prophet? What I do venture to surmise—but merely to surmise, mind you!—is that Theodore Roosevelt, fairly on the warpath for the Republican nomination, may corral it. His resources and ingenuities are still potential. He can threaten certain defeat if he be rejected. He has always shown himself relentless. The Republicans are at fingers-and-thumbs—out at elbow—and, Lord, how cold it grows! But, if he be able to big-stick his way through the National Republican convention, there will stand across his way the third-term gorgon; Cazat with the rabble at his heels, threatening the end of the republic of Washington and Lincoln.

As God is wise and just, I do not believe that Theodore Roosevelt will ever come back.

H. W.

New Orleans
    December, 1915

Red Blood Versus Red Tape

(April 11, 1917)

The proposal of Theodore Roosevelt to enlist in the World's Army of Freedom and go to one of the fronts in Europe leading a body of American soldiers may not be whistled lightly down the wind as the melodramatic performance of a man who has a positive genius for the spectacular. It should be considered very seriously. What is war but spectacular? What is glory but spectacular? Men are reached equally through their imagination and their patriotism, and, except for the sympathetic and emotional in man, there would be no armies.

We learn from the National Capital that, although Theodore Roosevelt's plan of raising a division of American volunteers for service in France is not regarded as practical by the General Staff of the Army, there is a general belief that President Wilson will avail himself of the ex-President's offer of service in some form or other before hostilities have got well under way.

The President is known to be deeply impressed with the manner in which Colonel Roosevelt has thrown all partisan feeling to the winds, and friends of the Administration say that any assistance which the White House can consistently give to the Roosevelt plan for raising volunteers will be given.

The difficulty so far, we are told, is that there is no plan on foot calling for volunteers. It may come later, but General Staff officers are not enthusiastic over the idea. They are against the volunteer system because they fear it will not bring in men fast enough, and men in round numbers are needed in a hurry.

This being true, the circumstance adds to the force of the Roosevelt offer. He can raise more troops and quicker than any other man. Agreeing that the draft plan must be resorted to Colonel Roosevelt could raise his division and have it ready to go whilst Congress and the Army Staff were getting the draft machinery started.

As there seems to be some misunderstanding touching the precise nature of the ex-President's offer it may be well to correct the impression that he wishes to command an expeditionary force. He expressly disavows this, advocating a full army corps for service abroad, and pressing his claim as "an ex-President of the United States of previous military experience" for the command of a division in this corps. In other words, all that he asks is permission to raise his division and then to lead it to the battle line under a corps commander selected from the regular service. The Colonel's only suggestion as to the corps commander is that he shall be "one of our first-class regular Major Generals."

Here is a statement prepared by himself which tells its own story and makes its own argument:

"The American people are united behind the President in the determination to wage effective, aggressive war for our own rights and for the rights of humanity and civilization.

"I believe that our people now realize that the system of universal military service is the only effective and the only democratic system. I, of course, most earnestly hope for the passage of legislation establishing the principles of universal and obligatory military service and training.

"In addition, I believe that the American people desire that in the immediate future we send abroad an expeditionary force. It is an excellent and indispensable thing to raise money for and furnish supplies to our allies. This must, of course, be done. But more than this must be done. The American people wish to do their own fighting. They do not wish merely to pay others to fight for them.

"They believe that we owe it to ourselves and to the national honor to send a fighting force of at least an army corps, under the American flag, to the front at the earliest moment. This army corps should be commanded by one of our first-class regular Major Generals. It might consist of three or perhaps only two divisions.

"I have asked permission to raise a division, which would be in this army corps and under its commander. No unwise precedent could possibly be created by permitting an ex-President of the United States of previous military experience to raise such a division and to serve with it at the front under the command of the General who heads the army corps."

It is easy to find objections to all this and easier to declaim against it. Yet there are two sides to it and in no event should we make light of it. Red tape is always the rule with the Army Staff and the War Department, and, of course, Red Tape is very necessary to organization. But just now, whilst Red Tape is considering precedents and statutes, Red Blood might be doing its part. We should not allow the opportune moment to pass. If it be requisite, Congress should enact the legislation enabling Colonel Roosevelt to raise his Division. He will raise it in a hurry. That is the Roosevelt way. And, it will do more to hearten the fighting line in Europe and to encourage recruiting in America than any other single agency.

As the *Courier-Journal* has already said, the appearance of an ex-President of the United States carrying the Star Spangled Banner over a body of American soldiers to the battle front in Flanders will glorify us as will nothing else. It will electrify the world. In fancy we can see this sublime spectacle circling round the Arch of Stars and marching down the Champs Elysées, up through the Rue Royale, and, passing the Madeleine, out the Boulevards to the Column of July, thence to the front, by that time, let us hope, across the Rhine. Teddy might be constituted a special messenger, his boys a body of videttes, avant couriers of liberty, sent ahead to carry the news to Wilhelm in Potsdam that his race is run, that his dynasty is down and out, and that, Germany rid of the Hohenzollerns, the war is over! It is worth all it costs us either in Red Tape, money and equivocal precedents.

WILSON

During 1910 and 1911 Mr. Watterson referred to Woodrow Wilson as "the light of Democracy," and for a time it seemed that he had found another public man whom he would value as he had valued Tilden. But misunderstandings arose toward the end of that year and on January 21, 1912, the editor arrived in Washington with the announced intention of doing everything he could to prevent Mr. Wilson's nomination. In his autobiography the editor discussed this chapter in his life as fully as he desired and there is no point in adding to that personal narrative.

But in a political sense Mr. Watterson's withdrawal from

the Wilson camp lost Kentucky to the Governor of New Jersey, which, otherwise, he would readily have carried. The editor's influence turned the delegates to Champ Clark.

From the moment of the break onward Mr. Watterson wrote frequently and lengthily about Woodrow Wilson. His personality in varying semblances enters the editor's writings in connection with general topics like the World War and the campaigns of 1912 and 1916. But the three subjoined articles are definitely about Mr. Wilson and they are included in this division of this volume because they cover the whole public ground of the Wilson-Watterson relationship.

The first is that call to the Democrats of Kentucky which changed the character of things political in the editor's state; but none of his writings on this topic, so absorbing to him, is more thoughtful, friendly and impersonal than the second reprint below, "The New Dispensation." It was written just after the election of 1912. Mr. Watterson again conducted his favorite autopsy, for "the Republican party is dead" and will soon be swallowed by the Bull Moose. Within four years events reversed the prophecy, but the incidental political indigestion had not yet been allayed.

The last article in this group was written in 1918. The editor, as a leader of American thought, was standing firmly and admiringly at the right hand of the commander-in-chief and calling on his countrymen to do the same.

To the Democrats of Kentucky

(February 21, 1912)

I

In a lighthouse tower, watching the ships that toss at sea, may not an ancient mariner trim his lamp, and, as the sun goes down, send its beams across the darkling waters without offense to the man-of-war's-men that make merry in the offing, all unconscious of the coming storm?

Dealing with party interests, I shall write from a party point of view. Indeed, considering some recent home developments, I shall write from a Kentucky point of view. Now, as ever and always, my aim shall be truth, and truth alone. It shall go ill with the Democrats of Kentucky if they do not listen, nowise ill to me; for I am beyond the reach of the revenges and reprisals of this world, and have long been proof against the poison of printer's ink.

Nor am I under the least illusion. I know full well that the risk of speaking out in meeting is proportioned to the good intended; the honest having but a single tale to tell, the dishonest fifty shifts and an hundred tongues to promote their selfish plans and schemes. As a rule, the vicious are not wanting the foolish to keep them company, to follow after and applaud them.

So much heat and perversion have entered into the recent Wilson-Harvey affair that a plain consecutive narrative, even at this late day, may not be without interest and profit. The story divides itself into two parts; first, the break between Wilson and Harvey, to which I was only a witness; and, second, the issue of veracity forced upon me by Governor Wilson, through which, in a sense, I became a principal. This latter incident involves his turpitude or mine. He has sought by assuming an attitude of superiority and silence, having previously adopted a course of levity and belittlement, to whistle me down the wind of a dignity which I take leave to believe is purely fanciful. The public intelligence is left to decide whether Governor Wilson so transcends me in standing, character and value of service as quite to destroy the relations of equality between us man to man.

I have related how in the beginning, and as it were upon the ground floor, I was lured into the Wilson movement. Its aspects at least looked good to me. When the time arrived for launching it I was ready to do my part.

Delegates to Conventions, let me observe by way of preface, do not shape themselves always and wholly out of the insubstantial vapors of popular opinion. Popular Opinion itself is not the offspring of nebulous conditions descending from Heaven. Agitation is essential to organization, and both require money. It is a sordid fact, it is a discreditable but recognized method. Taking a hint from the prize-ring and the stage, presidential candidates, like pugs and prima-donnas, have latterly had their literary bureaux, their advance agents and their publicity promoters. Too many of them have had their stunts of political advertising and personal exploitation. It should go without saying that, being for Wilson, I was not insensible to the need of money. Neither were he and his managers. Even now, as then, they are reaching out after all the money they can get. Else who is paying for the most costly political machine known to modern times since the death of the late Mark Hanna?

In the beginning many names of possible subscribers to a campaign fund were canvassed. Among the rest the name of Thomas F. Ryan occurred to me. He is a rich man. He is a Democrat. He is a Virginian. Whether he liked Wilson or not, being, as I believed, beyond the reach of a President of the United States to hinder or help him, I hoped he might be induced to aid toward the nomination of the Governor of New Jersey.

I may say in passing that if it be a crime to take the hands of Morgan and Carnegie and Ryan, I shall have to plead guilty, for I know the three of them very well. I have an impression that none of the mammoth fortunes will bear too close scrutiny. But I have never constituted myself a Congressional Committee of Investigation, and, wanting nothing for my own use, have not thought that, if money were required for any purpose held by me to be good, I might not with propriety go to them, or any one of them, nor deem it requisite that I look a gift horse in the mouth.

Before speaking to Governor Wilson I spoke to his managers about the Ryan suggestion, and, like Roosevelt and Harriman, being practical men, they were no wise shocked, but, on the contrary, highly pleased. When I spoke to Governor Wilson he hesitated, thought the name of Ryan, if it got out, would do more harm than good, and declined to accept what he declared rather rudely to be "dirty money." That, of course, settled it. I made no insistence. I did not even resent his implied censure and discourtesy by representing that I never touched an unclean dollar in my life either coming or going, along with the natural inquiry—since the Carnegie Pension would be unequal to his need, in case he finally got it—where he expected to find a capitalist with wings?

I am at pains to recur to this episode because it has been made the basis of many attacks upon me and of great exploitation to Governor Wilson. It was the basis, indeed, of the applause which greeted his dismissal of Harvey and which he silently accepted although he knew as far as Harvey was concerned that it had no foundation in fact. The truth of my first statement, made upon the insistence of Colonel Harvey, in corroboration of the publication in *Harper's Weekly* accounting for its change of attitude toward the Wilson candidacy, was denied by Governor Wilson and his agents. The Wilson-Harvey letters, of which I knew nothing until later, fully confirmed it. My averment as to my own relations to the Wilson campaign was given the lie direct by Governor Wilson. In such matters, since records are not usually kept, such an issue might easily arise. It happens, however, that in this case I hold the amplest proof. This I have offered to produce under proper restrictions safeguarding the rights of others, Governor Wilson refusing and insisting that I have lied.

Again the public intelligence and at the same time the sense of public justice are left to decide whether an honorable man, who has himself raised an issue of veracity, is at liberty to decline any sure means of arriving at the truth and whether his refusal is not in itself a confession of judgment.

II

Truth being stranger than fiction, and strange as the romance of the White House must be allowed from the most casual reading of its history, the transit from the Presidency of a University to the Presidency of the United States at a single bound and within two short years would seem inconceivable.

The upward flight of Napoleon in times of revolution and war was scarcely so precipitate. All things great, however, are simple, and Governor Wilson's plan of campaign has been simplicity itself. It embraced merely a stepladder and a flying machine. His idea was to mount from literary to political preferment by the stepladder and then kick the stepladder from beneath him; and, having thus reached a point of vantage, to send the antecedents of a lifetime packing, in order that he might outrival the most radical in the profession of radical principles and policies, relying upon his flying machine to carry him across the intervening space between his dangerous elevation and the prearranged place of safety.

That he seems to have satisfied the most suspicious and exacting is proof of the extraordinary intellectual equipment and amazing audacity which has easily misled a man so credulous, appreciative and sympathetic as I am. Yet, since many of the Democrats caught by his spectacular conversion—including Mr. Bryan—are men of brain and heart, it is wonderful that they can see nothing ominous and sinister in the succession of events which have marked the meteor-like career of their new "Saul of Tarsus": the acceptance of the nomination for Governor of New Jersey out of the hand of James Smith, and, the battle gained, his ruthless dismissal of Smith; the recantation of Eastern connections and heresies so plausible as to seem real, though concurring with interests the most obvious; the tuneful and well-timed apology to Mr. Bryan having the same self-seeking concurrence; the abrupt dismissal of Harvey to point the moral and adorn the tale of complete emancipation from the influence of "predatory wealth." Allowing Harvey to be a bad man and Smith if possible to be worse, is there no such thing as honor among thieves and loyalty among politicians, and may a man who has held antecedents and friends so lightly be depended upon to stand faithfully by organisms and principles?

III

The Democratic Party has never had to meet a greater responsibility than that which confronts it. The split among the Republicans gives us the hope that we shall elect our ticket no matter whom we put up. Hence the supreme importance of making no mistake in the choice of a candidate.

There was on the face of it something very alluring in the idea of going outside the arena of professional politics and taking a scholar and a gentleman out of one of the universities, who professed to be a Democrat and had actually been a student of Government.

In the case of the Governor of New Jersey the attraction was enhanced to the Democrats of the South by the accident of his Southern birth. The combination appealed strongly to me. Circumstances favored it. There was even, though distant and indirect, a domestic connection, my own end of it held to tenderly by me. Why should I break away from such a leading? Why should I turn against Governor Wilson?

I saw and heard him grossly misuse—"shameless" is the word employed by him in his ultimate confession—a loyal fellow-servant and colleague in his service. I discovered that, though I was faithfully engaged advancing his cause, he was in secret correspondence with my bitterest enemies in Kentucky. From these personal and private matters I was led to review his more recent public record and came to the realization that this was equally crooked. In a word, beneath the veneering of scholarly polish lay the coiled serpent of unscrupulous ambition.

It was because I was convinced that Governor Wilson made the heartless break with Harvey for the exact purpose—deliberately worked out in his own mind—which this incident has achieved, that I resolved then and there to go no further under such a leader. It was as a flashlight revealing a character and personality not before visible to the naked eye. Even as Colonel Harvey owed an explanation to his readers did I owe an explanation to my readers. That was their right and it was my right. Hence the warning of my party against a man whom my immediate intercourse had disclosed to me as likely, if elevated to the Presidency, to unite the unhappy qualities which the Republicans found in Harrison—a man of many intellectual gifts and personal virtues —which the Democrats found in Cleveland—a strong-minded, patriotic man of the best intentions, yet a very bull in a china shop—each of whom did his part toward his party's undoing.

Something more, fellow-Democrats, than intellect and scholarship are required of the President of the United States. He should be a man of experience, tact and judgment. He should have a good as well as a strong heart, a broad no less than a bright mind. Of Governor Wilson's talents and accomplishments there need be no question. Because I thought and said I had found him a schoolmaster and not a statesman, I have been roundly taken to task. I might as well be accused of saying I found a blacksmith a blacksmith and not a watchmaker. Socrates and Plato were doubtless very good schoolmasters indeed, but if either were living now

I should doubt his fitness to be President. I certainly should vote for neither to be the next Democratic nominee for President.

What was I to do? With the ink not yet dry on the extollation of Governor Wilson for giving Colonel Harvey a blunt answer to his direct question touching the support of *Harper's Weekly,* my critics assail me for giving the public a plain statement of my reasons for withdrawing my support from the Wilson candidacy. It is even charged that there was a conspiracy "to destroy Woodrow Wilson." Who are all the conspirators? Waiting a fortnight and fearing that he had overdone the ingrate to Harvey in seeking to placate the radicals of the West and South, Governor Wilson writes to Harvey. Then, figuratively, they kiss and make up. So Harvey cannot be one of the conspirators. Am I a conspirator because I am less forgiving than Colonel Harvey and more sensible of the public obligations involved?

It might be well to look a little closer into the rather theatrical reconciliation of Governor Wilson and Colonel Harvey. It appears that immediately after the interchange of the touching letters indicating Wilson's contrition and Harvey's magnanimity, Damon and Pythias spent a day and night under the roof of the same hotel in Washington without improving the opportunity to rush into one another's arms. But a little while ago they again attended a banquet in Philadelphia, and, though not twenty feet apart, were conspicuously ignorant of one another's presence. Can Wilson have thought to eat his cake and have it, Harvey, for the sake of their common business interests in the Harper publication, consenting?

Such considerations are nothing to me. I am thinking solely of the public interest as affected by private character and the party interest as menaced by a formidable array of college clubs backed by a literary bureau rolling in mysterious luxury and wealth and circulating lies unspeakable. Whilst there is yet time I would save Democracy a fatal misstep. I would put my fellow-Democrats as wise as events have put me.

In Governor Wilson we should have a candidate every step of whose way through the whole campaign would be over the hidden pitfalls of a career yet to be explored. We should have a candidate who has made a deathbed repentance of lifelong convictions, ably expounded, to secure a presidential nomination. Happily, before I had gone too far in urging this candidacy its specious quality, as by the falling of a screen, became despicably apparent.

It may be that I take my political life in my hands when I make known to the public what circumstances made known to me. That is of small account. On less provocation and with even more at stake, I have often done this before. I have not very far to go before I reach the end. Please God, every step of the way

shall be on high, firm ground and in the open. I know not how
else to fight. And so I salute my enemies from one end of the
State to the other and invite them to come and enjoy themselves.
The harder they hit and the oftener will best suit me, because
when the winter is over and I get back to "God's Country" I am
going to do some hitting myself!

HENRY WATTERSON.

Naples-on-the-Gulf, Florida

The New Dispensation

(November 9, 1912)

I

Now that the election is over and the battle won, and that the
shouting has had time to subside into a sigh of satisfaction and
relief, let the mind's eye of thoughtful Democrats, glancing from
heaven to earth, from earth to heaven, body forth to the less
thoughtful some of the giants and dragons which will presently
rise across the party's line of march to divide its counsels and
obstruct its progress.

They may seem just now to unreflecting and optimistic enthusiasm but airy nothings, mere figments of overwrought or of prejudiced imagination. Yet are they real, and it will not require the
poet's pen to give to each his form and presence; even to distinguish each by a tag bearing a local habitation and a name.
History tells that after Bull Run the victory disorganized the
Confederates almost as much as the defeat had demoralized the
Federals. In the long run, however, it was the Union, not the
Confederacy, which reaped the harvest. This lesson should not
be lost upon Democrats.

The Democratc party out of the two terms of Grover Cleveland got nothing except agreeable interludes from the monotony
of Republican partyism. Woodrow Wilson is abler and far more
highly equipped—much better qualified to make a really great
Democratic President—than was Grover Cleveland. But the
obstacles which Cleveland had to meet and overcome were foot-
hills by comparison with the mountains already rising across the
highway that stretches out before Wilson.

Within Mr. Cleveland's easy reach, if he had known how to
profit by them, were men of the first order of intellect; men trained
to the responsibilities of Government; men used to the affirma-
tions of public policies; men who had sat in the high places of
legislation and administration. Mr. Wilson will have to rely for
the most part upon discoveries and creations of his own; political

amateurs new to official life; novitiates to practical and large affairs. Barring a few members of the house—a few Senators—having chiefly negative experience, he will at once encounter in the lower branch of Congress a top-heavy majority, with possibly a divided leadership, and, in the upper, if support at all, yet too close for comfort.

Public opinion is nowhere crystallized. It is in a fluid state. The historic issues that first divided parties pass from the scene, the problems of the future but arrive upon it; he who saddles and bridles and successfully rides the monster without a head called Democracy, must be possessed of the gifts of the nation-makers of old and in addition must be attended by the good fortune which genius sometimes attracts and sometimes compels.

II

The objections which were generally offered to Woodrow Wilson as a nominee—that he was rather a schoolmaster than a statesman—if not tyrannous and intolerant, yet tactless—incapable of making common cause and working to harness, and lacking a high sense of personal obligation—assuming them found in fact—may, or may not, show themselves to be weaknesses in the elected President.

Upon the threshold he will have rough work to do. It is safe to say the onrush of office-hunters will surpass anything ever known before. A gentle, kindly, grateful man would find himself submerged beneath the cross-currents of sentiment and duty. It will require the most obdurate of masters, used to the disciplinary and ungracious, to resist the appeals, some of them real, but most of them spurious—which will echo through the living rooms of the White House; which will assail him during all his waking hours, and pursue him in his sleep and dreams; morning, noon and night never escape from the mean and sordid and brazen in the rank ignominy of self-seeking. He who does not stand like a statue of wrought iron, with "no" constant upon his lips, who does not bare his bosom to the storm, knowing in advance what of obloquy and abuse betide, might easily break his heart before the arrival of a Congress bound still further to test his manhood and try his soul.

In spite of Mark Antony's tearful orations, we do not understand that Cæsar gushed over his friends, or that, though not unmindful of them, Washington much consulted his personal likes and dislikes in the choosing of his instruments. Now and then a tradition which tells of a leaning toward the chivalric comes to us from Henry of Navarre and Andrew Jackson. But the rule among Kings of men has inclined to the Doric. They have been made of sterner stuff and have cultivated the reserved and unyielding. Leadership implies self-confidence, dominancy, and will-power. Mr. Cleveland had plenty of these. But he lacked the fullness of knowledge which comes from life-long intellectual habitudes, and the definite purpose which takes its cue from special study and original research. He got his political economy by absorption and at second hand. He possessed strong natural gifts; Within the reach of his mental vision no man saw clearer; within his competency no man governed wiser, or truer. He was obstinate, however, rather than firm; not at all resourceful in dealing with men; and, temperamentally tactless, likely to grow impatient under stress of circumstances. Thus he wrecked his party—wrecked it after it had reached what seemed a safe harbor—and left it a very hulk upon the wide, wide sea.

Woodrow Wilson comes to the head of affairs a full grown man. He is mature in all his powers. For good or ill, his character is ripened and all his own. Sprung from a race of scholars and thinkers, he has, from his cradle, played with books—devoured them, written them—a publicist learned in the schools; a politician, astute, acute and up to date; a popular speaker of the modern type, at once effective and attractive. The opportunity before him is resplendent, the pitfalls many and deep.

What he will do with Congress remains to be seen. What Congress will do to him remains to be seen. Democracy needs a Jefferson to initiate, a Jackson to execute. How many of the swan-songs of the campaign can be translated into statute law? What rival ambitions may take the field—at first under cover and then in the open—to confuse and thwart his highest aims? Shall he find a Bentonian tower of strength in the Senate as Jackson did? Shall he be able to organize a group in the House such as held up the hands of Jackson with men like James K. Polk and Franklin Pierce and James Buchanan, Andrew Stevenson and Richard M. Johnson in the lead? Shall be prove himself another Old Hickory?

Time alone shall tell us. His nomination and election look very like a destiny. The times need a man; they need a schoolmaster; they need an academician; they need one who knows and can discriminate; who sees and can do; who is honest and not afraid. Roosevelt has some great qualities. No doubt of that. But Roosevelt is yet a boy. He is a boy crazy after a bird's nest it is not good for him to have. Events will show us what Wilson is.

III

Meanwhile the Republican party is .dead. Its leaders, with Taft at their head, may not think so; but it is as dead as a door nail. As the institution of African slavery killed the old Democratic party has the Protective Tariff System killed the modern Republican party.

Like slavery, Protectionism, laid in false economic theories, is untenable. It has outstayed its welcome. The American manufacturer will find Protection a Chinese wall as the Southern planter found slave labor a broken reed. The vast income required by the Government to be got through the customhouses will upon a fairly adjusted revenue tariff furnish the manufacturers all the protection they could ask against their foreign competitors, who have to cross the seas to bring their wares to market.

It is inevitable that the Bull Moose party, under the leadership of Roosevelt, will swallow what is left that is worth having of the Republican party. By the advent of Wilson and the Democracy the Bull Moose becomes the party of protest. Slowly, but surely, all the elements of discontent will gather around it. Whilst Wilson is giving the people the "marble heart" of enlightened practical and orderly administration, Roosevelt will be giving them "the song and dance" of Armageddon.

Take out of the Democratic party the "Progressives," as they call themselves, and join them to the "progressives" who rally to Roosevelt, and no man can predict the state of the country and the complexion of the Congress. As Wilson strives to fulfill the promises of the Democratic platform and to meet the requirements of national progress, will the standards of Progressivism be raised. All who do not bow down and worship at the shrine of Bull Moose—having no responsibilities to carry and playing to the fanciful, the emotional and the poor, whom we have always with us no matter what laws Congress may pass and what wisdom and virtue may reside in the White House—all who do not demand the preposterous will be described as Reactionaries and be relegated to outer darkness. By 1916 it will be a contest between the possible and the impossible in government, complicated by Democratic factionism and the ghost of Republicanism, unknowing, or unwilling to admit, that it is dead.

The Bull Moose propaganda is a religious cult, not a political programme. The one tangible thing embodied by it in the campaign just ended was a Third Term for Theodore Roosevelt. That could only mean life-tenure and an absolutist autocracy. The pretension that it would not Mexicanize the Government and Diazify the Presidency is the milk-and-water which conspiracy employs to dupe the immature and credulous.

That the zealots of the Woman Suffrage crusade should be caught by it attests their incapacity to discriminate and their unfitness for political leadership. Stripped of Third Termism, bereft of the Roosevelt resources and activities, nothing remains of the Bull Moose scheme of regeneration except its rescript of humanity which, as sprung from the teaching of the idealists of Christendom, belongs to the ethics of life and holds but an indirect relation to the science of Government. Yet, the visionary and hysterical are carried away by the sheer passion of "Onward, Christian Soldiers," just as during the war of sections they marched to battle chanting "John Brown's Body"—the song, the shibboleth, not any fixed, coherent idea, in their minds.

There is nothing fanatical about either Democracy, or the new leader it has elevated to the Chief Magistracy. The country has come to a parting of the ways between the government of organized corruption which we have had and "a new birth of freedom" which we seek. Before we attain this latter we shall surely pass through fire. The horrible story of how the Presidency term-in and term-out has been bought and sold will go far and for a long time to protect us against the machinations of the Money Devil. The dangers ahead are of quite a different kind. They will spring from the sentimental and impracticable who call themselves Democrats and fancy that, now the skies have fallen, the poorest will be able to catch larks.

It has been observed that we are teaching everybody to read and nobody to think, whilst steadily enlarging the area of suffrage. That means that the law of Force, which has ruled so long, will be succeeded by the law of Numbers. Woodrow Wilson will be the first among American Presidents to meet the revolution and to adjust its problems to the actualities and possibilities of government "by the people, of the people and for the people."

God give him wisdom and grace and send prosperous gales to the ship of state about to be entrusted to his keeping!

The President, the People and the Press

(June 8, 1918)

It is given out from Washington—doubtless by some querulous partisan if not some downright enemy of the Administration—that "the President begins to show signs of impatience, if not resentfulness, of criticism."

The *Courier-Journal* takes leave to believe nothing of the sort. A man less versed in affairs, less invested with responsibility and less read in history than Woodrow Wilson, might rise superior to the confused chatter which springs spontaneous to the lips of the public anxiety, and finds casual expression in a newspaper press not always considerate or well informed. Nervous irritability is not a Wilsonian weakness.

Obviously, parties are not dead yet. Their labels at least survive. The fall elections are at hand.

In voting extraordinary powers to the President neither the Congress nor the people should lose sight of the difference between a state of peace and a state of war. We may quarrel therefore with no man's reluctance to vote extraordinary powers. Yet these are essential to the Commander-in-Chief of the forces in time of war. The simple canons that rule in times of peace must give way to the stern rules that apply to marching and fighting armies.

The pathos of the Lincoln story is nowhere more poignant than in those passages which represent him bravely facing the enemy in the field whilst enduring the nagging of those restless friends in the Congress and in the press who thought they knew better than he did how to conduct the armies and fight the battles. As we now know, he had made himself a most capable soldier. The record shows that, surveying the entire field, he, more than anyone, intellectually dominated it and was right in his military conclusions.

The lesson of Abraham Lincoln throws a light along the pathway of Woodrow Wilson. It pleads for generous treatment of Woodrow Wilson. We need not deify him. But we must trust him. He is not only our leader but the world's leader. Lloyd George was right enough. The issue lies between Hindenburg and Wilson. If Wilson does not beat Hindenburg good-bye to Civilization.

The President has been accused of being over self-willed. It were a venial fault—a virtue if he wins the fight. Truth to say, there have been occasions when he seemed to need prodding on the warrior side and the *Courier-Journal* did not fail to prod him. But, always as a friend, never as an enemy. We thought, for example, that he should have made resolute and resonant protest on the invasion of Belgium. We thought he should have dismissed Bernstorff after the going down of the *Lusitania*. Being an academician, clever with his pen, by his deliberation he invited a certain apprehension on the part of those who, with the *Courier-Journal,* believed war with Germany inevitable.

We made free to say so. That is the business, the duty, of a newspaper which is worth its salt. The President is surrounded by selfish interests of every kind. Washington affords an ill point of view. If our good Woodrow should give, not indeed his days and nights, but a chance moment now and again to the perusal of these columns, he might not rise always smiling—the rather thoughtful—maybe at times vexed a bit—yet never a word unkindly writ, nor counsel lacking the support of reason and experience.

"We are no longer Democrats—we are no longer Republicans," said Abraham Lincoln, and, as he meant them, the words are as true to-day as they were when he uttered them. War knocks the filling alike out of politicians and parties. It is too early for forecasts. We have as yet scarce wet our toes. We are just pressing through the bloody surf into the surging depths beyond. What storms shall come no man can say. The skies look ominous enough. The waves are mounting high. But, thank God, we are a united people. Our hearts beat brave and strong. Our leader that was a schoolman has put his qualms and books aside and drawn his sword. At length he has girded his loins and his neck is clothed in thunder. It is ours to believe and to follow.

Hence, we say, a truce to criticisms. They will advance nothing—mend nothing. Whether they emanate from a self-seeking politician or a disgruntled newspaper, they play in some sort to the hand of the enemy.

We need not question the patriotism of our effervescent ex-President to challenge the wisdom of his vociferation. The present occupant of the White House will, if he lives, hold his place nearly three years yet. In case the war be not completely won and well over by 1921, not to say 1920, Heaven help us. It will be time enough then to concern ourselves with national politics and domestic affairs. The *Courier-Journal* would have Woodrow Wilson in the interim put foot upon the meaner things of party interest and personal ambition. When he wins the war a diadem would not enhance his glory. It would only relegate and reduce him to the category of the successful adventurers who have gobbled up whatever was in sight, nor thought of elevating humankind and vindicating the ways of God to man by supreme renunciation and sublime self-sacrifice.

It will be Woodrow Wilson's opportunity, having led his country to victory, to lead his countrymen to the renewal of the old faith; to the recall of the old traditions; to the spiritual recognition and readjustment by the people of the new birth of freedom which is all we shall get out of the war. In that way, and in that alone, may he hope to make a good third to Washington and Lincoln. To hanker further after the gaudy things of public life —even to tamper with the intrigues of politics—would not only lower his place in history but tend to debauch the popular character.

After the winning of the war the President should nurse but a single thought—one, constant, luminous ideal—the return of the Government to the design of the fathers and the regeneration of political society by the widest reach of the Declaration, the Constitution and the Christian religion. Let him not turn away in cynical despair. The ancient garden flowers of liberty will bloom again. The simple, bygone music of the Union will well again in the people's hearts. The mists of greed and gain, of wealth for wealth's sake, will roll away, and we shall see, as upon a screen in Heaven, "the old Continentals in their ragged regimentals," and the brave, the good and the true that followed them, and shall know that freedom, honor and prosperity can only be achieved by the love and service of God and the equal fellowship of man.

LINCOLN

To the greater number of Americans Mr. Watterson was known in person as the most attractive lecturer on Abraham Lincoln on the circuits. A few knew him socially; a few thousand had heard and seen him at national conventions; but his point of greatest contact was as a lecturer, and his most successful lecture was the "Lincoln." This is published in his book "The Compromises of Life."

The article below on the same subject is less famous, but more informing, than the lecture. It was published in the *Cosmopolitan Magazine* and is reprinted here by permission. Its serious purpose was to establish the legitimacy of Lincoln's birth, and the article is the closest approach to the Life which Mr. Watterson had hoped to write about the President he most admired.

The second article introduced by this note was written in the *Courier-Journal* and is devoted to a development of Mr. Watterson's theory that a personal God has directed the destiny of the American Republic. The occasion which the article signalized was a celebration at the Lincoln Memorial near Hodgenville, Ky. The editor sent it in to his paper from Florida, for he had already begun to remain away from public functions.

Abraham Lincoln

(February 7, 1909)

A Reminiscence of the Man and a Study of His Character

BY HENRY WATTERSON

(Reprinted by permission of International Magazine Co.
(*Cosmopolitan Magazine*). Copyrighted 1908)

I

I was engaged by Mr. L. A. Gobright, the Agent of the Associated Press in the National Capital, to assist him and Major

Ben Perley Poore, a well-known newspaper correspondent of those days, with their report of the Inaugural Ceremonies of the 4th of March, 1861. The newly-elected President had arrived in Washington ten days before—to be exact, the morning of the 23rd of February. It was a Saturday. That same afternoon he came to the Capitol escorted by Mr. Seward, and being on the floor of the House at the time—the rules were not so strict then as now, and having the freedom of the Reporters' Gallery, and being personally acquainted with most of the Representatives, I often went or was called there—I saw him for the first time and was, indeed, presented to him.

"You are not a member," said he, kindly, observing my extreme youth. "No, sir," I answered, "I only hope to be." He said: "I hope you will not be disappointed," and passed on.

Early in the morning of the 4th of March I found thrust into the keyhole of my bed-room a slip of paper, which read "for Inaugural Address see Col. Ward H. Lamon." Who was "Col. Ward H. Lamon"? I had never heard of him. The city was crowded with strangers. To find one of them was to look for a needle in a haystack. I went straight to Willard's Hotel. As I passed through the big corridor of the second floor, spliced with little dark entree-ways to the apartments facing on Pennsylvania Avenue, I saw through a half-opened door Mr. Lincoln himself, pacing to and fro, apparently reading a manuscript. I went straight in. He was alone and, as he turned and saw me, he extended his hand, called my name, and said: "What can I do for you?" I told him my errand and dilemma, showing him the brief memorandum. "Why," said he, "you have come to the right shop, Lamon is in the next room. I will take you to him, and he will fix you all right." No sooner said than done, and, supplied with the press copy of the Inaugural Address, I gratefully and gleefully took my leave.

I cannot recall whether I carried it directly to Mr. Gobright, or to Major Poore, or to the telegraph office immediately over the way at the northeast corner of the Avenue and Fourteenth street. Major Poore records in his Memoirs that he put it on the wires, and very likely he did. I had time to run my eye over it, and distinctly remember that it had been clumsily typeset in some country office, and was considerably interlined with pencil marks.

Two hours later I found myself in the Senate Chamber, witnessing the oath of office administered to Vice President-elect Hannibal Hamlin and listening to his brief speech. Then I followed the cortege through the long passageway and across the Rotunda to the East portico, where a special wooden platform had been erected, keeping close to Mr. Lincoln. He was tall and ungainly, wearing a black suit, a black tie, beneath a turndown collar, and a black silk hat. He carried a gold or silver-headed walking cane. As we came out into the open and upon the temporary stand, where there was a table containing a Bible, a pitcher and a glass of water, he drew from his breast pocket the manuscript I had seen him reading at the hotel, laid this before him, placing the cane upon it as a paperweight, removed from their leathern case his steel-rimmed spectacles, and raised his hand —he was exceedingly deliberate and composed—to remove his hat. As he did so, I lifted my hand to receive it, but Judge Douglas, who stood at my side, reached over my arm, took the hat and held it during the delivery of the Inaugural Address which followed.

His self-possession was perfect. Dignity, herself, could not have been more unexcited. His voice was a little high-pitched, but resonant, quite reaching the outer fringes of the vast crowd in front; his expression serious to the point of gravity; not a scintillation of humor. Notwithstanding the campaign pictures of Lincoln, the boor, I was prepared to expect much. Judge Douglas had said to me, upon his return to Washington after the famous campaign of 1858 for the Illinois Senatorship, from which the Little Giant had come off victor: "He is the greatest debater I have ever met, either here or anywhere else."

It is only true to say he delivered that Inaugural Address as though he had been delivering Inaugural Addresses all his life. To me it meant War. As the crowd upon the portico dispersed back into the Capitol I was wedged in between John Bell, of Tennessee, and Reverdy Johnson, of Maryland. Each took me by the arm, and we sat down upon a bench just inside the Rotunda. They were very optimistic. No, there would be no war, no fight; all the troubles would be tided over; the country still was safe. I was a boy, just one and twenty. They were the two ablest and most renowned of the surviving Whig leaders of the school of Clay and Webster, one of them just defeated for President in the preceding election. Their talk marveled me greatly, for to my mind there seemed no escape from the armed collision of the Sections, Secession already accomplished and a Confederate Government actually established. There is in youth a prophetic instinct which grows duller with advancing years. As I look behind me, I not only bear this in mind, illustrated by the talk of those two veteran Statesmen that day in the Rotunda of the Capitol at Washington, but I feel it and realize it, so that I am much less confident, with a lifetime of experience to guide me, than I was when buoyed by the ignorance and bravery, but also the inspiration, of youth, the problems ahead read plain and clear as out of an open book.

II

The next three months I saw and heard Mr. Lincoln often in public, and on several occasions was thrown with him in private companies. He looked the picture of health. Serenity, however, not levity, was the prevailing mood with him.

To me he seemed a wholly resolute man. There was, in his habitual kindness, a most unfailing and a very firm note. I do not believe that at any turning he hoped for a reconciliation between the leaders of the North and South, who were already stripped for a fight. He had carefully measured the forces of combat, and made up his mind both as to his duty and the situation.

On either side it was a play for time and advantage. The signal-gun was fired at length by the South in Charleston Harbor. Promptly upon the attack upon Sumter came the Proclamation for troops from the White House at Washington. Extremism was destined to have its way. At last it had won. Blood was sprinkled in the faces of the people. Abraham Lincoln and Jefferson Davis were perhaps the only two living men who thoroughly understood what was about to happen.

It will be remembered that Mr. Lincoln was but fifty-two years of age. His practical knowledge of National affairs had been limited to a single term in Congress. His nomination and election to the Presidency were regarded as accidental—he was an untutored, a very homely and awkward child of fortune. Seward and Chase, Fessenden and Trumbull, Simon Cameron and Zachariah Chandler were, each in his way, the accepted authorities of the time. There was not a Member of his Cabinet who did not consider himself a bigger man than his master. Even so keen an observer as Seward wholly missed the dominating features of the Chief he had reluctantly come to serve until he got his answer in that queer letter of his of the 1st of April, 1861, which, as by a flash of lightning, revealed the truth and brought him to his intellectual knees, never to rise again. Somehow, I had a great impression of Mr. Lincoln from the first, and, during the four succeeding years of War, though serving on the opposite side, this never left me.

Toward the preparation of an address upon Abraham Lincoln, required in 1895 by the Lincoln Union of Chicago—though I thought I understood his life and character very well—it seemed prudent to gather whatever I might of a biographic description. There could not have been fewer than half a thousand volumes and pamphlets. These were replete with contradictions and discrepancies. Even the epoch-making work of Nicolay and Hay was imperfect through lack of data discovered after it had gone to press. The "call" for a complete life seemed as urgent as it was apparent, and, in 1896, believing that my exit from daily newspaper work would be final, I went to Geneva, in Switzerland, where my children were at school, to obtain leisure and repose for the composition of such a volume or volumes. Subsequent events quite diverted me from my purpose. But I penetrated the subject at that time far enough to be struck by the mass of inconsistency staring me in the face, and the need for a connected story separating the tangled web of fact and falsehood, and partly at least removing the incongruities of prejudice and partyism.

Nothing, for example, has been more misrepresented and misconceived than Lincoln's pedigree and birth. Some confusion was originally made by his own mistake touching the marriage of his father and mother, which had not been celebrated in Hardin County, but in Washington County, Kentucky: the absence of any marriage papers from the courthouse at Elizabethtown, the county seat of Hardin County, leading to the notion that there had never been any marriage at all. It is easy to conceive how such a discrepancy might occasion any amount and all sorts of campaign lying, thence distorted into popular belief among the ignorant and inflamed. Lincoln himself died without knowing the truth that he was not only born in honest wedlock, but of an ancestry upon both sides of which he had no reason to be ashamed.

The name of Lincoln came from excellent sources, and was borne by good people. The Lincolns were among those who overcrowded Norwich jail in England because "they would not accept the ritual prepared for them by the bishop"; who pelted the tax-collector with stones, and finally, in order to "rid themselves of an odious government," who bravely sailed out of Yarmouth harbor in 1636, crossed the ocean, and founded the colony of Hingham, in Massachusetts. It was these land-owners, wheelwrights and iron-mongers whose descendants thence migrated southward into New Jersey, Pennsylvania, Virginia and at last into Kentucky. The Abraham Lincoln who was fifth in descent from Samuel Lincoln, of Hingham, and who had become owner of considerable tracts of land in Kentucky, fell by the bullet of a lurking Indian in the sight of his three boys—Mordecai, Joseph and Thomas—the latter a six-year-old lad who was saved by the timely crack of the rifle in the hands of his older brother, to become the father of the future President.

Thomas Lincoln was not the irresponsible ne'er-do-well that most of the biographers of Lincoln have represented him. A fairer estimate has yet to be made. Nor was the Hanks family so obscure as used to be thought.

For a long time a cloud hung over the name of Nancy Hanks, the mother of Abraham Lincoln. Persistent investigation has, however, brought about a vindication in every way complete. We owe this largely to the researches of three women—Mrs. Hobart Vawter, Mrs. Hanks Hitchcock and Miss Ida M. Tarbell. Mrs. Vawter's grandmother was Sarah Mitchell of Kentucky, a second cousin of Nancy Hanks. She it was who discovered the marriage bond of Thomas Lincoln and the marriage record of Jesse Head, the Methodist minister who officiated at the marriage of Thomas Lincoln and Nancy Hanks the 17th of June, 1806. Mrs. Caroline Hanks Hitchcock took upon herself the task of tracing the genealogy of the Hanks family, thus throwing a flood of light upon the maternal ancestry of Abraham Lincoln, and consequently upon the foundations of his character and genius.

It is related that two brothers of the name of Hanks received "the commoners' rights in Malmsbury" for service rendered in defeating the Danes, and we are told that the name of Athelstan, a grandson of Alfred, is on the deed. Thomas Hanks, a descendant, who was a soldier under Cromwell, had a grandson who came to America in 1699. This Benjamin Hanks became the father of twelve children, the third of whom was William, born February 11, 1704; William migrated to Pennsylvania, and his son, John Hanks, married Sarah, a daughter of Cadwallader Evans and Sarah Morris. The record reads: "John Hanks, yeoman, Sarah Evans, spinster." A grandchild of this union was Joseph Hanks, who was borne southwestward upon the tide of emigration, headed by Daniel Boone. Joseph Hanks crossed the mountains with his family of eight children, horses, herds of cattle and household goods. He had bought one hundred and fifty acres of land for his homestead near Elizabethtown, Kentucky. The youngest of the eight children in this migration was little Nancy, five years of age when they left the Valley of Virginia. After four years of home-making in the wilderness, Joseph came to his death. His will, dated January 9, 1793, probated May 14, 1793, has been discovered, and a facsimile appears in Mrs. Hitchcock's book.

This document settles once and forever the legitimacy of the parentage of Nancy Hanks.

The mother survived the father but a few months, and the orphaned Nancy, then nine years old, found a home with her uncle and aunt, Mr. and Mrs. Richard Berry, near Springfield, Kentucky, Mrs. Berry being her mother's sister. Here she lived a happy and industrious girl until twenty-three years of age, when Thomas Lincoln, who had learned his carpenter's trade of one of her uncles, was married to her on June 17, 1806. The whole official record is still in existence. The "marriage bond" to the extent of fifty pounds, required by the laws of Kentucky at that time, signed by Thomas Lincoln and Richard Berry, was duly recorded seven days before. The wedding was celebrated as became prosperous country folk. The Uncle and Aunt gave an "infare" to which the neighbors were bidden. Dr. Christopher Columbus Graham, of Louisville, who died in 1885 (he was the father-in-law of the late Governor Bramlette and of ex-United States Senator Blackburn, now Governor of Panama), wrote at my request his remembrances of that festival and testified to this before a notary in the 98th year of his age. He said:

"I know Nancy Hanks to have been virtuous, respectable and of good parentage, and I knew Jesse Head, Methodist preacher of Springfield, who performed the ceremony. The house in which the ceremony was performed was a large one for those days. Jesse Head was a noted man—able to own slaves, but did not on principle. At the festival there was bear meat, venison, wild turkey, duck and a sheep that two families barbecued over the coals of wood burned in a pit and covered with green boughs to keep the juices in."

The traditions of the neighborhood tell us that Nancy's disposition and habits were considered a dower. She was an adept at spinning flax, and in the spinning parties, to which ladies brought their wheels, she generally bore away the palm, "her spools yielding the longest and finest thread."

She was above the average in education. She became a great reader; absorbed "Æsop's Fables"; loved the Bible and the hymn-book; possessed a sweet voice, and was fond of singing hymns. Old people remembered her as having "a gentle and trusting nature." A grandson of Joseph, Nancy Hanks's brother, once said to Joshua F. Speed, from whom it came to me:

"My grandfather always spoke of his angel sister Nancy with emotion. She taught him to read. He often told us children stories of their life together."

The first child of Thomas and Nancy Lincoln was a daughter, Sarah. Three years after marriage arrived the boy, Abraham. Another son named Thomas was born; he lived but a few months, though long enough indelibly and tenderly to touch the heart of the elder brother. Before the Lincolns started for their new home in Indiana he remembered his mother taking her two little children by the hand, walking across the hills, and sitting down and weeping over the grave of the little babe before she left it behind forever.

The last recorded words of Nancy Lincoln were words of cheer. A few days before her death she went to visit a sick neighbor. This neighbor was most despondent. She thought she would not live long. Said Mrs. Lincoln: "O, you will live longer than I. Cheer up." And so it proved. The dread milk sickness stalked abroad, smiting equally human beings and cattle. Uncle Thomas and Aunt Betsy Sparrow both died within a few days of each other. Soon the frail, but heroic, mother was taken to bed. "She struggled on day by day, but on the seventh day she died," says the brief account. There was not a physician within thirty-five miles; no minister within a hundred miles. Placing her hand on the head of the little boy, nine years old: "I am going away from you, Abraham," she said, "and I shall not return. I know that you will be a good boy; that you will be kind to Sarah and to your father. I want you to live as I have taught you and to love your Heavenly Father."

Thomas Lincoln sawed the boards with his whip-saw from the trees he felled, and made the coffins with his own hands for the Sparrows and for his wife.

Pitiable story; one can scarce read it with dry eyes; but it lifts the veil forever from the cruel mystery which so long clouded the memory of Nancy Hanks. I here dwell upon and give the details, because it ought to be known to every American who would have the truth of History fulfilled.

III

The War of Sections, inevitable to the conflict of Systems, but long delayed by the compromises of patriotism, did two things which surpass in importance and value all other things; it confirmed the Federal Union as a Nation and it brought the American People to the fruition of their manhood.

Before that War we were a huddle of petty Sovereignties held together by a rope of sand; we were as a community of children playing at Government. Hamilton felt it, Marshall feared it, Clay ignored it, Webster evaded it. Their passionate clinging to the Constitution and the Flag, bond and symbol of an imperfect if not tentative compact, confessed it. They were the intellectual projenitors of Abraham Lincoln. He became the incarnation of the brain and soul of the Union. "My paramount object," said he, "is to save the Union, and not either to save or destroy Slavery. If I could save the Union without freeing any Slave, I would do it. If I could save it by freeing all the Slaves, I would do it—and if I could do it by freeing some and leaving others alone, I would do that."

In the sense of security which his travail and martyrdom

achieved for us we are apt to forget that it was not a localized Labor System but Institutional freedom which was at stake; that African slavery was the merest relic of a Semi-Barbarism shared in the beginning by all the people, but at length driven by certain laws of Nature and trade into a Corner where it was making a stubborn but futile stand; that the real issue was Free Government, made possible by the Declaration of Independence and the Constitution of the United States, and inseparable from the maintenance of the Union. If the Union failed, Freedom failed.

The trend of modern thought was definitely set against Human Slavery; but outside the American Union, the idea of human freedom had gone no farther than limited monarchy. Though he came to awaken the wildest passions of the time, the Negro was but an incident—never a principle—to the final death grapple between the North and the South.

No man of his time understood this so perfectly, embodied it so adequately, as Abraham Lincoln. The primitive Abolitionists saw only one side of the Shield, the original Secessionists only the other side. Lincoln saw both sides.

His political philosophy was expounded in four elaborate speeches: one delivered at Peoria, Ill., the 16th of October, 1854; one at Springfield, Ill., the 16th of June, 1858; one at Columbus, Ohio, the 16th of September, 1859, and one the 27th of February, 1860, at Cooper Institute, in the City of New York. Of course he made many speeches and very good speeches. But these four, progressive in character, contain the sum and substance of his creed touching the organic character of the Government and at the same time his personal and party view of contemporary affairs. They show him to have been an old-line Whig of the school of Henry Clay, with strong emancipation leanings; a thorough anti-slavery man, but never an extremist or an abolitionist. To the last he hewed to the line thus laid down.

It is essential to a complete understanding of Mr. Lincoln's relation to the time and to his place in the history of the country, that the student peruse closely these four speeches; they underlie all that passed in the famous debate with Douglas; all that their author said and did after he succeeded to the presidency. They will always stand as masterpieces of popular oratory. The debate with Douglas, however—assuredly the most extraordinary intellectual spectacular in the annals of our party warfare—best tells the story and crystallizes it. Lincoln entered the canvass unknown outside the State of Illinois. He ended it renowned from one end of the land to the other.

Judge Douglas was himself unsurpassed as a ready debater. But in that campaign, from first to last, he was at a serious disadvantage. His bark rode an ebbing tide; Lincoln's bark rode a flowing tide. African slavery had become the single issue now; and, as I have said, the trend of modern thought was set against slavery. The Democrats seemed hopelessly divided. The Little Giant had to face a triangular opposition embracing the Republicans, the Administration, or Buchanan Democrats, and a remnant of the old Whigs, who fancied that their party was still alive and might hold some kind of balance of power. Judge Douglas called the combination the "allied army," and declared that he would deal with it "just as the Russians dealt with the allies at Sebastopol—that is, the Russians did not stop to inquire, when they fired a broadside, whether it hit an Englishman, a Frenchman, or a Turk." It was with something more than a witticism that Mr. Lincoln rejoined: "In that connection I beg he will indulge us whilst we suggest to him that those allies took Sebastopol."

He followed this center-shot with volley after volley of exposition so clear, of reasoning so close, of illustration so homely and sharp, and, at times, of humor so incisive, that though he lost his election—though the allies did not then take Sebastopol—his defeat counted for more than Douglas' victory, for it made him the logical and successful candidate for President of the United States two years later.

What could be more captivating to an outdoor audience than Lincoln's description "of the two persons who stand before the people as candidates for the Senate," to quote his prefatory words?

"Judge Douglas," he said, "is of world-renown. All the anxious politicians of his party . . . have been looking upon him as certainly . . . to be President of the United States. They have seen in his round, jolly, fruitful face, post-offices, land-offices, marshalships, and Cabinet appointments, charge-ships and foreign missions, bursting and spreading out in wonderful exuberance, ready to be laid hold of by their greedy hands. As they have been gazing upon this attractive picture so long, they cannot, in the little distraction that has taken place in the party, bring themselves to give up the charming hope; but with greedier anxiety they rush about him, sustain him and give him marches, triumphal entries and receptions, beyond what in the days of his highest prosperity they could have brought about in his favor. On the contrary, nobody has ever expected me to be President. In my poor, lean, lank face nobody has ever seen that any cabbages were sprouting."

As the debate advanced, these cheery tones deepened into harsher notes; crimination and recrimination followed; the gladiators were strung to their utmost tension. They became dreadfully in earnest. Personal collision was narrowly avoided. I have recently gone over the entire debate, and with a feeling I can only describe as most contemplative, most melancholy.

I knew Judge Douglas well; I admired, respected, loved him. I shall never forget the day he quitted Washington to go to his home in Illinois to return no more. We sat down together in a doorway. "What are you going to do?" said he. "Judge Douglas," I answered, "we have both fought to save the Union; you in your great way and I in my small way; and we have lost. I am going to my home in the Mountains of Tennessee, where I have a few books, and there I mean to stay." Tears were in his eyes and his voice trembled like a woman's. He was then a dying man. He had burned the candle at both ends; an eager, ardent, hard-working, pleasure-loving man; and though not yet fifty, the candle was burned out. His infirmities were no greater than those of Mr. Clay; not to be mentioned with those of Mr. Webster. But he lived in more exacting times. The old-style party organ, with its mock heroics and its dull respectability, its beggarly array of empty news columns and cheap advertising, had been succeeded by that unsparing, tell-tale scandalmonger, Modern Journalism, with its myriad of hands and eyes, its vast retinue of detectives, and its quick transit over flashing wires, annihilating time and space. Too fierce a light beat upon the private life of public men, and Douglas suffered from this as Clay and Webster, Silas Wright and Franklin Pierce had not suffered.

The presidential bee was in his bonnet, certainly; but its buzzing there was not noisier than in the bonnets of other great Americans, who have been dazzled by that disappointing mirage. His plans and schemes came to naught. He died at the moment when the death of those plans and schemes was made more palpable and impressive by the roar of cannon proclaiming the reality of the "irrepressible conflict" he had refused to foresee and had struggled to avert. His life-long rival was at the head of affairs. No one has found occasion to come to the rescue of his fame. No party interest has been identified with his memory. But when the truth of history is written, it will be told that, not less than Webster and Clay, he, too, was a patriotic man, who loved his country and tried to save the Union. He tried to save the Union, even as Webster and Clay had tried to save it, by compromises and expedients. It was too late. The string was played out. Where they had succeeded he failed; but, for the nobility of his intention, the amplitude of his resources, the splendor of his combat, he merits all that any leader of a losing cause ever gained in the report of posterity; and posterity will not deny him the title of statesman.

In that famous debate it was Titan against Titan; and perus-

ing it after the lapse of forty years, the philosopher and impartial
critic will conclude which got the better of it, Lincoln or Douglas,
much according to his sympathy with the one or the other. If
Douglas had lived he would have become as Lincoln's right hand.
Already, when he died, Lincoln was beginning to look to him and
to lean upon him. Four years later they were joined together
again on Fame's Eternal Camping Ground, each followed to the
grave by a mourning people.

As I have said, Abraham Lincoln was an old-time Whig of the
school of Henry Clay, with strong free-soil opinions, never an
extremist or an abolitionist. He was what they used to call in
those old days "a Conscience Whig." He stood in awe of the
Constitution and his oath of office. Hating slavery, he recognized
its legal existence and its rights under the compact of the organic
law. He wanted gradually to extinguish it, not to despoil those
who held it as a property interest. He was so faithful to
these principles that he approached emancipation not only with
anxious deliberation but with many misgivings. He issued his
final proclamation as a military necessity; and even then, so
fair was his nature that he was meditating some kind of restitution.

Thus it came about that he was the one man in public life who
could have taken the helm of affairs in 1861, handicapped by none
of the resentments growing out of the anti-slavery battle. Whilst
Seward, Chase, Sumner and the rest had been engaged in hand-
to-hand combat with the Southern leaders at Washington, Lincoln,
a philosopher and a statesman, had been observing the course of
events from afar, and, like a philosopher and a statesman whose
mind was irradiated and sweetened by the sense of humor.
Throughout the contention that preceded the war, amid the passions inevitable to the war itself, not one bitter, proscriptive word
escaped his lips or fell from his pen, whilst there was hardly a
day that he was not projecting his great personality between some
Southern man or woman and danger.

Under date of February 2, 1848, from the hall of the House
of Representatives at Washington, when he was serving as a
member of Congress, he wrote this short note to Herndon, his law
partner at Springfield:

"DEAR WILLIAM: I take up my pen to tell you that Mr.
Stephens, of Georgia, a little, slim, pale-faced, consumptive
man, with a voice like Logan's" (that was Stephen T., not
John A.) "has just concluded the very best speech of an
hour's length I ever heard. My old, withered, dry eyes" (he
was then not quite thirty-seven years of age) "are full of
tears yet."

Thenceforward he had a great opinion of Alexander H. Stephens and a high regard for him.

After that famous Hampton Roads conference, when the Confederate commissioners, Stephens, Campbell and Hunter, had traversed the field of official routine with Mr. Lincoln, the President, and Mr. Seward, the Secretary of State, Lincoln, the friend, still the old Whig colleague, though one was now President of the United States and the other Vice President of the Southern Confederacy, took the "slim, pale-faced, consumptive man" aside, and, pointing to a sheet of paper he held in his hand, said: "Stephens, let me write 'Union' at the top of that page, and you may write below it whatever else you please."

In the preceding conversation he had intimated that payment for the slaves was not outside a possible agreement for reunion and peace. He based the suggestion upon a plan he already had in hand to appropriate four hundred million of dollars to that purpose.

Many foolish and overzealous persons put themselves to the pains of challenging this statement when it was first made by me many years ago. It admits of no possible denial. Mr. Lincoln took with him to Fortress Monroe two documents that still stand in his own handwriting; one of them a joint resolution to be passed by the two houses of Congress appropriating the four hundred millions, the other a proclamation to be issued by himself, as President, when the joint resolution had been enacted. These formed no part of the discussion at Hampton Roads, because Mr. Stephens told Mr. Lincoln they were limited to treating upon the basis of the recognition of the Confederacy. "In that case, Stephens," said Lincoln sadly, "I am guiltless of every drop of blood that may be shed from this onward." Thus in point of fact the conference died before it was actually born. But Mr. Lincoln was so filled with the idea that next day, when he had returned to Washington, he submitted his two documents to the members of the Cabinet. Excepting Mr. Seward, they could not agree with him. He said, "Why, gentlemen, how long is the war going to last? It is not going to end this side of a hundred days, is it? It is costing us four millions a day. There are the four hundred millions, not counting the loss of life and property in the meantime. But you are all against me, and I will not press the matter upon you."

I have not at any time cited this indisputable fact of history to attack, or even to criticize, the policy of the Confederate Government, but simply to illustrate the wise magnanimity and the far-reaching sense of justice which distinguished the character of Abraham Lincoln.

IV

Tragedy herself hung over the humble pallet—for cradle he had none—on which the baby Lincoln lay; nestled with him in his mother's arms; followed him to the little grave in the wildwood and attended him to the fall of the curtain in the brilliantly lighted Theater of the National Capital. "Now he is with the ages," said Stanton in the gray dawn of the winter day as the stertorous breathing ceased and the great heart was stilled forever. His life had been an epic in homespun; his death, like that of Cæsar, beggars the arts and resources of Melpomene of the mimic scene.

"Within the narrow compass of that stage-box that night," says John Hay, "were five human beings; the most illustrious of modern heroes crowned with the most stupendous victory of modern times; his beloved wife, proud and happy; two betrothed lovers with all the promise of felicity that youth, social position and wealth could give them; and a young actor, handsome as Endymion upon Latmus, the idol of his little world. The glitter of fame, happiness and ease was upon the entire group; but in an instant everything was to be changed with the blinding swiftness of enchantment. Quick death was to come on the central figure of that company . . . Over all the rest the blackest fates hovered menacingly; fates from which a mother might pray that kindly death would save her children in their infancy. One was to wander with the stain of murder on his soul, with the curses of a world upon his name, with a price set upon his head, in frightful physical pain, till he died a dog's death in a burning barn. The stricken wife was to pass the rest of her days in melancholy and madness; of those two young lovers, one was to slay the other, and then end his life a raving maniac!"

Had Lincoln lived? In that event it is quite certain that there would have been no Era of Reconstruction, with its repressive agencies and oppressive legislation. If Lincoln had lived there would have been wanting in the extremism of the time the bloody cue of his taking off to mount the steeds and spur the flanks of vengeance. For Lincoln entertained, with respect to the rehabilitation of the Union, the single wish that the Southern States—to use his familiar phraseology—"should come back home and behave themselves," and, if he had lived he would have made this wish effectual as he made everything effectual to which he seriously addressed himself.

His was the genius of common sense. Of admirable intellectual aplomb, he sprang from a Virginia pedigree and was born in Kentucky. He knew all about the South, its institutions, its traditions and its peculiarities. "If slavery be not wrong," he said, "nothing is wrong," but he also said, and reiterated it time and again, "I have no prejudice against the Southern people. They are just what we would be in their situation. If slavery did not now exist among them they would not introduce it. If it did now exist among us, we would not instantly give it up."

His idea of paying the South for the slaves did not by any means originate with the proposal he was prepared to make at Fortress Monroe. It had been all along in his mind. He believed the North equally guilty with the South for the existence of slavery. He clearly understood that the Irrepressible Conflict was a Conflict of systems, not merely a sectional and partisan quarrel. He was a considerate man, abhorring proscription. He wanted to leave the South no right to claim that the North, finding slave labor unremunerative, had sold its negroes to the South and then turned about and by force of arms, confiscated what it had unloaded at a profit. He recognized slavery as property. In his message to Congress of 1862, he proposed payment for the slaves, elaborating a scheme in detail and urging it with copious and cogent argument.

"The people of the South," said he, addressing a War Congress at that moment in the throes of bloody strife with the South, "are not more responsible for the original introduction of this property than are the people of the North, and, when it is remembered how unhesitatingly we all use cotton and sugar and share the profits of dealnig in them, it may not be quite safe to say that the South has been more responsible than the North for its continuance."

This is the language not only of justice, but of far-reaching Statesmanship.

The celebration of the Centenary of the birth of Abraham Lincoln will not be bounded by Sectional lines though it will recall from many points of view the issues and incidents through which he passed in life, and of which in history he remains the foremost figure. I am writing from the Southern standpoint. All of us must realize that the years are gliding swiftly by. Only a little while, and there shall not be one man living who saw service on either side of that great struggle. Its passions long ago faded from manly bosoms. Meanwhile it is required of no one— whichever flag he served under—that he make renunciations dishonoring to himself. Each may leave to history the casting of the balance between antagonistic schools of thought and opposing camps in action, where in both the essentials of fidelity and courage were so amply met. Nor is it the part of wisdom to regret a tale that is told. The issues that evoked the strife of sections are dead issues. The conflict, which was thought to be irreconcilable and was certainly inevitable, ended more than forty years ago. It was fought to its conclusion by fearless and upright men. To some the result was logical—to others it was disappointing—to all it was final.

With respect to Abraham Lincoln, I here, as a Southern man and a Confederate soldier, render unto Cæsar the things that are Cæsar's, even as I would render unto God the things that are God's.

Something more than two hundred and sixty years ago there arrived at the front of affairs in England one Cromwell. In the midst of monarchy he made a Republic. It had no progenitor. It left no heirs-at-law. It was succeeded, as it had been preceded, by a line of sovereigns. But from the Commonwealth of Cromwell date the confirmation and the consolidation of the principles of liberty wrung by the barons from John, their unwilling King. From the Commonwealth of Cromwell date the grandeur and the power of the English fabric, the enlightened and progressive conservatism of the English Constitution, the sturdy independence of the English people. Why such cost of blood and treasure for an interval of freedom so equivocal and brief puzzled the wisest men; remained for ages a mystery; though it is plain enough now and was long ago conceded, so that at last—dire rebel though he was—the name of Cromwell, held in execration through two centuries, has a place in the history of the English-speaking races along with the names of William the Conqueror and Richard of the Lion Heart.

That which it took England two centuries to realize we in America have demonstrated within a single generation. Northern or Southern, none of us need fear that the Future will fail to vindicate our integrity. When those are gone that fought the good fight and Posterity comes to strike the balance sheet it will be shown that the makers of the Constitution left the relation of the States to the Federal Government and of the Federal Government to the States open to a double construction. It will be told how the mistaken notion that slave labor was requisite to the profitable cultivation of sugar, rice and cotton, raised a paramount property interest in the Southern section of the Union, whilst in the Northern section, responding to the impulse of modern thought and the outer movements of mankind, there arose a great moral sentiment against slavery. The conflict thus established, gradually but surely sectionalizing party lines, was wrought to its bitter and bloody conclusion at Appomattox.

The battle was long though unequal. Let us believe that it was needful to make us a Nation. Let us look upon it as into a mirror, seeing not the desolation of the past, but the radiance of the present; and in the heroes of the New North and the New South who contested in generous rivalry up the fire-swept steep of El Caney, and side by side re-emblazoned the National character in the waters about Corregidor Island and under the walls of Cavite, let us behold hostages for the old North and the old South blent together in a Union that recks not of the four points of the compass and long ago flung its geography into the sea.

Abraham Lincoln

(February 12, 1909)

I

That God, of whose actuality the mind of man is not able to conceive, but whom we prefigure as an all-wise Deity, who, from the building of an empire to the fall of a sparrow, concerns Himself with mortal affairs, has had the American Union in His holy keeping, can be doubted by no one who has studied its history.

All the incidents and accidents of the Revolutionary War made for the Continentals and against the British; all the incidents and accidents of the War of Sections made for the Federals and against the Confederates.

The law of good and ill-fortune extended itself to the leaders in each instance. Why George Washington, the Virginia Colonel of Militia, instead of Colonel Lee, the accomplished English soldier, with a European career and reputation to commend him? Why, with all his handicaps, did Grant, the greatest of modern fighters, forge to the front ahead of McClellan and Sherman and Sheridan, brilliant officers, but clearly unequal to the final issue, and why were Albert Sidney Johnston, the rose and expectancy of the young Confederacy, and Stonewall Jackson, Napoleon alike of the Sword and the Cross, struck down at the decisive moment? How came Ericsson's little "cigar box" to crawl into Hampton Roads just in the nick of time, to do the work and then go to the bottom of the sea, and how was it possible, except through the direct help of some power divine, that Cushing was able to creep up York River, both banks studded with Confederate batteries, to "fix" the second and last of the Southern iron-clads? And, finally, why Lincoln, the rustic lawyer, the so-called rail-splitter, instead of Seward, the matchless leader, or Chase, the magnificent? God, God, and God alone!

By all the rules of political calculation, Lincoln should have been the Illinois Senator in 1855. If he had been, there is every reason to conjecture that he would never have attained the Presidency. Had he defeated Douglas in 1858, it is possible that the nomination of 1860 might still have come to him; but it would have put him face to face with Seward at Washington and have brought him into dangerous prominence. Seward aside, McLean too old, made it easy, among the lesser entries, for the knowing ones to choose Lincoln.

The Democratic party had committed harikari betimes. Through the breach made by Douglas, his life-long rival, in the wall of Democracy, Lincoln, at the head of the Republicans, marched in triumph. How else; yet in the light of after events, his destiny was the destiny of the Republic; for nothing can be surer than that he was the one and only man who could have lived through the dark days succeeding Bull Run and the *Trent* affair, as Washington was the one and only man who could have survived the winter of Valley Forge.

Richard Watson Gilder quotes John Hay as saying, in answer to a question put to him, whilst, in collaboration with Nicolay, he was writing the Life: "As I go on with the work, to me Lincoln grows greater and greater." It is even so. No one can read the documentary history of Lincoln's Administration and doubt it. By the side of him the others seem mainly pasteboard men.

II

There remain no more hidden chapters, not even any more disputed passages, in Lincoln's life. Individually, he was as transparent as the day. His was the genius of common sense. He had all the distinguishing characteristics of the politicians of the mid-period of the last Century; their craft, plausibility and cleanliness; their inclination toward doctrinal discussions; their loyalty to party organization and engagements; their vital love of their country and their pride in its institutions. A "conscience Whig" he was and a "conscience Whig" Lincoln continued to the end.

Lincoln excelled Douglas in his devotion to an idea, its probable consequences and all that it implied. Thus, in the famous debate, he gained the advantage which the whole-hearted logician must always gain over the hair-splitting opportunist. He was less of an egoist than Douglas and therefore less selfish. Douglas would never have yielded to Trumbull as Lincoln did. He would have got the Senatorship to lose the Presidency. Yet Douglas was as great a party leader as ever lived—not incapable of sacrifices—inferior to Lincoln only on the moral side. When the supreme test came their fortunes fell apart. Douglas' bark rode an ebbing tide. Lincoln's bark rode a flowing tide.

His intellectual dignity was paramount. It shone through the uncouth youngster who studied law by a tallow candle and told stories to the rude habitués of the little country store. His first public address reveals it as plainly as his last. There is extant a letter, written when he was not yet five and twenty, which is a model of simple manhood and at the same time of clever argument and elevated style. He was a tamer of women no less than a master of men; as all-too-late the puissant Jessie Benton Fremont found to her cost; as in spite of the gaucheries and angularities, the refined, aspiring Mary Todd very early discovered.

The sums in single-rule-of-three he had painfully worked out upon a white pine shingle taught him as much of patience as arithmetic. The mysteries of the savage-haunted backwoods and the sublimity of the ocean-like prairie awakened and kept alive in him the reverence for God and nature which goes to the better making equally of the seer, the poet and the statesman. His dreams came to express themselves in deeds.

In short, and in fine, Abraham Lincoln learned his humanities as he had learned his philosophies and his efficiencies, out of the horn-book of experience and the lives of men. Hence was he ripe and ready for his part when the prompter's bell rang for the curtain to rise. Having obeyed humbly, he commanded grandly. To him, politics was not a game of ten-pins, nor Government a play of chance, though he knew both; as a matter of fact, was both in the field and in the council an athlete and an expert, as Seward and Chase and Stanton came, each in his order and his way, perfectly to understand.

Nor is it mere panegyric to say so. In many cases and contingencies, page and line may be cited; the gentle but consummate answer to Seward, when Seward proposed as a favor to Lincoln to take upon himself the whole management of affairs; the easy but canny disposition of Chase before heaping coals of fire upon him in the Chief Justice appointment; the whimsical but not mistaken complacency under the surly, and sometimes trying virtues, which made Stanton so necessary to his place and so fitted him to the alternating duties of upper-servant, policeman and watchdog of the Treasury. No man, indeed, knew better than Lincoln, in the everyday trivialities of personal intercourse as well as the larger concerns of official conduct, how to draw the line, and where to draw it, to suit the word to the act, the act to the word, seeking only, and always seeking, results.

The duty he had been commissioned to do was to save the

Union. With an overwhelming majority of the people the institution of African slavery was not an issue. In his homely, enlightening way, Lincoln declared that if he could preserve the Union, with slavery, he would do it, or, without slavery, he would do it, or, with some free and other slaves, he would do that. The Proclamation of Emancipation was a war measure purely. He knew he had no Constitutional warrant, and, true to his oath of office, he held back as long as he could; but so clear-sighted was his sense of justice, so empty his heart of rancor, that he wished and sought to qualify the rigor of the act by some measure of restitution, and so prepared the Joint Resolution to be passed by Congress appropriating four hundred millions for this purpose, which still stands in his own handwriting.

He was himself a Southern man. All his people were Southerners. "If slavery be not wrong," he said, "nothing is wrong," echoing in this the opinions of most of the Virginia gentlemen of the Eighteenth Century and voicing the sentiments of thousands of brave men who wore the Confederate gray.

Not less than the North has the South reason to canonize Lincoln; for he was the one friend we had at court—aside from Grant and Sherman—when friends were most in need. Poor, mad John Wilkes Booth! Was he, too, an instrument in the hands of God to put a still deeper damnation upon the taking off of the Confederacy and to sink the Southern people yet lower in the abyss of affliction and humiliation which the living Lincoln would have spared us?

III

There will gather the 12th of February, 1909, about the spot where Abraham Lincoln first saw the light an hundred years before, a goodly company. The President of the United States will be there, as a matter of course. He will come to give emphasis to the occasion and to feel himself both honored and distinguished by it. There will be music and banners and speech. What boots it to Lincoln?

He is immortal now. The screen has rolled away. He knows the truth at last. The final earthly word of him was spoken long ago. There is need for not another. All is said that can be said by the poets, by the orators, by the varying pens of a myriad of pressmen. Turn we exalted from the scene; but, Mother of God, must we go before we have looked into the Heaven above us in unutterable love and homage with the thought of a spirit there which knew in this world nought of splendor and power and fame; whose sad lot it was to live and die in obscurity, penury, almost in want and squalor; whose tragic fate it was after she had lain half a lifetime in her humble, unmarked grave, to be pursued by the deepest, darkest calumny that can attach itself to the name of woman: the hapless, the fair-haired Nancy Hanks?

Years ago, somehow, I took her story home to myself. My own grandmother was born less than an hundred miles away about the same time, and, though she was the daughter of a man famous in his day, and came of grandiose people for those times, I could not prove as much of her as Robert Lincoln can prove of his grandmother; because, in my case, the family papers were lost in a great conflagration, whilst the Lincoln-Hanks papers remain intact.

No falser, fouler story ever gained currency than that which impeaches the character of the mother of Abraham Lincoln. It had never any foundation whatsoever. Every known fact flatly contradicts it. Every boot-heel of circumstantial evidence stamps it a preposterous lie.

It was a period of heroic achievement tempered by religious fervor. It was a decent, God-fearing neighborhood of simple, hard-working men and women. Debauchery was wholly unknown. Double-living was impossible. Nancy Hanks came of good stock. So did Thomas Lincoln. Historically, it would not matter who were the parents of Abraham Lincoln any more than it matters that he whom the English monarch rejoices to call his progenitor was a bastard; but it offends the soul of a gallant and just manhood, it should arouse in the heart of every good woman a sense of wrong that so much as a shadow should rest upon the memory of the little cabin in which Nancy Lincoln gave to the world an immortal son, born in honest, unchallenged wedlock, nor thought of taint or shame anywhere.

Let not the throng assembled there pass down the slope and fade away without a heart salute to the gentle spirit of Nancy Hanks Lincoln, that maybe, somewhere beyond the stars among the angels of the choir invisible, looks upon the scene, serene and safe at last in the bosom of her Maker and her God!

"Let us here highly resolve," the words ring out like a trumpet-call from the printed page, "that these men shall not have died in vain; that this Nation, under God, shall have a new birth of freedom; and that government of the people, by the people and for the people shall not perish from the earth." Repeat we the declaration as we stand upon the hillside where he was born. And, along with it, let us highly resolve that we will follow no leader, that we will heroize no favorite, who, in his private life and public counsels, does not practice the moderation, emulate the justice and display the fortitude and patience of Abraham Lincoln.

H. W.

Naples-on-the-Gulf, Florida

A FREAK OF NATURE

In his own book of memoirs Mr. Watterson has dealt at length
with his love for music and his education in that art. The
editorial which follows this note deals with an oddity of musical talent, the celebrated negro, Blind Tom, who was a sort of
human pianola-victrola and caused much remark in his time.

"Blind Tom"

(June 16, 1908)

Tidings of the death of "Blind Tom" at Hoboken, "where
he had been living in retirement," the wire tells us, "and sub-
sisting on charity," reach at least one heart that loved and pitied
him, and summon from the land of shades and dreams many a
ghost of days and dear ones long since departed. I must be his
oldest living friend. It is not true, as I have sometimes seen it
stated, that I taught him what little he knew of music; but I was
in at the outset of his strange career and am familiar with all its
beginnings.

I first heard of him through Robert Heller—William Henry
Palmer, best known in his day as a popular magician, but a most
accomplished pianist. It was at Washington and in the autumn of
1860. Palmer had just come up with "Blind Tom" in Louisville,
I think, and had been of course and at once perplexed and amazed
by his extraordinary characteristics. His crude, often grotesque,
attempts to imitate whatever fell upon his ear, either vocally or
on the keyboard, were startling. He had heard Judge Douglas
speak and graphically reproduced a few sentences. He had heard
a reigning Prima Donna sing and repeated her soprano in a few
bars. The Bethune girls, daughters of General Bethune, of Columbus, Ga., his Old Master, had taught him a few jingles, which he
rattled off upon the piano. He knew nothing very complicated, or
very well. But he was blind and clearly an idiot; in short he was
a prodigy.

Palmer gave him several "lessons"—that is, he played over
and over for him such pieces as Thalberg's "Home, Sweet Home,"
Mendelssohn's "Spring Song," and the salient passages out of some
of Liszt's transcriptions. Excepting a few additional "lessons"
of this kind had later along from Eugene Baylor, who taught him
his famous "Margrae Danse," Tom made little further progress
and learned nothing new.

He would spin about the piano, like a baboon, mumbling to
himself whilst Palmer, or Baylor, played, and, if they stopped,
he would rush headlong to the instrument and try to follow after

them precisely as they had phrased. Two or three of such "lessons" sufficed, and though he learned nothing accurately, nor played with any other expression than they had rendered, what he did was surprising, even to those who knew the process and the limitation.

There was on the Tennessee line a certain Major Macconico, who had a great barytone voice. He taught Tom to sing "Rocked in the Cradle of the Deep," very much as he sang it. There was a tailor in Griffin, Georgia, by the name of Hanlon, whose tenor voice was fetching, and he taught Tom two or three love ditties, which Tom repeated in rich though rather guttural tones, yet in undoubted tenor. It was something more than a phenomenon of memory. Though blind, he could handle the keyboard readily, whilst his vocal imitations from bass to treble, from deep barytone to mezzo soprano, were sufficiently accurate and individualized to be recognized.

Tom seemed a woman-hater. Whether it was pure misogyny, of a kind of shyness manifesting itself boorishly, I know not. I well remember in Atlanta, where a party of us had him with us off and on for two or three months, a young lady one day sat down at the piano and began to play. Tom was at the dark end of the chamber, spinning upon hands and heels and mumbling to himself. He caught the sound of the instrument. He stood for a moment still and upright. Then, like a wild animal, he made a dash and swooped down upon her. Terrified, the poor girl shrieked and ran, whilst the rest of us held him, writhing and trembling with what seemed to be rage. "She stole my harmonies," he cried over and over, "she stole my harmonies," and never again did he allow her to come near him. If she were even in the room, he knew it somehow and became restive and angry.

In the autumn of 1865, Tom reappeared at the North under the management of his old master's family, quite impoverished by the war, and an attempt was made to "liberate" him from what some mistaken and over-zealous humanitarians called his "enslavement." Happily, this failed. The case showed for itself, and Tom was left with those who had cared for him from his babyhood, had been most kind to him, and knew, as none others could, his real wants and needs.

The notion that the Bethunes had a gold mine in his performances was not true. They made at the height of his popularity hardly much more than a living, and I suppose that eventually this failed them. They must be all of them dead now. How Tom came to live in want at Hoboken, just how he was separated from his old friends, and how he dropped out of public notice, I cannot say. His mother was alive as late as the early eighties; but I doubt if she, or any of the Bethune family survive.

The last time I saw Blind Tom was in London, away back in 1866. General Pinkney Howard and one of the Bethune boys had brought him over. It had been then nearly three years since I had been with him in Atlanta. From the beginning of our intimacy Tom had been greatly impressed that, with a maimed hand, I could still strike a few chords and run an octave on the keyboard. To his poor, half-wit mind it seemed a miracle. Upon a Sunday afternoon I came into the little hall on or near Leicester Square, where Tom was to appear. He was back of the scenes spinning as usual hand over heel, and mumbling to himself. As we came upon the stage General Howard said, "Let us see whether he knows you." I called him. He slowly uncoiled himself and listened. I called him again. He stood irresolute, then ran across the boards, seized my hand, assured himself of the withered stump and joyously called my name.

What was it? Memory? Yes, it was memory without doubt; but what else? Whence the hand power that enabled him to manipulate the keys, the vocal power that enabled him to imitate the voice?

When he was a tot of four of five years old he strayed from the negro cabin into the parlor of the mansion and hid himself whilst the children were having a concert. When they had gone, leaving the room, as they supposed, quite empty, they heard the piano tinkle. They ran back, and there to their amazement, sat the chubby little black monkey on the stool, banging away for dear life, yet not without sequence and rhythm, trying to repeat what they had just been singing and playing. From that time onward he was the pet of the family.

I cannot trust myself to write of him as I feel. It is as if some trusty, well-loved mastiff—mute but affectionate—closely associated with the dead and gone—had been suddenly recalled to be as suddenly taken away. The wires that flash his death lighten a picture gallery for me of the old, familiar faces. What was he? Whence came he? Was he the Prince of the fairy tale held by the wicked Enchantress; nor any Beauty—not even the Heaven-born Maid of Melody—to release him? Blind, deformed and black—as black even as Erebus—idiocy, the idiocy of a mysterious, perpetual frenzy, the sole companion of his waking visions and his dreams—whence came he, and was he, and wherefore? That there was a soul there, be sure, imprisoned, chained, in that little black bosom, released at last; gone to the Angels, not to imitate the seraph-songs of Heaven, but to join the Choir Invisible for ever and for ever.

H. W.

Mansfield
June 15, 1908

BRYAN

Mr. Bryan is one of the figures upon the editor's painted panorama that, like Roosevelt and Wilson, ranges through every division of his writings and cannot be confined under a sub-heading. But the following article discussing what Mr. Wilson should do with Mr. Bryan after 1912, and what Mr. Bryan would probably do to Mr. Wilson, is included in the division of Personalities as the nearest approach to a confined writing on this prevalent topic.

Mr. Bryan and the Cabinet

(December 21, 1912)

Naturally the composition of Mr. Wilson's Cabinet is of great and general interest, and inevitably the newspapers are full of speculation as to this, that and the other possibility. These are at best but guesswork. They may for the most part be described as the idlest chatter. Not a little of this chatter eddies around Mr. Bryan.

Obviously Mr. Bryan cannot be ignored. Obviously he should not be ignored. Thrice defeated, he received with each defeat more votes than were polled for Mr. Wilson, elected, and, in the last National Convention he put himself forward in his rôle of dictator and had his claim allowed.

He is superman in the eye of his following if not in his own eye. The plank he inserted in the platform, touching a single term for the nominee and the point he made of this in the campaign, raises the not unreasonable presumption that he is looking to the succession in 1916. That, upon the threshold, is a serious matter for the President-elect to consider.

As early as 1844 the question of an unselfish, homogeneous Administrative family had taken such shape that Mr. Polk in offering portfolios to the gentlemen invited to become members of his Cabinet exacted of each of them the promise that in the event he became a candidate for the Presidential nomination in 1848 he would at once resign and withdraw.

If Mr. Wilson should not require this promise of Mr. Bryan could he hope for a wise, disinterested counsellor, and, if he should couple his offer by its exaction, would not Mr. Bryan's self-esteem regard it as an insult? "No candidate for the Presidency," wrote Mr. Polk in his Diary under date of Feb. 21, 1848, referring to Mr. Buchanan, his Secretary of State, who had given the pledge and failed to keep it, "ought ever to remain in the Cabinet. He is an unsafe adviser." Elsewhere Mr. Polk says he would have dismissed Mr. Buchanan except for public exigencies which he names.

The experience of Lincoln with Chase and of Harrison with Blaine gives emphasis to the Polk dictum. With these records and examples before him can Mr. Wilson afford to have Mr. Bryan in his Cabinet? Would Mr. Bryan not be from the start a marplot?

There is yet another reason, what one might call a "disqualifying clause," with respect to Mr. Bryan, and that is a certain intellectual deafness which seems incurable. He is temperamentally at least a leader. He is incapable of playing second fiddle. Having posed as captain so long, can he come down to lieutenant? Woodrow Wilson is something of a captain himself, and how long might the twain artificially joined be expected to dwell together in harmony—

> "Two souls with but a single thought,
> Two hearts that beat as one?"

Mr. Wilson was represented the other day as quoting Burke to the effect that a complete political family should embrace two types, the party leader and the official worker; but it is safe to surmise that the President-elect will consider himself as supplying the first, whilst choosing the second from those subalterns who may be relied on to do as he bids them.

In such a fabric Mr. Bryan would be wholly out of place. No single set of harness would be strong enough to hold both of them. Like the agricultural sailor's spiked team of two oxen and a mule, the larboard ox would get on the starboard side, whilst the mule got afoul of the rigging, resulting in "a pretty kettle of fish." Two dogs and one bone—the saying hath it—two cats and one mouse, two women and one house, can never agree. As to Mr. Wilson and Mr. Bryan that appears about the size of it.

But the President-elect must treat Mr. Bryan with consideration. There is but one other place after the Secretary of State which would fit Mr. Bryan's dignity, and that is the Embassy to the Court of St. James. In 1853 Mr. Buchanan accepted it as an honorable exile and final political interment. Yet it proved the one thing needful to making him President, for it took him out of the country during the queer politics of 1854 and 1855, and thus rendered him most available for the Democratic Presidential nomination in 1856.

Mr. Bryan might study that chapter of American history not without profit to himself. If he accepted, the problem would be solved and the knot be cut. If he refused, the President-elect would have done his part and could leave the rest to the providence of God.

One thing seems certain, if Mr. Wilson is going to have a fight with Mr. Bryan it will come better early than late, and rather from the outside than on the inside.

TWO EMINENT VICTORIANS

In Mr. Watterson's middle life a man was wont to range himself as a champion of Thackeray over Dickens, or the contrary. The editor was a Thackeray man, and whenever in his later life he chanced upon a morsel of news bearing upon the great literary controversy of the Nineteenth Century he would write about it.

The following article is interesting for its sprightliness and its opinion, but perhaps the most striking thing about it to this generation is the reminder that the public once warmly discussed whether "Vanity Fair" was not too immoral to be read!

Thackeray and His Detractors

(March 15, 1908)

It seems that Andrew Lang, a professional bookmaker—though it does not appear that he ever followed the races—a Scotchman and a Tory, has, incidentally to his customary Grub Street handicraft, undertaken to make a case for the Last of the Stuarts. Since most of the black sheep of History—quite all the way from Nero to Cesare Borgia and Aaron Burr, have had their defenders, it is not surprising that the uncrowned King James III, as even George the Fourth was willing to call him, should come in for a coat of whitewash. But, the better to float a new volume commemorating a rather obsolete and wholly fanciful hero, Mr. Lang lays sacrilegious hands upon a much more important personality who, he rightly conceived, would not want for a host of friends aroused by a sense of just resentment. The would-be victim is Thackeray, the Author of "Henry Esmond," the literary creation which our thrifty iconoclast says was stolen bodily from a novel of Sir Walter Scott, to-wit, "Woodstock," a claim he tries to sustain by an affected identification of the dramatis personæ of the two fictions.

The "plagiarisms" of Shakespeare were long ago laid upon the shelf and ticketed "adaptations." The Bard of Avon filched only from the dry bones and dead languages of far-away lands and times. He worked his "stolen goods" into new and improved fabrics. He vitalized what would probably never have been heard of more. And, "there are others," Byron and Longfellow, charged with wholesale "translations."

Nothing is easier than the discovery of "likenesses." In real life the discoveries are as a rule whimsical enough; for the most part the emanations of individual affection, or aversion. In works of the imagination the room for assimilation and surmise is broader still, and a very much greater authority than this Mr. Andrew Lang would be required to fasten upon the Author of "Vanity Fair" an act of burglary into the conspicuous and well-guarded storehouses of the Author of "Waverley."

One grows sick and tired, as the saying is, of seeing penny-a-liners seek to disport and exploit themselves at the expense of the most original, independent and upright literary man of his time. If there be blemishes upon Thackeray's work there are blemishes upon the work of Michael Angelo, whose name at least he appropriated. Of mannerisms there are plenty; but they are his own, nor more pronounced than the mannerisms of Fielding, or those of Macaulay. His was a many-sided intellect, and his experience had been both voluminous and variegate; albeit, whatever he was, or was not, nothing could be farther from the truth than the ascription which dogged him to his grave that he was a cynic.

His earlier humor is sometimes ribald, and sometimes heedless. He was but trying his wings. He could scarcely have been a valued contributor to *Punch,* else. Much, I dare say, of the "puppyism" he describes in "Arthur Pendennis" was reminiscent. All impressionable, aspiring youngsters in literature and art must pass through their period of adolescence, happy he who has not committed his follies, "of record."

Thackeray got his wisdom quite soon enough to make it effectual for all the serious purposes of life and letters, and it shows itself not less in "Vanity Fair" than in "The Newcomes," though differently; the Titmarsh genius a cross between the realistic and the romantic; deeply learned in fiction, French and English; presumably familiar with Stendhal and certainly with Balzac and Victor Hugo and the elder Dumas, whom he did not despise; a close student of the Queen Anne men and an adoring pupil of that scion of the younger branch of the House of Hapsburg, who in "Tom Jones," as Gibbon assures us, left a monument that will outlast the Escorial.

Touching "Vanity Fair," Mr. Harry Thurston Peck has a rather discriminating article in the March issue of *Munsey's Magazine.* Professor Peck is not incapable of sound judgment where his prejudices are not engaged and when he lets his reason with his choler question. He seems a lover of Thackeray and comes bravely to the rescue of the Satirist's fame.

Yet does he, like so many of the others, dwell over-long upon the sinister in Thackeray's realism, not sufficiently considering the make-weights on the side of his romanticism. He allows too much to the stereotyped spirit of perverse detraction, and the immature, not to say ignorant, perceptivity taking its cue from this, which, for fifty years, have marked the larger part equally of English and American criticism, denying to Thackeray what it has conceded to Balzac.

The one pictured English life and manners with the same fidelity, reach, breadth and artistic finish which the other brought to the portraiture of French life and manners, each of them a realistic romanticist of the very first rank. Naturally, their treatment has been very different. If "Père Goriot" was a French "Lear," what were "Colonel Newcome" and "Major Pendennis"? "Becky Sharp" was something rather better than "Madame Marneffe." But nobody has ever taken Balzac to task as everybody— almost everybody—has taken Thackeray to task.

Mr. Peck drops into the procession. His writing seems, for a friend, half-hearted, at least not whole-hearted, just a trifle too apologetic. He saddles Thackeray with "the tacit assumption that all the world is peopled by such types as we discover in 'Vanity Fair,' and that there are none who are wholly pure-minded, generous and noble," which is not true in fact, and, considering the circumstances, the "ground plan," and ultimate development of "Vanity Fair," will not hold true in theory. He quotes a certain Mr. Whibley, whoever he may be, to the effect that Thackeray "seems to snigger amid sobs," a very shallow and paltry suggestion, and, under his own responsibility, he speaks of the little essays with which, following the lead of Fielding, Thackeray's novels abound, as "smug sermons," in one instance spoiling "a passage of fine pathos with a kind of cynic leer."

For a single offense of the kind in Thackeray—if any exist at all—the like of which has escaped this present deponent—a dozen, an hundred, might be cited of Dickens, whom, nevertheless, Mr. Peck declares to be "universal," Thackeray being the "provincial." He elaborates this in the course of a homily still inclining to depreciation, as follows:

"Thackeray was an Englishman of London, while Dickens was an Englishman of England; and his imagination, grotesque and strained as it sometimes is, reaches out beyond the sphere of the particular up into the illimitable spaces of the universal. His pathos may be at times theatrical. His humor may be often farcical. Yet, in his mightier moments, he appeals to something to which every human heart responds. Thackeray, on the other hand, is technically the greater artist. He is the truest realist that England has produced, except, perhaps, his contemporary, Trollope. . . . Yet unless you are a Londoner, unless you are worldly-wise, unless you have yourself a touch of cynicism in your nature, you will not greatly care for Thackeray. To prefer him to Dickens gives proof of a certain sort of cultivation. To prefer Dickens is to show yourself more broadly human."

It will hardly be denied that in melodramatic building-power and many-sided character-creating power, Dickens had a touch of the Shakespearean; as had Dumas; as had Byron; for the matter of that, they all breed back to Homer; but that Thackeray "was far more insular, far more local, than Dickens"; that he "could draw individual Frenchmen and Germans from life with the deft touch of a portrait-painter," but "could never have given us that marvelous, impressive, overwhelming picture of France in the throes of the Revolution which Dickens spread before us in 'A Tale of Two Cities,' we cannot think at all." On the contrary, if Thackeray had had the handling of "A Tale of Two Cities," we feel quite sure that he would have made a better imitation of Dumas than Dickens has left us.

Professor Peck, accepting the accusation of cynicism, explains that it was the influence of club life and "of Bohemianizing about London and Paris," listening to club talk, "made up of risque stories, of hinted scandal, of cynical observation and of worldly aphorisms," a rather narrow view of club life, closing with the statement that "the club window was the nest on which he settled down as other men repose before their firesides."

Except for the club, it is true that Thackeray could hardly have made his full-length portrait of "Major Pendennis," nor, except for knocking about town, his charcoal sketches of "Costigan" and "The Kitchen." But Dickens could not have given us "The Marquis of Steyne" and "Becky Sharp" portraits quite as vivid and lifelike and as "universal" as "Fagin" and "Mrs. Gamp." Dickens himself, the greatest of fireside singers, had a shipwrecked home, as we know, and played to the groundlings, though, like Edmund Keen and Edwin Forrest, he played so strong that "the whole house rose to him."

The New York *Times,* to return to the text from which we started, thinks that, in revealing the analogy between "Henry Esmond" and "Woodstock," Mr. Andrew Lang "has sprung a bomb." If he has, its fragments are likelier to fall about the head of the apologist of the Stuarts than they are to disturb the pedestal on which the Master Satirist of modern England so firmly stands.

"The real James," the Scotchman tells us, "was not a hard drinker, a gamester, a pursuer of women, a false friend"—though he was— and anyhow, what matters it—for, as the *Times* remarks, "Thackeray's picture of high life in London in the time of William and Mary is full of the true historical perspective," adding, with truth and force, that "history cares very little for the claims of the ousted Stuarts, whilst 'Henry Esmond' is a work as fresh and vital now as it was fifty-six years ago."

Thackeray did, indeed, as the *Times* reminds us, have to submit to his full share of hostile criticism in his lifetime, but if the charge was then made that he ever, consciously or unconsciously, borrowed intrigue and characters from the Wizard of the North, it has not survived.

It is impossible to consider him, however, without many sideglances at his personality. Thackeray projected himself into his writing more than any man of letters of his time. As a consequence, he has come in for a certain animadversion which no other writer of that literary era has encountered. He wrote a fanciful sketch of an evening party and was straightway charged with lampooning his hostess. He wrote some fugitive pieces about "Snobs," which were collected into a volume, and straightway the word went forth that he was the greatest of snobs. Then, with "Vanity Fair" came the only thing left the spiteful to say of such a masterpiece—that it was "heartless" and that its author was "a cynic." All this while the man behind the puppets, who showed himself a little too often, overflowing with redundant energy and ardor, and human interest of all kinds, including self-interest, was the reverse of a cynic; a joyous, robust creature, spite of his tragedy; who laughed and swore consumingly; with resonance and abundance; but who could no more "sneer" than pick a pocket!

Thackeray dearly loved to guzzle and gabble with his friends— overgiven perhaps to the pleasures of the table. This tendency was early and highly developed—maybe it was misleading. Maginn and Mahony were not the best exemplars for a very young man of letters, for all their bonhommie and brilliancy. Nor was the *Punch* "round table" a very proper School either of Sentiment or Ethics. With Fleet Street on the one side and Pall Mall on the other, Thackeray had no lack of opportunities to ripen whatever of cynicism was in him. Yet we have the best of evidence that the home influence never relaxed its hold upon him; that "the old Major," his stepfather, and "the Kinikins," his daughters; in short, his "fambly" including a mother to whom he was all devotion, constituted his "solar system," round which his labors circled, to which he returns again and again, a great overgrown boy, Society, the world worldly, merely a workshop and an asset, a source of supply and a playground.

The criticism that sees no good in "Vanity Fair" would deny holy writ if it became the fashion to do so. The book is full of sympathy and sentiment. The women? If "Amelia" was a fool and "Becky" a sharper, was not that inevitable to the purpose of the piece? How else could the man have pointed his moral and adorned his tale? He was not painting a gallery of the goody-goody, nor finding his adventures in a nursery. He had already made a pastel of "Caroline Gans." He afterward did her at full length, and gave us "Laura Bell" and "Ethel Newcome" and "Warrington," "Colonel Esmond" and "Colonel Newcome," wholly to disprove a calumny, which sought to injure the man, failing wholly to injure the books.

Thackeray's place in literature is as fixed as that of any of the immortals. It is a waste of words to discuss his writings. It is his personality which is brought to question, though in the case of no one of his contemporaries have we ampler material for a just estimate. He was, in truth, a typical, strapping Englishman who at forty looked sixty. In spite of his broken nose there was something very winning in his countenance. His voice was not untuneful—even when he sang his droll songs in a kind of *sotto voce* treble as Moore is said to have sung his. Before an audience his clumsiness became an advantage rather than a disadvantage, a guarantee at once of sincerity and the absence of affectation. He ate and drank heartily—having a better head than stomach—never wanted to go to bed—and though built for four score died at fifty-two, a victim of his own deafness to nature's calls, the result of preoccupation, of overwork and of insufficient rest. Had he taken better care of his health, his life might have been prolonged to a great old age, and, if it had been, he would have outlived the rancors, both social and literary, which insisted upon distorting everything he said and did.

Instead of being a cynic, Thackeray was a sentimentalist. There was simply nothing mawkish about his sentiment. One does not like to think ill of Dickens, but in real integrity and sturdy manhood, in true, self-respecting and honorable sensibility, Dickens was as a child to Thackeray. The completed story of the Brookfields, like everything else at one time maligned, sheds light upon the upright character and tender heart of one of the most affectionate of men, but the Baxter episode tells a story from which there is no escape. No one can read the letters too tardily given to the public, and contemplate the circumstances and meaning of the friendship begun in 1852, to end only with the great man's life in 1863—a friendship exceptional in every way—without fully comprehending the fact that the underpinning of Thackeray's personality and genius was Love, and that more than any author of modern times he exemplified in his writings the Coleridge dictum:

> "All thoughts, all passions, all delights,
> Whatever stirs this mortal frame,
> All are but ministers of Love,
> And feed his sacred flame."

Naples-on-the-Gulf
  Lee County, Florida

ON THE AUTHOR OF PICKWICK

"Dickens was neither a genuine man nor a gentleman," is a Wattersonian thrust which reveals the vigor with which the editor ranged himself with admirers of Thackeray in the Victorian literary controversy. The following article pursues his favorite argument that Dickens was (his most severe craft epithet) "a space-writer."

As to Charles Dickens

(October 15, 1910)

We reprint from *The Bookman* some timely, and on the whole judicious, remarks touching the approaching Dickens Centenary and the proposed fund for the impecunious children and grandchildren of the great English novelist.

What we may owe to the "Genius" of Charles Dickens we have measurably paid in hard cash and are paying every day, and will continue to pay through all time, in ever-increasing appreciation. What we owe his "Memory" is another matter. He was not even to his familiars a very admirable person; to us he turned his darker side.

Doubtless, most of what was said in "Martin Chuzzlewit" and the "Notes," was true enough. But the spirit was venal and paltry. At a moment of international tension he came over deliberately to write an anti-American book that would sell. Thackeray might have done the same and done it better—only he did not—and having perpetrated this spiteful and vulgar piece of penny-a-lining, twenty-five years later Dickens had the effrontery to come again in quest of the adulation and dollars of the generous and forgiving people he had lampooned.

A self-respecting man would have scorned to do this. The truth is that Dickens was neither a genuine man, nor a gentleman. He was a man of transcendent gifts, but quite as wanting in true nobility as either Bacon or Byron. Whatever debt we may owe

his genius, **we** have paid. We owe his memory and his progeny
nothing.

CARRIE NATION

Because Mrs. Nation represented in her person and activities two
unforgivable crimes in the Watterson calendar—meddlesome-
ness with private matters, and prohibition—he marked her
death with the following:

(*July 13, 1911*)

Yesterday all that was mortal of poor, old Carrie Nation was
laid to rest in an obscure Missouri churchyard. Poor, old Carrie
Nation! She was a crazy Jane, wasn't she? How many drunkards
did she reform, how many would-be drunkards did she rescue,
how many innocents turn away from the dram-shop? She seems
to have done very well in the business of saloon-smashing and
hatchet-selling. If mad at all, there was a method in her madness.
Did she really suffer from the hysteria into which she threw herself, or enjoy the excitement and notoriety? Who shall tell?
Poor, old hag! Peace to her ashes. Witches of the blasted health,
spirits of dead priestesses of pagan fable—maybe the soul of Meg
Merrilies herself—attended her wanderings from Dan to Beer-
sheba, which she did not find all barren, and they will e'en follow
her to her grave. Born in Kentucky, 'twas fitting that she should
die in Kansas. "I shall come again," said Meg Merrilies, "I shall
come again, long, long after these crazed old bones have lain whitening beneath the mould." Will Carrie Nation come again? Not
to Kentucky. Here at least emotional politics is beginning to yield
to sanity and common sense at last.

JEFFERSON DAVIS

One of the final shakes given to the Bloody Shirt was when, in
1909, an Indiana congressman sought to prevent the bas-relief
of Jefferson Davis from appearing on the silver service which
the State of Mississippi wished to present to the battleship of
that name. Upon this congressional effort Mr. Watterson
launched a formidable attack. He was in an excellent position
to do this because he, a former Confederate and a whole-
hearted Southerner, had pleaded the cause of the North and
the genius of Lincoln in the post-bellum South. This editorial
illustrates the skill with which the editor used the devices of

journalism—one of them, his mock forgetfulness of the name of the offending congressman, being an invention of his own.

A Wornout Hate

(May 11, 1909)

"Strange, as in looking back over the past the assertion may seem, impossible as it would have been ten years ago to make it, it is not the less true today that Mississippi regrets the death of Charles Sumner, and sincerely unites in paying honors to his memory."—Lamar's Eulogy upon Sumner.

"Jefferson Davis, than whom there never lived, in this or in any land, a nobler gentleman and a knightlier soldier—Jefferson Davis, who, whatever may be thought of his opinions and actions, said always what he meant and meant always what he said—Jefferson Davis declared that next after the surrender at Appomatox, the murder of Abraham Lincoln made the darkest day in the calender for the South and the people of the South. Why? Because Mr. Davis had come to a knowledge of the magnanimity of Mr. Lincoln's character and the generosity of his intentions."—Watterson's Eulogy upon Lincoln.

Forty years ago, contending against the passions of the hour and the prejudices of the Southern people—natural, if not reasonable, inevitable though impolitic—the *Courier-Journal* said: "If we want the North to do justice to us, we must do justice to the North, and, before we can expect the Northern people to accept our heroes, we must accept their heroes."

On no other basis could complete reunion and lasting peace have been established.

We have lived to see it assume the force of law and to become a universal National sentiment. When William McKinley signed the commissions of Wheeler and Lee in the Regular Army—having previously signed those of Butler and Castleman and other Confederate Soldiers in the Volunteer Army—proclamation was issued to America and the world that the War of Sections was over; but, when the South, no less than the North joined in celebrating the Centenary of the birth of Abraham Lincoln, official action was given popular sanction, and the decree was made absolute and final.

In the face of an issue thus achieved, responsive to an impulse so patriotic and generous, dissonance from any quarter would seem perverse; but that the spirit of enmities long ago cooled and for the most part hushed in death, should crystallize into a formal resolution and appear in the Congress of the United States, with Jefferson Davis for its inciting cause, is truly surprising. It is of a piece with the aspersions recently cast upon the fame of Alexander Hamilton by a Senator who insists that a statue ordained in his honor shall not be erected in the National Capital. As well might we go back to the fulminations of Calender and refuse our homage to Thomas Jefferson, or dig into the forgotten memoirs of Franklin, to find that the old Doctor was not a Prohibitionist and therefore that he is unworthy of further commemoration. The names of the Representative and the Senator who betray such lack at once of human sympathy and a sense of the fineness of things, are so obscure that the present writer cannot recall them without recurring to the roster and will therefore leave unmentioned.

Jefferson Davis was the Civil Chieftain of a cause which, whatever may have been its errors of judgment, or the paradoxical character ascribed to it, stood for well-defined ideas of self-government. During four years of battle against incredible odds, it engaged the ardent devotion of substantially the entire white people of the South. If he was guilty of treason, so was every white man, woman and child, in the South. Attainder of him attaints us all. But why should he, long since gone to his account, be excepted from amnesty? What principle, what party interest has a motive for stigmatizing his memory?

The years glide swiftly by. Most, if not all of us, have come to see that two mistakes of the first order were perpetrated by the people of the United States the latter half of the Nineteenth Century. It was a mistake of the South, for any cause whatever, to precipitate a war of sections, and it was a mistake of the North, after the overthrow of the Confederacy, to undertake a reconstruction of the Union by force of arms. That the country has survived mistakes of such magnitude is proof of amazing vitality; of a vitality that draws its sustenance from the adaptability and the flexibility of free institutions and from a popular character equal to all emergencies, military and civil. Man proposes and God disposes, and often we build wiser than we know. But who shall say that the very mischances of these forty years of domestic controversy were not needful to make us the Nation we are today? It was Grant, himself, who issued the order finally withdrawing the troops from the South, as it was none other than Grant who stood between the Confederate soldier and a surrender that might have been most dishonoring to American manhood and most humiliating to our National annals.

The truth is that the battle ended forty-four years ago and its provoking issues have become historic and academic; the best thinkers of the country have arrived at the belief that if the South wanted justification it might find it in a long line of plausible, if not attractive, argumentation in favor of the right of a State to withdraw at its own will from the Union, beginning with Josiah Quincy and his associates in New England and ending with Jefferson Davis and his associates in the Gulf States. The framers of the Constitution found themselves unable clearly to determine this point. So they left it open. After years of contention—complicated by the irrepressible question of slavery carried to the ultimate of the irreconcilable—the well-intentioned omission of the Fathers to fix the exact relation of the States to the Federal Government precipitated the two Sections of the Union into war, and out of this war—although we did not see it at the time—we emerged more homogeneous as a people and better equipped as a nation than we had ever been before.

But, to come to the point: if Jefferson Davis is to be outlawed, Mississippi is outlawed; because Mississippi and Jefferson Davis are historically synonymous, one and inseparable. Why name a battleship after Mississippi and forbid Mississippi to place the effigy of its greatest citizen and best fighter upon the customary presentation service of silver? It was not in the armies of the Confederacy, but of the United States, that Jefferson Davis won his laurels as a fighter. There would seem a singular fitness, therefore, in his association with a National fighting ship bearing the name of Mississippi, to say nothing of the right of the people of Mississippi to pay homage to their most distinguished and representative man, accused by no one of any manly deficiency, regarded by all the world as a type of manly excellence.

The member of Congress, whose name we fail to recall—though we believe he hails from Indiana—might, not without instruction to himself, before introducing his defaming resolution have torn a leaf out of the records of Congress and have carefully perused it.

On the 11th of March, 1874, Charles Sumner died in Washington. More than any other of the Ante-bellum leaders of the North he had drawn the fire of the South. After the War, he had stretched forth the hand of peace to his old enemies and the South did not refuse it. But it seems a coincidence that it was a Mississippian who, when that hand lay cold in death, stood up in the same House which is now asked to dishonor the memory of Jefferson Davis to honor the memory of Charles Sumner. Lamar's words rang from one end of the land to the other. His eulogy upon Sumner is immortal. It ranks with the masterpieces of the world's orators; with Pericles and Bossuet; and Mississippi—the Mississippi which it is proposed now wantonly to affront—indorsed it, applauded it, never wearied of heaping honors upon its author, Lamar, Jefferson Davis's closest friend and immediate representative, Jefferson Davis, himself, still alive to say "Amen!" Shame, shame, shame, Mr. ————!

It was at Buena Vista, February 22, 1847. General Zachary Taylor and his army had fought their way across the Rio Grande via Palo Alto and Resaca de la Palma and Monterey to the heart of the Coahuila country Old Santa Aña thought he had Old Rough and Ready in a hole.

The Mexicans greatly outnumbered the Americans. For awhile things looked dark. The first ray of light came with the charge of the Mississippians under Colonel Jefferson Davis. The last desperate attempt to break our line was met by the Mississippians under Colonel Jefferson Davis.

There were no supports. The odds were three to one. It was the crisis of the battle. On came the Lancers furious and flashing and brilliant with color. Colonel Davis formed his men in the shape of a V, open toward the enemy, and thus exposing him to a murderous fire, soon sent him decimated and reeling, flying in every direction, ending the decisive engagement with a glorious victory.

Colonel Davis was desperately wounded, but he kept his saddle to the last, when his gallant but irate old father-in-law, never quite reconciled to the marriage of his daughter, rode up and exultingly thanked him.

Buena Vista, if nothing else, constitutes reason enough why Mississippi should never forget Jefferson Davis; why all good Americans should be proud of him, and why the face and figure of such a fighting Mississippi fighter should be identified with a National fighting ship bearing the illustrious name of Mississippi. "My countrymen," said Lamar at the bier of Sumner, "know one another and you will love one another." That was thirty-five years ago. Have we gone backward or forward in National unification and reciprocal pride, the one section of the other? Anyhow, to Mr. ———— of Indiana, and to the few who take his narrow, unpatriotic and proscriptive view, we may repeat the lines,

> "You cannot chain the eagle
> And you dare not harm the dove;
>   But every gate
>   Hate bars to hate,
> Will open wide to love."

OLD ROUGH-AND-READY

One day Mr. Watterson came down to his office and sent for the managing editor. "I see the War Department," he said, "has adopted the *Courier-Journal's* suggestion to name our camp for Old Rough and Ready. If you ever let it get in the paper as 'Camp Taylor,' I'll have your hide, hair and horns." And on the one or two occasions when the slip was made, Marse Henry would put a huge ring around the passage and urge the managing editor to burn or slay the office wight who had thus offended.

Other Louisville newspapers declined to acknowledge the point of his contention and continued to call the area "Camp Taylor," so he expressed his feelings on the subject in the attached editorial and announced to his staff that folks who could not understand that "hadn't never been nowhar and didn't know nothin'."

"Camp Zachary Taylor"

(October 2, 1917)

The more one thinks about it the surer is he likely to become that there is much in a name anyhow that there is more than was dreamt of in the philosophy of the famous young lady of Verona; in a word that old Capulet's daughter was mistaken when she said that a rose would smell just as sweet if it were called a squash. Suppose her own name, for example, had been Samantha and her lover's, Simeon, and, instead of "Romeo and Juliet," the play had been put on the bills "Simeon and Samantha," what then? That is the conundrum the gentleman-up-a-tree would like to have somebody answer.

Hence it is that the *Courier-Journal* sticks to "Camp Zachary Taylor," in lieu of "Camp Taylor." It marks the "General Orders" of the War Department. It takes heed equally of official propriety and the admonitions of eternal justice. There old "Rough-and-Ready" lies—that, by the way, were not a bad name for the cantonment!—down yonder by the river's side. It may not be precisely the spot where:

> "He sighed and she sighed,
> And then they sat side by side."

but nevertheless a good place for a couple to sit and sigh and sing the "Star Spangled Banner" and saying between kisses and sighs: "To Hell with the Hohenzollern and the Hapsburg!"

However, let us avoid profanity! Old Rough-and-Ready rests at last in his modest grave "down by the river side." He sleeps his last sleep. He has fought his last battle. No sound can awake him to glory again. And yet, as his spirit walks its solemn round hearing some knock-kneed, bow-legged, bandy-shanked newspaper reporter say "Camp Taylor," the poor ghost might be pardoned for asking "which Taylor, yer son-of-a-gun?"

It were a reasonable question. Because, d' ye see, there are Taylors and Taylors, just as there are Smiths and Smiths, and Browns and Browns. But there is only one Zachary Taylor, who at Buena Vista—the Mexicans ten to one—told Santa Aña to go to grass, or words to that blooming effect, and said, "a little more grape, Cap'n Bragg."

It makes an inspiring story. The boys of the Cantonment should know it by heart. He was a fighter—Old Rough-and-Ready—from way back—from Bitter Creek, as a body may say—high up and north side! The lads in khaki can not do better than study his career. Then they would know what to do with a mean, splenetic creature who would deny him his right to be called not Taylor, but Zachary Taylor, and the Cantonment's right to its true and legal designation of "Camp Zachary Taylor."

To the duck-pond with the dirty dog who says "Camp Taylor" instead of "Camp Zachary Taylor!"

PROFESSIONAL

PROFESSIONAL

THE BET WITH THE *WORLD*

The average editor deems himself fortunate that few of his readers remember his prophecies. In the course of human events, many of them go awry. This volume necessarily contains passages which, while they seemed certain of realization at the time they were indited, came to inglorious refutation.

But the three editorials which follow relate to a stunning and amusing triumph of prophecy by Mr. Watterson. It was bold. Thousands of those who read it did not foresee a possibility that, within a given time after November, 1909, Mr. Taft and Colonel Roosevelt would be "at daggers' points."

The New York *World,* whose emanation was responsible for the prophecy, did not believe it and merrily accepted the bet of a large dinner in Washington to be paid by the loser.

When the mists of the future had parted, Mr. Watterson was a triumphant victor, and some of the comments which appear in this group of editorials are in his finest jocose manner. For various reasons the dinner was never held, the *World* complaining that there was no way of getting Mr. Watterson to fix a date. He tried, however, to line up his distinguished guests; but when the writer, then his Washington correspondent, found that a death in the family would prevent the presence of Chief Justice White, the editor gently disclaimed the *World's* forfeit.

It is interesting to note that in the list of proposed guests Mr. Watterson included that very Vice President Sherman who, before he had met him, the editor looked upon as a representative of a very fearsome "money devil."

Later Mr. Watterson said that the dinner never was intended to come off and that the only reason he went so far as to ask the Chief Justice was because "Joe Pulitzer had hounded him into it."

A Fair Offer

(November 22, 1909)

Says the New York *World:*

"We should hardly have expected that Henry Watterson
would take 'the return from Elba' seriously, yet he is convinced that there is a strong movement on foot to bring about
the renomination of President Roosevelt, and believes that
'the result will be a division between the Taft and Roosevelt
men, which may split the Republican party.' The Colonel has
lived with the Republican party ever since it was born, and he
ought to be better acquainted with it. There is no 'strong
movement' to renominate Mr. Roosevelt—merely much gossip,
more or less wounded vanity and a friendly disposition on the
part of the radical Republicans to scare the Taft Administration. At present there is no more danger of a Republican
split over Taft and Roosevelt than of the Colonel's voting the
straight Republican ticket in 1912."

This is but an easy, surface view. It fails to take account of
certain underlying conditions. It does not sufficiently consider
human nature. There is now and again a good deal of human
nature in politics. Mr. Roosevelt has been more than once suspected of it, and in the end it may be found that behind the calm
exterior of the President, and beneath that broad, expansive smile,
a few stray embers lurk.

Sometimes one has to go away from home to get the news.
the *Courier-Journal* gave no credit to the story that there was a
dicker between Roosevelt and Taft to take turn and turn about,
in the White House. Neither did it question Mr. Roosevelt's
sincerity when he announced that he would not accept a nomination for a "second elective term." That he was disloyal to Taft
at heart, expecting a stampede in the convention that would force
its candidacy upon him—which his enemies yet persist in charging
—we did not believe and do not believe. Nor do we regard the
"return from Elba" chatter seriously. Either the *World* misses
the point, or else Mr. Watterson failed to make it as clear in the
expression as it is in the conception, that the Taft-Roosevelt situation would make a break likely, if there were no busybodies to
agitate it, but that, with a host of keen and selfish politicians to
see in it at once their profit and their revenge, it seems inevitable.

Mr. Watterson did not say, or did not mean to say, that
"There is a strong movement to nominate Mr. Roosevelt." That

would be putting the cart before the horse. He said that there is a well-organized conspiracy to make a breach between the President that is and the President that was, and this is true. Whither it will lead and where it will end, it is too early to speculate. Men of importance are engaged in it. Our esteemed New York contemporary would be surprised if we named them.

Having delivered itself as above quoted, the *World* proceeds to moralize as follows:

"The Republican party is tough and efficient. Its discipline is magnificent. The habit of party loyalty is firmly established in national affairs. If Mr. Taft lives he will be renominated, unless he abdicates. There is less Republican opposition to him than there was to McKinley during McKinley's first term, or than there was to Roosevelt during either of Roosevelt's terms.

"Talk is very cheap between elections. It is about the only thing left in the country that is cheap, and everybody that does not get his mail promptly, or is overcharged by a railroad, or has trouble in borrowing money at the bank for the next two years will be condemning the Taft Administration. This will be the case especially in the Middle West. But when the time comes for decisive action there will be few politicians who care to quarrel with the National Administration and nobody of influence to lead the Roosevelt third term movement, unless Mr. Roosevelt leads it himself.

"If he returned from abroad determined to be a candidate for President again at any cost, eager to betray his friend Taft and ready to manage his own campaign he might be able to split the Republican party, but even Mr. Roosevelt's worst enemies think better of him than that."

Now let the *Courier-Journal* moralize a lick or two.

Men like Theodore Roosevelt do not do something for nothing. He is a most astute practical politician. He is but just turned fifty, in the very middle and high noon of life. "What is an ex-President to do but die or get drunk?" a dictum which used to be ascribed to one of them, does not apply to Theodore Roosevelt. His African journey was sagaciously planned. It is being systematically achieved.

The reception which awaits the hero will beggar anything of the triumphal kind the world has ever seen. In Berlin and London and Paris, not to mention Rome, they are waiting for him, the Kaiser and the kings, for their cousin-german, the people behind their monarchs, for their fling, the Parisians for their spectacular, which they will make an extravaganza; the "Teddy Bears" for

Teddy himself! There is nothing, we are told, which succeeds like success.

Nor is there anything which is so easy as the raising of misunderstanding between friends. A wink and a nod and a word by chance, and the trick is turned; presto! a blow is struck. The go-between in love, the marplot in hate, Othello and Iago and sweet Desdemona! Shall the Republican party play the rôle of Desdemona?

We agree with the *World* that the Republican party "is tough." Yea, verily, and sly and hard to down, a roaring militant, triumphant organization, with perfect discipline, vast resources, and the habit of loyalty. So was the Democratic party fifty years ago. Buchanan and Douglas are dead, but human nature remains intact.

Whether the Republican party is able to hold together against the strain of the protective tariff system, as the Democratic party was not able to hold together against the strain of slavery, remains to be seen. Whether the Democratic party has vitality enough to profit by a Republican split is very doubtful. The Republicans who are planning to horn Taft off and to whoop Roosevelt on are of the opinion that the Democrats are not worth considering. Meanwhile is the President that is, whilst he waits the coming of the President that was, casting an anchor to windward that he is so gracious to us Democrats, especially to us ragged rebels—not so ragged as we were—of the South? Teddy, let us remember, is half a Southron.

Nor let us be too cock-sure of anything, and yet, albeit opposed on principle to games of chance, we have a wager to offer the *World,* not of money, but of wittles, with maybe a drop or two onbeknownst to the W. C. T. U. to wash 'em down, to-wit: a dinner for twenty-four, to be given in Washington City, District of Columbia, on or before the first Monday of December, 1911, the *World* to invite twelve, the *Courier-Journal* to invite twelve, the Chief Justice of the United States, the Vice President, and the Speaker of the House of Representatives to serve as judges and referees, and to sit at table as additional, ex-officio, guests—or words to that effect—the proposition to be that Taft and Roosevelt are at daggers' points by the *Courier-Journal* in the affirmative, the *World* in the negative.

What sayeth our esteemed New York contemporary? Has it a mind to do business? Shall we count it "in"?

To Joseph Pulitzer, Greeting!

(November 27, 1909)

"Sir, respect your dinner."—Thackeray.

The New York *World* is a thoroughbred and comes worthily to the scratch. Nay, it comes jauntily. Joseph Pulitzer was ever a dead game sport, and, though wealth and years may have somewhat abated the buoyancy of the journal which he rescued from ruin and made young again, not to mention the boys who will live after him, knows no such word as "backdown," fully conceiving that God hates equally a coward and a quitter!

Our esteemed contemporary accepts the wager of a dinner for a dozen on a side—"four and twenty blackbirds all in a row"—including the Chief Justice, the Vice President and the Speaker of the House, as make-weights and referees, tendered it by the *Courier-Journal;* to be given in the City of Washington, District of Columbia, on or immediately before the first Monday of December, 1911; the gauge being that then and there, or thereabouts, the President that was, in other words Theodore Roosevelt, and the President that is, in other words William Howard Taft, will be reaching after one another's vitals, tearing one another's hair, and otherwise disfiguring one another's personal and political record, the *Courier-Journal* taking the affirmative, the *World* the negative of that interesting proposal.

It looks a fair scheme. It seems certainly more equal-like than two similar schemes, the mention of which may not be irrelevant. The 16th of February, 1881, the late Noah Brooks and the Editor of the *Courier-Journal* accepted from Mr. Elisha W. Vanderhoff, of the Union Club, New York—the loser to pay a dinner forfeit—his offer of these three propositions; first, that if Mr. Folger were not Secretary of the Treasury upon the organization of the Cabinet, already chosen and to be announced within two weeks, he would be at the end of a year; second, that if Mr. Blaine were Secretary of State on the organization of the Cabinet, he would not be at the end of a year; and third—this latter in the teeth of the knowledge of both Mr. Brooks and Mr. Watterson that Mr. Allison had been agreed upon for Secretary of the Treasury—that Mr. Allison would not be in the Cabinet at all.

A year later, the 16th of February, 1882, each of Mr. Vanderhoff's postulates having come true—it required two deaths and an attempted suicide to win his dinner—the wager was paid by the losers.

The night of the adjournment of the National Democratic Convention at Chicago in 1892 the Editor of the *Courier-Journal* bet Mr. Frank A. Richardson, of the *Baltimore Sun,* a dinner for twenty that Cleveland and Stevenson would be elected, and that Illinois would cast her electoral vote for the Democratic ticket. Mr. Richardson gave the dinner in Washington after the inauguration of the new administration. A bully good dinner it was, whereat there were much rejoicing and a rare outpouring and consumption. But why particularize?

It will be seen from these that the present proposal by the *Courier-Journal* to the New York *World* is in the line of safe and equal precedents. Victuals are always in order. It is never sinful to gamble for food. On the contrary, angels preside over that board where plenty hobnobs with cheer and song and wit and fellowship maketh hearts to be glad, no matter who pays the reckoning; which, in this case, the *Courier-Journal* will willingly do, for it makes the bet wanting to give the *World* a dinner and, therefore, hoping it will lose, taking no stock in ill-humors of any kind, nor seeking ever to set even Republican friends and neighbors by the ears; a peacemaker, yea, a merrymaker, and a believer in the philosophy of the revelers who sang, " 'tis better to laugh than to be sighing," though having the poisoned chalice at their lips; all of which Mr. Roosevelt and Mr. Taft would do well to put in their respective pipes and to smoke upon it the coming eighteen months, d'ye mind!

The fact is it was the cock-sureness of the *World* which instigated the offer of the *Courier-Journal.* The *Courier-Journal* does not like being laughed at, or sworn at, or addressed with disproportioned positivity. Mr. Pulitzer's young gentlemen possess that total lack of the consciousness of fallibility which has become the distinguishing mark of metropolitan journalism. Now, the *Courier-Journal* when need requires has a certain faculty for the oracular and can on occasion affect the toploftical in great shape. It has girded its loins many a time against barbaric hordes and studied the cue-papers of heathen lands. Where the royalties of intellectual combat are at issue, and brickbats are to fly and razors to do their appointed office, it may usually be found somewhere about the middle of the fray, or words to that effect; albeit, not a friend of war for war's sake; just a plain, everyday pilgrim with brass boot-tips and a pop-gun, ever prepared to go its pile on its judgment.

In its response to the *Courier-Journal's* invitation our esteemed New York contemporary says:

"The *World* accepts. The Colonel can count us 'in,' and we have only two conditions to impose:

"First—Win or lose, the Colonel shall personally order the dinner and supervise its preparation.

"Second—He shall stand by and see it through, from the caviar to the coffee.

"Bring on your feud or your food, Colonel."

There lurks here a levity which ill becomes the gravity of the occasion and the subject. Obviously, the *World* has not sufficiently reflected. The covert innuendo—we shall not say the implied disparagement ("surely, now, Sir Anthony, you speak laconically") that "the Colonel shall stand by and see it through from the caviar to the coffee"—is unworthy the chivalric spirit which we are sure animates every one beneath the gilded dome of Printing House Square. In the famous Cocke-Wise duel, when the two antagonists were placed in position, Cocke, a dead shot, whispered to his second loud enough to be heard fifteen paces away, "I call you and God to witness that I am guiltless of this man's blood," and Wise sang out "—blast your—soul, look after your own blood," and straightway shot Cocke through the body.

We waive the flagrant affront. Maybe it was unintentional. Boys will be boys. They know not what they invoke. Nor do they fully conceive the latest thing in dinners, or they could not fall into the somewhat belated alliteration about the "caviar" and the "coffee." If "the Colonel" should order the dinner, it will not begin with the one, nor end with the other. That part of it, however, will keep.

It is not such matters of technique that move us. A more serious question presents itself. Why should the *World* touch so lightly upon a theme which should be the subject of the deepest contemplation? "The Colonel" order the dinner? Why, man alive! before it is given, millions will discuss it; every dish should be a work of art, and London and Paris will be all agog; the *World* should unite with the *Courier-Journal* in sending abroad a demand for sealed proposals; John Chamberlin is dead, more's the pity; though Oscar and Sherry and Martin are still alive; and there is that little hole-in-the-wall down at Ninth Street and University Place! Nobody will order the dinner. It will order itself. It will be its own creation. It will become a *cause célèbre*. It will grow and bloom, and build itself in the sunshine of educated palates and the hothouses of gastric thought from Cairo to St. Petersburg, from the Bosphorus to the Caribbean Sea, with contributions from the chefs of Christendom and the crowned heads of Pagandom; great pyramids of smoking rice and pillars—again to quote the immortal Titmarsh—savory kids, snow-cooled sherbets, luscious wine of Shiraz, enough to stagger a Barmecide and beggar an Arabian Night's entertainment!

Yet softly! Let not the horns proceed too far in advance of the hounds! There are two years in which to arrange the menu and sound the bold anthem; none too few, yet enough, and so, with the Thanksgiving spirit playing like an oriole about the pen, and many birds outside singing still of summer in full-throated glee, it is up to you, dear Joseph Pulitzer, to take heart of heart from an old friend; to look with glad mind to our coming dinner; may it see our poor old Democratic party united and strong once more; may it see you restored to health and strength; the light come back to those shadowed eyes; that luminous brain as resistless and alert as in days gone by; and all as merry as a marriage bell, dear Joseph Pulitzer! Not to put too fine a point upon it, we looks toward you, Joe!

So confident was the New York *World* in 1909 that it should win its dinner-bet with Marse Henry (see chapter under Political Campaigns) that Mr. Cobb wrote the following sportive article about his Kentucky colleague:

That Dinner

(New York World, December 4, 1909)

"The fact is, it was the cocksureness of the *World* which instigated the offer of the *Courier-Journal*," remarks Colonel Watterson, perhaps by way of explanation, perhaps by way of apology for his impatience. "The *Courier-Journal* does not like being laughed at or sworn at or addressed with disproportioned positivity."

We like that expression, "disproportioned positivity," knowing as we do that the offense is not so serious as it sounds and that the language adds dignity to the indictment. Much is to be said in favor of "disproportioned positivity." Without it there would never have been a horse race in Kentucky, and we remember as if it were yesterday when the good gray Colonel's own disproportioned positivity needed neither whip nor spur in its dash for the wire.

Times change, of course, and the Colonel changes with them. After fifty years on the firing-line, with his own gun-barrel so covered with notches that there is no place to file another, the Colonel likes his *otium cum dignitate* and a little nap along with his after-dinner cigar. It annoys him mightily if one of the boys disturbs his repose by taking a pot-shot at some tempting political proposition that is skulking among the trees in the neighborhood.

Now this Roosevelt-Taft thesis of the *World* against which Colonel Watterson has impulsively staked the dinner of dinners is no more a matter of disproportioned positivity than is that decent confidence in six times seven which comes from a familiar acquaintance with the multiplication table. We pretend to be nothing more than a plain journeyman prophet with a union card, working eight hours a day, and price and a half for overtime. The Colonel backs his dinner with his recollections of the quarrel between Buchanan and Douglas. We back our dinner with casual knowledge of the psychological processes of Theodore Roosevelt. Now that the dinner is guaranteed, we have no objection to taking Colonel Watterson into the cabinet, turning on the light and showing him how the thing is done.

Roosevelt cannot quarrel with Taft without confessing that Taft was a mistake—his mistake, for he forced Taft's nomination as a Man of My Type. When did Theodore Roosevelt ever plead guilty to a blunder? When did he ever lay a desecrating hand upon the doctrine of his own infallibility? Can the Colonel recall an instance?

If Taft messes up My Policies it will prove only that Thor alone can wield Thor's hammer. Taft will be doing as well as any mere creature of flesh and blood could have been expected to, better indeed than anybody else could have done, for I trained him; I selected him; I revealed to him the sacred mysteries. I personally conducted him behind the veil of the temple. But My Policies are transcendent. They are part of the great world riddle and are to be solved only by the master mind that conceived them. You could not have Me, and you must learn that any substitute for the Real Thing is at best imperfect, unsatisfactory and fallible.

Our own guess is that when Mr. Roosevelt comes back he will be found in the ranks of Mr. Taft's outspoken defenders. We submit to one qualification, however, which is that before the return from Elba, William Howard Taft shall not have acquired too great popularity. The Little Father could forgive failure easier than too much success. He could tolerate Taft in the White House for eight years, but not Taft in the hearts of his countrymen. Should Taft happen to become the idol of the uplifter, the muck-raker, the cowboy and the plain people of the prairies, that would be another story. We should count the dinner as good as lost; for then the fur would indeed fly; then the tug of war would begin; then the shorter and uglier words would start to paw the earth and tug at the leash, while the only living ex-President shed his Rough Rider hat and proceeded to give an imitation of a human cyclone.

Maybe the Colonel's history is better than our psychology. We

shall see what we shall see. But in the meantime we look askance
upon the Colonel's suggestion of outside assistance in arranging
the menu. The *World* is just as Democratic as Colonel Watterson,
but a good dinner cannot be determined by a plebiscite or by the
initiative and referendum. It must be bossed by a benevolent
despot, and that is why we specified that the Colonel himself must
order the dinner and see it through from start to finish. If the
Colonel needs the counsel of a cabinet of chefs, well and good;
but we shall hold him personally responsible for the finished
product.

To the New York "World," Greeting!

(January 13, 1912)

"The break between Theodore Roosevelt and William Howard
Taft is at last complete, both political and personal," says the
New York *World*.

On, or about, the 27th of November, 1909, the Editor of the
Courier-Journal, just returned from abroad, was asked by the
newspaper reporters who gathered about him, what he thought
of the "Back from Elba" talk, and he answered that he thought
there was in it a forecast of coming events, that it meant the
possible reappearance of the ex-President in the political arena,
certainly collision between Theodore Roosevelt and William Howard Taft.

Thereupon the Editor of the *World* jumped all over the Editor of the *Courier-Journal;* whereupon the latter observed to
the former, "a dinner for four-and-twenty that the first Monday
of December, 1911, William Howard Taft and Theodore Roosevelt are at daggers drawn, the wager to be decided by the Chief
Justice, the Vice President and the Speaker of the House as
between us," and the former observed to the latter, "it is a
whack," or words to that effect. Then and there the Hon. Joseph
G. Cannon arose to say that he was a virtuous man and opposed
to all forms of gambling and would have nothing to do with a
business so obnoxious and nefarious, or words to that effect.
And the Editor of the *Courier-Journal*, having the love of the
Republican leader deep down in his heart of hearts, consolingly
remarked that Uncle Joe need not distress himself, "because on
the first Monday of December, 1911, he will not be Speaker of
the House."

The first Monday of December, 1911, has come and gone,
and the Editor of the *Courier-Journal* wins on both propositions.

Shall we have another Democratic Peace Dinner, with every

Presidential aspirant at table, or an all-around love feast, having
no party complexion, with Uncle Joe Cannon in the seat of honor?

*   *   *

Marse Henry

(January 16, 1912)

The New York *World* is what the more æsthetic members of
the Young Men's Corinthian Association would call "a dead,
game sport." It is in point of fact a thoroughbred. It comes
handsomely and promptly to time. If the Editor of the *World*
had known that the Editor of the *Courier-Journal* is the only
child of the seventh daughter of the seventeenth son in a straight
line from Shohr Thynge, in early ages the boss-prophet of Cale-
donia—that, as a matter of fact, the Editor of the *Courier-
Journal* never missed his forecast but once in his life and that in
and enduring the High Waters of '49, which don't count—our
esteemed contemporary would not have ventured upon a predes-
tined trial of anticipatory mind-reading. Yet, since wagers-of-
chance for victuals smell sweet to Heaven and blossom in the
sight of angels, the forthcoming dinner shall be without a blem-
ish; a very affair of the gods. Let us have every proper and
all possible ceremony. To that end there should be and need be
no haste. Why not make it the occasion for fitly celebrating
the next anniversary birthday of Thomas Jefferson? Time must
be given the poets to sing, the orators to prepare, the caterers to
provide. Even the newspapers might be taken into counsel and
confidence and an invitation be extended the more suggestive
for sealed proposals. We pause for breath and a reply.

INTERVIEWING HIMSELF

The editor made his own profession the butt of a joke when,
sojourning on the west coast of Florida in his active year
of 1908, he wrote an interview with himself in mock protest
against the methods of the American reporter. The com-
munication attracted widespread attention in the United
States, as Mr. Watterson knew it would, and was an example
of his facility in going out with one stone and bringing home
a bagful of game. He used this article as a reminder of his
life-long aversion to reporters' free-hand interviews and
his practice in always writing out for the press a desired
quotation. But he also employed this "authorized interview"
to dispose of some prevalent fallacies touching himself.

Every Man His Own Boswell

(February 19, 1908)

I

To him who journeys overland there are other perils than those of the impact of locomotives and the unseen broken rail. There is the hold-up in the station and there is the ambuscade in the lobby of the hotel; sometimes it is a pair of callow legs with a moon face attachment, sent out by the City Editor "to try it on a dog"; and sometimes it is Mr. Hawkeye, the famous journalistic detective, under direct and special orders from the Managing Editor himself. Occasionally a whole bunch of the boys swoop down upon you, and then it is "take my reputation, but spare my life," or words to that effect.

To be bidden abruptly to stand and deliver; to be required to furnish copy for somebody else's composing room when you would not obey a call from your own; to be caught by the nape of the neck and the seat of the breeches and tossed heels over head into print, willy nilly—another man undertaking after five minutes of random talk to tell the public what he thinks you think on every imaginable subject, but in your name and the first person singular, with quotation marks, as if he were quoting your precise language, though he has never taken a note nor used any characteristic form of expression, not even made a scratch of pencil—these are some of the dangers which give an added terror to modern travel.

I have been so often a victim that I sometimes wonder I am yet alive. That I retain any public respect is a miracle. Vainly have I advanced my own pretensions as a newspaper reporter; have urged the folly of carrying coals to Newcastle; have represented that birds of prey should spare one another; that there should be humanity among chevaliers of industry, discrimination among wolves, honor among thieves. "Come down out of that tree, Mr. Coon," says Capt. Scott, from the Night Assignment; and if you don't come down and look pleasant, too, next day you shall see the picture of Mrs. Winslow or Mother Eddy decorating the outside page of the Daily Bumble Bee as your very latest!"

Now, I am grown mighty tired of this and I am resolved, at least once in my life, to be accurately reported. I want a first-class job, and as the sole means to that end, and at the same time as a sample of my particular handicraft, I am going to report myself. I have the warrant of so good an authority as Dr. Oliver

Wendell Holmes for this. "Every man his own Boswell," the
Autocrat put upon his title page. Let me at least try to follow
in his illustrious footsteps.

II

Colonel——! They always say "Colonel"—why I know not!
(The Colonel took another whiff from the long Cuba-six—) It
is true that I have never used tobacco, nor smoked a cigar in my
life; but think of a Kentuckian without his weed! He might
as well be without a mustache, or a gun."

"What is it you want, young man?" says the Colonel kindly.
"Have you lost anything?"

"No, sir, but I shall lose my job if you refuse to talk."

"Refuse to talk, you jackanapes! What am I here for but
to talk? What was this station built for but to shelter me whilst
I talk? What is that train waiting for but to hear me talk?
Do you see this grip, sir? It contains nothing but six-shooters,
mint juleps and talk, sir! Fire away, sir, and I will talk! I will
talk you, sir, like any nightingale, so that the ladies shall say,
let him talk again."

"Well, Colonel——"

"Yes, sir, go on, sir, don't be bashful, sir." (It will be observed that they insist upon the "sir," though they mistakenly
print it "sah," when, if they had any ear for music and verisimili-
tude, they would spell it "suh.")

"What do you think of Teddy?"

"You mean the President, I suppose, sir? Young man, when
you speak of dignitaries, give each his proper style and title.
Never call a Captain Lieutenant, nor a General Major. The
President's name is Theodore, not Teddy. His other name is
Roosevelt. Oblige me by saying either Mr. Roosevelt or Mr.
Theodore Roosevelt, or just plain the President. I think very
well of him around about in spots, sir. He ought to have been
the Editor of a daily newspaper. The last time I was in London
I heard the Lord Chancellor say to the Archbishop of Canterbury
that if Mr. Theodore Roosevelt had charge of the London *Times*,
he would double its circulation in a fortnight. The learned prelate concurred in the remark of his noble friend."

"But as Mr. Roosevelt is not the Editor of the London *Times*,
nor likely to be, how about him as President of the United
States?"

"Now there you corner me." The Colonel obviously began to
be interested, to drop the tone of sarcasm with a k. and to wear
the air of a man who was ready to get down to business. "There
you put me to thinking, sir. If Teddy were Billy—excuse my
French!—the thing would be dead easy. But, Teddy being

Teddy, Theodore being Theodore, Roosevelt being Roosevelt—
and all of them Republicans—it is a kind of conundrum."

"But that last message of his," the Reporter ventured; "wasn't
that a corker?"

The Colonel frowned. "Young man," says he, "never use
slang. Nothing so ill becomes a writer for the press as slang.
Nothing so gives a reporter away as slang. Say sockdolager, sir.
It was a sockdolager. Too long for a pert paragraph—too
piquant and spicy for a sermon—it most reminded me of one
of Mr. George Bernard Shaw's prefaces—musically speaking, a
prelude in G sharp—taking the high C, as, in the olden time, an
Irish thoroughbred might take a six-barred gate."

"Its philosophy?"

"Splendid."

"Its morality?"

"Sublime."

"Its politics?"

"A cross between Felix Adler and Cæsar's Commentaries,
with a dash of Tom Lawson! The President is a many-sided
man. He must delight in private theatricals as much as in outdoor
amusements such as bear hunting and riding or walking through
the rain. And he is a good actor, too. When he puts on some
of those togs he stole from Mr. Bryan when Bryan thought
he was swimming and marches down to the footlights to fire off
the two hoss pistols he looks just like the peerless Nebraskan.
One can fancy he sees Bryan just behind doing the gesture play;
though, to complete the impersonation, Mr. Bryan should extend
one hand through the arms of Mr. Roosevelt, and twirl the fingers from the Presidential nose as if to say, 'Don't we apples
swim?'"

"Champ Clark seems to be delighted."

"Why not? We are all delighted. John Tyler saved the
country from High Tariff and The Bank. Andrew Johnson
rescued the Nation from the Mexicanizing process of old Ben
Wade and Thaddeus Stevens. But Roosevelt is as a giant to
these. He has taken the hydra-headed monster of Plutocracy
by the jaws and split him wide open, spilling his entrails all
the way from the Rockeyfellowships of the Chicago University
to the Oil Tanks of Wall Street, and forced the Republican party
to fall in behind and applaud his act. That is a miracle. Who
made the Standard Oil Monopoly? The Railways under the
patronage and inspiration of the Republican Party? Who made
the Steel Kings of Pittsburgh? The Protective Tariff, per-
petuated by the Republican Party. To what Campaign Fund did
Old High Finance pour out his millions? The Republican Campaign Fund. Yet, here we have the recipient of all these favors

—the residuary legatee of the usufruct of High Tariff and High Finance—completely taking the wind out of all other Radical sails—turning on the light upon predatory wealth—pouring a flood of sunshine into the dark places made hideous by Harriman & Company—with the intrepidity of a Ben Tillman and the daring of a Bob La Follette, to say nothing about the unction of a Bryan and the incisiveness of an Arthur Brisbane. It is incredible; not, as Dr. Johnson said of the dancing of the dog that, considered from a Democratic standpoint, it is so extraordinary in itself, as that a Republican President should do it at all."

"What will be its effect?"

"By all rules, its immediate effect should be the defeat of the Republicans in the coming Presidential election. To all intents and purposes the President says to his party: 'You must take Taft, or me.' They don't dare take him. He would not dare to run. If Bryan cannot beat Taft, he cannot beat anybody. I allow for the disaffection. But this will cut both ways. The Republicans only saved Hughes out of the wreck in New York a year ago. Can they pull Taft through? And what about Ohio? The Eastern writers figure it on paper that Bryan cannot carry a state on the Wall Street side of the Alleghenies. I am not so sure about that. Cleveland's chances were not so good when, in 1892, he went away from Chicago to face a party in New York sullen and divided. The Homestead riots arrived in the nick of time. Inside of a week the Labor Unions were transferred bodily from the Republicans to the Democrats. I see no reason for believing that times are going to mend measurably between now and November. The argument against Mr. Bryan is tolerably cogent. I know, because time and again I have made it. But, in relying on that, the Republicans will lean upon a broken reed—idle hands and empty stomachs have no ears for oratory and do not listen to reason. Besides, if Taft, the heir-at-law of Roosevelt, why not Bryan, his own progenitor? Taft, with a Republican Senate, might play havoc; but what could Bryan do against a Republican Senate? Even predatory wealth—Mr. Roosevelt's Criminals of Plutocracy—might take this view. In other words, the President has made Mr. Bryan seem a Conservative."

"Would you vote for Mr. Bryan yourself?"

The Colonel frowned again. "Young man," he said solemnly, "what do you take me for? I never crossed a Democratic ticket in my life. As I have often indicated, there are many things in Mr. Bryan's idea of Democracy which I do not approve—some articles in his confession of faith which I reject—but our objective point, the good of the many, not the benefit of the few, has ever been and now is the same. The points I have made against him have related rather to the practical than the ethical. I have not taken him at his face value. I have challenged his proceedings often. But, outside my objections, enough remains to make a case. We agree in many essentials. Just as I believe in a certain rotation in office as indispensable to the justice and vitality of party organization, do I believe in the rotation of parties in the Government as indispensable to that equilibrium of power without which our institutions would veer perilously close to oligarchy. Long tenure begets proscription. The Democratic party grew so strong in power that it was able to make its exit thence the signal for a bloody war. The Republican party should not be kept in power so long that its leaders will forget that there is a Constitution, that there are a people and a God. Of course, I shall vote for Mr. Bryan, sir. You must take me for a dam'd fool, sir—a dam'd fool!"

(The Colonel did not actually use those exact and profane words, but that is the way the boys like to trim off their copy, and, as a true craftsman, I do not like to go against usage!)

"What about Hughes?"

"Well, it begins to look as though Roosevelt can prove one too many against Hughes as Cleveland proved one too many against Hill. The President is a mighty clever practical politician, let me tell you. That last message kind o' brings the ceiling down—anyway, the cornice. Yet, if he does not nominate Taft on the first ballot, Hughes would seem the logic on the second."

"And Fairbanks?"

"The Vice President is the worst-used public man of his time. He is a gentleman of high merit, of real ability, and an orthodox, lifelong Republican. If antecedents and opinions expressed the logic of the situation he would be the nominee. Defeat with Fairbanks might prove less disastrous than victory with Taft. It would at least leave Republicanism normal. That cocktail affair was discreditable to the Methodist Church. The enemies of the Vice President in his own party have used it disgracefully. If I were an old-line Republican I would be for Fairbanks. If I were Fairbanks I would pool my issues with Hughes and Uncle Joe and play Warwick to the new administration."

"And 'Uncle Joe'?"

"Alas," said the Colonel, "Uncle Joe has no more committees to make, no more chairmanships to give—not in this Congress, anyhow—and when the Representatives separate and go to their several homes, their enthusiasm is likely to ooze out at the palms of their hands, as it were, like Bob Acres' courage."

I vouch for the foregoing. It may not be quite up to date—
this is a long ways on the offside of nowhere—but it is authentic.
It is like the author's autograph, genuine. I know because I
wrote it myself.

H. W.

Naples-on-the-Gulf
   Lee County, Florida

THE *COURIER-JOURNAL* AT FORTY

It was an omnium gatherum of wise saws and ancient instances
which the editor set down in his newspaper on that Sunday
morning that marked the fortieth birthday of the *Courier-
Journal.* He discussed the principles which had guided his
editorial career; the private newspaper cemetery which the
Courier-Journal had filled with its rivals; the death of its
own prosperous weekly in the Free Silver fight which he
declares to have been his newspaper's "one indisputable
mistake." He lovingly strummed a few of his famous old
phrases like "Democracy, Unterrified and Undefiled" and
"Back to the Constitution" and "A tariff for revenue only."

Retrospective

(Sunday, November 8, 1868—Sunday, November 8, 1908)

I

The *Courier-Journal* was born forty years ago today. On
the morning of Sunday, the 8th of November, 1868, the people
of Louisville awoke to find upon their doorsteps, instead of the
old *Journal* and the old *Courier,* which had contended for
their suffrage and divided it, a sprawling and a stranger sheet,
with a big, hyphenated headline which announced the *Courier-
Journal.* It had come without warning and it took the town
completely by surprise; the negotiations that led to the union,
involving the purchase and ultimate absorption of the *Democrat*
having been so quietly conducted that, until the eve of the Sunday
in question, they were unknown to any but the parties to them.

The surprise was very great, nor was it a pleased surprise, for
each of the contracting papers had its enemies and its friends,
yielding the newcomer a divided welcome, and presaging a public
opinion at the outset suspicious and for a time hostile, but always,
and from that day to this, critical and exacting.

The City of Louisville was as a child in swaddling clothes.

There were not exceeding a hundred thousand people, all told, collected around the Falls of the Ohio. Facing Northward, the commercial leaders of this little community saw Chicago directly in the foreground, with Cincinnati on the East and St. Louis on the West, double and treble its own size, its rivals, and rather disdainful rivals for the trade South of us.

Experience had clearly demonstrated that two newspapers of the first class, though equally dividing the local business, could not possibly exist, and this had led to a consolidation whose aim was, by stopping a ruinous competition, to give Louisville an organ which could adequately fight its battles against Chicago, St. Louis and Cincinnati, in place of three weak and warring contestants cutting one another's throats, as it were, for a patronage which was wholly insufficient.

The *Courier-Journal* was thus the pioneer in the movement toward the readjustment of newspaper properties which, after the War of Secession, was forced upon the farseeing and has since marked the journalism of the greater Cities of the Union, as its present nomenclature attests, the *Post-Dispatch,* of St. Louis; the *Record-Herald,* of Chicago, and the *Commercial Tribune,* of Cincinnati, with the *Courier-Journal* leading the van of progress and prosperity.

II

Independence was the lodestar which hung over the *Courier-Journal* at its birth, and has steadily guided its onward way; pecuniary independence—for the honor of the cloth; intellectual independence—for the public good.

Anterior to its coming, the newspapers of Louisville had largely looked to Main Street for their business, to Frankfort for their party order. None of them was strong enough to stand upon its merits and its rights, and to go its own gait, regardless of the merchants and the politicians. The *Courier-Journal* flew the flag of freedom from the first. It proposed to be its own master—to do its own leading—and, if die it must, to die fighting.

Long, indeed, and bitter was the strife, unyielding, over-confident its struggle for existence. Twice the disgruntled party managers raised great sums of money and put forth all the agencies of prejudice and misrepresentation to destroy it. Many minor enterprises arrayed themselves against it; most of them vituperative; none of them proposing to allow it any quarter; the unvarying purpose not to live and let live with the expanding growth of the city, but the extermination, root and branch, along with the disgrace, of what had in reality become an institution. With a single exception the *Courier-Journal* felt none of these assaults. It easily ran down and sank the antiquated and lumbering old hulk of the Bourbons, which, top-heavy with distinguished party leaders and loaded with party spoils, opened fire upon it in the early Seventies, from guns that did more execution at the breach than the muzzle. The succeeding penny-whistles that sought to pepper it with mustard seed, and generally in the afternoon, proved laughable to the public without so much as ruffling its equanimity. Thus till well into 1896 the paper enjoyed plain sailing. It had crossed the stormy seas of the Reconstruction era and had weathered the headlands of Greenbackism—riding a flowing tide—and it seemed to be entering a snug harbor, when it struck a snag in Free Silver.

Within a year it lost one half of its daily circulation and nearly the whole of its mammoth weekly circulation. The three succeeding years it cost more of patient endurance, of unremitting tact and judgment to save the property than thirty years before it had cost to create it. But it was saved. It was not only saved, but revitalized; so that the elder of its founders was spared to see two record seasons, nineteen hundred and nineteen hundred and one, before at a great and honored age he was called to his account, having served faithfully and given generously during a life of signal usefulness, of singular devotion to its obligations and of very inadequate compensation.

III

Between the Sunday of its arrival, November 8, 1868, and this present Sunday, the 8th of November, 1908, forty years of shine and shower have passed over the good gray head of "the Old Lady at the Corner," who, like her sister, the venerable Old Lady of Threadneedle Street, may say, "there was drought. I withstood it; there were panics, I mounted and rode them; empires have risen and fallen; republics have come and gone; armies and parties have mustered and marched. I have seen them all and have survived them all; great is the goodness of God and great the glory of Duty done for Duty's sake!"

That Sunday in November of 1868, when its eyes first opened to the light, they looked upon a great Democratic disaster in the defeat of Seymour and Blair, as now they look upon another in the defeat of Bryan and Kern. During the four decades intermediate there were times when the world showed dark, not only for the Democratic party, but for Constitutional Government. For a while the Opposition had not votes enough in Congress to order a roll call. The people owed to seven brave and upright Republicans their escape from the Mexicanization of the Republic, threatened by the impeachment of a President who had committed no legal wrong. Not one Republican, either upon the

Supreme Bench or in Congress, was found brave and upright
enough to rescue the country in 1877 from the fraudulent count
of the Electoral votes and the seating in the Presidency of a
man not elected to it.

The Democratic party leaders had not the wisdom to follow
up their advantage in 1880 by an appeal to the public conscience
on that issue, as they had not the wisdom to improve their opportunity to reduce the Tariff to a revenue basis, when they
were given the chance by the popular verdict of 1892. It got
to be a kind of truism that the Democrats could be relied on
to perpetrate some folly at the critical moment, the patient donkey
becoming the accepted and seemingly the appropriate party
emblem.

In Kentucky, especially, we came upon evil days. Faction begot faction. Reason fled to the rear and passion forged its way
to the front. The pall of tragedy fell over the sea, the very angels
wept, so that one Kentuckian speaking to another might not un-
truly, nor unfitly, repeat the words of Antony:

> "Then I, and you, and all of us fell down,
> Whilst bloody treason flourished over us."

A great President had already fallen beneath the assassin's
blow, when the *Courier-Journal* was born in 1868, and two more
were to follow him, the buoyant, intellectual and affectionate
Garfield and the gentle, sweet-natured, most lovable McKinley;
proof of the wickedness of party strife o'erleaping the limitations
of patriotic manhood; warnings to the people against faction; for
none of our martyrs to the Cause of Liberty and Popular Government had been charged with official malfeasance or private
wrong.

Throughout all the vicissitudes of time and chance, the
Courier-Journal, striving ever to stand upon its feet and upright,
has sought also and always to keep the middle of the road and
to go straight ahead. Its battles have been aggressive, never
defensive. Yielding combat to all comers, it has refused it to
those only whose dishonest perversity insured nothing but mud-
slinging, responsive not to truth, surely hurtful to the common
weal.

Almost continuously it had been compelled by its convictions
of right and duty to choose between alternatives, to fight with
its arm in a sling—as in 1872, in 1880, in 1900 and in 1904—or
else, as in 1896, to separate itself from its life-long party associates and to make a brave, but futile sacrifice for nothing; its
one indisputable mistake, for which it was made to pay, and
justly to pay, very dearly indeed.

It had stood by a sound currency and the Nation's credit, from first to last. Neither was in reality menaced in 1896. The paper might as well have saved its money and its credit by doing in that year what it had to do four years later to save its life. And—irony of fate, after all—it came to regard the Boanerges of Free Silver—the boy orator of the Platte—as one of the simplest, purest and ablest of public men; to believe that his election to the Presidency tendered the people a change of parties needful to the cause of freedom and reform; and to regard his defeat as a national misfortune.

The time will probably never come when the *Courier-Journal* will be exempt from the accusations of corrupt motives, which invariably assail it whatever it says or does. Originally, it was represented by its enemies as a preacher of the Freedmen's Bureau, because it stood for the habilitation of the negroes of the South according to the terms of the three last amendments to the Constitution of the United States, and fought for the obliteration of the old, obsolete black laws from the statute books of Kentucky. Then, because it fought Greenbackism, it was a hired minion of the Bloated Bondholders. Then, because of the support it gave Samuel J. Tilden, it was in the pay of the Sage of Gramercy Park, which held mortgages upon its buildings and its columns. Then it was rolling in wealth furnished by the Gold Bugs. And now—"last scene of all" to this immediate moment "that ends this strange eventful history," it is the attorney of the Breweries and Distilleries, for no other reason than that it is opposed to a prohibition that does not prohibit, that it is opposed to paternal government and sumptuary invasions of personal liberty, and that it would save Kentucky from the ignominy of Maine and Georgia, where the liquor laws promote hypocrisy, favor lawlessness and foster smuggling and adulteration; the ready recourse in both states of the red-nosed angels of Religion and the rascally Grafters of politics.

Time, which usually reveals all things, proves nothing if not the disinterested and unselfish devotion of the *Courier-Journal* to its intellectual convictions and the public good as it has been able to see it.

Not infrequently the false charges directed against it have been actually true of those that made them. In every instance where, with respect to the policy to be pursued, it has differed with its party, the final results have vindicated its forecasts, its mental and moral probity; most notably in its attitude toward the various realignments immediately succeeding the War of Secession; in its attitude toward the revision of the Tariff, "for revenue only"; and in its attitude toward a sound and stable monetary system. Often has it had to take its life in its hands to rescue its own people from themselves. Always has it been subjected to the enmity of the vicious and the venal—to the organized misrepresentation, constant, unscrupulous and methodical—the tribute that envy pays to success, having for its basis its secret admiration which even the self-conscious bad sometimes entertain for the prosperous and the upright.

To all such its silent answer has been and will ever be, "we shall consider ourselves as increasing in honor the farther we diverge from you."

It will be gratifying to its friends to learn that never in its history has the *Courier-Journal* carried so great a volume of business patronage—both as to circulation and advertising—as at this moment, whilst the result in Kentucky of the latest election, when it led its party to the recovery of the state lost to it by bad leadership, is most gratifying to it. Upon the same principles of policy and conduct it will continue to preach the Gospel of Democracy, Unterrified and Undefiled. "Back to the Constitution" is the only hope of Good Government. The *Courier-Journal* will make that its shibboleth. A scorner of shams, it will fight as it has always fought extremism of every sort, whether arrayed on the side of self-seeking Pharisaism, or visionary sentimentalism, or hysterical morality. A friend of Temperance, it will fight that sumptuary legislation, which is aimed alike by political interest and fanatical bigotry, to abridge the freedom of the individual and to interfere with the habits of the people. It will contend for home rule in the States, in the counties and in each community; meeting crazy prohibition, which, being ever the sport and prey of corrupt partyism, has always been a failure, with local option laid in popular sentiment, and looking to regulation consonant with sane public opinion. In Louisville and in Kentucky, it will be found, as it has always been found, on the side of order and law; in the Nation for the strict letter of the Constitution of our fathers, for the representative character of the two Houses of Congress; for the separation and independence of the three co-ordinate branches of the Government; for an honest and progressive administration of the affairs by the Chief Magistrate and the Executive Department, and, Keynote to all else, for "a Tariff for Revenue Only."

From these ideas and aims it will make no departure; as it has been, it will be, and, Democrat or Republican, "Dam'd be he that first cries, hold, enough!" its motto being now, as in the beginning, borrowed from Burke's noble dictum, "applaud us if we run; console us if we fall; but let us pass on—for God's sake—let us pass on!"

ON JOURNALISM

Himself a conspicuous example of a personality bursting through the editorial mask, Mr. Watterson always contended that personal journalism was the best. In his day and his section of the United States responsibility and identity were necessarily associated, he said, but the reason in this instance for the man being as famous as the newspaper is because the newspaper was the man. He possessed a considerable share of the stock of the company, and by an arrangement with his partner he was the master of the editorial column. In this way the editor was able to develop his own ideas and ideals, and the inevitable result was what is called personal journalism.

Mr. Watterson was fond of saying that, even "with the purse commanding the sword," journalism need not lack any of the force or influence which he himself developed in it. But the fact remains that he never experienced a condition of this sort, and no editor who did has ever emerged from his page in the full light of his own personality, as Mr. Watterson did.

The following article on personal journalism is selected from many he wrote on the subject as it includes the characteristics of all of them. It contains certain apparent conflicts of statement and takes a gloomy view of the future of the editorial. Yet Mr. Watterson lived to recant his statement that, without possessing editorial control, an editor could speak his full message; and also his statement that editorializing was a dying art. For in 1919 he retired as Editor Emeritus of the *Courier-Journal* because he did not agree with the policy of its new owner toward the League of Nations. And during the World War he used the "dying" editorial form of expression to do some of the most effective work of his career.

One sentence in the following, however, is calculated to cheer many American newspaper men to whom it applies: "The humble anonymous writer is not likely long to remain either humble or anonymous if he has something of special value to communicate . . . and knows how to put it."

Personal Journalism

(March 2, 1909)

I

An "argufication" between the eminent Dr. Parkhurst and Mr. Arthur Brisbane on the subject of his "anonymity" in newspaper writing presents some suggestive features and moves a rather old hand at the bellows to "a few remarks."

The point of view is the main point. Doctor Parkhurst and Mr. Brisbane cannot agree. They argue from opposite premises. The one is nothing if not an individualist. The other is still masked—though not half concealed—by his service. Every man is more or less the creature of his environment. It may not be thought obtrusive in a veteran invited to this debate if he take into account his own experience.

I began my newspaper career a devotee of impersonal journalism. I had lived and earned my living in London and been impressed by the dignity of the editorial anonym. The broad columns, the clear type and the absence of title lines had a charm for me. When the negotiations which made me the successor of Mr. Prentice were completed they included a provision for his retention—much against his wish. He wanted to go to California, where his brother-in-law, Calhoun Benham, had a ranch to which he had been urged to come and pass the remainder of his days.

I refused to listen to it. It seemed to me unmeet that Prentice and the *Journal* he had founded should ever be separated whilst he lived. "My dear young friend," at last he said, "you will build up the *Journal,* and in building it up you will build me up. I may live a long time. It is not fair that your work should be hid behind the shadow of my fame."

The very last thing I thought of was fame. I was a young fellow of eight and twenty, with a wife and a brood of children already in sight, and my sole aim was to improve my worldly fortune and condition. Mr. Prentice survived nearly three years. I was more than content to work behind the shadow of his fame; especially as the work proved very remunerative. I had as little personal vanity as Mr. Haldeman, who had none at all. When Mr. Prentice died we agreed that now we would have a newspaper as absolutely impersonal as any published in England. Alack the day! That was not the rule in the country—it was particularly not the rule in Kentucky—and it was not to be. Personal detraction, taking license from the absence of retort, amounted to personal defamation. The public could see, not virtue but only cowardice, in silence. I was at last impelled to indite a paragraph some five columns in length bearing the descriptive caption, "Exclusively Personal," which took in each individual assailant having any responsibility and embraced the whole field of misrepresentation.

Then and there my scheme of impersonal journalism went down, if not with a dull thud, yet quite beneath the wave, never to flutter again; though I can truly say that there have been times when I became so sick seeing my name in print that I have wished the letters that spelt it might be lost from the alphabet.

This autobiographic résumé, however egotistical, may serve to throw some light upon what I shall have to say touching the opinions of Doctor Parkhurst and the opinions of Mr. Brisbane in the matter of anonymous newspaper writing; because whatever I may think about it springs from many opportunities for observation along with some serious reflection and actual knowledge.

II

To the newspaper drudge the futility of all newspaper writing must often edge its way into his tired fancy. The best of it seems so quickly swallowed by the ocean of currency, like waves upon the beach, each day succeeding the other to efface its existence. Words, words; even thoughts, thoughts; what does it matter?

Yet to those of us who live, move and have our being in the grind of daily journalism and in none other, it matters a great deal; so that, after a bit of rest—a night of sleep—under the spur of the news of the morning—maybe under the inspiration of some principle, or dogma, or measure—we take up the pen again, and rush along the page, and blot out and interline and read the proof and revise it amid the glow of the effusion and the glare, if not the glory, of print, inwardly exclaiming, "Now that is something like!" to see the poor, ephemeral thing, as a skyrocket, come down like a stick, its coruscations lost forever in the darkness of illimitable space.

Says Dr. Parkhurst:

"The matter of anonymous authorship is of practical importance to all readers of newspapers and magazines.

"To read an article by an unknown author is to put one's self under the instruction of an unaccredited teacher.

"The worth of an opinion is approximately measured by the moral and intellectual competency of the man or woman by whom the opinion is expressed, so that to yield one's self to the influence of productions that are not guaranteed by authorship known to be authoritative is to treat one's mind in the same way that a mountain climber treats his body when he commits himself to a guide who shows no license and no credentials.

"For to whatever degree we may think we may hold our convictions in reserve, our opinions do have direction given them by the things that we read.

"With the abundance of literature that is in the field it is too much to ask of readers in these hurried days to find out for themselves whether what is put before them is worthy of their perusal, when their time might have been saved them by a distinct announcement of the name and credibility of the author.

"Of course anonymity is a device practiced by publishers in the interest of economy, as it enables them to pad their columns with matter that is cheap without its being known, that it emanates from a cheap writer."

In the main Dr. Parkhurst is right. It may not be that publishers through economic considerations prefer cheap writers and cheap writing. It is the rather that, unable to obtain better, and unwilling to abdicate power and transfer authority to any mere wage-earner, they content themselves with padding. Hence the degeneracy of what is called the Editorial Page. Emanating from anonymous persons having no original jurisdiction, nor sense of responsibility, or conviction, it lacks equally strength and continuity of thought. To that extent its weight is lessened, its hold is loosened and its influence is abridged.

All of the great newspaper properties are passing into the ownership of corporations or estates. As a consequence the opportunities for individualism of any sort are few. They are likely to grow even rarer still. Dr. Parkhurst's intimation that they are edited from the Counting Room, however, is not necessarily a reproach. To the extent that it means that the newspaper, like other fabrications, is made to sell to yield a profit—that it seeks to be self-sustaining, in order that it may achieve "the glorious privilege of being independent"—it realizes an aspiration, indeed the yearning, of a time when the newspaper had a hard struggle to keep alive, more or less the slave of the niggardly advertisers and the local ringsters, often ill-able to call its soul its own.

Authority must be lodged somewhere. In the person of a visible Editor, it seemed to carry with it a certain guarantee wanting to the impersonal and anonymous; but, there is no reason why the Counting Room, conducted with integrity on business principles, should not render the public equally valuable and disinterested service. There needs to be a perfect understanding and agreement between the Editorial Room and the Counting Room if good results are to follow, either to the people or the paper. Because of the change from individual to family, or corporate ownership, the modern trend, undoubtedly, inclines toward the Counting Room. He who holds the purse commands the sword. The great journal of the future may be as exact, as metallic and as rayless as a banking institution, dealing exclusively in news, editorializing a lost art.

Nevertheless, I agree with Dr. Parkhurst that the reader wants to know whom he is reading after.

Primarily the Daily Newspaper is the History of Yesterday. If it should perform this function simply, having no other end in view, its value to the community would be priceless. Intelligent readers, intrusted with the facts and unhindered by pressure, could reach their own conclusions. But, as a rule, the Daily Newspaper accepts no such limitation. It sets up for a Teacher as well as a Historian. It would influence—"mould," I believe, is the word —public opinion; yet it is not always the public—too often it is some private—interest, which colors its narrative and shapes its oracles, fitting the one into the other, without that sense of accountability to God and Truth which ought to lie at the bottom of every man's purpose, and which does lie at the bottom of every good man's heart. Here is where personality, direct, individual responsibility comes in.

The Editorial Page is valuable in the degree that it aids the reader to digest the news. Under the changed conditions it is becoming, if it has not already become, a rather useless appendage —not even ornamental—reminding one of those clusters of artificial flowers which at the more pretentious railway eating houses are supposed to decorate the tables and to deceive the way-farer. Yet ought it, after the exhilaration—the distractions and excitement—of the News pages, to be as a raised dais in the center of a great hall, a seat of power and charm; an elevation from which to survey the passing show, having its lights adjusted the better to set forth this passing show, and its ready chorus to explain it.

An Editorial Page thus conceived and executed could not fail to impress itself upon the thought of the time at once an influence and a feature, an arm of the service and a commercial asset.

Beneath the rule of a supervision wholly adequate it would soon rival the News Departments in point of popular interest. One single editorial, embodying the rationale of the situation and appearing each day of the year, would come to be sought by intelligent readers as an essential part of their morning paper; how much more a page covering the entire range of the day's doings, dealing with each topic according to its quantum and its kind, "from gay to grave, from lively to severe."

Except it be thus delivered the Editorial Page were best extinguished. To set apart a certain number of columns for the equivocal dignity of big type, to fill these columns with perfunctory matter; with matter as lifeless as dolls stuffed with sawdust; equally wanting the elements of conviction and constancy; one thing today, another tomorrow; unirradiated by any gleam of light, undiversified, even by a trick of fancy, uniform only in flippancy, or dullness, is to disfigure the Page, to degrade the Editorial. But directed and made up by a man of intelligence, not necessarily what is called an able or a brilliant man—merely a man of sound understanding, painstaking and conscientious in his work, upright and elevated in his aim, having a sufficient knowledge of affairs, a sincere spirit and a level head—the good of such an adjunct of the daily news—such an index to the History of Yesterday—were incalculable; and, though it lead to the personal journalism which Mr. Brisbane discredits, it would at least embody a responsible journalism; much to be preferred to prevailing tendencies, which, I cannot help thinking, were better honored in the breach than the observance.

Thus far I agree with Dr. Parkhurst and disagree with Mr. Brisbane.

III

We live in a world not merely of facts but of men; of human sentiments and ideas. Strictly speaking, the impersonal is impossible. Somebody is always behind the fact, behind the idea, behind the expression.

"In newspaper and magazine writing," says Mr. Brisbane, "a great part is to some extent perfunctory, part of a routine. It should be well conducted, careful and accurate, but it need not be made personal or individual. If pictures are for sale, you want to know the name of the artist—but you do not demand to know the name of the man who wrote the catalogue.

"If pictures are for sale, one wants to know that they are genuine and that the dealer is trustworthy. Neither the newspaper nor the magazine can be well conducted unless there be some capable and responsible head who is at once visible and accessible. He need not press his personality upon his readers; but in proportion as he is known of men, and respected, will his publication command the public confidence."

Mr. Brisbane continues:

"Somehow or other, when we behold the poor anonymous writer, with his little nose rubbed in the dust by the powerful

Dr. Parkhurst, we are moved to quote in feeble protest:
'They also serve who only stand and wait.'

"Ours is a voracious national brain. It devours great
quantities of reading matter. Not all of those that write can
be powerful and convincing like Dr. Parkhurst, or important
in themselves by virtue of past accomplishments as he is.

"The humble, anonymous writer who only stands and
waits hoping that some day he, too, may be worth while,
*has his little place in the world in which words have become
so important.*

"The humble anonymous writer" is not likely long to remain
either humble or anonymous, either obscure or poor, if he has
something of special value to communicate to the public and
knows how to put it for what it is worth. No man's nose need
be, nor can be, rubbed in the dust except he be some witling or
weakling unable to stand alone. The "silent singers," of whom
Dr. Holmes tells us, are everywhere; they to whom opportunity
has never come; they who, when it came, let it pass them by; but
can Mr. Brisbane think that any really great piece of writing was
ever wholly lost?

I quote again:

"There are all kinds of writers, all kinds of writing, as there are
all kinds of work in the world.

"When you hear Wotan, with a patch over his eye,
growling away, you want to know the *name* of that Wotan,
whether it be a Van Rooy or somebody else. You want to
identify Caruso and Tetrazzini. But you do not care so
much about the name of the man hidden in the stomach of the
dragon, and rumbling out the words, 'Lass mich schlafen.'

"You care even less about the name of the very worthy
people that sing in the chorus. You would be rather indignant
if the operatic managers insisted upon making you read all
the names of all the chorus singers and scene shifters—yet
they are important in opera.

"If you go to a famous restaurant in Paris, and if you
happen to know anything about eating, you may want to
know the name of the chef, the scientist in the white cap, that
does the cooking. But you do not insist upon knowing the
name of the waiter or the cashier."

Here, if Mr. Brisbane will allow me to say it without offense,
he confuses the physical and material with the moral and spiritual.
Surely writing, for all its varieties, is not as singing or cooking.
Nor is it, however picturesque it may be, as painting, which speaks

from the canvas to the eye and shows for itself. But ethical writing—the writing of ideas, convictions, sentiments—political, polemical writing, aimed to persuade, to convince, to convert—that must carry with it some credential attesting the character and authority of the writer if people are to listen and to heed, to read and to believe.

Neither the name nor the credential need appear at the mast-head of the publication, or the bottom of the column; Mr. Dana's name did not appear over the editorial page of the *Sun;* but, all the same, the public wants to know—and soon or late it will find out—in case it matters—who is responsible for what it reads in its accustomed newspapers.

But, let Mr. Brisbane proceed:

"Dr. Parkhurst, as it happens, is mistaken in his idea that 'anonymity is a device practiced by publishers in the interest of economy.' The Reverend Doctor, of course, has had no experience in the actual conduct of a newspaper. If he had had such experience he would know that nothing is more difficult to find, and sometimes nothing more *expensive,* than the really competent anonymous writers who *make* the news-paper and keep it going. It is an interesting fact that many anonymous writers are extremely well paid; one of them in one of our cities is paid more than the famous Mark Twain, several times as much as William Dean Howells, as much as the people pay to the President and about one-half of the Cab-inet put together; in short a very respectable salary, and all for anonymous work."

Here again Mr. Brisbane is confusing. He refers rather to the writers of narration, the staff of special writers, than to the writers of what the English call "the leading article," save in his own case, which is wholly exceptional; nay, as Mr. Brisbane puts it, apocryphal; because, although his name is blazoned nowhere upon the Hearst publications, he is coming to be as well known as Mr. Hearst himself. In the person of Mr. Brisbane many anomalous and fortuitous circumstances and conditions have met.

The London *Times* in the days of Delane was the apotheosis of the impersonal. Yet the personality of that eminent man could not be hid, whilst the Walter family through three generations stood as the embodiment of English conservatism and rich re-spectability, a kind of guarantee that the Thunderer was an Understudy of the Almighty. Indeed, it is not possible to conceal for any length of time, and it is not desirable to have concealed, the personality of any man of striking character, exercising power over a popular publication; to say nothing about those shining qualities of genius which, whether for good or evil, will elude the most obdurate anonym and penetrate all disguise; as in the case of Sir Walter Scott and George Eliot, and many old-time newspaper workers whom I might name, who wrote without signing their names to their screeds, but whose identity could not be kept in the dark.

In the following, with which I shall close these suggestive extracts from the writing of a man who, though the latest among newspaper workers to come to the front, is already well at the front, Mr. Brisbane is either at fault in his theory or else his observation and experience are at variance with mine.

"The fact is that a newspaper has or *ought to have*, its own character and individuality. That character is the sum of the effort and conscientiousness of various anonymous workers that do their best to build up a good machine. The newspaper is a machine for supplying information and promoting thought. It needs brilliant individuals. It is made much stronger by the signed work of such a man as Dr. Parkhurst. But it couldn't live without the steady, daily grind of the anonymous men.

"There is one other matter involved in the writing of signed articles, and that is the important matter of human vanity. It is a pathetic fact that many men write well, thinking of nothing but facts and the public, while they write anonymously. And the same men, especially when young, become foolish, egotistical, strive after unnatural and unwholesome effect, the moment their names are signed.

"It is often a great injustice to allow a young, inexperienced man to sign his name. His work in a newspaper like this goes into the hands of millions of readers. The importance which is due to their numbers he imagines due to himself and his own ability, and he is apt to be changed from a promising boy into a pretentious freak.

"Unless a man has a good deal of character, on the day that he signs his name he is apt to forget about the public and the matter intrusted to him, and begin thinking about himself."

The make-up of a successful newspaper involves an autocracy. A single master-mind must preside over it. Whether this emanate from Upstairs or Downstairs, from the Editorial Room or the Counting Room, it will give to the finished product offered the public whatever of individuality, or character, it has. No great newspaper was ever established, or created, upon any other plan.

Organization goes without saying; mechanical, typographic,

distributive; the placing of the commodity on the market to the best advantage; requiring in the publication department tact and judgment and enterprise and integrity. But the newspaper being made to sell should have, and the successful newspaper does have, a certain consistency of its own, sprung from a definite policy and in time acquiring a distinct constituency; its popularity, certainly its staying quality, measured by its attractiveness; its influence in the long run by its disinterestedness; the elements of ability and amiability playing important parts toward its acceptability.

The personal equation should augment the sense of public responsibility, not diminish it. He must be a very shallow person who thinks to exploit himself by his writing apart from the cause or occasion, the service or the subject matter. Such a writer would not last very long and could not acquire any serious standing.

The old personal journalists, such as Greeley and Prentice, Raymond and Forney, James Gordon Bennett and Sam Bowles and Father Ritchie were exploited in spite of themselves. Each of them was first of all true to his flag. The triumphs of each were due to himself and after their kind. But, they were very marked men. They lived in times and places less crowded than now. Individuality was easier and commanded a greater premium perhaps. But the throng is not even yet so great that rare men doing good work may be shut out from the public view. In short, personal journalism has merely changed some of its methods; its contemporary actors are not so idiosyncratic, or so much in evidence; but the individual character is there, and must be there; in New York, at least, a statute requiring the publication of responsible names; so that, to revive the old system, only a few more Brisbanes are required, and these are likelier to come than to stay away.

H. W.

Naples-on-the-Gulf, Florida

QUEER VIEWS ON WAR NEWS

Having been a newspaper publisher during the War of Sections, Mr. Watterson was not alarmed about censorship suggestions in 1917, as were most American proprietors of journals. Around and about the Confederate camps in Tennessee he had been the maker of a curious newspaper called the *Rebel,* and in the following article on press censorship he coolly and with amusement related an incident of how he misled his Union readers in the interest of the Confederate strategy. While the passage will make most American editors shudder, it exemplified Mr. Watterson's belief that news columns during a war were unreliable anyhow and they might as well be used to help the army. He had no faith in what he read between column rules during the World War and felt that censorship, real or by request, was working in every nation engaged.

During times of peace, on the contrary, this editor was a very lion against any suggestion of abridging the news by government or private activity. In war he was willing to reserve for free expression and relation only the editorials of his newspaper. But, in war or peace, he would not suffer the least infringement of those columns of opinion.

The Freedom of the Press

(April 25, 1917)

I

In the Senate's consideration of the Press Censor Bill the debate naturally took a wide range, both of subject matter and point of view, and inevitably much was said of a desultory and not wholly enlightening kind.

Even among newspaper men the precise relation of the newspaper to the official fabric has never been surely fixed. It remains for the most part a go-as-you-please. Like statesmanship, journalism is an indefinite quantity. Yet, publicity a kind of wherewithal of contemporary life, the press constitutes an actual and important department of the public service—called not inaptly the Fourth Estate—and Congress undertakes a delicate, if not a dangerous performance when it attempts by statute to regulate, especially to curtail, its manifold duties.

In times of peace the newspaper may be safely left to public opinion and the libel laws. How far these modifying agencies should in time of war be supplemented by legislative enactment is an open question. Neither freedom of speech nor of the press stands in such need of protection as they seemed to require when the First Amendment to the Constitution of the United States declared that "Congress shall make no law respecting an establishment of religion or prohibiting the free exercise thereof; or abridging the freedom of speech, or of the press; or the right of the people peaceably to assemble and to petition the Government for a redress of grievances."

Just as the sedition laws, intended to restrain license, ran in their execution to excess, were these guarantees, brought round by the popular reaction, adopted and imbedded in the organic chart. There they stand to be invoked against tyrannous repression. But they are supported by a compelling force in the trend of modern thought which inclines to the fullest liberty of expression and by a more educated sense of their duty in the men charged with editorial responsibility.

Let us say at once, therefore, that the leading newspapers of the country are not alarmed—or even agitated—by the disposition shown by some of the politicians at Washington and elsewhere to lay axe upon the First Amendment to the Constitution of the United States. They expect somehow to say their say and to have their fling. No President is likely to be over high and mighty in the exercise of censorial jurisdiction. The true objection to laws meant to be restrictive—and in reality vexatious—relates to their probable enforcement by subordinate officials upon the lesser newspapers.

As a rule shoulder-straps, clothed in a little brief authority, can and does make himself, as the darkey in the play observes, "very insuffensive." Redress is not usually right at hand. Hence official inhibition should be gingerly applied and its lines be clearly drawn.

There is no reason to doubt that the course pursued by Lord Northcliffe in this world war has been of inestimable value to England. Yet a drastic Government would have suppressed him. At the Confederate capital, during the War of Sections, John M. Daniel, a distinguished journalist of his time, through the Richmond *Examiner*, held the Administration of Jefferson Davis to rigorous account and in wholesome check, and, had it lain in any power to help the doomed cause of the South, his criticisms of the conduct of affairs would have served a good and not a bad purpose. That however is never the official view.

II

The publication of news is quite another matter. In war time military necessity has everywhere the right of way. Its censorship must be thorough and unquestioned.

An actual example may not be irrelevant, nor uninteresting. During the spring and summer of 1863 the Confederate army, commanded by General Braxton Bragg, opposed the advance of the Federal army, commanded by General W. S. Rosecrans in Middle Tennessee. There was a newspaper published at Chattanooga called the *Rebel*. It was a breezy, certainly a newsy little sheet, which had a habit of talking out in meeting and calling a spade a spade. This had brought its editor in collision with General Bragg. Except that behind 'him in more or less of personal intimacy and close concurrence, and sympathy, were most of the other generals of the army down in front, serious trouble might have been made for him and he might have been brought to a round turn.

But, wholly loyal, he was not without his own sense of responsibility. It happened that between the chief of the Military Secret Service, Colonel Alexander McInstry, and himself exceedingly friendly relations had long subsisted. He went to this officer and said:

"I know as well as you and General Bragg know the danger of unguarded newspaper publication directly in the rear of a fighting army. I must print something to meet the demand for news. What I do print is picked up helter-skelter here and there by gossip, grapevine and otherwise, and, hit or miss, is worked into the *Rebel's* daily situation article. It is without method, purpose or authenticity. I can never foresee what harm I may be doing. I want to do good, not harm. But I must have this newspaper feature. Now why should you not take it in hand and use it as a part of your secret service? With your actual and abundant information you can give me a much better situation article than I can possibly obtain. Your adjutant is an expert newspaper reporter. Let him prepare this and each night wire it to me. It shall appear just as you send it. Thus we shall commit no indiscretion and I shall be enabled to satisfy my public."

The offer was at once accepted, and from that time to the fall of Chattanooga, the *Rebel's* triple-leaded feature of features, "The Front," was composed and edited by the Secret Service Department of General Bragg's army, nobody the wiser or the loser, except those who took it for imprudent garrulity, as the Federals sometimes did, for one of McInstry's aims was "to mislead the enemy."

In Colonel Freemantle's famous book, "The South at Arms," published in London in 1864, appears this sentence under date of Shelbyville, May 10, 1863: "Everybody about headquarters is abusing the Chattanooga *Rebel* for its publication in today's issue of important army movements," the "important army movements" being improvised to mislead the Federals by Provost Marshal General McInstry and wired the *Rebel* from Army Headquarters the night before.

Let us hope that before the proposed measure is finally enacted by Congress it will be wholly stripped of its objectionable features and perfected so that it may not become under the hand and rule of the subordinates charged with its enforcement a machine for petty oppression and vainglorious exploitation. Meanwhile we are not at all alarmed on general principles about the freedom of the press. This is equally beyond the reach of bumptious shoulder-straps and small fry politicians who rattle around in Congress.

ESSAYS AND TRAVELS

ESSAYS AND TRAVELS

EVERY NATION FOR ITSELF

While Mr. Watterson was living abroad in 1896 the foreign relations of the United States began to be a topic of particular interest and concern to him. The following, which bears the date-mark of Paris, marks the first point in his writings where the phantom of a League of Nations appeared. This he greeted with instant distrust. While the accompanying article conceded that "isolation" was a finished theory of American governmental policy, it recommended a sort of substitute international arrangement whereby every nation would think strictly of No. 1. This article will be recognized as "Wattersonian" in style, and perhaps its most pertinent suggestion is that the Ambassadors of the United States should be barred by statute from making speeches—a thought not unknown to editors before and since.

Jingoism

(May 14, 1896)

As Old as Human Aspiration—Moses the Original Jingo—Americans in Europe—The French Republic Has Come to Stay—Hero Worship and False Gods in the United States—Duty of Our Diplomatic Representatives Abroad.

I: THAT VENEZUELAN TEN-STRIKE

Jingoism, as a term, is of purely modern usage, but, as a principle, it dates back to the very beginning of the strife for ascendancy among the races of man. It is, therefore, of tribal origin; and has for its most illustrious exponent in ancient times that magnificent old Jingo, Moses. Moses did not exactly "get there," as the phrase hath it; but he pointed the way, and from Moses to Beaconsfield, the most successful representatives of national aspiration have been jingoes.

Like most pseudonyms, expressive of some prevailing word or thought, begotten by chance and bred in the popular fancy—it is made subject to many uses and abuses. The unambitious toad, who did not want to be a butterfly with wings of gold, but preferred to remain a worm,[1] priding himself the while upon his conservative character, regarded self-assertion of every kind as jingoism. Per contra, the other poor toad who tried to swell to the dimensions of an ox, found out, when it was too late, that self-assertion may be sometimes carried too far. Decatur put the true theory exactly in his famous toast: "Our country," said he, "may she ever be right; but right or wrong our country!"

Five thousand miles away from home, an ocean rolling between, and a hundred millions of more or less hostile foreigners within easy reach, the very writing of the lines makes the heart to swell.

The brotherhood of man, indeed! We shall see it when the millennium arrives. Meanwhile, it is every nation for itself, the devil to get the hindmost, as he generally does.

Mr. Cleveland builded very much wiser than he knew in his Venezuelan message. Whatever his motive may have been, and however limited his perspective, he called down "the despots of Europe" and, reminding them of the existence of the American Union, served notice upon them that, hereafter in human affairs, that Union will have to be reckoned with—first. The shock to the nerve-centers of monarchy was instant and prodigious. The indignation and outcry knew no bounds. But the President of the United States, sitting calmly in the White House, might observe to the noisy protestants, as Ransy Sniffles on a certain occasion observed to his recalcitrant critter, "You may kick and you may jump and you may prance, but I kin hold you, gol ding you, I kin hold you!" Anyhow, the surprised Kings and Queens pretty soon found out how the matter stood and began to cool off and to mend their manners, and, as a consequence, the dons and other war dogs, and the counts and no-accounts, fell in line and followed suit so that ever since, to be an American in Europe is to be something more than the proverbial illustration of a fool and his money, or a nobody to be whistled down the wind of every titled donkey's pretended nobility!

Let us all go and take something; and you, Mr. Cleveland, you get the largest glass and the biggest lump of sugar because, though maybe you didn't know it, you spoke the right word at the right time.

II: AMERICA'S MANIFEST DESTINY

I remember very well how it used to be myself. I was over here in the darksome days just after the war—our own little

---

[1] Mr. Watterson was seldom guilty, as here, of mixed figures, however hastily he wrote.

unpleasantness, I mean. Such trivial distinctions as Federal and Confederate were unknown. To the European imagination, all of us, without distinction of race, section or condition, were Yankees. I was glad enough to get an obscure corner among the ample folds of Old Glory, and, finding the place so comfortable and congenial, I have stuck to it ever since and advised the rest of the boys to do likewise.

To be sure there be men who go to excesses as there be men who do not go at all. Never a popular book, or drug, but hosts of spurious imitations. The proposal to have Congress take a hand in the criminal jurisprudence of a foreign State—appropriately emanating from the Senate—was certainly cutting the jingo pattern rather low in the bosom and scant about the waist; and, except for the prompt intervention of wiser modistes, one might well have entertained fears for the goddess. But it is safer to err in excess than to commit the folly of refusing to see that everything which concerns humanity concerns us. We are no longer a huddle of petty States held together by a rope of sand. We are no longer a squalid Democracy, secure chiefly by reason of our isolation, a Pariah among the governments of men. We are a Nation—with the biggest kind of an N—a great imperial Republic destined to exercise a controlling influence upon the actions of mankind and to affect the future of the world as the world was never affected, even by the Roman Empire—itself.

The ocean is but a ferry. New York and London are at this moment nearer together than in the days of the Cæsars were Athens and Rome. It is only a question of time when we shall have five hundred millions of people crowding the continent from the Atlantic to the Pacific precisely as the continent of Europe is now crowded. Already, the touch of a spring in Berlin or Vienna is felt in New York and San Francisco. The struggle of the future will be the survival of the fittest. Why should we not begin to look about how things are going and to cast about for our particular interest and glory?

There is a difference, certainly, between mere inflation and buncombe and a policy of sagacious aggression. With the average American newspaper, jingoism is a very convertible form. Now you see it and now you don't, and it makes a good deal of difference whose ox happens to be gored. We are ever too ready to draw the line upon political differences. The beautiful unanimity which responded to the Venezuelan message attested the real, underlying thought of the people. Mr. Cleveland had struck a popular chord and he had struck with a strong hand. If the performances of the President only equalled his manifestoes, he would be indeed a leader where he is only a master. But master or leader, he hit the nail on the head, whether he drives it home or not, and, as I said before, it did a world of good to Americans and Americanism in Europe.

III: MONARCHY VERSUS REPUBLICANISM

The tourist, coming to Europe for a summer's holiday, is likely to be misled by the superficial aspect of things.

As a rule, he has so much money to spend. He has left care behind him. He means to have a good time; and the way to a good time is straight and open before him. There are no obstacles or frictions of a serious kind to be encountered. The pleasure-making machine is in excellent repair and thoroughly greased. The undercurrents of society are for the most part invisible. He does not concern himself about the philosophy of Government. It looks all right. Everything seems more fixed and solid here than with us. There is an air of repose in the established order, and his sensibilities are not jarred by the constant and boisterous ebullitions of political activity, which mar the serenity of the rich man's existence in America.

To those who have the leisure and the wherewithal to enjoy life, it matters little whether the State be called a monarchy or a democracy. But no man can look deeper, can take account of that which relates to the well-being of the greatest number, without having his belief in Republicanism strengthened and his love of liberty refreshed, by all that he finds in the theories and methods of Government on this side of the Atlantic and, though in less degree, even here in France, which has emerged from feudal dogma and practice and is on the high road to all that can truly benefit a people and ennoble a nation.

I have sometimes thought that, as France advances upon this highway, we, in the United States, are showing a tendency toward retrogression. The aristocracy of wealth—the plutocracy—which seems inevitable to our ever-expanding resources, is a dread menace if it be not held in check by a sturdy, independent, enlightened character among the masses of the people. In France, the individual is all that he should be, or could be, in his character of citizen. He is brave, self-reliant, intelligent. He loves his country. He knows his rights and dares those rights maintain. He has overcome immense obstacles in wrenching his present freedom; has swum rivers of blood, handicapped by centuries of oppression. We, on our own part, know not what freedom is, what freedom means. We were born to it. It came to us in our natal air. We are too often victims of illusion. We see dangers where there are no dangers, and glide over thin ice oblivious of the turbid depths below. We are still a very young, a very emotional, and, for all our boasted smartness, a very ignorant people. Heroes and hero-worship still play a great part with us. We make an ideal, invest it with imaginary virtues, set it on a pedestal, call it by some name or other, and proceed to apotheosize it. Only when it is too late do we stop to closely examine—to inspect and dissect—our idol of pasteboard and saw-dust. Hence we are perpetually running after false gods, when we should worship only that God which, ruling the winds and the waves, finds a lodgment in all our minds and all our hearts if we would but look within.

The experience of history, not less than the cynicism of mod-ern life, has considerably abated the spirit of hero-worship in Europe. Even in France every candidate for the Presidency is not heralded a Jupiter Tonans by his partisans. Boulanger's day was but a short and a sorry one. Of course, in countries like England and Germany, the few who eddy about the inspired circle worship at the shrine of the divine right and the Lord's annointed. Every Englishman loves a lord, of course. Every German at least pretends an affection for the Kaiser. But in these coun-tries, force is the mainspring of action; and where men univer-sally must, they are not likely in general to do much else.

One thing is quite certain, there is not a monarchist in Europe who does not hate America. Sometimes the hate is veiled by wonder. Sometimes it is restrained by prudence. But it is there all the same; and the one way to meet it is to hold it in constant reminder that we, too, are great and strong, that we, too, believe in something; that we, too, have rights which they must respect. Soft words butter no parsnips. The Ambassador from the United States to one of these monarchies should be interdicted from making speeches of any kind. He should be instructed to main-tain at all times and under all circumstances an attitude of armed complacency. It is true that, after exercising a world of patience and using his private influence to coax the powers that be, Eustis succeeded in liberating a perfectly worthless negro, who had vio-lated the law and earned all he got. But France is neither Eng-land nor Germany.

We gain nothing by toadying to court favor. He who does so merely ingratiates himself in the rather disdainful tolerance with which the man with a title looks down upon the commoner.

"Sire," replied John Adams when George III reminded him that, having been born an Englishman, he should love England, "Sire," said the brave old Republican, "I love no country except my own."

H. W.

Boulevard de Courcelles

THE PATHS OF GLORY

Mr. Watterson was in the habit of making frequent journeys abroad. He knew his Paris, his London and his Berlin like a native. He would always, as he expressed it, "earn his salt" with brilliant editorial correspondence such as the subjoined. It deals with the loves of Napoleon and Josephine and is tinted with the atmosphere of that Nineteenth Century Paris which he knew and loved. Old Paris never seemed to interest him, and all his articles bore references to the metropolis of the Emperors, not the Kings. The Place Vendome, not the Place des Vosges, was his promenade; and his favorite doggerel was Thackeray's, "his ways is fine, his manners easy, a gayer, finer gent than he ne'er strode along the Shonz Eleezy, or on the Rue de Rivoli."

The following article is an example of his essay style and is notable for that rhythmic swing and sparkling diction which were his to command. Nor did he leave the theme without descanting on the price Bonaparte paid for his glory. He believed in the Æsopian construction, with the moral at the fable's end.

Malmaison

(April 24, 1907)

I

The environs of Paris, hardly less than Paris itself, are deeply impressive. They awaken all that is responsive in the heart, all that is thoughtful and intelligent in the mind of cultivated man. From Mount Valerian upon either hand round the magic circle of wood and dale, Versailles and Fontainebleau, the hill of St. Cloud and the terrace of St. Germaine, the villages of Ville D'Avray and of Barbaison, every footstep leads across the migrations of love and daring, over the tombs of all that was stubborn in patriotism, heroism and romance when knighthood was in flower and valiants were ready to look danger in the eye and laugh death in the face for sake of a blue ribbon or a bunch of violets. But among the many spots which memory gives to the Odyssey of tears none arouses interest of the sentimental sort more than Malmaison, sometime the home of a twain whose names will live forever in mundane sympathy or controversy—perhaps in both—Napoleon Bonaparte and Rose Tascher, generally called Josephine Beauharnais.

To the munificence of a rich Hebrew, the late M. Ostris, Paris owes the reclamation and ownership of Malmaison. Though yet rather bare it has been thrown open to the public and already the increasing tide of pilgrims attests with what attraction. It is a plain country place of no architectural or regal pretension, but, for a French château, very well adapted to living comfort.

The grounds are ample, with plenty of outhouses and stables such as one might have seen in Virginia during the Colonial period. There is a little adjacent private chapel. A brook wimples through the lichens. The swards are beginning to be swept, the trees to be trimmed, the flower beds to be tended, and, as the encroachments of the advancing city have not quite reached thus far inland, there is not wanting an air of rustic isolation, which falls in agreeably with the sense of fitness.

The day was overcast, as it should have been, when we went there. Only now and then a glint of sunlight broke through clouds that were not of the spring, but of the autumn. An officer in uniform showed us through the more than half empty rooms and halls, and up the winding stairs, unchanged for a century. This was the music room—in it the harp of the first Empress, presented by the Second—and here was the cosy, rather than elegant, dining room, with a set of table ornaments, very inelegant, presented to Napoleon by the King of Saxony. Above were three connecting apartments; first, that of the Emperor, then a primitive bathroom opening into the bed chamber of Josephine, the bed upon which she died undisturbed, and at last the boudoir of Hortense; all extremely light and airy, overlooking the garden in the rear. The house is oblong, having very little decoration except a pair of gables at either end and two miniature obelisks, presumably brought by Napoleon from Egypt, along with a number of Egyptian portraits that adorn one of the reception rooms.

The library looks like a library. In it are several of its original furnishings. The floors, growing a little creaky, are of hardwood. They had abundance of fuel in those days, and, it being cheap, they were not afraid to burn it in deep and wide fireplaces, redolent of the olden time.

I dare say from year to year contributions will swell the contents of the old house, so that in the end it will become a veritable museum of relics as well as the resemblance of a living mansion. Naturally, it is now rather ghastly in its nudity, though there is enough of the reminiscent to take the fancy and hold it.

Whatever may be thought of the immortal Corsican, he remains the most startling and picturesque figure the drama of the ages has thus far produced upon the stage, either of history or romance.

II

I have had my Napoleonic education in three separate installments. First came the schoolboy's conception of the all-conquering soldier; then the man's reaction against ruthless ambition and cruel war. Each of these impressions, if not crude and false, was undiscriminating.

Historians of the Headley and the Abbott variety fed the one, the flood of anti-Bonaparte literature which was let loose by the fall of Louis Napoleon fed the other. They seem to me now to have been exaggerative and unjust. The last ten or twelve years I have been studying the subject for myself, with the result that in many ways I have modified most of my earlier opinions and changed some of them.

Napoleon was certainly an idealist and a day-dreamer, largely a man of the affections. There can be little doubt that he possessed a credulous and a loving heart. He made a good son and a more than good brother. The whole of them were an unruly lot. He showed himself a loyal friend. He got little else than ingratitude. He adored Josephine. She returned his adoration with infidelity.

That he ever put a crown upon the head of a woman so faithless and frivolous can only be accounted for by the fact that he idolized her and forgave her, for her misbehavior was not unknown to him. He loved her when he put her away from him and suffered more than she did. It was the stepping down and out of the regal splendor, not the breaking of conjugal bonds she had never respected, nor the sundering of ties of companionship she never appreciated, which brought the tears the poor woman shed. A light-headed Creole, reared in the school of the decadence, demoralized, if not debauched, by the horrors and excesses of the French Revolution, Napoleon came across the disc of the loose life she was leading; first as a Little Monster and then as a queer prodigy, whom she took because she could do no better, and whom she never understood.

He need not have married her at all. But, he loved her; he was essentially a chivalric man, and along with her he took to his heart the children she had to all intents cast away.

The divorce was certainly a mistake. Josephine, whatever else she may or may not have been, was Napoleon's Mascotte. During his mismated life with Marie Louise he often visited Malmaison and passed hours with this the wife of his youth and his bosom, much to the worry of the frowsy and ignoble Austrian woman he had for reasons of State and dynasty taken in her stead and who had brought him nothing but trouble and ill-fortune.

When Napoleon returned from Elba, Josephine having died

during his absence, hither he came as to an altar of mourning. Hortense showed him silently into the room where she had breathed her last and gently closed the door. He stayed an hour and when he came out his eyes were red with weeping. Yet there are those who would have us believe that this was a man of blood and iron.

Why is it that strong men so often become the prey of weak women?

III

When the Allies entered Paris in 1814 they found Josephine at Malmaison. They paid her much attention. It was their cue to defame Napoleon and the ex-Empress served the purpose exceeding well. To represent her as a miracle of goodness and virtue was to paint Napoleon an ogre. The fiction lived for more than half a century.

Intellectually, Napoleon had some serious limitations and physically some dreadful handicaps. He was the world's greatest specialist in the art of war. That he could not see his way to accepting the peace which Metternich offered him seems proof that he lacked the genius of constructive statesmanship in spite of the proof to the contrary furnished by his recreation of France after the Revolution which he had captured and made his own. He was a soldier every inch of him—though a soldier of fortune—glory, not the good of man, the god of his idolatry, and being thus a gambler, luck finally deserted him.

All critics agree that during the Hundred Days he surpassed himself. Not the allied armies, but the elements overcame him. Destiny. It was unintended by the human plan that one man should rule the universe; especially a man so human as Napoleon. Yet, he came perilously near it. What if the rain had not descended the night before Waterloo?

At St. Helena we see a querulous, prematurely old, old man. That was the woman in him. Monsters are made of sterner stuff. Had Josephine lived, and they had permitted her, she would have gone to him, and, instead of a sublime tragedy, we might have had an idyl of Darby and Joan.

I do not think Josephine was a bad woman; she was a weak, a vain and foolish woman, who could not rise to her fortunes. Except for her insufficiency she could have held her place to the end. She died the 29th of May, 1814, at Malmaison, and was buried June 2, in the little Parish of Ruell, hard by. Over her grave a monument, bearing the figure of a recumbent and weeping woman, was placed by her two children. It bears the inscription, "A Josephine" and below "Eugene and Hortense." In 1837 Hortense died and was brought here for interment by the side of her mother, the Emperor Louis Napoleon, her son, later along, erecting a monument over her grave.

Our party, the guests of the Consul General and Mrs. Mason, and of Mr. Donald Harper, Counsellor of the Embassy, visited the little old church and stood by the grave of these two frail, fair and unfortunate women; least fortunate in their splendor. I have stood by the tomb of Napoleon many a time—the emotions varied and varying—and the emotions here, though mingled, were mostly of pity and sadness. Do you remember the visit of Col. Henry Esmond to the grave of his mother in the lowlands, the shadow of the crosses upon the hillside, the tinkle of the bells in the valley? Well something of that visitation crept over me as I stood in this church of Ruell. Here, too, was a woman who had climbed high in dreamland, like a star to fall, never to hope again. Who shall judge her? Surely not Paul Barras. Nor the shade of Tallien point finger at her. Not even the ghost of Bonaparte.

There is in Père la Chaise an upright shaft of granite above the last resting place of a woman of genius—of surpassing beauty and genius—whose life was a defiance—poor Ada Isaacs Menken—bearing the two significant words—"Thou Knowest." And so with Rosa Tascher, otherwise Josephine Beauharnais, whilom Empress of France.

Yet, let us not forget the man in the case. He too suffered. He too fell. Nor all the gorgeous trappings beneath the gilded dome that rises over the Champ de Mars, nor the drums and tramplings of the legions that idolize his memory, may soothe one aching heart-throb, nor lessen by a single drop of blood or tears, the usurious price he paid for his glory!

H. W.

Paris,
April, 1907

THE SECOND CUBAN REPUBLIC

A trained writer and observer like Mr. Watterson could not so thoroughly succumb to the *dolce far niente* of the tropics as to make him forget the use of his eye and his pen. Therefore, from the south of France, Florida and Cuba, his favorite lounging places, the editor was accustomed to dispatch to his newspaper those delightful letters on many subjects of which the following is a sample.

At this time in 1909 Mr. Watterson and other Americans were concerned with the future of Cuba. Would the Republic last? Since that time the island self-government has survived fourteen years and a world war.

Again "Cuba Libre"

(January 29, 1909)

I

These are fateful and feverish days for Cuba, and for the Cubans. The Cubans are presently to be freed from the gentle despotism which has flung round their political cradle the spell of a prospering but to them an oppressive ministration. In other words, Magoon has furnished benevolence galore without finding the least assimilation.

The Cubans, to a man, want the Republic—their own Republic —but if they must be governed by a foreign power they would prefer Spain, which for all the ugly bygones, speaks their own language, has their own modes of thinking and doing, and, though at times hideously misusing them, did not offend their self-love by any such show of superiority as they have encountered in the Yankees. This may, on the surface, seem paradoxical. Yet it is wholly true. If we should take the case to ourselves we might better understand it. As between the English, the German or the French, in the event that we had to submit to an alien yoke, we should choose the English. In the teeth of benefits so great and obvious, of every kind and on every hand, one might fancy a different state of public opinion and feeling. Magoon, the Magician, is the proper name for him. His work here has been far-reaching. It has been all-embracing. He has caused two blades of grass to grow where but one had grown before. The story is replete both with interest and instruction.

When the Provisional Government, which is about to give place to what may be called the Second Republic, was set up in September, 1906, it found the population of Cuba divided into two hostile camps, each inflamed by bitter hatred against the other; it leaves the island with the Cubans united and everybody swearing to forget party and to place the Nation above all other considerations.

When Magoon came here, most unwillingly be it said, chaos reigned supreme. The land resounded with the clash of arms. It was clouded by the smoke of burning property and military campfires. He leaves it echoing with the hum of industrial activity and overspread by the aroma of nearly one hundred mills grinding day and night in their effort to take care of an enormous crop of sugar cane. He found the Government discredited and the pillars of the republic tottering because of a general belief that the elections of the previous year had been fraudulent, that, instead of registering the people's will, they had registered the will of a cabal enforced by the intimidation of the electorate. He quits Cuba with substantially every elective office filled by officials elected at two popular elections, participated in by a surprisingly large percentage of the population, at which the ballots were cast without police surveillance or any kind of espionage, elections that were as fair as were ever held in any country, and which command and receive not only the acquiescence of the people of Cuba, but the admiration and commendation of all who witnessed the proceeding.

"The past two years and four months," I quote from the admirable speech delivered by Gov. Magoon at the Farewell Banquet, "have been filled with conditions calculated severely to strain and test a state much older and better established than the Cuban republic. In 1906-07 there were floods, a revolution, a collapse of government, a foreign intervention, a cyclone, a poor crop of tobacco and a low price of sugar; yellow fever appeared in numerous places throughout the island, obliging the establishment of quarantine against shipping and passengers from Cuban ports. In 1907-08 there were long-continued strikes in practically all the industrial trades that did great damage to commerce and development; the worst drought in many years inflicted great injury upon agriculture and stock raising; and in October, 1907, came the world-wide panic with resulting money stringency and trade depression. Naturally enough these matters caused creditors to seek collection of debts due them, and this period of enforced payment of private indebtedness has gone on in Cuba and other countries. It is safe to say that in Cuba more than 50 per cent. of the private indebtedness has been paid and that credit is again fully established and the producers of the island are relieved of a large annual interest charge."

Governor Magoon gives a gratifying account of the moral peace which the advent of the Provisional Government inaugurated. He thinks, as a result of his observation and experience, that the people of Cuba are capable of self-restraint, and can face and overcome, without disturbance, conditions calculated to produce wide and great discontent. The records of the courts, he tells us, of the rural guard and the municipal police, show a remarkable decrease in crimes of every sort during the last two years in Cuba, while in other countries where similar conditions have prevailed, crime has increased. This, he thinks, is one of numerous reasons justifying the belief that the Cubans are capable of self-government.

I learn from Governor Magoon's statement that when the Provisional Government was established in September, 1906, it found in the treasury $9,893,993.23 of cash available for general expenses. But it was compelled to use this money in paying the obligations of the former government to provide for the national defense against the forces of the revolution and the damages incident to that revolution. It was necessary to meet the additional cost of the increase of the rural guard authorized by the Cuban Congress from 3,600 to 5,000 men. There were other large and urgent outlays forthcoming. Among the first of these was the cost of the extirpation of yellow fever. Then, in order to restore the Government to normal conditions, new elections had to be held. This made it necessary to take a census, prepare electoral lists, provide election supplies and actually to hold two elections. These disbursements more than exhausted the money in the treasury. Nor was this all. It was found that the Cuban Congress, by special acts and general legislation, had appropriated $9,134,537.73 to be used in starting certain public improvements. The completion of the roads and bridges alone thus authorized, as had been estimated by competent engineers, would cost $20,286,500. At the time the Provisional Government was established it was feared that the public revenues would diminish and that the republic would have to face a deficit. Instead of diminishing, the revenues increased and it soon became apparent that the public improvements contemplated could be carried out within the surplus revenues.

These revenues were sorely needed. They were essential to the progress and development of the island. Governor Magoon frankly declares that the Provisional Government would have gone ahead with them under normal conditions, but the conditions prevailing as a result of the industrial and commercial depression made the action taken imperative as a means of relieving the public distress. Most of the works have been completed and paid for; those remaining under contract are not less than 60 per cent. completed and paid for, whilst the treasury contains $2,000,000, with revenues showing a steady increase.

This exhibit, which I abridge from the Governor's banquet speech, is certainly encouraging and justifies the eloquent words with which he closed that speech, which I quote as follows:

"I look toward the future of the Republic with confidence inspired by experience and observation that has shown me that the overwhelming majority of the Cuban people are sober, industrious, peace-loving, law-abiding citizens, inspired by a love of family and a love of country, passionately desirous that Cuba should be a free and independent state. My hope is inspired by the events of the past two years, during which the island has been blessed with moral peace, public tranquillity, a wholesome regard for law and the rights of others, popular elections participated in by all and challenged by none; peace and prosperity restored and the Cubans reunited by the bonds of friendship and good will; the new government resting upon the franchise and favor of a large majority of the electors and well assured of the consideration and assistance of its political opponents; opposition without obstruction and co-operation in all things to promote the progress and preserve the stability of the State and the preservation of the republic. The world is watching Cuba, not without apprehension, but with the best and kindest wishes that the efforts of the Cuban people in the past, the present and in the future will be crowned with success."

II

Will the Republic last? Can Gomez play Diaz? "I dun'no." Quien sabe? The iron hand seems the only rule for the Latin. Magoon has carried it swathed in velvet. His own figure-of-speech tells of an oil can and a feather brush. Notwithstanding and nonetheless, the mailed grip was there, backed by an unlimited power, and the discipline has been good for the Cubans.

It may last them a long time. Before another revolution ripens they may be educated to the point of settling their political battles other than by a resort to arms, calling down upon them the final intervention of the United States. Most of them, perhaps all of them, understand this. They love their country. They want to be left free to enjoy it in their own way. However one may doubt their capacity for self-government and discredit their racial character and disapprove their methods, their right is indisputable, and he is not a good American—that is, not loyal to the principles of our institutional freedom—who refuses to concede it to them.

Upon the threshold we are met by the eternal conflict between the spiritual and the concrete. Quite a lot of money has been invested in Cuba since the close of the Spanish War. Much of this came with the get-rich-quick idea. All of it was, and continues to be, more or less speculative. Avaricious and timid, progressive, enterprising and unscrupulous, it sees in the end of the Provisional Government the menace of every kind of uncertainty; for the Cuban hardly less than the Castilian is a devotee to "the good old vices of Spain."

This capitalistic element will prove the hardest with which

Gomez will have to deal; because it is convinced that its safety lies in the return of the Americans and it will work to that end. The circumstance imposes upon the opposition the need of a restraint which can only emanate from a prudent, far-seeing and self-denying patriotism.

In a region such as this it takes but little to make a revolution, or the appearance of one. The average American mind has not yet learned to grasp questions of foreign policy which do not carry some stirring domestic interest. We are apt to accept without sufficient discrimination the first story that comes to us. There is a growing belief that we made a mistake in not taking over Cuba along with Porto Rico and that the Teller Resolution was sentimental tommy-rot. Be this as it may, we are ourselves responsible for the idea of Cuba Libre and of independent government, which moves the spirit of the present generation of Cubans.

There are, of course, a few Cubans who believe, sadly but sincerely, that their countrymen are incapable of self-government and who know that if this be affirmed, the manifest destiny of the island is, geographically and logically, as sure as was that of Texas. But the mass and body of the people are otherwise bent. To them there is a repellance in the Yankee which was not in the Spaniard. They resent what they regard as our affection of disinterestedness. They resent a self-complacency which irritates where it is silent and are indignant before a dominancy which is too often blatant. Blood is thicker than water. The petty tyrannies of old Spain are forgotten—the brutality and horrors are fading away like the wreaths upon the patriotic statues and the bombs. Weyler was not so bad after all. It is the pebble in the shoe, not the scar upon the back, or the brand upon the forehead, that gives disquiet.

I must confess that, being a crank about liberty, if I am a crank about anything, I quite understand these sentiments and sympathize with them.

"'Tis an ill-favored thing, but mine own," says Touchstone, twanging a chord that makes the whole world kin. Applied to Cuba, 'tis a Paradise, and "by God," said an old Cuban friend of mine, educated in Germany and passing most of his life in Paris, "we don't intend to give it up."

I see in Gomez a simple and brave soldier and in Zayas a resourceful, not merely scheming politician, and I doubt not, a patriotic man. But, the riff-raff; Lord, the riff-raff; injin, nigger, beggar man, thief—

> "Both mongrel, puppy, whelp and hound,
> "And cur of low degree."

Havana is no more Cuba than New York is America. In Havana "Cuba Libre" has not a little of the tra-la-la to it. Out in the provinces it is stilly conviction. The Havanese hate us, but would not fight us. The "rurales" do not hate us, but would fight for the republic we have promised them. When the pie is cut, when the offices are all filled, what of the rejected ones? Will each turn conspirator?

For Gomez, there's the rub. Zayas tells me he is full of confidence. He needs to be. May his faith be fulfilled abundantly!

Most of our fellows say they are glad to get out of here. They go with that sort of pleasure which shows itself chiefly in convivial ebullitions of reluctance and is much too ostentatious to be quite honest. On the whole they have had a good time and all sorts of a good time. Havana is a glorious city. Brother Burbridge makes the browsing around about the top of the Prado very fetching and there are excellent pickings with Brother Dick over by the Sevilla and down in the Café de Paris, not to mention the rosy dawns and the starry nights and the drives from the Malecon—

> "When moonlight o'er the azure sea
> Her soft effulgence beams—"

away up and beyond, the Dedado, where the royal palms stand sentinal, at once, and signal tower, to liberty, and the plaintive laurel sighs love and sorrow into listening groves of orange and mango over which the giant Ceiva, like ogre of old, holds watch and guard. Dear! Dear! There should not be any doubt about the future of such a Garden of Eden. We are all of us republicans, are we not?

> "But what avail the plow, or sail,
> Or land, or life, if freedom fail!"

H. W.

Hotel Sevilla
Havana

ROUGE ET NOIR

Monte Carlo, "the loveliest spot in the world," was Mr. Watterson's favorite vacation-land. He published enough descriptive matter about the place to fill a book of its own, but an article he wrote in 1911 is here reproduced as the leading exhibit on the subject. It is done in his best journalese and includes an interesting discussion of gambling.

The Real Monte Carlo

(April 1, 1911)

I: HOW SATAN BAITS HIS HOOK

A deal of nonsense of one sort and another is written about Monte Carlo. I should certainly not advise mothers to send their pet lambs here for religious instruction. There are more "swears" than "prayers" under the frowning walls of Tete de Chien and down among the red roofs of la Condamine.

The Casino, for all its resplendency, its columns of porphyry and alabaster, its choirs dedicated to song and dance, and its chapels dedicated to fashion and chance, its wealth of stained glass and old gold, is yet singularly unlike a Cathedral. Set amid gardens that seem enchanted and are celestial, upon a castellated crag between the mountains and the sea, it might easily be mistaken for the mundane home of a Greek god. It lends itself to whatever treatment the mood of the observer may care to bestow upon it.

To the loser, it is hell; to the winner, heaven. The cynic may choose one point of view, the philosopher another. Books have been written upon all sides of it and every aspect.

The best and fairest of these, because the most informed and the least partisan, is that of the Hon. Victor Bethell, a son of the second Baron Westbury, and the head of the Monte Carlo branch of the Comptoir National d'Escompte de Paris, a hard-headed banker, who knows it well, has neither prejudices nor illusions, and in his "Anecdotes and Systems of Play," aims only to "put the public wise" touching the actualities of the place. In his preface to this really illuminating and readable volume Mr. Bethell says:

"As long as the world exists gambling is sure to continue. Of late years it seems to have increased its hold upon the members of the upper classes. Fortunately, most of them take to it more as a pastime than a vice. They gamble to amuse themselves, and few of them lose more than they can afford. They visit Monte Carlo and Ostend because all their friends go there, and, having arrived, they find that they are "out of it" unless they join in the universal pastime of roulette.

"There are many to whom it matters not whether they win or lose; in fact, the majority come fully prepared to part with a certain sum. But there are many others, to whom it does make a difference, and, although they may not expect to come away large winners, it will probably quite spoil all the pleasure of their trip if they lose more than a very limited sum. To these—the less fortunate of the gambling community—I dedicate this little book, in the hope that each one may find herein a system suited to his or her taste. A player without a system is like a ship without a compass, and, although there may be few which lead to fortune, there are a considerable number which will give the visitor to Monte Carlo plenty of play for his money, and insure him against any heavy loss. I am informed by a gentleman who has frequented gambling establishments for most of his life that many of my so-called systems are erroneously described as such. They are not 'systems,' he says, but only 'methods of play.' From my point of view, however, every individual may be said to have a system who takes into the gambling rooms a certain capital with a prearranged plan how he will play it—not only as regards how he will stake his money, but as regards how much it is his intention to win or lose at a sitting.

"I am not sanguine that the publication of this book will cause the Administration to put up their shutters, but I do believe that if every visitor to Monte Carlo would only adopt some prearranged method of play, and religiously stick to it, the dividends of the shareholders would be considerably reduced.

"It is the players who vote systems a bore, and can never muster up the strength of mind to come out of the rooms when they are winners, who contribute most to the profits of the Bank."

There is nothing perfunctory, but a world of truth here. To many, games of chance are a business, involving more or less of real labor and fatigue. But, to most, they yield merely pastime and pleasure; and somehow, it does not seem to have been incorporated as a part of the eternal plan that man should derive a money profit off his recreations.

The "system" which Mr. Bethell commends imposes imperturbability and self-denial, forecast and patience. These are scarcely the virtues of the average gambler, who is usually filled with the get-rich-quick hysteria. Composure and sagacity as money-makers can do better anywhere than at the gaming table.

There are queer old women here who make a meager living by the "piking" process; but only a few. The "Labouchere System," as it is called, requires considerable capital. The Earl of Roslyn had his "system," knocked as high as a kite by Sir

Hiram Maxim in a dummy play. Indeed, there is no "system" that will hold water, because each "spin," is in itself a "system," and, although once in a while there is a certain "run" of the colors or the figures, the sun of each day's play and the developments of the various tables defeat—in point of fact render impossible—reliable calculations of any sort and all sorts.

The experienced and astute man of business may anticipate the market. But no prescience can anticipate the little ball that goes merrily round to drop at its own sweet will into a red or a black receptacle, numerically ranging from 0 to 36. The best system, therefore, is not to play at all; but in case one does play, to cut and run the moment he finds himself ahead.

It was not, however, of the games and gaming at Monte Carlo that I began to write, but of the Principality of Monaco, as a whole, and its drama, as a continuous performance. Nowhere on earth can any theater be found so brilliant and varied. At this, the high-noon of the season, it is the very apex of the swelldom of the universe, with its vast retinue of hangers-on and sightseers; reigning sovereigns to be encountered on every hand; the celebrities of all lands lost in the crowd of patricians, millionaires and nobodies; to eat, drink and be merry the single refrain from the highest to the lowest. Nature made Monte Carlo the loveliest spot in the world. Art and money have completed the work of nature. The *mise en scène* is as finished as a state setting. Pictorially nothing remains to be done.

II: BUT CATCHES ONLY SINNERS

There are inevitably, amid the waste of rhetoric and moral energy trolled off at its expense, many misconceptions about Monte Carlo. One is that the loss of individual fortunes is common. Another is that enormous gains are frequent. The Casino gets its profit of the many, not of the few. The big player has a chance to win his money back. It is the little player who, lagging behind, can never catch up. He falls a victim to the unlimited capital of the bank and his name is Legion.

The suicide stories are as baseless as the tales of wondrous strokes of luck. During the twenty-five years that I have at intervals dropped in and out of the place no instance of suicide traceable to losses in the Casino has come to my knowledge. He who "goes broke" has only to appeal to the Administration to be furnished with money enough to reach his home, however distant it may be. The transaction is duly recorded. If he ever returns and wants to play again, he has only to make good and be reinstated to full membership, for it must be understood that the Casino is a chartered club, its title being "La Société des Bains de Mer."

Citizens of the Principality of Monaco are denied access to the tables.

Of late years the increase of patronage has been so great that the Casino has been enlarged to twice its original size. The rabble quite swallowing the quality, the management found itself obliged to set aside a suite of rooms, admission to which could only be had for a consideration. These rooms became quickly as crowded as those that are free-for-all. Then, still ministering to the aristocratic element, an International Sporting Club, under drastic requirements, was organized. This, too, is crowded, but with the élite. The more distinguished people make it their rendezvous. The company there being select, the tone and the play are higher. Not merely reigning sovereigns, but world-famous statesmen and renowned millionaires throng the palace in which it makes its home, quite apart from the democratic Casino, where rag, tag and bobtail elbow one another and rudely push for the chance to lose their money. Often the tables are crowded three files deep. Seats are at a premium and are sometimes liberally paid for. Every day servants, valets or maids, are sent in early to secure and occupy them, playing for small stakes, until the master or mistress arrives.

Next, after adulterated wines, the artificial woman, though to the initiate perfectly obvious, like the doctored wines to the connoisseur, is very successful in imposing herself upon the credulous. She is much in evidence at Monte Carlo. Usually she has, or she appropriates, a title. On the Continent, especially in France and Italy, titles are as plentiful as Colonels in Kentucky. They are for the most part unimportant and meaningless. Even where they are not bogus they are worthless. The "Princesse" is to be held at least at arm's length; the "Comtesse" to be a suspect. Only the fool Americans are taken in by the titular nobility of mock heraldry and the tin-shop. A close second to the titled ones of Utopia comes the ghastly procession of what Ben Ridgely used to call "the battle-axes," case-hardened old women who play from morn to noon, from noon to dewy eve, with a few five-franc pieces, year in and year out, season after season, some of them looking like the hags upon the blasted heath whom Macbeth encountered. Time was when they had beauty and money. Even the croupiers pity and tolerate them.

Then the woman and the dog appear upon the scene, sometimes the woman leading the dog and sometimes the dog leading the woman. And every manner of dog from Great Dane to tiny spaniel; dogs that bark in a single lingo, English or German; cosmopolite dogs that bark in all languages; mongrel, puppy, whelp and hound; but never a cur of low degree; high priced dogs; aristocratic dogs; each of them more or less petted and spoiled. The playgrounds for the little people in the gardens overlooking the sea are the most beautiful in the world. They make a perpetual carnival of flowers and children and dogs.

Not long ago Marc Klaw was over here. Next to him at one of the tables in the Casino sat a little old lady. Losing together, and then winning together, they picked up a chance acquaintance. At last they rose together, Marc gallantly conducting her to the door and thence to her automobile. As they passed through the vestibule the orchestra was playing the "Ave Maria" of Gounod. "Isn't it lovely," said Marc, tears coming to his eyes, "the last time I heard it sung was by Christine Nillson." The old lady smiled and said: "So long ago?" As Marc turned back into the Casino and the auto sped away a friend said: "Do you know who that was?" Marc said he did not. "It was Christine Nillson," said his friend.

On the whole, the moralizing having Monte Carlo for its text is time wasted. Nor is it always quite sincere. Many years ago, seated upon a lounge in the foyer of the Casino, the head of one of the great historic houses of England, a man of wisdom as well as wealth who, as Daniel Webster once described the Duke of Devonshire, "had never made a bargain in his life," observed as we surveyed the throng passing in and out,

"These people have no right to complain if they lose. They come to win and they hope to win. It is their own fault if they are ignorant of the chances against them. Most of them are sightseers lured by curiosity. Win or lose, they will scarcely come again. Half the others are pleasure-seekers with money to throw to the birds. Part of it goes to the tables. Those that are viciously inclined are doing less harm than they do elsewhere. At least there is no concealment. The infatuated gamblers are few indeed. Some of them actually pick up a living, such as it is. The cleanliness and order are much to be commended. The animus of the customary abuse of the place is its enormous yield to the shareholders. You people in America resent Standard Oil, which has brought to every man's door and cheapened a commodity of universal need and use, not so much that it is Monopoly as that it pours such riches into a few pockets. So is it with Monte Carlo. Its profits are incredible and they are inevitable. But Europe must have some vent for its idlers who do less mischief squandering their money at Monte Carlo than they might if left to their other and many devilish devices."

I asked this aristocratic philosopher what he thought was the most reprehensible feature of gambling.

"The disarrangement of the sense of values," he promptly replied. "All commerce is more or less a gamble. Life itself is a gamble. In trade each is seeking to get an advantage of the other. In table gambling, days, weeks and months are concentrated into minutes and seconds. The action is so quick that the player takes no account of money or time. When he goes broke, as you Americans say, he is up and away. If he can he comes back and wins. Then he spends his money as if he were a Rothschild and goes broke again, to rail at fortune and lampoon the Casino. As often as not he is a cheat and a rogue and generally a bit of a liar."

I told him of an epigram we have in Kentucky touching the gambler's life, "chickens today and feathers tomorrow." And, not noting the humor, he said with great gravity, "In England we have men who call themselves gentlemen and derive a sure income playing cards—bridge or baccarat—in the clubs and at week-end parties. For myself I would as soon trust one of these poor croupiers and, as for my money, would much prefer to invest it at roulette or trente-quarante."

There is one aspect of Monte Carlo that might appeal to a stoic or a saint: the moonlit nights amid the gardens and upon the esplanades. As I have said, the place is finished. Nothing of loveliness is wanting. There is not anywhere a ragged edge or a gaping waste spot. Look where you will, the eye falls only upon the exquisite blending of art and nature.

Charles Garnier put his magic touch upon the architecture, which is made to fit, decorate and illumine the winding walks and ways whether they lead to the seaside or climb into the mountains.

By night the contrasts of light and shade are startling. Standing upon the parapet overlooking the *tire aux pigeons,* the moon sailing in mid-heaven—let us say toward the wee sma' hours—the good and evil of the world, the strength and weakness of humanity, the grace and beauty of youth and love, the grime of living and the inequalities of life, spread out like a scroll of the ages tracing back to Theseus and Perseus, gorgons and the golden fleece, and coming down to the days of miracle. Rockefeller able to put Midas out of business and Carnegie to make Crœsus look literally like thirty cents! The blaze within the Casino has faded away, as some guilty thing, and a faint twitter of guitars steals upward from the all-night palace below, whither the swells have gone to supper. The yachts ride with proud expectancy in the little harbor. Upon the hill yonder the Prince's beacon shines. The surging of the sea, like the monotone of an organ from the Cathedral of the deep, penetrates the soul. Out of the shadows stalk the wolves of thought. All is hushed. The tired gamblers are asleep, only tireless pleasure is awake! Tomorrow and tomorrow and tomorrow!

H. W.

Hotel Metropole
Monte Carlo

MISCELLANEOUS

MISCELLANEOUS

OUR BRUSH WITH SPAIN

Mr. Watterson believed in the cause of Cuba Libre, and from a mass of his writings on the war with Spain the following editorial of April 20, 1898, is selected as representative of his whole position in the matter. It reveals him confident that the war would be brief: his theory was that Spain would make "a mere feint" at fighting as a matter of politics with her Jingoes. The editor hazarded the guess that stronger hands in diplomacy than those of President McKinley and Secretary Sherman (toward the latter he was ever harsh) might have averted a war, but he was confident that only good for the United States could come of it.

This editorial is written in the oratorical, or inspirational, style which won him a wide and admiring audience and reflects that antipathy to slavery which he always felt. For though a Confederate soldier, as he has himself related he was always a Union, anti-slavery Democrat.

In Hoc Signo

(April 20, 1898)

The resolutions upon which Congress finally agreed as expressive of our notice to Spain and the causes which impelled it are representative of the mind, heart and power of the American people. There are some who preferred another phrasing, some who would have written them differently, but all in all they embody the truths and the purposes upon which we rest our case with mankind and appeal to the tribunal of battle. As Congress in the end sank minor differences of declaration and united upon this indictment of Spanish wrong, this proclamation of Cuban independence, this demand for Spanish abdication, this order to the Executive for the enforcement of that demand, and this disclaimer of our own intention to control the sovereignty of Cuba, so the people, ignoring similar differences, proclaim the voice of Congress the voice of themselves, and will make their own the action of the President in giving to their words the force of deeds.

It is given out that the President will today sign the resolutions and transmit them along with his ultimatum, allowing Spain a short time—say twenty-four hours—to comply, or take the consequences.

All this, however, is a mere formality. It is the ceremonious preliminary to the duel. Spain's reply is already discounted. There is no probability—there is hardly a possibility—that it can be anything but a refusal of our demands. That reply received, the war will be on. Within an hour afterward the orders for the movement of our forces against Spain should be issued; by the opening of the coming week Havana should be invested, if not captured.

It is not for the *Courier-Journal* to predict the course of events or to map out the campaign. We shall be surprised, however, if the war, so long in beginning, be not soon over. We doubt if Spain really intends to make much more than a feint at fighting, in order to propitiate her belligerent domestic elements, save the throne from the Revolutionists and turn loose Cuba with "honor." If the war should be protracted it will be either because of serious reverses of our navy in its first engagements, or because the Spaniards choose to pursue the policy of avoiding direct conflict, and devote their energies to keeping out of the way of our warships, harrying us by privateering depredations and scattering sallies wherever their cruisers may find a weaker prey. This policy is not altogether improbable unless we should make such quick work of our eviction of Spain from this hemisphere that she may be brought to terms before she fairly begins such a policy. Certainly we do not expect hostilities to be prolonged by the reverses or destruction of our fleet. Say what one will about Spain's navy—grant, even, that her ships are a match for ours—we shall never believe that her seamen are a match for ours until they have proved it by a trial of skill. We have never yet met seamen who vanquished ours on equal terms, and we have met and conquered seamen of better fighting blood than any that flows in Latin veins. The American navy, always unequal in ships to its antagonists, has always defeated its antagonists gloriously, and until it has been demonstrated that its men have sadly degenerated or that they are in no degree the masters of seamanship as applied to the modern development of the man-of-war that they were as applied to the man-of-war in its less advanced stages, we shall never believe that they cannot overcome a fleet even much superior to their own manned by the fire-eaters of Spain.

Be that as it may, and whether the war be long or short, it is a war into which this nation will go with a fervor, with a power, with a unanimity that would make it invincible if it were repelling not only the encroachments of Spain, but the assaults of every monarch in Europe who profanes the name of divinity in the cause of kingcraft. We do not mean to say that there are not good people in this country, aside from the patriots for revenue only, who are not earnestly and conscientiously opposed to this war. There are many others who believe it could have been averted, with the concession of all our demands, if a stronger hand had been at the helm of our diplomacy before the congressional crisis was reached. But all these will be as one with their countrymen in vigorously prosecuting the war, now that it is inevitable, to a splendid triumph for Americanism, for civilization, for humanity.

And that is what this war means. It is not a war of conquest. It is not a war of envy or enmity. It is not a war of pillage or gain. From the material side it is a war of tremendous loss to us, involving burdens of millions, not one cent of which can we hope to recover. There are those who diet on rice and peer through blue goggles who whine that on legal grounds we have no right to interfere with Spain's belaboring her own ass, to dispute her sovereignty over Cuba, her own territory. If they had prevailed, America today would be a slave-holding nation. They are deserving of no more serious consideration than the feather-headed maniacs who are bellowing for war only for war's sake. We are not going to the musty records of title archives to find our warrant for this war. We find it in the law supreme—the law high above the law of titles in lands, in chattels, in human bodies and human souls—the law of man, the law of God. We find it in our own inspiration, our own destiny. We find it in the peals of the bell that rang out our sovereignty from Philadelphia; we find it in the blood of the patriots who won our independence at the cannon's mouth; we find it in the splendid structure of our national life, built up through over a hundred years of consecration to liberty and defiance to despotism; we find it in our own giant strength, attained in the air, and under the skies of freedom and equality, which has not only won and guarded the world's bulwark of liberty and law in our Republic, but which has laid down and enforced the decree that liberty and law on this hemisphere shall not be further trespassed on by despotism and autocracy, and which now, in the sight of the Powers of the earth and the God of nations, takes one step more and says that liberty and law shall no longer be trampled upon, outraged and murdered by despotism and autocracy upon our threshold.

That is the right of our might; that is the sign in which we conquer.

THE CANAL AND THE FORTY THIEVES

On the adventures of France and the United States in Panama
Mr. Watterson wrote many editorials. "The Fly by Night
Republic of Panama," was one of his repeated phrases in
lecturing Colonel Roosevelt on that piece of Caribbean statecraft. Bunau-Varilla, the French promoter of the Panama
route, he invariably referred to as "Vanilla Bean," and his
associates were always the "Forty Thieves of the Forty Millions." For years Mr. Watterson fought this battle alone,
and when the New York *World* and the Indianapolis *News*
joined him in 1910 he welcomed them without enthusiasm,
for he and Senator Morgan had lost the fight for the Nicaragua Canal. Nevertheless, for auld lang syne the editor
stood by his belated colleagues when Colonel Roosevelt sued
them for libel, refraining from all but a few ironical digs at
them for getting into trouble over using language far more
polite than the *Courier-Journal* indulged in.

While the selected editorial does not contain many of the
phrases which Mr. Watterson was wont to employ in this
connection, it gives his side of the controversy more succinctly
than any other. It was at this point in the row that the
words "a crook and a jackass" were said to have been applied
by Colonel Roosevelt to a judicial figure connected with the
trial of his case.

A Tragic But Timely Story

(February 4, 1910)

The lack of serious purpose, as well as continuity of thought,
the levity of the average daily newspaper—expressing itself sometimes in terms of ridicule and sometimes in terms of abuse, but
oftenest in terms of indifference, if not silent altogether—is one
of the most discouraging features of our public life.

The press should be, and perhaps in the long run and in the
final sum-total it is, the bell-tower of good government; the source
and resource of the liberties of the people; the very outpost of
freedom. But there are weary reaches of time when school does
not keep for it, dreary interludes when it goes to sleep, miles and
miles along the border-line separating truth from falsehood with
never a watch-fire burning, nor a sentinel on guard. Thus does
organized rapacity get in its work upon unorganized society; corruption overreach the unknowing and the credulous, or seduce the
weak and mercenary; picking off a laggard here and chloroform-

ing a delinquent there, the deed done, the treasure gone, the thieves away before the camp is awake, the house is astir, and the officers of the law, aroused to their duty, are alive to what has happened.

The Isthmian Canal transaction is a most illuminating case in point. All the early expert surveys and official reports favored the Nicaraguan route. Until a questionable French company came upon the scene the Panama route was regarded as impracticable where it was considered at all. Behind the Nicaragua scheme there was neither organization nor money. It embraced a plain, open-and-shut proposition; no cost for right of way; no price for territorial concessions or franchise grants; no lobby at Washington nor junta at Granada; a straight line and easy digging up the San Juan River to and through Lake Nicaragua, and thence across a narrow strip of land to the Pacific. For a sum not in excess of two hundred millions the canal could have been completed and except for the interception of the Panama project it would now be completed.

The Panama Canal Company of France has culminated in shipwreck. It had gone under in scandal and tragedy. Those who invested in it had lost their money. It was bankrupt. At this point certain Americans arrived in Paris with a scheme of resurrection. Their plan was to organize a new company to take over the holdings of the old company. This was not hard to do, and, being done, both cheap and easy, the Yankees keeping out of sight, its French manipulators appeared in Washington.

They had in reality nothing to sell but a few worthless pots and pans, some excavations and mud-heaps on the Isthmus of Panama, and the fag-end of a ten-year concession from the Republic of Colombia. The whole hand-me-down and layout was the merest stock-jobbing operation, hot air and water, backed by impudence and the promise of pelf. But it gained a footing and it got a hearing.

As soon as the wolves smelt blood they turned loose. Engineers who had time and again reported Panama impossible were induced to reverse their judgment. Nothing so good had turned up since Credit Mobilier and Pacific Mail. Not alone the agents of the French company were on the ground, their jackets lined and their pockets stuffed with lottery tickets good if the steal went through, but the Trans-Continental Railway Pool, aiming to beat both Panama and Nicaragua, took a hand. One could actually, almost physically, see the old familiar crowd, who, in days of Reconstruction, had mustered so blatantly under "the old flag and an appropriation," tumbling over themselves to get beneath the banners of the Panama Company of France.

Upon its face this company showed its fraudulency. It began

by demanding a hundred and fifty millions of dollars; fell to a hundred millions, and finally offered to take, and did take, forty millions. A more palpable confidence game, a greater robbery, was never perpetrated upon a people's treasure house.

There was a certain resistance. But it proved unequal and abortive. One gallant old man threw himself into the breach and stood to his guns. The Congress cannot claim, the public men of the time cannot pretend, the newspapers cannot say, that they proceeded without advisement. Morgan held to the field until he fell dead in his tracks, denouncing the infamy and telling the truth. Nothing braver, more tragical and pitiful, was ever witnessed in Legislative Halls. All men knew him to be as unselfish as he was fearless. But he was old, he was alone, he fought single-handed against odds, he could not last forever. So they said, and seeing him badgered and insulted, outwitted and obstructed without coming to his rescue, they saw him fall at last, whilst corruption flourished and the devil danced the can-can throughout the lobby at Washington and the bucket-shops of Paris.

Hands lifted, hats off, to the memory of John Tyler Morgan, of Alabama! Every word that he uttered has more than come true. Forty millions to the forty thieves was but a mouthful to the birds of prey who, gathering over the remains of the De Lesseps carrion at Paris, had swooped down upon Washington. thence to swoop down upon Bogota, thence to swoop down and to settle down in Panama, having gorged themselves with quite forty millions more—to require how many hundreds of additional millions no prophet can tell, nor even at this rate giving us any assurance of a canal which shall return a dollar of the millions it has cost us.

From first to last the *Courier-Journal* stood by Morgan. It was his only prop and backer outside his own immediate newspaper constituency. All it got for its pains were a bored public and a press, where not apathetic, abusive.

Years afterward, when Morgan had long lain in his grave and the enriched thieves had severally dispersed, each to his lair, leaving not a trail behind them, two American newspapers ventured to echo the charges which Morgan had made and the *Courier-Journal* had repeated in the teeth of the scoundrels whilst they were engaged in the actual work of robbing the Treasury without their daring to defend themselves—theirs being a still-hunt and play for time—and what happens? The brigands, backed by a foolish Administration, grow bold again. Not a scrap of incriminating evidence left outstanding and no chance of reprisal or recovery, they come out of hiding. The newspapers are hauled into court to answer a criminal libel.

They have come off free—indeed with feathers in their caps. We congratulate them. But, alas and alack the day! If the *Courier-Journal*, if grand old John Tyler Morgan could have had the New York *World* and the Indianapolis *News* by their side, whilst it was yet not too late, Linden might have seen another sight, the country saved and the Treasury intact.

PANAMA TOLLS

In April, 1914, Mr. Watterson and George Harvey were fighting side by side with Woodrow Wilson for the honor of the nation in upholding the Hay-Pauncefote treaty as to coastwise shipping tolls in the Panama Canal. This is one of the few times the three principals in the famous Manhattan Club affair were shoulder to shoulder on an issue where there was any great division of opinion. But to Mr. Watterson and the President, particularly, the attempt to maintain the remission of Panama Canal tolls to American vessels was cheating. The following editorial fully represents the editor's views.

The Nation's Honor and the Coastwise Shipping Steal

(April 29, 1914)

I

In the May number of the *North American Review*, Colonel George Harvey continues the series of salient articles he has been writing upon the state of public affairs with a close, searching inquiry into the tolls questions. He takes the right end of the argument, of course. But he reaches his conclusion through a process of reasoning which seems at times to concede overmuch to the other side.

For our part we can see nothing in the act remitting the tolls in favor of the coastwise shipping trust—a prosperous monopoly—but subsidy pure and simple; in the approval given this by the National Democratic platform only a piece of sharp practice worked upon the committee and the convention amid the confusion and excitement of the closing hours; and in the opposition to its repeal something very like selfish demagogism, more or less cowardly and dishonest.

Colonel Harvey, writing like a statesman as well as a publicist, goes about his work with deliberation and candor, pursuing it from one citation to another, through a long line of authorities, pro and con, arriving finally at the terms of the Hay-Pauncefote treaty itself, which, Rule I., Article 3, reads as follows:

> "The canal shall be free and open to the vessels of commerce and of war of all nations observing these rules, on terms of entire equality, so that there shall be no discrimination against any such nation, or its citizens or subjects, in respect of the conditions or charges of traffic, or otherwise. Such conditions and charges of traffic shall be just and equitable."

There cannot be two readings of this. It is as plain as words can make it. There is no need to go behind it in quest of the intention of its framers. Yet Colonel Harvey, seeking more than justice for the offside of the fence, of argument there being none, asks, Does the phrase "all nations observing these rules" include or exclude the United States; does the phrase "vessels of commerce" include coastwise vessels of the United States in the matter of the application of the language of the treaty; does the exemption of American coastwise vessels from the payment of tolls constitute such a discrimination against the vessels of other nations as is forbidden by the treaty?

These queries seem to us superfluous. Lord Pauncefote and Secretary Hay were straightforward and honest men. They knew the meaning of the language, and when they agreed upon the words of the treaty they carried out the fundamental principle of their diplomacy. "So far as I know anything about that Diplomacy," says Mr. Choate, who being Ambassador to England knew a great deal about it, "during the six years I was engaged with them their rule was to mean what they said and to say what they meant."

It happens, however, that there is more direct testimony than that even of Mr. Choate. This comes from John Hay himself. In an interview with Mr. Willis Fletcher Johnson, a journalist of the highest standing and credit, had as late as 1904, the American Secretary of State spoke with his wonted clearness and candor. Recalling the incident Mr. Johnson, as quoted by Colonel Harvey, says:

> "I asked Colonel Hay plumply if the treaty meant what it appeared to mean on its face, and whether the phrase 'vessels of all nations' was intended to include our own shipping, or was to be interpreted as meaning 'all other nations.' The Secretary smiled, half indulgently, half quizzically, as he replied:
>
> "'All means all. The treaty was not so long that we could not have made room for the word "other" if we had understood that it belonged there. "All nations" means all nations, and the United States is certainly a nation.'

" 'That was the understanding between yourself and Lord Pauncefote when you and he made the treaty?' I pursued.

" 'It certainly was,' he replied. 'It was the understanding of both Governments, and I have no doubt that the Senate realize that in ratifying the second treaty without such an amendment it was committing us to the principle of giving all friendly nations equal privileges in the canal with ourselves. That is our Golden Rule.' "

Going outside the language of the treaty—which were altogether needless—this would nail it down, leaving nothing more to be said. But Colonel Harvey does not stop here. He remembers that the Senate is a part of the treaty-making power and proceeds elaborately to quote what was said concurrently in that august body. It does not fease the case held by the people against the attorneys of the Coastwise Shipping Trust.

Colonel Harvey thinks, as fair men must, that "there is no escape from the conclusion that exemption is, as President Wilson has said, in plain contravention of the treaty with Great Britain," and that consequently "the large thing to do is the only thing we can afford to do—a voluntary withdrawal" from a false position, from which we must retreat or forfeit what Jefferson depicted as "decent respect for the opinions of mankind," and then he sums up as follows:

"True, we built the canal; we own it; true, Great Britain will derive greater advantage from its construction than all other nations combined; true—and to this extent we agree with Mr. Roosevelt—it ill behooves the British Government, under the circumstances, to raise the question of our coastwise traffic at all; true, if we repeal exemption now we do it for all time and admit foreign possession of a partial veto power which approaches more closely that we enjoy to a subtle encroachment upon the Monroe Doctrine; true, if you like, we made a bad trade, the terms of which would have been modified long since but for the utter inadequacy of our diplomatic service.

"But we have pledged our faith as a nation; and that is the beginning and the end of all argument. England may—in fact, surely will—derive vast material gains by holding us fast to the hard bargain which she drove so shrewdly and successfully, but if ultimately she profits as a nation from so flagrant a demonstration of narrow selfishness, her experience will be unique in the history of the world. With that we have nothing to do; it is her own affair.

"Our sole concern relates to our honor, and that must be preserved inviolate."

We cannot think that it was a hard bargain. Considering our shipping interests on the Lakes and what Canada did in the matter of the Welland Canal and her end of the Soo Canal, and might reverse if we persist on going back upon our word as to Panama, it is of the first moment that we repeal the Exemption Act. Every member of the Senate who votes to sustain the subsidy makes himself party to a breach of faith to promote an economic fallacy.

II

The "truckling to England" gag is an emanation of surpassing impudence. The "restoring the flag to the high seas" through subsidy is the economic fallacy. If we want to subsidize our ships let us by all means do so; let us do so openly and aboveboard. If our Irish friends want to jab England let them choose some fitter opportunity. But down with humbug. As far as the *Courier-Journal* is concerned, wherever it sees a politician hiding behind a subterfuge it will expose him no matter who he is or by what party name he calls himself.

Much has been said in these discussions about the transcontinental railways—especially the Canadian Pacific—and a line is sought to be drawn from the enormous grants of land made from time to time. In those days corruption was unbridled. They furnish neither argument nor precedent. On the contrary, they should warn us against repeating the crimes which were brought to light by the look into Credit Mobilier and Pacific Mail.

Neither should any American delude himself into the belief that subsidy will restore our lost carrying trade. Colonel Harvey seems himself to fall into this error when he says:

"What we do know is that forty-five years ago thirty-five per cent. of American shipping was carried in American vessels, and that to-day it hardly reaches nine per cent. of all seaborne traffic. Under the circumstances, we are disposed to believe that it would be sound economic policy to open the gates of the canal wide to revivification of the American mercantile marine, if we had the legal and moral right to do so."

It was our Navigation laws—the fruitage of high protection— that drove our flag from the high seas. Repeal those laws and it will quickly reappear. Under the Walker Tariff eighty-five per cent. of our foreign trade was carried in American bottoms. Let us build our ships free from high duties on everything that enters into their construction or buy them where we may buy them cheapest—that is, get them at as low a cost as our marine competitors, and we shall see this again.

The traditional Democratic position in the matter of subsidies was, and is, and ever will be, right. Why should the people tax themselves for the benefit of any special industry or interest? One enterprise has just the same right to claim help as any and every other. That which is not self-supporting should be gently permitted, and has been generally permitted, to go to the wall. Hoisting the flag above it means nothing and should not avail. The Government has no right, either in equity or law, to levy a dollar of taxation except for its own support.

The President does not pass unchallenged in some of his attitudes. When he said "I ask this of you in support of the foreign policy of the Administration. I shall not know how to deal with other matters of even greater delicacy and nearer consequence if you do not grant it to me in ungrudging measure," he went either too far or not far enough. The phrase has evoked an amount of speculation. It is, indeed, most inept. We agree with Colonel Harvey that it is not only so vague and mysterious as to be susceptible of many kinds of misconstruction, but is directly contrary to the President's professions of publicity as a worthy and effective force, and evinces an impolitic distrust of the leaders of the very co-ordinate branch of the Government to which he makes his appeal. The growing restiveness of Congress may be in part ascribed to this rather characteristic bit of Wilsonian tactlessness.

Again, Colonel Harvey takes the President to task for saying, "Whatever may be our own differences of opinion concerning this much debated measure, its meaning is not debated outside the United States; everywhere else the language of the treaty is given but one interpretation, and that interpretation precludes the exemption I am asking you to repeal," and comments as follows:

"The meaning of all this, of course, is that the United States should acquire in the judgment of other Powers, irrespective of our own opinion, without debate. We squarely dissent from any such doctrine. We agree with the London *Times,* which says frankly that 'such a notion is naturally unpalatable to a high-spirited people who feel themselves entirely competent to deal with all their foreign problems on the merits of each and without extraneous assistance.' Even admitting, although the evidences are not as yet forthcoming, that all other nations stand with Great Britain in this matter, we are nevertheless the party more directly and deeply concerned, and surely we are entitled to a hearing. We are unable, moreover, to see how President Wilson can sustain such a position with any degree of consistency while, at this very moment, he persists doggedly in refusing to recognize the de facto Government of Mexico, in plain defiance of the unanimous opinion of the civilized world. No other self-respecting nation on earth, least of all Great Britain, would make such an admission; and, whatever may be our final action on the Repeal Bill, the fact should be made indubitably clear that we do not."

This is sound doctrine no less than gospel truth. The President is never happy when treading upon foreign ground. His studies have been invariably domestic and economic. In this business he is right in his conclusion but wrong in his argument. It is a subsidy pure and simple and a clear violation of treaty obligation.

It is said by Mr. Wilson's critics that he was surprised by the opposition his stand in this matter provoked and that if he had foreseen it he would not have taken the stand. Let us hope and believe this to be an injustice. Anyhow, Colonel Harvey clears the decks of hair-splitting demagogy and other rubbish in his luminous article. If beneath his impressive writing the keen knife of the journalist sometimes thrusts itself, he yet writes like a statesman and a publicist, increasing the regret of many that he and not the inconsequent Page was sent as Ambassador to England; an appointment betraying the President's lack of perspective as well as his clouded discernment, in preferring among publishers that one least qualified as a kind of emphasis of disfavor to the other so admirably qualified and suited to its varied and complicated requirements.

T. R. AND THE TENNESSEE COAL DEAL

Morgan, Gary, Stanley, Littleton, Roosevelt, Mrs. Malaprop and Sir Anthony Absolute are but a small group of the many brilliant portraits which Mr. Watterson placed upon his editorial easel in his discussions of the Steel Trust investigation by the special House Committee in 1911. As a social entity, he was interested in these cross-examinations of his friends among the Nabobs, and charming passages like the pen picture or Morgan were the result. As an editor, he found excellent copy in the proceedings; and as a Democrat he perceived his party's mint piling up a good deal of political capital. So on this topic he wrote gleefully and at great length, and two of these articles are appended with their suggestions of the now dim, but once vivid, Tennessee coal and iron deal; and their final warning against mere destructive agitation. Marse Henry, despite his attacks on the "Money Devil," was a genuine Conservative.

As Good as a Play

(August II, 1911)

Mr. Stanley, of Kentucky, is making good upon the *Courier-Journal's* forecast of his character and abilities. He is getting at the bottom of the Steel Trust iniquity. The case is worse than anybody at the outset believed it was possible to be.

The pivot about which the investigation has thus far revolved has been the taking over of the Tennessee Coal and Iron Company by the United States Steel Corporation. Judge Gary began the story and Mr. Lewis Cass Ledyard has just completed it. There would seem to be nothing material more to tell. The great firm of Moore & Schley, loaded to the guards with Tennessee Coal and Iron, was about to go under. Its failure threatened to carry other great houses—maybe some great banks—along with it. To stay a still more destructive panic than had yet appeared upon the scene of Wall Street and to avert wide-spread, impending ruin over the country at large, recourse was had to that wizard of Art, Archæology and Finance, Mr. J. Pierpont Morgan.

Judge Gary made a fine figure in the witness chair. He is an example of the fact, so often noted in these columns, that the really potential men of the time are not in politics, but in business. Mr. Lewis Cass Ledyard is another shining example. Mr. Morgan, however, is the most world-famous Colossus of contemporary fortune-builders. He strides the oceans and is equally at home in Rome and Berlin, in London, Paris and New York, a commanding personality and power in each of the political and commercial capitals. We take off our hats to Mr. Morgan; a truly eminent American, typical of the masterfulness of his race, the genius and prowess of his country; son of Junius Morgan, the brains of George Peabody, grandson of John Pierpont, Poet and Preacher, inheriting from the one the imagination to conceive, from the other the wisdom and daring to execute; beloved among bankers and welcome among Kings, having the most lordly spirit and the worst manners to be found anywhere betwixt Hell-for-Sartin and Kingdom-Come! If Mr. Stanley calls Mr. Morgan he will get a daisy crossed on a cockle burr! Let him do so, by all means.

But softly; we must not forget the matter immediately in hand. Mr. Ledyard's testimony is vivid alike with narrative and suggestion. Well may it serve as prelude, or opening chorus, to the coming of the Master. After relating the conditions which led up to the edge of the threatened Moore & Schley catastrophe the grandson of Lewis Cass continued with this stirring recital:

"Sunday morning I called on Mr. Morgan in his library. When I described to him in detail Moore & Schley's predicament he expressed surprise and the most serious concern. He said that, as Moore & Schley were in the worst fix, attention ought to be given to that house.

"After I had talked with him an hour or more he telephoned for Judge Gary and Mr. Frick to come to his library.

"When I rejoined them at the conclusion of their conference and laid before them the proposition of Moore & Schley for the steel corporation to buy all the stock of the Tennessee Coal and Iron at par, Judge Gary was distinctly reluctant to do so.

"He said the Tennessee stock was not worth par; he doubted if it was worth more than sixty or sixty-five. I told Judge Gary the question was not as much what the exact commercial value of the stock was at the moment; that it was either to save Moore & Schley or to permit a situation to be brought about which meant the failure of other big banks and trust companies and an extension and intensification of panic conditions, and the end or result of which no man could foretell.

"I told him that if he should wait until the Tennessee Coal and Iron went, say, to 25, the steel corporation would not be in a condition to buy anything.

"That night, as I afterward learned, Messrs. Gary and Frick went to Washington.

"Before going away Mr. Frick asked me earnestly if, in my judgment, Moore & Schley could be saved by the steel corporation exchanging its second mortgage 5 per cent. bonds for the entire issue of Tennessee stock on a basis of 84 for the bonds and 119 for the stock, or about par for the stock. I told him I thought it could."

They were parlous hours. To lighten the shadows and beguile the strain, the princes, the viziers and the satraps gathered about Haroun-el-Raschid, put their heads and their purses together. "Judge Gary," Mr. Ledyard continues, "Judge Gary offered to loan Moore & Schley $5,000,000 of the steel corporation's money to help tide them over. Colonel Oliver Payne offered $1,000,000; George F. Baker, president of the First National Bank and brother-in-law of Mr. Schley, offered to loan them $1,000,000. One or two more millions in loans were offered by individuals, but Mr. Schley would not accept the loans. He declared they would not accomplish the purpose. He must make good his loans on about a hundred thousand shares of Tennessee stock, or his firm would fail, he said."

It takes one's breath away. These Muck-a-Mucks of Money-dom talk only in millions—not stage millions, either—and they carry themselves like field-marshals. The scene in the Morgan library is as thrilling as the best third act of the most successful popular drama. Here is a touch of the sure enough Arabian Nights:

"I remained with Mr. Morgan in his library Sunday night until 5 o'clock Monday morning. We were working every minute of the time.

"At 5 o'clock he told me to go home and get some sleep, but to be back in his library at 8:30 that morning. I went home, but could get no sleep. I took a cold bath, had some coffee, and in an hour returned to Mr. Morgan's house. When I arrived he was up and as chipper as if he had slept all night.

(He was then seventy years old.)

"He told me he had had a good sleep and a good breakfast and was ready for the day's work."

"Frick and Gary have gone to Washington. Nothing can be done," says Morgan to Ledyard, "until they get back. We shall have to wait."

Gone to Washington for what? To see the President of the United States and ask his consent to their breaking a law of the land, and, indeed, his co-operation whilst they did it. He gave his consent. And, there you are!

II

Every great affair, theatrical and financial, must have light and shade. The scene in the Committee room following the dramatic episode enacted by Mr. Ledyard was almost as good as a slice out of high comedy. Mr. Ledyard paused for half a minute at the point where he and Mr. Morgan were waiting for Frick and Gary to get back from Washington. Here, just like an ill-mannered Congressman, Mr. Martin Littleton broke in. Said Mr. Littleton:

" 'Did any money change hands in the transaction?'

" 'Not a dollar,' replied Mr. Ledyard.

" 'How much did J. P. Morgan & Co. receive as compensation for their work in this transaction?'

" 'Mr. Morgan charged not a penny for his services in this vitally important transaction,' quietly responded Mr. Ledyard."

That same afternoon, as Mr. Ledyard proceeded to relate, he and Mr. Morgan and the rest received a telegram from Messrs.

Frick and Gary that the Administration did not object to the deal, that the Government would not proceed against either company in the event the transaction were consummated, that all was well and quiet on the Potomac, and, in point of fact, then and there the comedy part of the proceeding came to pass. Thus:

> " 'But, Mr. Ledyard,' Mr. Littleton resumed, 'why did you have to go so far as to get the consent of the Government before closing this transaction?'
>
> "At this question Mr. Ledyard laughed until he was almost doubled in his chair.
>
> " 'Now, Mr. Littleton, you and I are practical men——'
>
> "The remainder of the sentence was drowned in a roar of laughter from the spectators and members of the Committee.
>
> " 'Are you using that expression in quotation marks or in its original sense?' inquired Mr. Littleton when order had been restored.
>
> " 'I did not intend to quote,' responded Mr. Ledyard, sheepishly, as if realizing that he unconsciously had plagiarized from an illustrious authority."

"Me, me, he means me," shrieks Mrs. Malaprop in the famous scene where Sir Anthony Absolute reads her the deprecating letter, and so Mr. Roosevelt might exclaim upon perusing the above passage. To bring it yet closer home, Mr. Littleton still, if not a bad man, a very bad-mannered Congressman, answering at once Mr. Ledyard's plea and query, speaks up and says he, or words to that effect, "shoo!" To which, "if you were counsel in a case involving the least doubt as to the legality of a desirable course, you would, I know, try first to find out what the Government's attitude would be before advising definitely what action to take, wouldn't you?" blandly urged Mr. Ledyard. And Mr. Littleton replied: "But what do you think about an administration that would permit such a transaction and guarantee immunity in advance?"

Springes to catch Teddy. Alack the day! Nevertheless it is given out that Chairman Stanley is seriously considering whether or not he will subpœna Mr. Roosevelt. To what purpose? The main facts are undisputed. Mr. Roosevelt could throw no new light upon them. He is quite beyond legal reach. We have no means of impeaching an ex-President. If Mr. Roosevelt cares to take the stand in his own defense that is quite another matter. But there would seem neither wisdom nor public benefit in seeking to bull-bait him with the view of driving him into a corner and humiliating him. That would hardly be a safe adventure either.

Toward the close of Mr. Ledyard's most interesting and wholly illuminating testimony, he took occasion to say: "I was born a Democrat, and am trying very hard to remain a Democrat. My grandfather was Democratic candidate for President, and nobody wants to be a Democrat more than I. But my party has of late wandered off after strange gods and I have not always been able to follow it. However, reason and sanity are returning to my party, I am delighted to see."

Between 1848, when Lewis Cass, of Michigan, and William O. Butler, of Kentucky, were the Democratic nominees for President and Vice-President, and 1911, many things have happened. In 1848, the government of the United States was a Slaveocracy. In 1911, as shown by these investigations, and the floods of light they have thrown upon the government of the country by the Republican party, which has been in power for the larger part of the last fifty years, it has been a Plutocracy. Having at the cost of incalculable blood and treasure escaped from the thraldom of Slavery, shall we be able with less cost to escape the thraldom of Money?

It is the opinion of the *Courier-Journal* that we may. But able and patriotic men like Mr. Morgan and Mr. Ledyard—who are assuredly both able and patriotic—will have to look farther and learn more than is now written upon the walls of the law-offices and bank chambers and directorates to which it may be said their lives are literally cabined, cribbed, and confined. When they talk politics they talk very like children. Most of them are open in their contempt for doctrinaires, all being doctrinaries who discuss the science of government, and yet they themselves know little else than the science of making money, which, deprived of its power to debauch, would, as far as politics is concerned, prove but a poor boy at a frolic.

In England money has measurably lost its corrupting influence. With the same safeguards over elections, covering legislative bodies, it will lose this power here. And both the millionaires and the commonalty will be the gainer by it. As long as money can buy votes, money will rule. When money can no longer buy votes, the people will rule. That may be a long way ahead. But it has started and is on the way.

The Steel Trust Inquiry

(June 5, 1911)

I

Never in the history of Government has such a flood of light irradiated the depths and revealed the mysteries of a subject of legislative inquiry as comes in answer to the summons of the Stanley Steel Trust Committee. Never the writer of romance had more startling tale to tell, or told it with greater effect, than Judge Gary, the head of the United States Steel Corporation. The hearings read like chapters out of Walter Scott or Alexander Dumas.

They are bewildering in the magnitude of the interests and the figures, breathless in the dramatic impressions, awe-inspiring in the portents and possibilities.

High Finance has in Judge Gary a High Priest worthy to sit upon Olympus. Steel, the magic wand of common life—the master-builder of the modern world—speaks to mankind through this wizard of constructive business in thunder-tones, and if good to man is to follow, these tones must be heard and heeded. It will remain for Mr. Stanley to show whether he is a constructive statesmen, or merely a party politician, for Mr. Littleton to indicate whether he is a leader, or just a lawyer. The opportunity for both of them is paramount.

The only good that is likely to come of the more or less insincere activities touching the Trusts and Trustism, in later years always prefacing a Presidential election, is publicity. The penalizing of one or a hundred violators of the law will bring no manner of permanent relief if the system be not completely overhauled and readjusted. Judge Gary makes this plain enough. We now know the truth about Tennessee Coal and Iron; about what actually happened; about what Morgan did, and Frick did, and Gary did, and Roosevelt and Root did. We know that all of them violated the law. What are we going to do about it? Was it a clear case of murder for money, or a case of justifiable homicide? There are undoubtedly mitigating circumstances put with persuasive force by Judge Gary. And there is the law itself—the double-dealing Sherman Act—to be taken into account.

II

It is not possible for any one familiar with the career, the character and the methods of the late John Sherman to believe that the Act of Congress which bears his name was intended to put a curb upon the Trusts and Trustism, or, in any wise, to restrain illicit gain.

John Sherman was nothing if not a slave of the Money Devil. He began his public life a poor young man and ended it a rich old man. Cold as an iceberg, unrelenting as wrought iron, he became in office the very Prime Minister of Plutocracy. He was an able, quick-seeing and far-seeing politician; the incarnation of the get-rich-quick spirit as applied to the evolutions of party through the operations of government; the engine-driver of predatory wealth, with one hand in the pockets of the people and the other upon the tiller ropes of legislation designed to rob the people under the forms of law.

The Tariff his fulcrum, public finance his lever, he knew precisely how and when to adjust and to balance, to hoist and to lower the power of corruption over the two Houses of Congress, in both of which he served so long, according to circumstances and conditions, the needs of his clients, the few, having never very long to wait upon the temper of the many, whom it was the business of his days and nights to hoodwink and pillage.

That such a man meant to serve the people, whom all his life he had consistently betrayed, and to obstruct or embarrass the masters who had enriched him, is inconceivable.

John Sherman merely saw that a tide was rising in the West which could not be resisted and must be ridden. Hence the Silver Purchase clause and the Anti-Trust clause of the legislation carrying the Sherman brand and trade-mark. They were springes to catch woodcock and they caught enough to victual the Republicans through twenty years of successful campaigning. What wonder that the Democrats had to repeal the Silver Purchase clause, and that the Supreme Court is put to its wits' end to find some reasonable interpretation of the Anti-Trust clause?

Judge Gary must revise his adjective. "Archaic," old fashioned, is not the term fittingly to describe the Sherman Act. "Tricky" is the word, "intended to deceive."

III

We, too, the people, will have to revise some of our proverbs. Is "competition the life of trade," under all conditions? Is "monopoly" always oppressive? Are there not circumstances which modify each of these ancient axioms? May they not, to use Judge Gary's term, be "archaic"?

Combination—"co-operation" Judge Gary calls it—is a rule of modern commerce which must be considered by a larger, if not a new, reading of political economy. The Trust—give a dog a bad name!—is here and it is here to stay. It can no more be extinguished than electricity, shut off than automobiles and airships. That which is wanted is to cure it of evil doing and this can perhaps be done through such Government supervision of it as will insure the same publicity as prevails with respect to the banks and is beginning to prevail with respect to the railways.

The Democrats in Congress, with Mr. Stanley and Mr. Littleton at their head, have as great an opportunity to render service to the country in the matter of Trustism, as with Mr. Clark and Mr. Underwood at their head, they have to render in the matter of the Tariff.

We shall gain nothing as a party, nor accomplish any reform which will outlast the season and inure to the benefit of the people, if we do not drop both the temper and the language of agitation, and drive at the evils to be actually reached.

Rome was not built in a day. Corruption cannot be driven out by a single session, limited to a single branch, of Congress. Already Mr. Stanley is getting at the facts of the business situation. Already Mr. Underwood is revealing the fallacies of Protectionism without pulling the house down upon us before we are ready to move. We have had at Washington thirty years of constructive statesmanship aimed chiefly in the interest of the favored few. That they have profited by it to the tune of piling up mammoth fortunes in less than a generation goes without saying and is not surprising. Scarcely any of these enormous aggregations of wealth would bear close moral scrutiny. Yet, short of anarchy, it is not probable that we can legally reach one of them. It is the system which is wrong, and the removal of this system to which we must address ourselves. And we must do this as doctors seeking remedies, not as demagogues seeking applause; as statesmen invested with the long-range glasses of truth, not as inquisitors wearing the death's cap and gown of judgment.

Meanwhile the great Steel Magnate has spoken the truth. He has spoken like a patriot and like a seer. He has suggested a way out. Neither he nor Mr. Morgan—nor yet Mr. Carnegie, who is later to appear—stand as culprits at the bar of criminal justice, but as Americans who have the right to speak and to be heard— and who will be heard—by their countrymen!

POLITICAL ADVICE FOR THE NEGRO

The social and political future of the colored race were always objects of thoroughly disinterested concern to Mr. Watterson. The first year of his editorship he conducted against a bogus Kentucky branch of the Ku Klux Klan a campaign which sent many of its leaders to jail. His voice was always raised for civil equality, and throughout the nation the negro race recognized him as its first Southern champion. In the subjoined he wrote a review of his contact with the colored race in an effort to prove the folly of racial solidarity at the polls. The negroes of Kentucky, however, are still voting the Republican ticket *en masse*.

The Negro and His Vote

(October 27, 1908)

We find the following paragraph floating around loose in the Republican papers:

"Henry Watterson says the negroes have paid their debt forty times over to the Republican party and should now vote the Democratic ticket. In this connection, might a wayfarer ask, what do the negroes owe to the Democratic party?"

This is a characteristic misrepresentation. The *Courier-Journal* is not advising the negroes "to vote the Democratic ticket." It is giving them reasons which it considers and which they ought to consider good reasons why they should cease solidly to vote the Republican ticket. Their true interest is to review the past, to revise the present, and to consider whether, having paid whatever debt they may think they owe the Republican party, they should not take account of their true situation and actual relation to the political, social and industrial fabric. They have everything to lose and nothing to gain by lending themselves to a body of selfish file leaders, who have used them only to abuse them.

They owe nothing to the Democrats and the Democrats offer them nothing. As an organism, the Democrats are not seeking their votes. If they were they would be fooling them precisely as the Republican party has fooled them.

On this question the *Courier-Journal* has always stood apart from all party fellowship and organization. It has put the race question above the mean and sordid interest of the potwollopers. The prosperity and happiness of the black people are indispensable to the prosperity and happiness of the white people. The *Courier-Journal* has stood steadily for giving the negro "a white man's chance." Ever for the under dog in the fight, it speaks for Society at large when it says that the interests of the two races are parallel and identical; that each has its place to fill; each its peculiar obligations and duties. Over and over again the Editor of the *Courier-Journal* has declared that he wants nothing for himself and his children which he does not freely concede the humblest black man and his children; yet, never has he sought the black man's vote, and he is not seeking it now.

Forty years ago the *Courier-Journal* was fighting for the rights of all men to live, move and have their being upon the readjustments established by the three last amendments to the Constitution of the United States. It fought to remove and it did remove the old black laws from the Statute books of Kentucky. It ran down the Kentucky Ku Klux, a bogus organization of night riders not remotely connected with the Klan South of us, whose chief exploitation was raiding negro cabins and shooting up inoffensive black people, and it put some forty of the leaders in the penitentiary. It secured the Negro his rights of locomotion in Louisville without the firing of a gun, or a bloody nose. In the matters of justice and law it has known no racial distinctions, and it has some claim—recognized by every colored man of intelligence in the City and the State—to the confidence of its Negro fellow-citizens.

Proceeding upon this claim, it has in this campaign advised them to stop a lick, or two, and look at the facts. What do they get out of the political wrangles of the whites? By voting as a unit with the Republicans they line up with a pitiful minority of whites against the mass and body of those who employ them. Yet it is to these latter that they look not only for employment, but for charity, sympathy and succor in time of need. Is this either wise or just?

At the North they are shut out from most of the paying occupations. In many communities they are told to "move on." In most they are "undesirable citizens." The South is their sure refuge. The white people of the South are their only true friends. If they give the South over to the foreign immigrant, as the North has been given over, they are lost. They can hold it forever by making themselves fit and proper work people.

They now constitute our labor system. We want them and they want us. But we don't want them if they are sullen and discontented. We want them as they are industrious and happy. The better class of whites are doing their best to make them so. The wicked and detestable whites are doing their uttermost to keep them in a state of ignorance, agitation and disorder. Every time, therefore, that a black man votes a Republican ticket he puts a cudgel in the hands of a mean white man to lay upon the back of the entire negro race, whereas, if he divided his vote, or refused to vote at all—showed some independence and enlightenment—he would soon see the difference.

This has been, and is, the attitude of the *Courier-Journal* toward the black people of the South, of Kentucky, and of the City of Louisville and of the County of Jefferson.

They should serve notice on the Republicans that they are not mere hewers of political wood and haulers of party water.

They should show the Democrats that they are not a mere body of hostile janissaries.

That is the lesson taught by Booker Washington. He is a great and good man. That is the lesson taught by Bishop Alexander Walters. He, too, is a great and good man. Their counsels will lead the Negro to peace and prosperity and contentment.

They will make him respect himself, and in proportion as he respects himself, will come to him the respect of other men. He is here, and he is here to stay. Shall he divide a labor field which he now monopolises with the Italian, the Slav and the riff-raff of Europe, inviting them here by his sloth and spleen, or shall he keep it inviolate and intact by making himself the better workman, the better neighbor, the better citizen?

The South wants him and it prefers him. But it wants a workman, not a politician, particularly a politician in the hands of hostile strangers and of local self-seekers, who are only after his vote and want to keep him down the better to make sure of this, using him as a club to beat the mass and body of the white population.

There are plenty of intelligent and upright Negroes here who perfectly understand these things. They are good citizens and patriotic men. They know that the *Courier-Journal* would take no advantage of them, and is not seeking their vote, but their prosperity and happiness, and that under every and all circumstances it is their constant friend and well-wisher.

TO CONFIRM BRANDEIS

So far as the writer of these notes was ever able to discover during an intimacy of many years, Mr. Watterson had no social or racial prejudices. In smiling speech he would now and then consign to Hades "a Cockney Jew" or an "Oirishman" or a "naygur," especially if these nationals were writing articles attacking him. But he judged and welcomed every man on his personal merits; and that Louis D. Brandeis was a Jew and a radical were added reasons why Marse Henry favored his elevation by Mr. Wilson to the Supreme Court. Brandeis and his family were known most favorably to the editor, and this article opposing the efforts to sidetrack the judicial nomination had its source in Mr. Watterson's heart.

The Persecution of Brandeis

(April 26, 1916)

The rule has been to select the Justices of the Supreme Court of the United States from among the more successful members of the Bar. The more successful members of the Bar have been for the most part those who are known as corporation counsel. Conservatism is no name for their immobility.

Not one of the learned professions has made less progress than that of the law. It clings with bigoted tenacity to its ancient practice and established ethics. Yet no body of men on earth is less fixed in the essential virtues of conscience. The fundamental principle and purpose of its being are to make the worse appear the better reason; sometimes to thwart justice and sometimes to quicken injustice; the law's delays and the subterfuges alike of courts and attorneys among the evils of government that have been hardest to reach and reform.

The medical profession long resisted progress. It, too, held to its "practice" and its "ethics." It held indeed like grim death, which it generally contrived to hasten. Through the centuries it opposed each and every upward and onward movement. "Specialism" was denounced as quackery. The "specialist" was outlawed. But the trend toward human relief was irresistible. As a consequence we have had within a single generation a scientific revolution.

The appointment of Louis D. Brandeis to the Bench of the Supreme Court of the United States was received by the average American lawyer very much as an old-time medicine man would have received the selection of a Homeopathist as Surgeon General of the Army of the United States. The legal profession was up in arms. Brandeis had sometimes fought corporations instead of always fighting for them. He had actually volunteered his services where a just cause was too poor to pay for its attorney. His learning could not be denied. So they began an organized assault upon his character. Lawyers were paid by rascally or revengeful corporations to go to Washington and assail his confirmation by the Senate. If he had been a malefactor he could not have been subjected to a more drastic and dishonest prosecution. And now it is pointed out by a corporation newspaper organ as an argument "that the president and seven former presidents of the American Bar Association regard Brandeis as unfit to be a member of the Court," and stated as a fact "that not a voluntary witness appeared to testify as to his reputation." "This," says the organ in question, "is most extraordinary. Had Mr. Brandeis no friends who could come forward to give him the support he so sorely needed to counteract the bad impression created by the large number of witnesses who testified that they regarded him as unscrupulous and untrustworthy, with a defective standard of professional ethics?

This is a falsehood outright, of course. There were as many witnesses for as against Mr. Brandeis, the difference being that those who testified in his favor were truthful, disinterested men, whilst those who testified against him were for the most part mercenary liars paid to go to Washington and perjure themselves.

Such ex-Presidents of the American Bar Association as Choate

and Root and Story inevitably regard a Jew on the Supreme Bench
as a desecration, whilst ex-President Taft found in Brandeis an
antagonist who put his Administration on the grill and left some
of its members in a hole from which they have never been able
to extricate themselves. That kind of opposition was to be
expected.

The Senate should go ahead and do its duty. Brandeis will
make both an able and a useful Associate Justice. The Court will
find in him what it really needs—an intellect not hidebound by
precedent, learning varied and profound, and immense capacity
for work. His rejection would be a shame and scandal for which
individual Senators would have to answer. Meanwhile here in
Louisville we know Louis Brandeis to be a man of the highest
integrity and merit.

"THANK GOD FOR GETTYSBURG"

No article which came from the editor's pen was more admired
than his semi-centennial treatise on Gettysburg, on the occasion of the celebration in 1913. There was not another
publicist in the United States so well equipped to discuss the
war of which Gettysburg is a symbol.

Gettysburg

(July 4, 1913)

1863-1913

I

It is historically agreed that Gettysburg was the decisive battle
of the War of Sections. Had the Confederates won it they might
have carried all before them. But, failing to win it, and having to
retire into Virginia and take up the old lines of defense South of
the Potomac, they could never hope again—

> "Above the bayonets mixed and crossed
> Men saw a gray, gigantic ghost
> Receding through the battle cloud,
> And heard athwart the tempest loud
> The death-cry of a nation lost."

It is claimed that if orders issued had been obeyed, Lee, and
not Meade, would have achieved the victory. Thus, if the claim
be true, chance determined the result. But, from first to last, this
mysterious agency interposed at every critical juncture to check-

mate the Confederates; the fall of Albert Sidney Johnston at Shiloh and of Stonewall Jackson at Chancellorsville; the timely arrival of the *Monitor* in Hampton Roads; the almost miraculous destruction of the *Albemarle* in Roanoke River, to name only the more important examples of what seemed special Providence. As if the disparity of forces was not enough, the cause of the Union was supplemented at every turning by the casualties of action. The best that can be said of the South is that it stood so long against such odds.

At Vicksburg, on the occasion of the unveiling of the statue to General Stephen D. Lee in the National Cemetery, a battered but beaming old Confederate made his way to the platform, and in a voice breezy with good-will exclaimed to General Frederick D. Grant, "Fred, old sport, I want to shake your hand, and with no hard feelings let me say that you never licked us—you just wore us out!"

That, taking into account the prevailing conditions, the South was willing to go to war seems now a kind of fatuity. No people were so happily situate. They had everything to lose, and nothing to gain, no matter what the issue might be. The trend of modern thought throughout the world was set against the institution of African Slavery. Even if it had been the most benign and economic of labor systems, which it was not, it was doomed. No single reliance of the more extreme and optimistic of Southern men held to the event: that cotton was King; that the North would not fight; that England and France would be compelled to intervene. All went wild.

Most wars that are not predatory may be described as illogical. Our War of Sections seems so when we reflect that after all its losses it left us where it found us. No problem was solved. We had to go back and build over again as best we might upon the old superstructure. "To bind up the nation's wounds; to care for him who shall have borne the battle, and for his widow and his orphan—to do all which may achieve and cherish a just and lasting peace among ourselves and with all nations"—immortal words that still ring out from the grave of Lincoln—they apply equally to the South and the North to the end that "government of the people, by the people and for the people shall not perish from the earth."

Thank God for Gettysburg!

II

The doctrine of Secession was born in New England. Slavery was brought to America in New England ships. Finding negro labor unprofitable, New England sold her slaves to the South, and, putting the money she got for them in her pocket, turned philanthropist; a gold-brick transaction worthy of the pious ones of Plymouth, who, reaching the Rock, "first," as Evarts phrased it, "fell upon their own knees and then upon the Aborigines."

Yet let not the South put up a poor mouth. Neither let her boast her superior manhood and morality. She made her bed and must lie in it. Too many Yankees migrated to Dixie in the early days for the South to claim and proclaim any exclusive blood canon, or exceptional code of ethics. There was, in good truth, never a greater fiction than the terms Puritan and Cavalier which an effete sectionalism once sought to affix as descriptive labels classifying and separating North and South, building verbal redoubts along a mythical line called Mason and Dixon over which there were supposed to be no bridges.

We do not hear nowadays much about Puritans and Cavaliers. Each was good enough and bad enough in its way; each in its turn filled the English-speaking world with mourning, and each, if either could have resisted the infection of the soil and climate they found here, would be still striving to square life by the iron-rule of Theocracy, or to round it in the dizzy mazes of the dance. It is very pretty to read about the Maypole in Virginia and very edifying to celebrate the piety of the Pilgrim Fathers. But there is not Cavalier blood enough left in the Old Dominion to produce a single crop of first families, whilst, out in Nebraska and Iowa, they do say that they have so stripped New England of her Puritan stock as to leave her hardly enough for farm-hands.

To readers of the *Courier-Journal* it is an old story, but it will always bearing repeating, that we are a wondrously homogeneous as we are an uncommonly united people, and have been always so. Long before our War of Sections there had been such a mixing up of Puritan babies and Cavalier babies that when it arrived the surviving grandmothers of the combatants could not, except for their uniforms, have picked out their own on any field of battle! Behold them to-day at Gettysburg.

Turning to the Encyclopedia of American Biography, we shall find, to come down to specific examples, that Webster had all the vices supposed to have signalized the Cavalier, and Calhoun all the virtues claimed for the Puritan. During twenty years three statesmen of Puritan origin were the chosen party leaders of Cavalier Mississippi: Robert J. Walker, born and reared in Pennsylvania; John A. Quitman, born and reared in New York, and Sargent S. Prentiss, born and reared in the good old State of Maine. That sturdy Puritan, John Slidell, never saw Louisiana until he was old enough to vote and to fight; a native New Yorker sprung from New England ancestors. Albert Sidney Johnston, the most resplendent of modern Cavaliers—from trig to toe a type of the species—did not have a drop of Southern blood in his veins; Yankee on both sides of the house, though born in Kentucky a little while after his father and mother arrived there from Connecticut.

And the Cavaliers who missed their stirrups somehow and got into Yankee saddles? The woods were full of them. If Custer was not a Cavalier, Rupert was a Puritan. And Sherwood and Wadsworth and Kearney and McPherson and their dashing companions and followers! The one typical Puritan soldier of the war, be it never forgotten, was a Southern, not a Northern, soldier; Stonewall Jackson, of the Virginia line. And, if we should care to pursue the subject further back, what about Ethan Allen and John Stark and Mad Anthony Wayne, Cavaliers each and every one! Indeed, from Israel Putnam to Buffalo Bill, the Puritans have had rather the better of it in turning out Cavaliers. So the least said about the Puritan and the Cavalier—except as blessed memories or horrid examples—the safer for historic accuracy.

III

After the reading of Lincoln's inspired speech—to each thought and word of which every true-hearted American may subscribe—the orator of the occasion at Gettysburg—it were fitting that he should be the President of the United States—should turn aside from the glories of the past to the dangers of the present.

Eternal vigilance is the price of everything, including liberty, and liberty often, like the cow in the nursery rhyme, "jumps over the moon," and one man is as good as another only whilst he behaves himself.

The whole history of government, as the *Courier-Journal* has often shown, is a record of force and fraud. Begun in the one to deepen into the other, it has offered, from the outset, boundless opportunities for robbers and cheats. The giant with his club, the first King of men, licked all the lesser giants in his neck o' woods. Then two or three giants of equal degree made a mill and contended for the belt. Thus the Nations. Finally, gunpowder having arrived upon the scene, it became necessary to establish classifications and degrees, based on something other than muscle. Thus the Nobility.

From first to last the scrimmage was a fight for land. The Court, with its corrupt favoritism—the freebooting Palatinate in Germany—the Harlotocracy in France—the Anglo-Saxon Hierarchy, "'alf and 'alf," in England—had four or five hundred years of the tyrannous exercise of arbitrary power.

The mud-sills at length began to show their teeth. First, after Jack Cade and Wat Tyler, Cromwell. Then the American Revolution. Then the French Revolution. The hewers of wood and the drawers of water became too numerous and too noisy for the giants. They insisted on a share of the spoil. They got a lot of notions into their heads about a new-fangled crazy quilt they called the Rights of Man. They demanded "a bill of particulars" and they formulated "a Charter of Liberty." After a while, they trolled into the walled precincts of Royalty a Trojan Horse they disguised under the name of Constitutional Government. The result is that now the Lord's Anointed in Germany and in England take off their hats and talk pleasantly as they pass by. The only club the modern giant relies on is a stuffed club; a club filled with sweetmeats and compliments, ribbons and stars and garters for the meritorious of the multitude, who serve him.

In France they have what they describe as a Republic. So have we in the United States. Yet, mark how with us the self-elect are constantly seeking to take matters into their own hands, to reduce the number of those who are to put finger in the pie, and otherwise to lord it over the many, to confirm their holdings and to keep their seats in the saddle.

Money has become to the modern King of the Commons—for so they delight to christen themselves alike in Monarchic Europe and Republican America—what gunpowder was to the earlier, feudal Kings. The club is succeeded by a sack of gold. And thus we have modern Politics, the most empiric of all the arts, if an art at all, the first lesson of which is how best to throw dust in the eyes of the voters. "Progress" is the word as "Freedom" was. Ambition, calling itself "Leader," declaims against "Bosses" and "Bossism." Each, according to his version, "stands at Armageddon and is fighting for the Lord." Yet the one and the other, the "big" and the "little," may be held at arm's length and sharply cross-examined before their drafts are accepted, and even then security should be required.

When Henry the Fourth, in France, or Henry the Eighth, in England, wanted an Estate—or a Woman—he just reached out after the object of his desire, saying simply, "Here! You! Come into camp!" The modern Would-be must be more circumspect. He poses as "a friend of the people," as "a lover of civil liberty," as "a guardian of law and order," or, consolidating all forms of demagogy into one big, nervy claim—he rattles around as "a Reformer." In proportion as he is blatant, he is likely to be corrupt. If he becomes very bitter, unresponsive to suasion, deaf to reason, be sure he has sold himself to the devil, and sold cheap. Precisely as the woman who boasts of her virtue will bear watching may we suspect the man who pretends to be braver and more honest than any man ought to be, or can possibly be.

Woodrow Wilson, being President of the United States, and having attended night school, knows all about these things and can tell the boys at Gettysburg lots. Recalling our War of Sections and what it cost us—how especially the fanatics on either side failed to get what they so clamorously wanted—recalling the period of Reconstruction, with its wrongs and mistakes—the chief, almost the only, lesson taught us is to beware of sentimental extremism. Now, as then, and ever and ever, implacable politics is corrupt politics, and the implacable politician a fool, when he is not a knave; because, if he be not feathering his nest along with his kind, he might as well be for all the good he does.

In public life, as in private life, the best men, whatever their opinions, are the just men. They are men of good sense and good feeling. To give and take—but always above the belt and in the open—to live and let live—to bear and to forbear—to abjure malice and to accept results—these are the bed-rocks of Government worthy to be called free; of citizenship worthy to be called Sovereign.

We live in untoward times. We have witnessed wondrous things. With the passing away of the old problems, new problems confront us. Modern invention has smashed the clock and pitched the geography into the sea. The map of the world, so completely altered that it really begins to look like the Fourth of July, lends itself as a telescope to the point of view. Concentration is becoming the universal demand, the survival of the fittest the prevailing law. The rule of Force by established usage is passing. The rule of the Many by Majorities is at hand. The idiosyncrasy of the Nineteenth Century was liberty. The idiosyncrasy of the Twentieth Century is markets. Be it ours to look to it that we steer between the two extremes of commercialism and anarchism, for, if we have not come to the heritage, which God and Nature and the providence of our fathers stored up for us, to employ it in good works, we had better not come to it at all.

Thoughtful Americans, true to the instincts of their manhood and their racehood, answering the promptings of an ever-watchful patriotism; carrying in their hearts the principles of that inspired Declaration to which their country owes its being as one among the Nations of the Earth; carrying in their minds the limitations of that matchless Constitution to which their Government owes its stability and its power; conscientious, earnest Americans can not look without concern upon the new dangers that assail us as we plow through the treacherous waters which, for all our boasted deep-sea soundings, sometimes threaten to engulf our Ship of State. But the people, the whole people, can never be corrupted. The history of a hundred years of Constitutional Government in America, the moral lesson and the experience of all our parties, may be told in a single sentence, that when any political organization, grown overconfident by its successes and faithless to its duty, thinks it has the world in a sling, public opinion just rises up and kicks it out. In that faith let us rest our hope of the future of the country; sure that in the long run wrong cannot prosper, and that an enlightened public opinion is a certain cure for every ill.

Hosanna! God bless us every one, alike the blue and the gray, the gray and the blue! The world ne'er witnessed such a sight as this. Beholding, can we say, "happy the nation that hath no history"? Perhaps, after all, the war was not in vain. God knows, and God is just and wise. And God is there to-day; upon the green hillsides, now decked with flowers, that ran with blood; in the blue skies once thick with powder clouds, now sweet with summer; marching heart-to-heart with the boys to the music of Heaven and the drum-beats of the Union "amid the cheers of Christendom." Hosanna, in the Highest!—

> "God lives! He forged the iron will
> That clutched and held that trembling hill.
> God lives and reigns! He built and lent
> The heights for freedom's battlement,
> Where floats her flag in triumph still!
>
> "Fold up the banners! Smelt the guns!
> Love rules. Her gentler purpose runs.
> A mighty mother turns in tears
> The pages of her battle years,
> Lamenting all her fallen sons!"

DOWN WITH THE MONROE DOCTRINE

In 1913 Mr. Watterson became alarmed about the Administration's Mexican policy. He blamed the Monroe Doctrine for all the troubles of the United States to the south. On February 22d of that year, alarmed by the Administration proposal for a Nicaraguan protectorate, he uttered a stentorian demand that this country abandon the Monroe Doctrine. It was a British inspiration, he said, and if pursued along the lines of intervention, policing and financing in Mexico and other Latin-American countries, it would result in untold loss of life and property. Annexation of the entire territory from Texas to Panama was worth considering, wrote Mr. Watterson, and for a while he headed a few editorials with "On to Panama." But if annexation were not to be the programme, he strongly urged the isolation of this country to the extent that it should "meddle no longer" in Latin-American affairs.

Taft was one of the American statesmen who took issue with the Kentucky editor, and there was a great deal of language exchanged back and forth on the subject. But Mr. Watterson remained confident that the United States was certain to get into war with Europe if it pursued a supervisory policy toward Latin-America, and in the four long editorials in the appended group he developed his theme over a period of two years.

The cataclysm in Europe which followed seven months after the final editorial of this series disposed of the topic of Latin-America forever, so far as Mr. Watterson is concerned, but he found fresh material for his thought when in the proposal of the League of Nations in 1918 he saw a meddlesome extension of the Monroe Doctrine to the entire world. Thus, what was an argument in favor of the League to most Americans was a poisonous objection from his standpoint.

The final in this group of editorials is remarkable in its revelation of how entirely innocent of the forthcoming calamity were the minds of average men. "There will indeed be no more earth-shaking wars," was written as late as January, 1914.

Away With It!

(February 22, 1913)

As most readers know, the Monroe Doctrine is not native and to the manner born. It was of British inspiration and sprang from the fertile brain of George Canning. In Mexico and South America the Spanish Colonies had risen to throw off the yoke of the mother country and to set up a chain of independent Republics. Spain alone was not able to whip them back. But, by the aid of the Bourbons in Austria and France, committed to what was called The Holy Alliance, there might be hope.

England regarded the combine with apprehension. It certainly menaced the British primacy. But the Canning Ministry could not see its way openly to oppose it. So, through the American Minister at the Court of St. James, it was intimated to the Administration at Washington that, if the Government of the United States, having a paramount interest in Republicanism, should warn Continental Europe to keep its distance, John Bull held himself ready in the event that trouble ensued to bring up the supports.

Thus the word came to be spoken by Monroe.

The idiosyncrasy of the Nineteenth century was Liberty. We, ourselves, had just attained it. To us, hatred and fear of kingcraft and priest-craft possessed a definite meaning. No Alliance, Holy or otherwise, should be allowed to cross the seas, and, overcoming the revolted provinces of Spain, obtain a foothold upon the free soil of America.

The Monroe Doctrine appealed to national interest, feeling and vanity. It met an immediate and eager popular response, and, the lost power of Spain in the New World being never recovered, it came down the corridors of time a very shibboleth of freedom and freemen. By 1865 its prestige had grown so great and was so conceded, that a wink was as good as a nod to the French in Mexico to pick up their doll rags and go!

The idiosyncrasy of the Twentieth Century is Commerce. Measurably the world has achieved its liberty. Everywhere institutional freedom, more or less, exists. America is no longer threatened by Monarchism. Europe is threatened by Republicanism. What further need have we of the Monroe Doctrine?

But this is not all. Who ever dreamed in Monroe's time that his Doctrine committed us to underwriting the sovereignty, the indebtedness, and the peace and order of the Latin-American States? Manifest Destiny, a sub-title given the Monroe Doctrine by modern jingoism, has been construed to mean many things. But nobody stretched it to cover the Governments of Mexico and Central and South America as a blanket.

There was indeed something like an outcry when in the Venezuela affair the Cleveland Administration put on the old mask as if to frighten England. Yet neither Cleveland, nor Olney, then Secretary of State, exceeded the limitation originally laid down by Monroe.

Each, seeking an exact definition, wrote of it. Said Cleveland: "The traditional and established policy of this Government is to oppose forcible increase by any European Power of its territorial possessions on this continent." Said Olney: "The vital feature of the Monroe Doctrine is that no European Power shall forcibly possess itself of American soil and forcibly control the political fortunes and destinies of its people."

What European Power is trying to get possession of a foot of territory in Mexico? How is the "Republicanism" of Mexico menaced by the "Monarchism" of Europe? In what are we more concerned for safety and order in Mexico than are England, Germany or France? Wherein does the Monroe Doctrine require us to assume all the responsibility? Even if it did, what relation had the purpose of the Doctrine as delivered by Monroe with any of the conditions which now prevail either in America, or in the world at large? Why should we not invite all the Powers to join us in the enforcement of order and law and the protection of life and property? What difference can be found in the situation in Mexico to-day and the situation which existed in China during the Boxer uprising?

Mexican intervention means war. It means the taking over of the Mexican country. It means a police army of occupation continued indefinitely.

We cannot hope to absorb the barbaric hordes of Mexico into our civilization. We cannot hope to govern them through the agencies of our political system. Who shall say that the attempt might not end with the overthrow of our own liberties?

But, in any event—Mexico apart—we should relegate the Monroe Doctrine to the lumber-room of things that were. It is Mexico to-day, to-morrow it may be another, the very thought of a protectorate over any of these semi-civilized aggregations of Indians, Negroes, Creoles, densely ignorant and savagely inclined, repugnant to good sense and good neighborhood.

It is not ours either to police them, or to indorse their credit. They already hate us because of our power and our patronage. We should leave them severely alone, rescind the Monroe Doctrine and go our ways rejoicing.

THE ADMINISTRATION'S NEW DEPARTURE

(July 26, 1913)

"Dunderhead" Not "Drumhead" Diplomacy

I

That the Administration, backed by the enormous resources and giving effect to the resistless power of the Nation, may set up and maintain a Protectorate, not alone over Nicaragua, but over all the Central American States, is plain enough. Thus far at least to the Southward, if no further, our fiat can be established as law. But, before we undertake a task so stupendous, shall we not count the cost?

Says Senator Borah, of Idaho:

"I am unwilling to take the first step until I have weighed all the consequences of the last step; and, therefore, I am opposed to a protectorate over Nicaragua until I am satisfied that we ought to take possession ultimately of all the territory from here to the Panama Canal.

"This proposed treaty is outside of any principle of the Monroe Doctrine as understood by its authors, and turns the principle of protection into the doctrine of aggression. For this Republic to assume the position of a protector over an independent government, that subtle form and specious guise by which deliberate aggression is always concealed, is, to me, unthinkable.

"When this three million is gone—what then? What is a treaty worth made by a kaleidoscopic government which may change in a fortnight? What will be our duty to American citizens who go in under a protectorate and make investment? When can we quit pulling up, and when can we withdraw?

"It is clear that 'drumstick diplomacy' can only end in ultimate and absolute possession and ownership. If we had not wandered so far from the concepts of our fathers this would startle the country; but as it is, I presume it will pass to a glorious fulfillment."

Here we have the language of a Statesman. Let us consider it. "This proposed treaty," to repeat the Senator's words, "is outside of any principle of the Monroe Doctrine as understood by its authors." It is outside every profession hitherto made by William Jennings Bryan. As for the Monroe Doctrine, we abandoned it long ago. To name no other instance we put foot upon its promise of noninterference with European affairs when we established ourselves in the Philippines and wrenched Cuba and Porto Rico from Spain. It will not do, therefore, to plead the Monroe Doctrine in support of an aggression having neither "manifest destiny" nor "benevolent assimilation" for a pretext.

"What is a treaty worth," says Senator Borah, "made by a kaleidoscopic Government which may change in a fortnight?" Verily, not the paper it is written on. Its sole binding power is battleships and marching armies. Declining to unite with any faction in Mexico, we propose to finance a faction in Nicaragua; and proceeding Southward, to take in Costa Rica, and Northward, to include the mongrel Republics of Salvador, Guatemala and Honduras—why not, since we have already despoiled Colombia of Panama, penetrate South America and give the protesting Latins sure proof at once of the truth of their fears and of our all-conquering intentions?

Whatever argument there may be as to Nicaragua is good for all the rest. The only argument for any is derived from the much-abused and ill-understood gospel of "expansion." That rests on conquest and conquest alone. It actually implies all or none. We cannot stop with Nicaragua. And, when we have taken over Central America, and invaded South America, what about Mexico? Can we safely leave Mexico outside the combine? By that time the jingo will be firmly in the saddle. He will require that we annex Mexico.

"If we had not wandered so far from the concepts of our fathers, this would startle the country," concludes the Idaho

Statesman, "but, as it is, I presume it will pass to a glorious consummation."

It may be so. The surrender of the Administration to the jingo spirit of the time—crossing the tracks of its professions of sanity, peace and reform—of progress on sober and orderly Democratic lines—invites alliance with the very System we came in to dethrone—that is, every questionable element in the land, the Armor Plate Trust, the Steel Trust, the Money Trust, all seeking outlet and deliverance from too close scrutiny of home affairs through a splendid, all-absorbing foreign policy, promising plenty of battleships and at one and the same time new fields for investment along with the safety of investments already made.

Nothing put forth by Theodore Roosevelt in his most ambitious and destructive mood—nothing suggested of him, or feared of him—was so far-reaching and fantastic as this half-baked scheme of mistaken national aggrandizement and wanton international spoliation.

The fly-by-night Republic of Panama, with William Nelson Cromwell working one end and Philippe Buneau-Varilla working the other—the Roosevelt Administration holding whilst those two adventurers skinned Colombia—the Gray Wolves of the Senate looking on complacent—the Forty Thieves of Paris and Washington to pocket the Forty Millions of swag—was bad enough. It wrote the blackest page in our Diplomatic annals. But it was a bagatelle by the side of this undertaking, when we contemplate its full meaning, its reach and consequences.

II

The canal is the pretext. Not satisfied with the discredit—or, shall we say the infamy—it has brought to our door—including the violation of treaty obligations, the clandestine bestowal of subsidy and the assertion of warlike purpose—we are now to extend our activities from the Isthmus to the Continent, that is the contiguous territory, beginning by the payment of $3,000,000 to the chance faction of half-breeds ruling in Nicaragua. For what? To safeguard the Panama Canal that is about to be against a rival Nicaragua Canal in Mr. Bryan's mind's eye. That anybody could sell a gold-brick to Mr. Bryan would surprise nobody. But, what about Mr. Wilson? He has been thought to be rather up to snuff.

Another canal is unthinkable. There is not a treasury in the world—not a group of financiers on earth—to consider such an enterprise. In the unlikely event that some "kaleidoscopic government" of Nicaragua should perform some confidence game upon some visionary collection of capital the other side of Mars, seeking moonshine investment, it would be cheaper for us to send Mulhall over, flanked by Lauderbach and Lamar,[1] to pull off a counter revolution.

But, the $3,000,000 we engage to embark will be but the beginning of the outlay which must surely follow. We paid $20,000,-000 for the Philippines, not counting the collateral expenses, and the Administration is considering the policy of giving them up. First and last, they have cost us a pretty penny, yielding us little in return except care and trouble. They are uncomfortably distant and expose us to many outpost dangers. But we have our copy-book precepts; trade goes with the flag; the Bible goes with trade; and, are we not a Christian people?

Recalling the McKinley formula for the World Power his Administration was escorting to the front of nations, and how Mr. Bryan especially railed against it, simple-minded and straightforward Democrats may well stand aghast before this measure of insidious revolution and incredible folly. It is a reversal of all our professions, built upon exigencies that do not exist and headed toward ends that stagger conjecture. We actually butt into Civil War and put a premium on insurrection. If we have found the Philippines a hard nut to crack, what shall be thought of buying a volcano and erecting it as a plaything in our back yard?

They are naming it "drumhead diplomacy" to distinguish it from "dollar diplomacy." Why—because we suppose the drum is the symbol, the drum-tap the signal, of war? We omitted no word to express our contempt for "dollar diplomacy." What shall we say for this "drumhead diplomacy"? Only this, that it is "dunderhead diplomacy."

III

We hear that, nevertheless, it is growing in favor at Washington. Senator Borah surmises that it will prevail. And why not? There is never a corrupt and corrupting interest which will not array itself in its behalf. There is not a beleaguered Trust menaced by the Sherman Act which will not hail it as a friend in need. Every speculation hanging on to the ragged edge in Mexico and Central America will take heart of hope and reach for the hand of Uncle Sam to help it out of its particular hole.

Nor is this all. The Lobby, driven for the time away from Washington, will find congenial occupation and rich pickings in Managua, Bogota, San José, and other Spanish-American capitals. The commercial world looks on and laughs. "Our South American trade is safe enough now," says England. "Yah, myn herr," says Germany, "ours too."

---

[1] These persons were then in the news, all dealing, somewhat apocryphally, with very large matters.

The President needs to look both to himself and to his Administration.

Ever since Mr. Bryan took the portfolio of the State Department he has appeared as a man in strange surroundings, if not actually dazed. A proper man within himself, his sense of social and official propriety seems not to exist. His mind is fertile of oratorical suggestion. He is a popular entertainer. He is at home only before an audience. When he gets down to brass tacks and boot heels he is lost. He should have been an evangelist.

This Central American trumpery is of a piece with the Railway Ownership foolishness. Truly, as Senator Borah says, if we had not traveled far away from our moorings to original principles and cardinal faith, it would startle the country. As it is, with parties at loose ends and politics in a fluid state—the politicians on the run and the masses as well as the combines on the make— the country does not stop to consider ethics that do not immediately strike its pocket.

It is itself on the gamble. Yet changeable, likely to strike back when hit though by a fancy, quick to unjust conclusions and artificial resentments. If the Administration loses the next House of Representatives it is gone. It cannot therefore afford too many experiments. Thus far its innovations have prospered. It should beware of overdoing. Ridicule is a terrible gorgon, and more than once the Presidential bark has run through funny waters perilously near the laughing rocks.

When, two years ago, Mr. Wilson resolved to take a shirt-tail shoot to the Southwest corner of the Bryan reservation, and ruthlessly to brush aside everything that might get in his way, he showed a subtle understanding of political conditions and acute foresight. It was keen, practical politics. The event justified it. He is now Chief Magistrate.

No one of his predecessors in that great office better knew the history of the country. Many of them have been commonplace men who were wise enough to do nothing—at least nothing out of the common. Obviously Mr. Wilson, a scholar and a thinker, means to do something. He is ambitious for the glory of his Administration.

Yet, after all, his peculiar experience has not wholly fitted him for so great a task. He is still on trial. He grew to manhood during times when chaos ruled as to principles, and at Washington the opportune was the only wear. It has become a sign of the obsolete to insist upon dogma—a proof of enterprise to go after the bizarre. For example, Theodore Roosevelt. But down beneath the surface, the full-bodied, clear and limpid current of old-fashioned Americanism still flows toward the goal of good government; of good government at home, before all else; laid in proper restraint under limitations fixed by law and a proper respect and sense of justice toward all mankind.

We need not go abroad to find work to do. We have plenty within ourselves. This Nicaragua project is only the entering wedge of a foreign policy regardless alike of peoples and consequences. It is a complete reversal of all our Latin-American pretensions. Central America is the very crater of revolution and the Central Americans the very offscourings of Christendom. If we require naval bases and coaling stations let us buy them and pay for them. There is nothing else in that quarter that we want or need.

A Protectorate in Nicaragua forecasts Protectorates over the other Central American States. Soon or late, we shall have Mexico on our hands. All this means imperialism; and, let us repeat, plays into the hands of the great Money Combine we affect to be so eager to quell. In short and in fine, Woodrow Wilson, the Schoolmaster, will do well to subject Woodrow Wilson, the President, to a course of philosophic study and intellectual discipline, whilst as for Mr. Bryan, the more he lectures and the longer he stays away, the better it will be for the Administration.

A Warning Lesson

(August 5, 1913)

I

With respect to the Nicaragua Protectorate Foolishness the *Courier-Journal* would by no means emulate the hero who—

> "Swore he'd killed ten thousand men,
> And thrice he slew the slain"—

—for the measure seems sufficiently dead—and yet one passing and parting word over the hole-in-the-ground to which, without benefit of clergy, the Foreign Relations Committee of the Senate has consigned it, may serve at once for epitaph and admonition.

A scheme of International policy at once more ill-judged and shortsighted could hardly have been devised. From every point of view it was positively senseless. It proposed precisely the things which wisdom and duty told us plainly not to do. To start with, it bore out the hurtful contention that our ultimate aim is the domination of the residue of the Continent south of us. It asserted a police power which cannot be maintained except at enormous cost, physical and moral, implying vast moneyed responsibility far-reaching in its consequences. And, finally, it committed us to an endless and dangerous crusade of warlike aggression, menacing to our liberties at home and our peace abroad.

Yet but one member of the Senate Committee—Senator Borah —in the beginning set himself resolutely against it; though truth to say, his colleagues, notably Senators Bacon, Williams and Clark among the Democrats, came bravely to time, when time was called.

To a gentleman up-a-tree it occurs that a spoonful of intelligence in the State Department would have saved us the equivocation in which this dead treaty still leaves us. It caused all Spanish America to sit up and take notice. The Greasers said, "What next?" Even as matters stand, they will go away brooding over what might have been. Those that are hostile to us will use it as fuel to feed the flame of anti-Yankee prejudice. Yet, for thirty-odd years we have been striving to lay the ghost of the Monroe Doctrine in the minds of our southerly neighbors.

What could Mr. Bryan have been thinking of? We established a Pan-American Union. We set up a Bureau at Washington and built a palace to house it. Mr. Root hied all the way to Buenos Aires, Chile and Brazil to disabuse the minds of those countries touching our intentions and to assure them of our disinterested friendship. "We consider," said Mr. Root, with the universal approval of his countrymen, "that the independence and equal rights of the smallest and weakest member of the family of nations deserves as much respect as those of the great empires. We pretend to no right, privilege, or power that we do not freely concede to each one of the American Republics."

This was to meet, and if possible, to dispel the ever growing suspicion of us which was discrediting our relations and destroying our commerce. Yet by one sweeping act in Nicaragua Mr. Bryan proposed to do away with all that had been done to reach a better understanding and again to raise before the eyes of all the Latins the old, odious black flag bearing the hated words "Monroe Doctrine." That was to confirm their fears and to enrage them further, to our loss and the gain of our trade rivals.

II

In view of the Mexican situation *in esse*, and our Central American and South American relations *in posse*, this would seem a good time for fishing the Monroe Doctrine, so-called, out of the basket of old clo's and taking a long, last look at it before transferring it to the dark closet of things no longer useful. It served its purpose and its turn. It was put to sleep by events. Nor has it ever been awakened except to be saddled with aims and ideas wholly foreign to its origination.

We had better let the French remain in Mexico. In no event

could we have since had worse neighbors. France is now a Republic. With England dividing North America with us— Mexico on the side—what have we to say against Monarchy? Yet Monroe declared:

> "The American continents, by the free and independent condition which they have assumed and maintain, are henceforth not to be considered as subjects for future colonization by European powers. . . . We should consider any attempt on their part to extend their system to any portion of this hemisphere as dangerous to our peace and safety. With the existing colonies or dependencies of any European power, we have not interfered and shall not interfere. But with the governments who have declared their independence, and maintained it, and whose independence we have, on great consideration, and on just principles, acknowledged, we could not view any interposition for the purpose of oppressing them, or controlling, in any other manner, their destiny, by any European power, in any other light than as the manifestation of an unfriendly disposition towards the United States. . . ."

"With the existing colonies, or dependencies of any European Power we have not interfered and shall not interfere," said Monroe. What about Cuba, Porto Rico and the Philippines? Then and there we bore false witness to our own promise—went back on our pledge—and, by the act, abrogated the Monroe Doctrine.

If we reassert it as to Mexico—as we did reassert it in Venezuela and proposed to reassert it in Nicaragua—it will not be the Monroe Doctrine at all, but some other gospel masquerading as such—a Policeman pretending to be a Statesman—a son-of-a-gun of a jingo deserving to be soundly whipped and thrown out.

We should never forget that the Monroe Doctrine did not originate with us at all. When it was promulgated by the Monroe Administration a situation, not a theory, confronted us. At the time the "foreign world" was wholly Monarchic. Monarchism being the antithesis of Republicanism, Monarchy was the bugbear of Republicans. The Monroe Doctrine, which still adhered to Washington's Farewell injunction, touching entangling foreign alliances, was intended to meet the specter which thus most affrighted Americans. The Spanish provinces in America had thrown off the yoke of Spain. The Holy Alliance was pledged, among other things, to help Spain to whip them back. We had hurried to recognize their independence. At this juncture, George Canning, the Premier of England, suggested to the Monroe Administration through Richard Rush, the American Minister at the Court of St. James, that his Majesty's Government would approve and support such an attitude, and, thus strengthened, the declaration was made. Alone, we were scarcely equal to it. But, backed by England it sufficed.

Yet are there those who, when the *Courier-Journal* urges that, with respect to Mexico we call England into council and concert, swear that this would be a desecration of the Monroe Doctrine, which we got of England, the same England that divides with us the possession of North America and is equally concerned with us to have peace and order—good neighborhood—established in that country.

III

In a recent private letter written by an old lawyer-diplomat learned in the lore of the State Department, we read as follows: "Somebody in high place at Washington—or assistant to somebody in high place—was surely 'in cahoots' with the bankers and promoters in exploiting Nicaragua for a beginning—as they are doing San Domingo, and thence extending, even if slowly, surely —to Patagonia! They can always buy the support of some bandit in temporary control who wishes to live in Paris! In one loan to Honduras these 'Financial' thieves allowed 6 per cent. to reach there, dividing the other 94 per cent. between themselves and the bandits. In San Domingo we paid a certain 'Professor' one large salary, whilst the poor San Domingans paid him another, to fix on their necks our protectorate, which is paying about ten times the amount the exploiters sent there. Who is behind the exploiters of the Nicaragua loan? Where do their tracks lead? Let us hope and believe not to the White House nor the State Department, though if so, of course, without the knowledge of either Wilson or Bryan; but surely the country, and especially the Democratic party, is entitled to know all the inside history of this nefarious plot."

The *Courier-Journal* notes, and glad it is to note, the attitude of Mr. Kent, of California, an Independent member of the House, who is said to own thousands of head of cattle yet votes for free meat, and who has large interests in Mexico yet opposes the sending of American soldiers down there to be killed in its defense. Mr. Kent went the extreme length, for a Congressman, of inserting a portion of the scriptures in the Record. He chose three verses from Proverbs, truly saying they absolutely put the kibosh on the Monroe Doctrine, which, as truly, he declares obsolete. Here are his Biblical citations foreshadowing the present situation:

"My son, if thou hast become surety for thy neighbor, if thou hast stricken thy hand for a stranger, thou art snared with the words of thy mouth."

"He that passeth by and vexeth himself with strife that belongeth not to him is like one that taketh a dog by the ears."

"He that is surety for a stranger shall smart for it."

Mr. Bacon cannot be too wary. No more can be Mr. John Sharp Williams and Mr. James P. Clark. The Democratic party is a newcomer. The Foreign reports emanate mainly from Republicans. Behold Henry Lane Wilson and stand on guard. Anybody can sell a gold brick to Mr. Bryan. Let the patronage go, Senators, and save the country and the party from the danger of tyros and tyroism in the Department of State.

It is to laugh. But it is well. Three lumps of sugar for each member of the Foreign Relations Committee who have done such good work, but the biggest three to the courageous, upright and sagacious statesman from Idaho, for he saw clearest and spoke first!

Need of Readjustment in Our Latin-American Relations

(January 21, 1914)

I

Dwelling awhile in the very heart of the Latin world, old and new, wandering at will among the winding vales and rugged hills that skirt the Mediterranean sea, pictures other than those of the Côte d'Azur will come and go across the fancy of one who has seen something of life, has read somewhat of history, and has thought a little on government

There was Julius Cæsar. I wonder if his ghost walks its round among the Alpes Maritimes? There was Napoleon Bonaparte. I wonder what his ghost is whispering to Cæsar's ghost?

Over there is Corsica, where the Little Man was born, and hard by is Elba, where they tried to shut him up, giving him dollrags to play with. Porto Ferrara could not hold him. Frejus received him. And then came Waterloo, Saint Helena and the tomb on the banks of the Seine, among the French people whom he said he loved so well.

Just up the coast is Genoa. They tell me Columbus was born there. And who was Columbus? At least he gave his name to the prettiest little city in Georgia and the State capital of Ohio. From Genoa across country a sleepy old town, fringing both banks of the Arno, marks the spot where the Commonwealth of Florence stood and the Medicii flourished. A trifle beyond some tumble-down palaces, throwing their lean shadows upon stagnant pools and gaping vacantly at the moon, are all that is left of the opulence and power of the Venetian Republic. Nay, still not very far away, we come upon Rome itself, nursing its ruins and vainly seeking to become a pinchbeck Paris. *Sic transit gloria mundi!*

Seated upon a ledge overhanging the Mediterranean sea—his heart full of home longing as his eye turns wistfully westward—one is moved to ask himself whether that strange agglomeration known as "the people"—the people of Rome, of Florence and of Venice—the people of America—ever stopped, ever stop, to consider and discriminate; whether nations *en bloc* are given the power of reflection and differentiation; whether, in short, the art of government is not as hidden as the science of death and the mysteries of the life beyond the grave.

Musing here awhile, alone, I wonder!

II

Old men are prone to be critical of younger men. They are apt to look askance upon change and to hold experience as wisdom's only anchor to windward. In them pessimism becomes a state of mind and by them innovation is met in a treble voice with, "What are we coming to?"

Nevertheless, when I read of the serious proposal that the Government of the United States, more Federal than the Federalists, shall purchase and operate the telegraph and telephone service of the country; that the Government of the United States shall establish a protectorate over one of the States of Central America, presaging in the Spanish-American mind the conquest of all of them; that the craze for direct elections having already revolutionized the method of constructing the Senate, shall so alter the machinery for the making of Presidents as must ultimately obliterate State lines—and recall that these startling schemes are heralded as the emanations of a Democratic Administration—I feel like indulging myself at least with "Whither?" and "What next?"

Federal ownership? Government censorship? Partyism by process of self-perpetuation? Hitherto it has required only a revolution to effect a change of parties at Washington. If the people, blindly paying the fabulous sums demanded, put these giant powers in the hands of any group of public men, it will require an earthquake. Progress, indeed; after the telegraphs and telephones, why not the railways; after the railways, why not all the public utilities? And then, as far as our old-fashioned Jeffersonian Democracy goes, why not the deluge?

I know not how to differentiate public measures from party leaders. They can never be separated. As the egg is to the shell, is the statesman to his case.

All the republics of which we have knowledge came to grief and were carted to the boneyard through the inability of the people to distinguish between the false and the true among their public men. In every age and clime the rescript for demagogy has been the same. It is as old as the hills, as simple and familiar as the selling of gold-bricks, yet apparently as attractive as ever.

I have always believed and have tried to maintain it to be the business of journalism and the obligation of journalists to enlighten the people as to men and measures; to do this fearlessly, constantly and unsparingly. It may be done most effectively by exposing not alone their fallacies of policy, but their deficiencies of character. Neither self-interest nor personal rancor should be allowed to enter the discussion, to warp the judgment and color the opinion. When a writer feels his indignation begin to rise in excess—righteous as he may think it—he should lay his pen aside.

Of the *Courier-Journal,* I can truly aver that it has steadily pursued this theory of public duty. If, in designating a spade as a spade, it has sometimes overworked that form of expression— having a passion for plain speaking and a preference for the single word that seems most descriptive—its aim has been without malice to be plain, specific and clear, not abusive, and it has held itself ready at all times to give reasons alike for its epithets and its sobriquets. To cite a case in point, I find myself taken to task for referring in a recent letter to Mr. Bryan and Mr. Roosevelt as "fakers." I meant neither to be offensive nor to call names, having no ill-will against either, but on the contrary the wish to think well of both.

Each has a taking way peculiar to himself; the one all orator, the other all showman. They catch the eye and the ear of the multitude. Perennial candidates for office, they seek to commend their aspirations by affecting a consuming, almost an exclusive, love for the people—the "dear" people, the "plain" people—exploiting along with themselves certain proposals which they conceive to be vote-catching, or which they expect to popularize. Mr. Bryan once accused Mr. Roosevelt of stealing his clothes whilst he was in swimming. They were, in point of fact, the clothes which Mr. Bryan had stolen from the demagogues who had gone before. Mr. Roosevelt merely had them made over to fit his figure and to suit his need.

That Mr. Bryan was thrice rejected as candidate for President, and that Mr. Roosevelt was thwarted in his purpose of Mexicanizing the Government and Diazifying the Presidency, might go to the credit of the discernment of the people. An optimistic view of modern times would readily incline to the belief that the people are after all learning a thing or two; that universal education is teaching them to discriminate; that they are not so simple and credulous as they used to be. I am not so sure about that. Was it not organized money, and plenty of it, that beat Mr. Bryan in 1896? Was it not organized partyism that beat Mr. Roosevelt in 1912? If the voters had been left to themselves, would they not have rushed into the morass of free silver in the one case and into the arms of Cæsarism in the other?

It was to protect the people against themselves that our system was created a representative Government and not a go-as-you-please Democracy. Neither Mr. Bryan nor Mr. Roosevelt is loyal to the principle thus established. Mr. Roosevelt is a patrician by birth, breeding and instinct. He vociferated agrarianism to get votes and office. That made him a "faker." Mr. Bryan is not nearly so agile and astute as Mr. Roosevelt. His agrarianism came to him by the accident of birth. Having the idiosyncrasies of a lay preacher, he employs the lay preacher's benevolent tone and conciliatory phrase. He seems sincerer, more natural, less artificial than Mr. Roosevelt—has not in his mock-heroics gone so far afield—but, with an abnormal love of money, he adopts, at least, debatable means of attaining it, reaches out after whatever he thinks will win, having little sense of propriety and the relations of right and wrong, his objective point, like Mr Roosevelt's being votes and office. This makes him a "faker."

No one of the schemes of regeneration offered by Mr. Roosevelt and Mr. Bryan will bear close inspection. One and all they promise far too much. They are for the most part vagaries to be dismissed either as spurious or illusory.

Mr. Cleveland, the third of the trio of popular heroes of the last five-and-twenty years, was of a different build. He was wont to promise little. He relied upon his profession of being a plain, blunt man—his character for diligence and integrity—to see him through, having some rough-and-tumble fighting qualities and a great deal of mother wit and common sense. He chiefly lacked the large and varied equipment essential to the statesman. He possessed the driver's power without the leader's insight. And so he played his part, quite wrecking a party that, under adequate leadership, had come in for a long stay.

I have said that in thus overhauling and at times chastising these three, the *Courier-Journal* has never had any selfish interest to advance, or malice to inspire it. The truth of this should demonstrate itself, and has variously demonstrated itself to candid readers. It did not hesitate to question them and to challenge their doings when they were at the height of their popularity and power—which ought to go to the account of its independence and patriotic intention—putting ever the public welfare before the occupant of the throne of grace and scorning the favor of the great at the cost of servility. It has pursued no man when he was down. The objects of its criticism were of full size always and abundantly able to fight back. Generally they wore official coats of mail and carried both the purse and the sword of power.

I know no reason why its attitude toward President Wilson should differ from the attitude it held successively toward President Cleveland and President Roosevelt and Mr. Bryan. Mr. Wilson is more highly qualified than either of the other three; very subtle as well as cocksure of mind, and as venturesome as he is able. He has arrived at an opportune moment. The country, having had its "new birth of freedom," needs now a new birth of integrity, public and private. To equalize the burdens of government—to moderate the rank and mad commercialism of the time—and to educate the people to some realizing sense of their duty to one another and the State, is the task set before him who would be a God-given leader of men.

It may be the destiny of President Wilson to head the revolution—or shall we call it the evolution?—of the masses, conducting them safely from the abyss of immoral business and politics to the uplands of what he has rather ostentatiously christened "the new freedom." For one, I am with him to that end, and shall follow him gladly and loyally. But I shall not follow him blindly, because he appears to me a most self-centered, ambitious man, and I dread the ascendancy of such men; because he is an undoubted experimentalist, and experimentation is a dangerous thing in government; and because, having a talent for the spectacular, he betrays a passion for surprises and the surprising. Statesmen of that type are to be held to rigorous accountability, nor taken too much on trust, nor given too great length of tether.

He has just achieved the second of two notable victories. The sycophants everywhere break into ecstasies of propitiatory applause. The time-servers as usual scud to cover.

I would not pluck a leaf from the President's crown of laurel. But no more will I crook the pregnant hinges of tongue or pen to make another image of the Cleveland-Bryan-Roosevelt variety. Applying to Congress the rod and the art of the schoolmaster, Mr. Wilson found Congressmen as pliant as the schoolboys he had been used to dealing with in the classroom—even as he had found the members of the Legislature of New Jersey—and, having worthy ends in view, he forced these through triumphantly. All honor to him for this, though it must not be forgotten that in the matter of the tariff he reaped where others had sown, and in the matter of the currency he had the public exigency behind him.

Before him now appears the danger line. Having put the home house in order, he must address himself to the premises over the way; in other words to the adjustment of the outer relations. It is here that our country has always shown weakest, having in reality had no foreign policy—and where he himself, as indicated by his diplomatic appointments and the mess he has made in Mexico, seems weakest—yet where incalculable injury may by meretricious agencies be done the welfare of the people and the credit of the nation.

III

To come directly to these foreign relations, let me say that I do not agree with those who threaten us with invasions and wars, and dire mischances, unless we abandon the Monroe Doctrine. For very different reasons I have urged its abrogation the last ten or a dozen years. Ethically it has been abandoned. That which appears to take its place, and in its name is being so widely discussed, is not the Monroe Doctrine at all, but a new doctrine to be called the Wilson doctrine.

I used to be something of a Jingo. It was long ago, when my country counted for little in the world at large, and Europe scarcely took the trouble to sneer at us. Europe has at length a tolerably clear perception of what we actually are and is mainly and discreetly silent. Yet the Europeans keep up "a devil of a thinking." They may not hate us. But be sure they do not love us.

Physically we need not care "a hill o' beans." We are quite beyond the reach of external enemies and enmities. But honor, good neighborhood and good repute should no more be disregarded by the nations than by individuals, and in this light it is for us to stand straight and to deal fair.

The Anglo-German trade strife and the Franco-German blood strife play to us. The Japanese "war scare" is a speculative red rag, a "bloody shirt" of the plate-armor people. We have nothing to fear on either hand of the oceans—either from the Orient or from the Occident. If all Europe should unite with all Asia concurrently to assail us, the worse for the combine and the better for us, because we need a body-blow from somewhere to arouse us to a sense of the distance we have traveled from the bases of commercial and political integrity. The upright and patriotic underpinning of the poorer days has long been feeling disastrously the effects of the swashing of fluid principles. We have as a nation too much money and too little conscience. Maybe a big dose of self-denial as an episode in self-defense would be good for us.

To be sure, there can be no union, European or Asiatic, against us. There will be indeed no more earth-shaking wars. The battles ahead are to be trade battles—the fighting for markets. The time has come, therefore, that we have a foreign policy enlightened, consistent and far-sighted.

If the Wilson Administration breaks down it is likely to be with respect to this foreign policy. It used to be said of Mr. Wilson at Princeton that he was given to "projects"; that he was "meddlesome"; that "visionary" and "restless," he would never "let well-enough alone." He seems to have brought this irritating spirit and unquiet mind with him to the White House. Applied to domestic matters pressing for adjustment and ripe and ready to his hand, the results thus far, if not conclusive and convincing, are yet greatly to his credit. But every good thing may be overdone. Writing from abroad, I shall not borrow trouble in the anticipation from things at home, I am mainly concerned as to the opening of the Panama Canal and what we are going to do about it—affecting our standing and relations in Europe—but more deeply and directly affecting our pocket in Central and South America, whose markets geographically belong to us, but whose people are being driven away by the bogey of the Monroe Doctrine and the menace of the Wilson Doctrine.

Accepting the President's Mobile speech as the keynote of the Administrative program, this Wilson Doctrine seems to me composed in very nearly equal parts of dissimulation and buncombe. The President is as skillful in manipulating the verbal commonplaces of the time as the acrobat in tossing balls. For illustration take the following sentences out of the Mobile speech:

"States that are obliged to grant concessions are in this condition —that foreign interests are apt to dominate their domestic affairs, a condition always dangerous and apt to become intolerable.

"What these States are going to see is an emancipation from the subordination which has been inevitable to foreign enterprises.

"I rejoice in nothing so much as in the prospect that they will now be emancipated from these conditions.

"It is a very perilous thing to determine the foreign policy of a nation in the terms of material interest.

"Human rights, national integrity and opportunity as against material interests—that is the issue which we now have to face.

"The United States must regard it as one of the duties of friendship to see that *from no quarter* are material interests made superior to human liberty and national opportunity."

So much of this as relates to the moral condition of other countries is merely sugar upon that part of it which forecasts intervention. The "uplift" passages are of the cant which has become so familiar to our political vernacular. The promised "emancipation" serves notice of "friendship," open to many constructions, but certainly unsought and undesired. Construed by the light of the Wilson interposition in Mexico, it implies and bodes an extension and amplification of the Olney dictum that the Government of the United States is sovereign in the Americas and that its fiat shall be supreme and final.

Such an assertion can only be maintained by force of arms. It does not make for peace. It makes for war. But war being out of the question, it makes for the permanent distrust and aversion of our Latin-American neighbors, and, as a consequence, commercial obstruction and loss of markets which a different policy might conciliate and secure.

Naturally the Latin-Americans dislike and suspect us. The racial differences would sufficiently account for this. In our war with Spain they were to a man with Spain. They resent our intrusion. They do not need our help. Brazil, Argentina and Chile are now great nations. They are not menaced by Europe, and, if they were, they are able to take care of themselves. The neighboring lesser nations have their pride—let us say their self-respect—and feel themselves insulted by our offer of patronage and threatened by our interference.

The proposed Nicaraguan Protectorate confirms every ill alleged against us. Ever since the Mexican War and our acquisition of California the Latins have something more than distrusted us. If this act of further advance Southward be pursued by the Administration and supported by the Senate, it will furnish conclusive evidence to their minds that further inroads upon their freedom—perhaps their autonomy—will remain only a question of time. Suspicion will become certainty; aversion will deepen into hatred. We cannot expect to draw custom and to keep customers with a stuffed club in one hand and a worn-out shibboleth in the other.

But, the exit—the outlet—we are upon the edge, if not in the middle, of a very bad fix; what shall we do to retrieve the blunders of the past and to obtain better conditions in the future?

I have respect for the opinions of Professor William Howard Taft, lately President of the United States. An able jurist, learned in public affairs and international policies and relations—a fair man always—very great weight attaches to all that he says. His recent defense of the Monroe Doctrine as a national "asset" is qualified. He describes the Doctrine as Monroe proclaimed it—

thus distinguishing it from its many later interpretations—and, in his speech to the Peace Society used the following language:

"The original declaration of the Monroe Doctrine was prompted by England's wish, when Canning was Foreign Minister, that England and the United States should make a joint declaration of such a policy. Everyone admits that its maintenance until recently has made for the peace of the world, has kept European Governments from intermeddling in the politics of this hemisphere and has enabled all the various Latin-American republics that were offshoots from Spain to maintain their own Governments and their independence.

"But now we are told that under changed conditions the Monroe Doctrine has become an obsolete shibboleth, that it promotes friction with our Latin-American neighbors, and that it is time for us to abandon it. It is said that it is an assertion of a suzerainty by the United States over both continents, that it seeks to keep under the tutelage of the United States great and powerful nations like the Argentine Republic, Brazil and Chile, and does not promote the friendly feeling that strengthens the cause of peace.

"Before we proceed to consider this proposition we ought to make clear certain definite limitations of the Monroe policy that are not always given weight by those who condemn it. In the first place, the Monroe Doctrine is a policy of the United States, and is not an obligation of international law binding upon any of the countries affected, nor, indeed, does it create an absolute obligation on the part of the United States to enforce it. It rests primarily upon the danger to the interest and safety of the United States, and, therefore, the nearer to her boundaries the attempted violation of the doctrine, the more directly her safety is affected and the more acute her interest, and naturally, therefore, the more extreme will be the measures to which she would resort to enforce it.

"The second great limitation of the Monroe Doctrine is that it does not contemplate any interference on our part with the right of any European Government for cause to declare and make war upon any American Government or to pursue such course in the vindication of its national rights as would be a proper method under the rules of international law. This was expressly declared to be a proper term in the statement of the Monroe Doctrine by Mr. Seward during the Civil War, when Spain made war against Chile.

"And Mr. Roosevelt, in his communications to Congress,

has again and again asserted that maintenance of the doctrine does not require our Government to object to armed measures on the part of the European Governments to collect their debts and the debts of their nationals against Governments in this country that are in default of their just obligations, provided only that they do not attempt to satisfy those obligations by taking over to themselves ownership and possession of the territory of the debtor Governments or by other oppressive measures.

* * * * * * *

"It is said—and this is what frightens peace devotees from the Monroe Doctrine—that it rests on force and ultimately on the strength of our army and our navy. That is true, if its enforcement is resisted. Its ultimate sanction and vindication are in our ability to maintain it; but our constant upholding and assertion of the doctrine have enabled us, with the conflicting interests of European Powers and the support of some and the acquiescence of others, to give effect to that doctrine for now nearly a century, and that without the firing of a single shot. This has given the doctrine a traditional weight that assertion of a new policy by the United States never could have.

"Much as the doctrine may be criticised by the press of Europe, it is an institution of one hundred years' standing; it is something that its age is bound to make Europe respect. It was advanced at a time when we were but a small nation, with little power, and it has acquired additional force and prestige as our nation has grown to the size and strength and international influence that it now has."

I have never of late years thought of the Monroe Doctrine with especial reference to Europe. In the beginning it was an assertion of Republicanism in America against the encroachments of European Monarchism. That aspect vanished long ago. At length Monarchy all over the world had to fight for its life against the ever-advancing Legions of Democracy. As far as interdicting "the despots of Europe," the Monroe Doctrine is a dead letter. The American Republics are in no danger. It is the Monroe Doctrine that is setting us at cross-purposes with the very neighbors it was put forth to protect, which during the last ten or a dozen years the *Courier-Journal* has urged upon the consideration of our people. Now comes Mr. Taft to say in the same speech from which the foregoing quotation is made:

"Were we to abandon the doctrine, and thus in effect notify European Governments that they might without objec-

tion on our part take possession of Santo Domingo, of
Haiti or of the Central American Republics or of any South
American Republics that might be disturbed by revolution and
that might give them some international excuse for intervention, it would be but a very short time before we would be
forced into controversies that would be much more dangerous
to the peace of this hemisphere than our continued assertion
of the doctrine, properly understood and limited."

We need not "abandon" the Doctrine, nor make any such
"notification." We just need to say no more about it. That, with
the opening of the Canal, we shall warn Europe away from needful naval stations—deny her access to indispensable fuel for her
ships—as indicated by the Lodge resolution—is a proposition that
should give pause to the sense of wisdom and justice in every
reflecting man. We cannot force the greater States of South
America, and if we go skylarking with the weaker in Central
America we shall soon fall upon unutterable corruption and
scandal.

The proposed Nicaraguan Treaty is a case in point. If it can
be dragooned through the Senate it will make great military equipment and preparation imperative and play to the lead of the very
Steel Trust and Armor Plate organisms the Administration is
committed to prosecute.

The scheme seems a piece of the Bryan passion for chasing
chimeras. It is full of explosives. No good can come of it.
Much evil will come of it. We have no more business in Central
America than in South America, in either than in Mexico, Mada-
gascar and Timbuctoo!

But Mr. Taft hits upon an expedient when at the close of his
speech he says:

"My hope, as an earnest advocate of world peace, is that
ultimately by international agreement we shall establish a court
like that of The Hague, into which any Government aggrieved
by any other Government may bring the offending Government before an impartial tribunal to answer for its fault and
to abide the judgment of the court as to the remedy or dam-
ages that shall be judged against it, if any."

Such a movement were in the right direction.[2] The idea is re-
enforced by some remarks of John Barrett, director of the Pan-
American Union, lately delivered before the Society for the
Judicial Settlement of International Disputes. Mr. Barrett de-

[2] So it may be observed that Mr. Watterson would endorse Mr.
Harding's efforts to gain American participation in the Court of International Justice.

clared that the time has come to evolve a principle from the Monroe Doctrine for all America, to be called the "Pan-American Policy," and continued as follows:

"The Pan-American Policy would adopt, absorb and enlarge the Monroe Doctrine as an original policy of the United States into a greater and 'all-American policy,' where each nation would have the same rights of attitude, the same dignity of position and the same sense of independence as the United States now has. By eliminating the attitude of absolute dictation and centralized power by the substitution of the word 'Pan-American' for 'Monroe,' and thus including all the American nations as sponsors, and substituting the word 'policy' for 'doctrine,' and thus removing the hard, unyielding, dictatorial and didactic suggestion, a long step will be taken toward a new era of Pan-American comity and confidence. The smaller Republics of the Western Hemisphere should be taken in by the United States, as junior partners, for the upholding of the policy against the rest of the world."

What other was the meaning, and what else was contemplated, when we established the Pan-American Union and built a palace at Washington to house it and establish within it a Bureau of which John Barrett is the head?

Dollar Diplomacy is the only kind of Diplomacy at the front in these degenerate days of trade and barter, and it is simple cant and pretense to deny it. The game of "freeze out" being played by Wilson and Huerta is none the less a gamble because Wilson calls it "The New Freedom," and opens each jackpot with prayer. I hope he will win; but, if he does, what do we get; and, if he does not, where are we? What we need is an overhauling of all our Foreign Affairs and a complete readjustment of our Latin-American Relations.

H. W.

Nice, France
Jan. 8, 1914

CHRISTOPHER SHAKESPEARE

On Sunday afternoons when the weather was mild, Mr. Watterson was accustomed to sit on the long porch at Mansfield, his country house, and talk of cabbages and kings. Those who were privileged to enter that family circle felt as if they had rubbed the lamp of Aladdin. Such fairy palaces of fact and reminiscence and opinion as Marse Henry would swiftly conjure up for them. Such clear glimpses of the great and the small, and always the interesting. When he talked it was well to listen, and many of his most attractive writings had their beginnings in these Sunday conversational ramblings.

"Do you know who wrote the plays of Shakespeare?" he asked one afternoon when the talk had turned to the literary. And then he related briefly his theory about Kit Marlowe and the brawl at Deptford, the theory which appears *in extenso* below. The delight and interest of his auditors persuaded him to make an article of this play of his fancy. He consented to a news room dictum that the writing must appear as a "feature" instead of on the editorial page and was as pleased as Punch when its advance syndication among other American newspapers brought nearly a thousand dollars in revenues to the *Courier-Journal*.

The Shakespeare Mystery

(April 23, 1916)

I

When Ignatius Donnelly was a member of Congress—morbidly obsessed by the Baconian theory of the Shakespeare authorship and on that account avoided by many of his colleagues as a literary bore—Proctor Knott resolved that he should have a hearing, and with this purpose in view asked a distinguished company to meet the Minnesotan at dinner.

Inevitably the then Kentucky Representative, Joseph C. S. Blackburn, and the renowned Kentucky humorist, Colonel Richard C. Wintersmith, were of the party.

Delighted with his opportunity, the Baconian enthusiast proceeded to state and elaborate his hypothesis and expound and elucidate his cryptogram. Colonel Wintersmith listened with the courteous attention which was his characteristic. But, as the story lengthened and the argument thickened, the wine, which at a certain point usually made the Colonel at least abruptly frank, got in its work. At length he could stand it no longer. "Mr. Donnelly," he said, "I cannot allow you to go any further on this line, because I know, as a matter of fact, that William Shakespeare, of Stratford-on-Avon, wrote those plays—every one of them." Donnelly, startled, said: "How could you know that, Colonel Wintersmith?" And, without a moment's hesitation, but with an air of finality, the Colonel replied: "Because I was there, sir, and I saw him write them." Though knocked almost speechless, Donnelly found voice to murmur, "Why, Colonel Wintersmith, it was three hundred years ago," and, turning placidly to Mr. Blackburn, the

Colonel said, as if exchanging a pleasantry, "Joe, how time passes!"

A more famous humorist of Kentucky origin, the late Samuel L. Clemens, equally as positive as Colonel Wintersmith, was sure that William Shakespeare, of Stratford-on-Avon, did not write the plays which stand in his name.

One of the last things Mark Twain did in life was to write and publish a book to prove this latter contention. It is a rambling, colloquial, reminiscential essay—broken here and there by autobiographic interruptions—spite of which, however, no one can read it without being seriously impressed. Mark Twain was not a Baconian. "Did Francis Bacon write Shakespeare's Works?" he asks, and promptly answers, "Nobody knows." At the same time he is confident that the "Claimant of Stratford," whom he laughs to scorn, did not write them, and adduces proof which ought to be regarded as conclusive that he did not and could not.

We scarcely need Mark Twain to tell us that the world loves a mystery and dotes on a paradox. The author of "Tom Sawyer" has a chapter upon the fakes and fakers of history from Perkin Warbeck and Lambert Simnel to the Count Cagliostro and Arthur Orton. He calls them "claimants," putting Satan at the head of the list, as with the "Bard of Avon," the greatest of all, "The Golden Calf, claimant; the Veiled Prophet of Khorassan, claimant; Louis the XVII, claimant; William Shakespeare, claimant," and so on, never one of them "that couldn't get a hearing, that couldn't collect a rapturous following, no matter how flimsy his pretension and obvious its absurdity."

It is but too true. There are people who credit Dumas' fiction about The Man in the Iron Mask. There are people who believe that John Wilkes Booth was not killed near Bowling Green, Virginia, but that he made his escape and died at last under an assumed name in Texas. What wonder that, with the title pages of ten thousand editions to sustain the assumption, the world accepts the preposterous Shakespeare fake? That Shakespeare himself, the producing theatrical manager of London and thrifty money-lender and land-speculator of Stratford-on-Avon, set no store by the authorship, is shown by the circumstance that, though the plays were frequently pirated, he made no protest. That the public of his day and generation held him and his alleged authorship in no great account is shown by the circumstance that his death was not made the occasion of particular remark in London, or ceremonial in Stratford-on-Avon. Barring Ben Jonson's apostrophe appended to a collection of the plays in 1623, seven years after his death, not a line of contemporary evidence can be found that Shakespeare was other than a trade-mark. Nor was he heralded as a poet—of whom nothing was locally remembered—

until he had lain in his grave three-quarters of a century. On this point Mark Twain's observations are striking. I quote as follows:

"When Shakespeare died, in 1616, great literary productions attributed to him as author had been before the London world and in high favor for twenty-four years. Yet his death was not an event. It made no stir, it attracted no attention. Apparently his eminent literary contemporaries did not realize that a celebrated poet had passed from their midst. Perhaps they knew a play-actor of minor rank had disappeared, but did not regard him as the author of his Works.

"His death was not even an event in the little town of Stratford. Does this mean that in Stratford he was not regarded as a celebrity of any kind?

"He had spent the first twenty-two to twenty-three years of his life there, and of course knew everybody and was known by everybody of that day in the town, including the dogs and the cats and the horses. He had spent the last five or six years of his life there, diligently trading in every big and little thing that had money in it; so we are compelled to assume that many of the folk there in those said latter days knew him personally, and the rest by sight and hearsay. But not as a celebrity? For everybody soon forgot to remember any contact with him or any incident connected with him. The dozens of townspeople, still alive, who had known of him or known about him in the first twenty-three years of his life were in the same unremembering condition; if they knew of any incident connected with that period of his life they didn't tell about it. Would they if they had been asked? It is pretty apparent that they were not. Why weren't they? It is a very plausible guess that nobody there or elsewhere was interested to know.

"For seven years after Shakespeare's death nobody seems to have been interested in him. Then the quarto was published, and Ben Jonson awoke out of his long indifference and sang a song of praise and put it in the front of the book. Then silence fell again.

"For sixty years. Then inquiries into Shakespeare's Stratford life began to be made of Stratfordians. Of Stratfordians who had known Shakespeare or had seen him? No. Then of Stratfordians who had seen people who had known or seen people who had seen Shakespeare? No. Apparently the inquiries were only made of Stratfordians who were not Stratfordians of Shakespeare's day, but later comers; and what they had learned had come to them from persons who had not seen Shakespeare; and what they had learned was not claimed as fact, but only as legend—dim and fading and indefinite legend; legend of the calf-slaughtering rank, and not worth remembering either as history or fiction.

"Has it ever happened before—or since—that a celebrated person who had spent exactly half of a fairly long life in the village where he was born and reared, was able to slip out of this world and leave that village voiceless and gossipless behind him—utterly voiceless, utterly gossipless? And permanently so? I don't believe it has happened in any case except Shakespeare's. And couldn't and wouldn't have happened in his case if he had been regarded as a celebrity at the time of his death."

II

Dwelling upon the ease, as well as the prevalence of the preposterous, in that queer little book of his, Mark Twain says:

"How curious and interesting is the parallel—as far as poverty of biographical details is concerned—between Satan and Shakespeare. It is wonderful, it is unique, it stands quite alone, there is nothing resembling it in history, nothing resembling it in romance, nothing approaching it even in tradition. How sublime is their position, and how overtopping, how sky-reaching, how supreme—the two Great Unknowns, the two Illustrious Conjecturabilities! They are the best-known unknown persons that have ever drawn breath upon the planet."

For the instruction of the ignorant he then proceeds to make a list of such details of Shakespeare's history as are facts—verified facts, established facts, undisputed facts—and not mere assumptions.

He was born on the 23d of April, 1564. Of good farmer-class parents who could not read, could not write, could not sign their names; at Stratford, a small back settlement which in that day was shabby and unclean, and densely illiterate. Of the nineteen important men charged with the government of the town thirteen had to "make their mark" in attesting important documents, because they could not write their names. Of the first eighteen years of the Shakespearean life thus ushered into the world nothing is known. They are a blank.

On the 27th of November, 1582, as Mark Twain, having examined the official records, shows, William Shakespeare took out a license to marry Anne Whateley. Next day William Shakespeare took out a license to marry Anne Hathaway, who was eight years his senior. He actually married Anne Hathaway. By grace of a reluctantly granted dispensation there was but one publication of the banns. Within six months the first child was born.

Two years followed, during which nothing at all happened to Shakespeare, as far as anybody knows. Then came twins—1585. Again two blank years, when—1587—he takes himself off for a ten-year visit to London, leaving the family behind.

Five blank years follow. During this period nothing happened to him, as far as anybody knows. Then—1592—there is mention of him as an actor. Next year—1593—his name appears in the official list of players. The following year—1594—he played before the Queen; a detail of no consequence; other obscurities did it every year of the forty-five of her reign and remained obscure. Three fairly full years are next accounted for; full of play-acting. Then in 1597 he bought New Place, Stratford.

Thirteen or fourteen busy years ensue; years in which he accumulated money, and also reputation as actor and manager. Meantime his name, liberally and variously spelt, had become associated with a number of great plays and poems, as, on the outside, author of the same. Some of them, in these years and later, were pirated, but he made no protest.

Then—1610-11—he returned to Stratford and settled down for good and all, and busied himself in lending money, trading in tithes, trading in land and houses; shirking a debt of forty-one shillings, borrowed by his wife during his long desertion of his family; suing debtors for shilling and coppers; being sued himself for shillings and coppers, and acting as confederate to a neighbor who tried to rob the town of its rights in a certain common, and did not succeed.

He lived five or six years—till 1616—in the joy of these elevated pursuits. Then he made a will, and signed each of its three pages with his name. It was a thoroughgoing business man's will. It named in minute detail every item of property he owned in the world—houses, lands, sword, silver-gilt bowl, and so on—all the way down to his "second-best bed" and its furniture.

It carefully and calculatingly distributed his riches among the members of his family, overlooking no individual member. Not even his wife; the wife he had been enabled to marry in a hurry by urgent grace of a special dispensation before he was nineteen; the wife whom he had left husbandless so many years; the wife who had had to borrow forty-one shillings in her need, and which the lender was never able to collect of the prosperous husband, but died at last with the money still lacking. No, even this wife was remembered in Shakespeare's will. He left her that "second-best bed." And never another thing; not even a penny to bless her lucky widowhood with. It was eminently and conspicuously a business man's will, not a poet's.

It mentioned not a single book. Books were much more precious than swords and silver-gilt bowls and second-best beds in those days, and when a departing person owned one he gave it a high place in his will. The will mentioned not a play, not a poem, not an unfinished literary work, not a scrap of manuscript of any kind.

"Many poets have died poor," sententiously interjects the creator of "Pudd'nhead Wilson," "but this is the only one in history that has died this poor; the others all left literary remains behind."

"If Shakespeare had owned a dog," he goes on to say, "I am sure he would have mentioned it in his will. If a good dog, Susanna would have got it; if a cur dog, his wife would have got a dower interest in it, sometimes I wish he had owned a dog, just so we could see how painstakingly he would have divided that dog among the family, in his careful business way."

He signed the will in three places.

In earlier years he signed two other official documents.

These five signatures still exist.

There are no other specimens of his penmanship in existence.

Was he prejudiced against the art? His granddaughter, whom he loved, was eight years old when he died, yet she had had no teaching, he left no provision for her education, although he was rich, and in her mature womanhood she couldn't write and couldn't tell her husband's manuscript from anybody else's—she thought it was Shakespeare's.

When Shakespeare died in Stratford it was not an event. It made no more stir in England than the death of any other forgotten theater-actor would have made. Nobody came down from London; there were no lamenting poems, no eulogies, no national tears—there was merely silence, and nothing more. A striking contrast with what happened when Ben Jonson, and Francis Bacon, and Spenser, and Raleigh and the other distinguished literary folk of Shakespeare's time passed from earth. No praiseful voice was lifted for the lost Bard of Avon; even Ben Jonson waited seven years before he lifted his.

So far as anybody actually knows and can prove, Shakespeare, of Stratford-on-Avon, never wrote a play in his life.

So far as anybody knows and can prove, he never wrote a letter to anybody in his life.

So far as anyone knows, he received only one letter during his life.

So far as anyone knows and can prove, Shakespeare, of Stratford, wrote only one poem during his life. This one is authentic. He did write that one—a fact which stands undisputed; he wrote the whole of it; he wrote the whole of it out of his own head. He commanded that this work of art be engraved upon his tomb, and he was obeyed. There it abides to this day. This is it:

> "Good friend for Iesus sake forbeare
> To digg the dust encloased heare;
> Blest be ye man yt spares thes stones
> And curst be he yt moves my bones."

Beyond the details thus given we know not a thing about him. All the rest of his vast history, as furnished by the biographers, is built up, course upon course, of guesses, inferences, theories, conjectures—an Eiffel Tower of artificialties rising sky-high from a very flat and very thin foundation of inconsequential facts. As a matter of fact, there was nothing to tell. He had no history.

Thus Mark Twain briefs the case. Not a single statement can be gainsaid. The conclusion is dead against Shakespeare.

III

The Baconians adduce some striking arguments in favor of their theory, including a few startling coincidences. Among these are certain passages in the plays that point to Bacon. In "Henry the Sixth" use is made of French historic archives that were unknown to the public in Shakespeare's day, but could have been known to Bacon, while Wolsey's famous speech in "Henry the Eighth," "Farewell, a long farewell to all my greatness," does not appear in any of the early editions, but does appear in the folio of 1623, two years after Bacon's fall and seven years after Shakespeare's death. I shall presently undertake to account for this.

Once, whilst I was visiting Whitelaw Reid, at Wrest Park, I spoke of it. "I don't believe it," Reid said. "Well," said I, "you have here in the library the means of verifying or refuting it." He raised his hand in deprecation, and exclaimed, "I would not if I could," meaning of course that, as American Ambassador, charged with affairs of moment, he could not afford to meddle with such a controversy; that he would make himself *persona non grata* to the English people if he did; wherein he was clearly right. I did not pursue the matter, nor look into the books, not caring a button who wrote the plays. Or, shall I say, knowing who did and not wishing or meaning to precipitate a contemplated scoop of my own?

The trouble with the Baconians is that they seek to prove too much. Their "cryptogram" is absurdly fanciful and far-fetched. It carries no weight with thinking people. It may be dismissed indeed as a figment of learning run mad.

During the spring and part of the summer of 1873 Sam Clemens and I were wandering in and about London, making

occasional excursions into the Warwick country, regaled the while
by the queer proceeding of the Tichborne trial, which was being
reported every day verbatim in the London papers and creating a
prodigious sensation all over the world. In his and my family,
closely connected by marriage (a great-uncle of his had married
a great-aunt of mine, his mother named after and reared by this
great-aunt) there was a legend that the Lamptons sprang from
the peerage and were entitled to English estates and titles. We
had a common cousin of the name of Leathers, who bred back to
the oldest of the Lampton brothers of Virginia, and who called
himself "The Earl of Durham." One day Sam Clemens, putting
aside the *Times,* from which he had been reading the performance
of Kenealy and his Fat Boy the day before, said in that irresistible
drawl of his—inherited, by the way, from Jane Lampton, his
mother, and not affected by himself—"I'll tell you what I'll do;
you put up five hundred dollars, and I'll put up five hundred, and
we'll bring Leathers over here and set him in as a claimant to the
Earldom of Durham."

He was so pleased by the conceit that he afterward wrote a
novel entitled "The Claimant." Another time, during that season,
as we were browsing among the rookeries of Fleet street, he
suddenly broke in upon a philosophic discourse of mine—"Say,
I went down to the Herald office yesterday and looked into this
Durham business; nothing to the story whatever; the Lamptons
not in it at all; went out a hundred years ago; the present Earldom a new creation; a rich Quartermaster of the Peninsula War
of the name of Brown or Robinson; but, all the same, we could
have lots of fun bringing Leathers over and it would be worth the
money." I have related elsewhere how, upon a hotel register in
Rome, many years later, I came upon the entry, "The Earl of
Durham—the Honorable Reginald Lambton—Lady Anne Lambton," indicating that Mark Twain was merely incubating his story
—there having been no visit to the Herald office—the Lambtons,
spelling it with a "b" instead of a "p," still in the peerage—with
which I taxed him, but not in the least disturbing his equanimity.

Pursuing the line of surmise applied to the Shakespearean controversy, is it inconjecturable that during this, or some succeeding,
visit to England, roaming around Leicester Square—maybe along
the muse-brooding banks of the Wye—I found— But let me not
anticipate. All in regular order.

IV

To come directly to the point, there is a simple but perfect
thesis in explication of the Shakesperean mystery. This relates
that the plays were written by Christopher Marlowe. They were

revised by Francis Bacon. Thus prepared for the stage, they were produced by William Shakespeare.

It is not true, as tradition reports, that Marlowe was killed in a tavern brawl at Deptford, June 1st, 1593. It was his antagonist who was slain. He and his friend Shakespeare, one of the managers of the Globe Theater, had gone for a lark across the Thames to the Surrey side after the successful performance of "The Tragedy of Dido." They fell in with a gay party, drank deeply, and in a tipsy quarrel between Marlowe and an actor named Herrick, who ventured to criticize certain passages in "The Passionate Shepherd," recently published and greatly admired, Marlowe, finding himself outclassed and underneath, used his knife to release himself, having no murderous or other serious intention. The incident seemed trivial and good humor was quickly restored. The company drank again and again. Suddenly poor Herrick staggered and fell to the floor. When they stooped to pick him up he was dead. An artery had been severed unknown to him or to any one, and he had bled to death.

Here was a situation, and what might have come of it no one can tell if at the moment of their dilemma young Francis Bacon had not driven by in a coach-and-six belonging to the Earl of Essex, on his way to the Privy Council.

Francis Bacon and Christopher Marlowe were the best of friends. They had been classmates at Cambridge. Marlowe was a poet and a scholar. Bacon was a philosopher, a lawyer, a statesman and a courtier, a man both of affairs and letters. There was mutual appreciation and genuine regard between them. But they had to keep apart in public. They could not be even seen together without hurt to Bacon.

At once Bacon realized the gravity of the case. Kit Marlowe was but a vagabond author hanging on to the theater and keeping company with the players, who were little better than outlaws. But he was a man of genius and promise; his chance victim an obscure varlet. Nevertheless, a gibbet loomed ahead. Bacon, ever fertile of resources and invention and prompt to action, suggested that the living man exchange his clothing with the dead man, and fly—fly for his life—and, to make assurance doubly sure, it being nightfall, he took him in the Earl's carriage to a point, whence his escape from England was easy. Next day it was given out that Marlowe had been killed, and, the penalty death for him in case he came to life again, it was ever after thus proclaimed.

Christopher Marlowe went first to Paris. Then he journeyed into Spain. Finally, all individual traces lost, he repaired to Italy and settled down in Padua. This will account for his love of Italian plots and characters, his familiarity with Italian scenes and themes, and his sometimes Latin tone of thought and turn of expression; though a Cambridge education would also have tended his mind in that direction. Be this as it may, he went to work as soon as possible with his handicraft of play-making, sending each play as it was written to his friend, Francis Bacon. The purely fanciful needed no revision. But, when the fruitful Marlowe genius was brought to grapple with medicine and law—when it had to deal with history, philosophy and court etiquette—the splendid technical equipment of Bacon was required to supplement and enrich the original text. Thus, in a way, "the wisest, brightest, meanest of mankind," shared authorship with the sublime dramatist and inspired poet, William Shakespeare, theatrical manager, now and then contributing a practical hint to their stage production, and—the names of Marlowe and Bacon in that connection out of question—giving his own name alike to the playbills and title-pages.

Bacon left no cryptogram. No more did Marlowe. But, in an early edition of the Lemounier Vasari, the Comte de la Borde, correcting one of the many errors of the Guida de Bassano, refers to a recluse of Padua, Pietro Basconi by name, who claimed to have nursed Marlowe in his last illness (Marlowe died in 1627, just a year after Bacon's death), and to have had from him the story and reduced it to writing. This strange composition came into the possession of Andreas Basconi, a descendant of Pietro, and was read, we are told, as late as 1843 by no less a person than Washington Irving, who, thinking it a doubtful yarn, and, with Whitelaw Reid, knowing it dangerous for a man of importance (he was then American Minister to Spain) to tamper with a subject so sacred to the British heart, wrote nothing about it, nor, indeed, spoke of it except to one or two intimate friends.

The original Pietro Basconi manuscript may or may not have been buried in the great conflagration that visited Padua in 1860; but why might not a rough, rather incoherent minute of this have been made from memory by Joel T. Hart, the Kentucky sculptor, long resident of Florence, and communicated by him to me, when in 1859, visiting his native land, the two of us shared an apartment on the south side of G street between Fourteenth and Fifteenth streets, Washington City, which is susceptible of proof? Or why, in 1873, when Mark Twain and I were rambling about London—he making pretended researches into British heraldry—may I not have fallen in with a ragged Italian in Leicester Square, who, born and reared in Padua, had an inkling of the truth and who tried to sell me a plaster cast of Christopher Marlowe, declaring that, if I would go with him on a dark night into a wood by the River Wye, he would produce from the hollow of an old oak tree the identical Basconi manuscript, which had escaped the flames, and was hidden there by a Gypsy relative of his and—?

Go to! Go to! I am not on the witness stand making oath to anything—only pursuing the usual Bacon-Shakespeare method. If our dear George Madden Martin can reconstruct out of the insubstantial pageant of a dream the boyhood of the Warwickshire lad who is known as the Bard of Avon, why may not I call from the shadows and the stars the strange story of Christopher Marlowe—the friend and schoolmate of Francis Bacon—at the moment of his supposed death the greatest of English poets and dramatists, who in "The Jew of Malta" anticipated both Shylock and Othello, and in "The Lascivious Queen," Cleopatra—who preceded Goethe in the idea, the philosophy and construction of Faust—many of whose early conceits, and some of his actual phrasing, to be found in the plays later ascribed to William Shakespeare? Did not Ben Jonson, cited in praise of Shakespeare, write also of "Marlowe's mighty line"?

Hazlitt quotes a number of single verses "struck out of the heat of a glowing fancy" that, as he says, "leave a track of golden fire behind them." The following are a few that might readily be ascribed to Shakespeare:

"I know he is not dead; I know proud death
Durst not behold such sacred majesty."

* * * * * * *

"Hang both your greedy ears upon my lips,
Let them devour my speech, suck in my breath."

* * * * * * *

—"From discontent grows treason,
And on the stalk of treason death."

* * * * * * *

"Tyrants swim safest in a crimson flood."

* * * * * * *

The two following lines—

"Oh! I grow dull, and the cold hand of sleep
Hath thrust his icy fingers in my breast"—

are the same as those in King John—

"And none of you will bid the winter come
To thrust his icy fingers in my maw."

And again the Moor's exclamation:

"Now by the proud complexion of my cheeks,
Ta'en from the kisses of the amorous sun"—

is the same as Cleopatra's—

"But I that am with Phœbus' amorous pinches black," etc.

Eleazer's sarcasm,

—"These dignities
Like poison, make men swell; this rat's-abane honour,
Oh, 'tis so sweet! they'll lick it till they burst"—

shows the utmost virulence of smothered spleen, and his concluding strain of malignant exultation has been but tamely imitated
by Young's Zanga:

"Now, tragedy, thou minion of the night,
Rhamnusia's pew-fellow, to thee I'll sing,
Upon a harp made of dead Spanish bones,
The proudest instrument the world affords;
To thee that never blushest, though thy cheeks
Are full of blood, O Saint Revenge, to thee
I consecrate my murders, all my stabs," etc.

"Comparisons are odious" and "Love me little, love me long"
are epigrams of Marlowe, and it must be allowed that he who
wrote "The Passionate Shepherd" could have written "Venus and
Adonis."

What boots it? Not a scrap of manuscript remains. This
side of the Judgment Day there will be none to tell us—perhaps
not then when all are busy. As Daniel Webster observed of "the
past" may we say of the plays "the are at least secure," whoever
wrote them. We have them. They will not get away from us.
Being immortal they will never die.

THE JANES, SALLIES AND RED-NOSED ANGELS

The two greatest topics of modern sociology and legislation, to
Mr. Watterson, were female suffrage and prohibition. He
wrote copiously on these themes and in moods ranging from
the abusive and the fantastic, to the exhortative and the
melancholy. Both of these developments of modern American thought the editor opposed with every force within him;
and nothing in his path during fifty years of writing ever
met with such furious and long-continued attack from him.

The leaders of the suffrage cause became "silly Sallies
and crazy Janes" in his catalogue of epithets, while the
political leaders of prohibition he assailed as "red-nosed
angels." It was not so much that women sought the vote
that disturbed him, but he believed firmly in the limitation
instead of the extension of suffrage. As for prohibition,
although an enemy of the open saloon, he distrusted the
purpose and method of the reform and wholly disbelieved in
the possibility of its enforcement. His autobiography contains his complete argument on both subjects; the files bulge

with articles grave and gay; but the two following are his leading contemporary writing on these topics.

The Most Momentous Question of Modern Times

(August 24, 1913)

I

The *Courier-Journal,* which has for nearly fifty years fought the woman's battle—holding woman the moral light of the universe—man's only anchor to windward—has felt it a supreme duty to consider and discuss the Woman Suffrage Movement as the most momentous question of modern times. If "votes for women" were the end of it and all there is to it, less account might be taken, for, under many conditions, women could by their votes do much good and womanly work. But "votes for women" is the least part of it. Beneath lies—nay, yawns—an abyss of revolution, menacing not only government and politics, but the whole human species.

At a time when the press is seeking to shirk its duty and to shunt the discussion, the *Courier-Journal* has given it a leading position and abundant space. We rather welcome the opportunity to discuss it and have the wise and good women of Kentucky consider it. We are not afraid of agitation. It is by no means a bad thing. Most of the good we see in the world has come on account of it. The air we breathe is cleared by lightning flashes. The ocean without its gales would be unwholesome, and life itself without disturbance would arrive nowhere. The unrest of women is a big disturbance, but every storm blows out in time, and, except we be doomed to the fate of the nations which have fallen victims to the feminism of other ages, so will this one.

It is, as we have shown, part of a disturbance that is epidemic all over the world; a disturbance caused by the uneasiness of great masses of people who find themselves cramped by the limitations or overstrained by the demands of the existing apparatus for the regulation of human life, or in whom the aspirations of an intelligence quickened by popular education demand opportunities and satisfactions had never before. They see but cannot share them, and, because they cannot, they agitate, thinking—often mistakenly —that they may. In art, in medicine, in business, in politics, there is the same insurgent disposition, shared by thousands, to smash the existing machine which denies them expression and make a new one that they fancy will serve them better. Humanity, says Edward Sanford Martin in that great essay of his, seems to have outgrown its old collar and to insist on having a new one. Instead of seeking one of the next larger size it seeks one that is preposterous.

Every considerable event the last fifteen years is part of that movement. The lesson of "room, brothers, room" was taught to Russia by Japan, was taught by the United States to Spain, was taught by Boers to British and by British to Boers, is proceeding in China, is proceeding in England, is going forward obscurely and dolorously in Mexico, is demonstrated in medicine by the Osteopaths and Christian Scientists, and in law by movements for the recall of Judges, and in the Roman Catholic Church by Modernists, and separation of Church from State in Italy, France and Spain.

II

In all this general ruction the woman movement has its place. Wrong as it is in directing so much energy toward the attainment of suffrage, the arguments of its individual apostles hopelessly bad and their specific aims wholly mistaken, the power of the movement is undeniable. Moreover, it has underlying causes of the first order of public moment.

The source and resource of these causes are economic. The restless women would not get so much leadership unless considerable masses of women were disturbed, and the considerable masses would not be disturbed nor follow restless, and mistaken, leaders if they were comfortable. Everybody nowadays nibbles at education; everybody reads and either has ideas or goes through motions of having them; and consequently everybody has something to express, and feels the need of expressing it. The natural way for women to express themselves would seem to be by means of husbands and children, but a proportion of the women affect to find that mode of expression either impossible, or so unsatisfactory that they turn to whatever else they can.

A certain proportion of the women do not look upon marriage either as their desire or destiny. They plan for it, but merely as a possibility, largely speculative, and with alternatives that look surer at least, and are more definitely attainable by their own efforts. The alternatives—the office jobs and factory and shop employments, and nearly all the independent vocations—would be right enough except for one thing, and that is that the women who take to them permanently might as well not be women at all, because they cannot conveniently combine with the service these occupations exact, the great and indispensable service of continuing the species. It was for that indispensable service, Martin argues, and argues not only with perfect truth but persuasive force, that women were contrived, and not for office work, nor factory work, nor work in shops. To the indispensable service the great mass of women undoubtedly are true, preferring it and undertaking it when it is attainable.

Machinery, which has upset the old domestic industries, has much disturbed the conditions of life and multiplied the employments alternative to marriage. Partly as a result of machinery, an overwhelming and compelling industrialism, engrossed in material progress, is ruthlessly set to turn the most precious assets of humanity and civilization into material wealth for immediate use. The same industrialism that deforests the land, skins the soil, devours and wastes the coal-beds and the iron mines, and squeezes the last drop of mineral oil out of the bowels of earth, stands ready, without any further compunction than a column of figures may signify, to divert the brains and hearts and fingers and bodies of women from the service indispensable to life to these temporary, sterile, and incomparably less important uses of commercialism. Somehow, in a world never so rich as now, the men seem less able than they used to be to take care of the women. Everything tends to be commercialized, all the commercialization tends to monopoly, and monopoly makes a machine. The race must yield to this, or starve.

That is one thing which machinery has done for us. It is nobody's fault in particular. It has just come to be because conditions produced it, and because conditions produced it, and because wealth is good, and because if you invent and make and run machines and organizations at all, you have to do it at a profit. The machinery of contemporary life is marvelously convenient and productive. The trouble is, as Martin shows, that the human race has been caught in the cogs of it, and is in danger of being ground up.

Thus it is that among the rest the women cry out. Something is the matter, and they, even as men do, feel it. Driven partly out of their own kingdom into man's, they demand equal rights, privileges, emoluments, in the man's kingdom. That is the old cure by a hair of the dog. It is not much of a cure. The better way is to make the woman's kingdom habitable again, and to get all the modern improvements into it, and win her back to live in it and rule it, or at least check her exodus.

But the suffragists are not willing to do anything of the kind. They are working to share the man's kingdom. Some of them want it all. Yet, if the woman's kingdom is to be restored and glorified the men must do it. It is the Crazyjanes who won't have it. They flout the old faith. Few of them are readers of the Bible except to reject it. Most of them scorn the Word. All of them are politicians. They aim to improve the condition of women by politics, and think that women's votes would help vastly in doing so. They take no account of the evil conditions and ghastly failure of politics everywhere. That is man's imperfect work, they say. Woman is to change all that and to make good, according to their scheme. Yet Senator Tillman was right. The thing tried before spelt degeneracy and preceded the dark ages.

III

This is for the most part an abridgment of the thesis laid down and elaborated in Martin's monumental work, "The Unrest of Women." Let us quote, without alteration or condensation, the exact language of our great essayist. It is, as everything that Martin writes, to the purpose, yet tolerant. No good and thoughtful woman can read the following without feeling the force of it:

"We have passed through a stage of national development when the chief good has seemed to the ablest minds to be the development of business, of transportation, of manufactures; the production of commodities, the construction of an enormous apparatus of civilization. Business has thriven; the railroads have been built, the apparatus has been constructed, and commodities in unprecedented volume have been produced. Comes along now all this disquiet and unrest, spreading and increasing until it has come to be more important than gains for the gainful, or commodities for all hands; until, indeed, it has become the subject that most engages statesmen's minds.

"The provision of bread and of bathtubs was never so great. But the people are not fed to their satisfaction, and cannot wash away their aches. There never was so efficient an apparatus of life. No one with any sense wants to make it less efficient or check its steady growth to meet increasing needs and cultivated wants. But now attention has been drawn away from apparatus to people. The chief problem is no longer 'How can we get more machinery?' but how can the spirits of men be fed?—how can life be made sufficiently satisfying to the mass of the people to induce them to sustain the Government?

"It isn't at all a case of women alone. It was not women's votes that turned the old Republican party out, or started the hammering of the trusts, the revision of the tariff and all the incidents of the new politics. It was a general revolt against politico-industrial apparatus that seemed to have grown oppressive. There is a great problem to be solved in politics, but it is not disproportionately a woman-problem, and it will not be solved, disproportionately, by women.

"The woman problem is a part, and especially a symptom,

of it. The woman's influence and thought will greatly affect the solution of it as they do of every human problem. But it has got to be worked out by the ablest political minds our country can produce, working continuously on it, and the ablest and least distracted minds for such matters are still the minds of the ablest men.

"The disquiet of the women cannot be allayed separately by anything done for women. It is part of the general disturbance and can only be soothed by measures that will also pacify the rest of society. It should have many good effects. The driving of so many women out into the industrial world cannot, must not, fail of valuable results in training, in development, in demonstrated capacity for many new undertakings and employments. At least this great adventure of woman into the man's kingdom is giving to the world a new appreciation of her value, both in those activities into which she has been constrained to intrude, and in that domain from which, in so alarming a measure, she has been evicted. Women are freer and more powerful and doubtless happier as civilization progresses, as justice grows more kind and reasonable and intelligent and even, and force and brute strength count for less in the transactions of life. The interest of women is all for the development and perfection of civilization and the purification of politics. We have lots of votes now, amply enough to express every form of discontent. The need is not of more votes, but of more dispassionate intelligence; not of more votes, but of knowing what to vote for.

"But politics will never do the whole business of pacifying human life and making people content to live it. It never did; it will not now. The great agent in that is religion. The great asset of our civilization, incomparably more important than all our astonishing apparatus for promoting physical comfort, is the mind of Christ. That mind penetrated all the perplexities of human relations and solved the problem of life in all its phases. It is on the spirit of Christ, working through individuals, and shaping and inspiring our politics, that we must count to straighten out the tangles in our affairs. That is the only force that is equal to so huge a task; that, working perpetually to bring justice, sanity and love into human concerns, can make men wise enough to be men and women patient enough to be women. That is the only force that can make labor duly tolerant of capital and capital duly considerate of labor; that can keep the spiritual in control of the material, and yet leave apparatus free to accumulate, and wealth to increase, and beauty to develop, and can bring

liberty and opportunity to all creatures to work out all there
is in them that is good."

The *Courier-Journal* has spoken not without feeling of the
men who enlist under the banner of "Votes for Women"—meaning, of course, immediate, unlimited suffrage to a body of people
wholly unprepared for it—doubling the present ignorant and
insufficient male suffrage—whom it has described as either weak-
lings or self-seekers. It is too much the fashion of the newspapers in their cowardly flight from irksome or disagreeable duty
to belittle the importance of the subject and seek to whistle those
who take it seriously down the wind of a rather lofty affectation
of superior foresight. The average newspaper writer deals only
with the concrete. He does not concern himself with causes or
effects. He shies at the unseen and quibbles with thought. Unless
you lam him over the head with a club you cannot reach him, and
then he prefers objurgation to reason. His reception of the truly
great speech of Senator Tillman is proof of this. Even Mr.
Martin takes an optimistic view; that the storm will blow over;
that Nature will assert itself and prevail at last; that wise women
will, in their order and in due season, come to the rescue; and
that, if they fail of this, man is not as big as he thought himself
and will deserve all that may be coming to him. Again we quote
from that incomparable essay:

"As for the men who fear feminism, they show a curious
distrust of the powers that are male. The only sound claim
the male creature has to be boss of the universe is based on
divine right. If the Creator intended that he should be boss
and equipped him with the facilities proper to that office,
boss he will be and nothing can stop him.

"Votes of women will have no more effect on his mastership than so many boiled peas. He may be gentle, he may be
patient, he may study to serve, he may shape himself to
controlled submission, but if natural mastership is in him,
master he will be. If it was not Nature's gift to him, and is
not a necessary incident of progressive human life, then the
sooner he finds his place the better. Anyhow, he can do very
little about it either way except to be himself, and the best
man he can.

"Petty tyrannies over women, dogmatic denial to women
of anything on earth or in life that they want and can attain
and handle, will avail not to keep man in power. Women
are very enduring creatures, who grow strong, and have distinctly grown to their present robust expansion, on petty
tyrannies and silly proscriptions. For centuries in China they

bound the women's feet to keep women in their place. And what did it finally come to? To- Tsi-Ann, the woman autocrat!

"What the insurgent women nowadays are after seems to be not so much power—for they have a vast deal of that already—as advertisement. That is a commodity that is not very filling at the price, and is very apt to prove incompatible with power itself. When a car wheel thrashes they take it off, when a machine goes noisily it goes to the shop. Advertisement is noise; it makes for jealousy, competition, hostility and retirement. The ladies are welcome to it if they like it, but it will not increase their power.

"Nature, seeking her ends and vindicating her laws, and ruthless in her proceedings, stands forever behind both women and men. Perhaps we shall be able in time to inculcate benevolence into our economic system. But Nature owns the road and will walk down the middle of it till the crash of doom, and run over everything that gets in the way without so much as saying: 'Honk, honk!' "

To repeat what we said in the beginning, "if votes were all." But "votes," which have proved so futile, are but the outer and visible sign. They are but the beginning of it. They will, as Senator Tillman says, drag down women without elevating politics, and better bad government than bad women.

Since this agitation became general, women have been distinctly going down hill in all womanly qualities. As the woman gains in what the he-women call "opportunity," she loses in character. These he-women are themselves essentially masculine. They are, like the male politicians, blatant and self-seeking. In the home life those of them who have had any home life have been failures. They are no more fit to lead decent and true women than if they were morally bankrupt; for their influence is wholly immoral.

It is not alone the idle rich who are a law unto themselves; who go abroad and buy titles by a process of shameless prostitution; who in their conduct and attire emulate the prosperous demimondaines of the European capitals; whose whole life is godless, graceless and sensual. They are merely occasional eyesores. The he-women whose cry for "sex freedom" rings out of bandwagons and echoes up and down the line of circus parades, elated by the enthusiasm of the poor drabs that follow—the Sillysallies and Crazyjanes of the rank-and-file—do not, or will not perceive that the multiplying tragedies and scandals of the day are the direct offspring of their teaching; that "sex freedom," to weak or vicious minds, means license; that adultery seems no worse in women than in men; that "opportunity" and "equality," as expressed by the lewd dances, furnish the woman the means, hitherto conceded to the man, of initiating sensual indulgence. The bad manners of the young women of the better class are everywhere conspicuous. They are being educated to the knowledge of evil. Sex barriers are thrown down. The forbidden is becoming the rule. The laws of God and nature are reversed. To meet the requirements of the he-women who seek to rule the roost self-assertion must take the place of self-denial; riding a single horse, the woman must insist upon riding before; and, as every woman has the right to choose the father of her own children—in case she be fool enough to have any—in case one father does not answer, she may get another, there being neither limitation nor responsibility to the dogma of "free love." Heavens! Rome had it; so did Athens; when the feminine New Jerusalem arrives, which of these he-women will play Aspasia? But much of this is Latin, and all of it is Greek, to the shock-headed boys who have come to the Editorial front of affairs from the baseball field through the City Editor's room, and who, where they do not welcome the arrival of Cleopatra and the rule of Catherine, are unable to consider any ethical question beyond its direct relation to the news of the day. Inevitably such writers see in the great South Carolinian only a figment of their own shallow creations, rejecting his philosophy because they cannot comprehend it.

If the evils foreshadowed by Senator Tillman are to be averted —if the degeneracy of luxury and wealth is to be arrested—the women, the true and noble women of our country—old-fashioned only in purity and grace—must take matters into their own hands.

The men are hopeless. Too many of them are only too willing to have woman degrade herself. Too many of them see nothing beyond the short range of their naked vision. The fathers in Israel, sure in wisdom and firm to duty, are conspicuous by their absence. It is the mothers of Israel who must come to the rescue. Chivalry may not be dead, but it seems on the wane, and the he-women are doing what they can to kill it.

For all its boasted progress and achievement, its wondrous inventions, its diffused intelligence, its vast engineries and accretions of what it calls enlightenment, the world does not increase in moral power and mental strength. There are more cranks and crankism than ever before. India was never fuller of fakirs. Hell breaks loose in unlooked-for places—and easier—and oftener —even in the heart of civilization, offering spurious remedies for fancied ills, sure cures for irremediable conditions.

The furies stand upon the battlements lashing the credulous to frenzy. The wanton girls of the he-girl-schools would abolish the Home. The wanton women in the band-wagons would abolish

Religion. As in France during the Terror they have constructed
a Supreme Being of their own and seated this in a Chariot to
whose wheels they bind the weakest along with the worst of men,
including not a few who call themselves ministers of the Gospel
of Christ. Yet there stands the Home; the Bible; the wife; the
mother; before their eyes emblazoned on the walls, the laws of
God and nature, and, except that Womanhood breathes into them
the life of action inspired by light from Heaven, we are lost.

Temperance Lecture

(February 9, 1919)

I

It rejoices me to observe that "there are others." Perhaps
before it is too late enough voters to count will open their eyes
and take notice of the moral fakers and knavish politicians who
put on the livery of Heaven to serve the devil of greed and cant
and fraud. Although it may not be said that—

> "Those now think who never thought before,
> And those who always thought now think the more,"

it yet seems to be true that certain among the hay-seeds who have
not lost the nasal faculty, howbeit their mental sight went long
ago, begin "to smell a mouse."

I note it gladly. From away out in the wild and woolly West
comes the cheering assurance that the Bolsheviki have not made
final and complete conquest of what was left of a once free people.
The Omaha *World-Herald* tells us that there are signs of a growing feeling in Nebraska that too much Government is not on the
whole an unmitigated good. This finds its expression, timidly
perhaps, but with increasing coherency and conviction, almost
everywhere that men and women congregate. Thence the question
arises how far it is safe and wise to go toward the surrender of
the people's liberties and privileges into the keeping and supervision of Governmental power?

The *World-Herald* does not fail to note that the spirit of
meddlesome authority thrives on what it feeds, just as do bigotry
and intolerance, remarking that it grows in Nebraska, "though
there are indications that popular fear and resentment are likewise
gathering force and volume," and then proceeds to say:

"Great abuses spring from small beginnings. A vast evil
may result from the combination of a number of little things,
each in itself seemingly harmless or even helpful, but which
become a precedent and gather accretions. Of a sudden they

give rise and authority to a system of laws, a body of doctrine, portentous and monstrous even in the sight of some of those who favored the numerous little separate parts that entered into its construction. It is then, sometimes too late, that people come to realize that great principles may not be violated with impunity on the sophistical excuse that good will result from the violation.

"Particularly is this true of governmental encroachment upon popular rights, upon civil and religious and personal liberty. It is just as true of the little acts and tendencies which conspire to centralize Government and magnify executive power at the expense of the direct control exercised by the people over the Government which presumably they choose not to be their master but their servant.

"An anti-cigarette law is a small—and silly—beginning. It is the forerunner, however, as we note in press reports, of movements for censorships of various sorts, of movements for putting the ban of law on tobacco in all its forms, and of correlated movements for 'putting the law on' tea and coffee and corsets and cosmetics. The prohibition of liquor many of us may like. But few of us like the swarms of Paul Prys that open our luggage on trains and in depots in search of it, or the promised prospect of squads of spies and informers to invade the sanctuary of the home and search for a pint hidden in the chimney. It seems not only harmless but salutary here and there to attempt a little political tinkering with the schools, and with the churches—and then some fine morning we wake up confronted with the necessity of battling to save churches and schools from political and partisan control. Peoples before now have listened entranced to the convincing exposition of the doctrine that by surrendering a little liberty here, a little power there, they may enjoy a more efficient and better unified Government—only to be faced later on by a Cæsar, a Man on Horseback, or a Kaiser with his junker court.

"It is in such ways that liberty itself is lost. The process, at first imperceptible and pleasing, becomes in the end a rushing torrent that threatens to sweep all before it."

II

I should not like to take the hand of a prohibitionist, if I knew him to be a prohibitionist. I should not like it because, in the event that he be not a fool outright who could nowise have my respect or interest, or concern me, he must be sterile of mind and heart as well as a traitor to the institutions of his country.

The Constitution of the United States assures to each citizen the right to life, liberty and the pursuit of happiness. These are essential to freedom, to a free country and to free men. In the exercise of his rights the individual man must not tread upon, or put in jeopardy, the rights of his fellow-man. Nor within this limitation must he allow his own to be ignored or abridged.

The case against prohibition, other than that it is a canting hypocrisy devised by rogues for the cheating of dupes, where it is not the broken reed of feminine hope, or a weak delusion of zealots, because in point of fact it does not prohibit, may be thus summarized:

First—It is the entering wedge to a sumptuary fanaticism which will not stop with the attempt at the denial of drink, but, given its bent and license, will set up a tyrannous supervision over every affair of private life and personal conduct, substituting for self-determination the will and rule of conventicle.

Second—It affects to establish virtue by law, substituting for the sense and sway of conscience the public acts and ordinances of assembly, thus making a political issue of religion and morality and removing it from the accountability of the minds and hearts of men.

Third—It is an assault upon the essential reason of our republican being, and the establishment of the spy-system, not to say the reinvestment of the star-chamber and the inquisition.

The quotation I have made from the oracle of Omaha reads like an editorial of, say, ten years ago, out of a certain ribald sheet of Louisville. Recently the New York *World* has taken up the same cry. I am afraid that my good brothers Hitchcock [3] and Cobb arrive upon the scene too late, that they reach the stable and propose to lock the door when the horse is gone, that, in point of fact, the Bolsheviki of prohibition have swooped down alike upon Hell-fer-Sartin and Yuba Dam, as well as upon New York and Nebraska, and that there is equally no balm in Gilead, nor sugar in the bottom of the glass.

The *World-Herald* closes its admirable dissertation with the following, which leaves little further to be said:

"Against such a tendency, if it continues to grow as it is growing to-day, the liberal and truly democratic forces of the republic will before long be compelled to organize and fight for the salvation of American liberty. The issue is becoming definite in Nebraska as elsewhere.

"The world has seen the end to which the magnified state with its 'Verboten' signs and its goose-stepping subjects led

[3] The *World-Herald*, owned by Gilbert M. Hitchcock, is edited by Harvey Newbranch, author of these excerpts.

Germany. All humanity has been drenched in blood on account of it. It was a logical end, the inevitable end. With quite different ideals our forefathers sought to set up institutions in America that would make a great people out of a free people; that would make the State the servant of the citizen and the responsible guardian of his liberties, rather than make the citizen into a puppet with the State his master.

"We have won a great war to put down Prussianism, but its spirit yet lives as it has lived always in various forms and guises. 'Under which flag, Bezonian'—bond or free—is a challenge which now, as in days long gone, each must answer for himself. And on the sum of the answers depends the fate of nations and civilizations as revealed in the ages-old rise of democracies and fall of despotisms. For it is the outstanding lesson of history that free peoples tend to become great and enlightened and virtuous while those in bondage sink into degeneracy of mind and will and conscience till finally even their proudest ruins are covered by the sands of oblivion."

III

I do not know much about whisky, having never drunk enough of it to learn—they tell me the Kentucky brands are the best ever and I can well believe it, taking the Kentucky women and the Kentucky horses as the world's standard of excellence—but I am an expert on beer, and, if I had the power, I would translate every distillery into a brewery. The cure for drunkenness, if there be any cure, is light wines and lager. The case-hardened prohibitionist who confesses himself unable to distinguish between a glass of grog and a stein of beer—nay, who still further discredits his intelligence by admitting that he is unable to realize the amazing contraries betwixt a bottle of whisky and a hole in the ground—is as much opposed to the one as to the other. He makes no discrimination. All drinks taste alike to him, each hell-bent and sot-breeding, the most innocent tipple along with the strongest swig. The experience of continental Europe is proof of my contention. There the wine and beer consumption is universal and enormous, with no drunkenness of the sort so common with us.

The question of prohibition is unknown. The teetotal zealot would be considered a crank. Beer is not only drink but food, for a large proportion of the people. The manufacture of beer is under the supervision of the law, rigidly enforced, and nothing but malt and hops can be used.

The consumption of concentrated alcoholic drinks in proportion to that of wine and beer is small. These latter constitute the Continental beverage equally for the rich and the poor. The

MISCELLANEOUS 371

many gardens where drinks are dispensed, having comfortable
tables and chairs and good attendants, are crowded during pleasant
weather with the most respectable classes of society ranging from
the highest to the lowest, all joining in a republic of pleasure,
drinking in moderation while enjoying the best of music. It is
the same during the winter months with the indoor places.

Upon many journeys through Germany I have never seen one
single case of drunkenness in any of these halls or gardens.
Treating, with its concomitant evils, is practically unknown. Each
man pays for what he orders, drinking no more than he desires.

I have never doubted that the relation of strong drink to crime
and of the lighter wines and beer to crime would, as indicated by
the police statistics in every land, show much to the advantage of
the latter as against the former. That the brewers of our country
have to answer for an overplus of dives set up by them
where liquors as well as beer are sold, is true enough. But the
fact does not affect the argument in favor of the vinous and malt
fluids.

Washington, though himself a distiller, was of this opinion.
Jefferson, who had seen more of the world—assuredly more of
the European world—than Washington, went the length of making a strenuous effort to introduce wine and beer to Virginia by
offering a bonus to the vintners and brewers who would come and
try the experiment. Wiser than Washington or Jefferson, the
American prohibitionists make no discrimination and allow no
distinctions. One and all, they are intemperate in what they call
their temperance, a single glass, according to their philosophy,
being the first mile-post on the road to perdition, a glass of beer,
or a glass of wine, and a glass of grog, one and the same. They
take their stand upon total abstinence, which is their right. But,
not content with adopting it for themselves, they seek to force it
by law upon their neighbors.

It is impossible to reason with such a spirit. It is of the very
essence of despotism. Gratified with respect to intoxicants, it
would next address itself to tobacco; then to such food as might
fall beneath its ban; and finally, to religious opinion, wearing
apparel and personal behavior. Tyranny accepted knows no
bounds. Fanaticism is relentless. In Europe the people know
this but too well, and the rulers dare not run counter to it.

IV

The moderate use of drink has brought as much happiness into
the world as its immoderate use has brought wretchedness. Even
in America there is not per capita in any community one sot to a
hundred moderate drinkers. Both in England and in the United

States drunkenness has steadily abated under the ministrations of an intelligent morality.

In the European beer-brewing and wine-making countries drunkenness of the kind common to us is unknown. The throngs that gather in the public gardens are a sight to see. They are perpetually crowded. Noblemen and workmen touch elbows. Women and children come and go. Disorder is unknown. Cheese and sausage are the food staples. This has been going on day in and day out for hundreds of years, and furnishes a complete answer to the dogma of the American prohibitionists "that we can no more conduct the liquor business without producing drunkards than we can run rattlesnake ranches without raising poison."

One might as well say that we cannot run banks without raising embezzlers; or railways without encountering accidents; or cucumbers and cabbage without the risk of cholera morbus, the thief, the wreck, the bellyache, like the drunkard, being the exception. Shall we have no more fiscal institutions, no more lines of transportation, no more truck gardens and no more cakes and ale? Perish the thought, for what has been and is in Europe can be in America or anywhere else where the rule of sanity is observed.

We pretend to think we are a free people and we agree that the world is too much governed. Yet nowhere is individual liberty so assaulted as in the United States. Thoughtful Americans must see that there are worse evils than the drink evil; evils more subversive of the character of a nation, because more general and pervasive, less obvious and less reachable. The drunkard is usually in evidence. He may be dealt with. It is otherwise with the varying forms of personal and political corruption. Virtue is self-resistance to vice, not enforced obedience to drastic regulation, morality itself being relative. That may be moral in one country which is immoral in another country.

The "common good," about which we hear so much, like the "general welfare" clause of the Constitution, has been worked to death. The "common good" is the veriest abstraction. It is nowhere the same. It has its variants. Who is to decide what is the "common good"? Time was when the church, through its close corporation of ruling prelates, alone decided. The "common good" was their belief, or pretended belief, in prescribed religious dogma. The "common good" embraced certain customs, manners and clothing decreed by canon law as orthodox. The penalties assessed against the delinquent varied from hanging to burning, from the rack to the thumbscrew. They were applied by whichever church party found itself in the ascendant.

After centuries of strenuous trial in the effort to make men good by force of arms and tortures, both a costly and a ghastly

failure, the self-ordained agents of God sowing the world in blood
and flame, were sent to the rear and the doctrine of toleration
—the bedrock of all freedom, of all enlightenment, of all good
government—was established measurably throughout Christendom, but absolutely, as the founders thought, in the United States.

This the prohibitionists would set aside and nullify. To do
so they fly in the face of Heaven itself. Treading the cloisters
of the past in Europe, or traveling the thoroughfares of the
present at home, I know but one torch to light the way, and that
is the Spirit of the Man of Galilee, whose teaching from first to
last was at war with force, appealing to the better nature and
the reason of man, not his brutal passions and combative parts.

V

I might as well rail at God for bringing sin and disease and
death into the world as seek to encompass them by sumptuary
legislation. Men may be made hypocrites by law, but never saints.
Religious truth has been rather obscured and retarded than ac-
celerated by theologic controversy.

Repressive agencies culminate in reactions. Radical puri-
tanism in England was succeeded by the debaucheries of the
Restoration; and prohibition laws in the United States have not
only not diminished drunkenness, but they have brought in their
train scandals and evils quite as hurtful to the community at
large as drink has brought to that limited section of the community given over to the excessive use of intoxicants; that is,
contempt for law, evasions of law, extortion and adulteration, the
corruption alike of the officials and the drink, lawful and needful
revenues extinguished in favor of lawless indulgences; the fanatical preacher and the grafting politician uniting to work the spy
system each for his own ends, but against the mass and body of
society.

I am being constantly asked how long I think that prohibition
will last. If it be not accompanied by the stimulation of the drug
habit, as in Turkey, where alone among the nations it has made
a permanent lodgment, the reaction will come with the knowledge
that in the cities it cannot be enforced. The constitutional inhibition may never be rescinded. But, like the fifteenth amendment
in the Southern States, it will become inoperative. "It will be
just as easy," says an old Mississippi friend of mine, "to get
a drink as to keep a nigger from voting."

Miami, Florida

"WAR OF THE KAISERS"

RETIREMENT

"WAR OF THE KAISERS"

RETIREMENT

"TO HELL WITH THE HOHENZOLLERNS"

When the bomb was launched at Sarajevo, Mr. Watterson was 74 years old. When the armistice was signed at Senlis he was nearly 79. Yet in this period he wrought the greatest and most effective work of his long career, a career which he confidently believed had ended. So certain was he that his tasks were over, and that he would spend his remaining days in writing only when it pleased him, that he had, in 1912, already begun to abstain from public appearance and to take long summer and winter vacations. One reason why this volume is empty of comment on many important events from 1910 to 1914 is because the editor left the writing to others.

But in 1914 he plunged into his heaviest labor with better equipment than any American journalist. He knew history and with fifty years of events, here and abroad, he had intimate acquaintance. He was familiar with the peoples and potentates of Europe. And when the cause of liberty in any form was at stake, Mr. Watterson was ever the first to mount the barricades.

That is the reason why he was far in the lead of the American press in the "War of the Kaisers," as he called it. To him, from the very first, the European struggle was the battle of autocracy against democracy. The men of '48 in Germany he had known well, and he understood conditions in that country from a long and loving association with its people.

The first reprint in this war group is the sulphurous slogan Mr. Watterson ran up to his newspaper masthead September 3, 1914, the war only a month old. "To Hell with the Hohenzollerns and the Hapsburgs," he cried, and in no profane or irreverent spirit. Throughout the war he repeated his war-cry until it became the spirit of those who were engaged in resisting the Kaisers. In England, through the admiring offices of Lord Northcliffe, it became as well-known as in Louisville. Now and then some camel-swallower assailed the invocation as profane, and Mr. Watterson would write such defenses of his parts of speech as appear, second, in the subjoined group. He lived to hear it echoed in press and pulpit everywhere.

To Hell with the Hohenzollerns and the Hapsburgs

(September 3, 1914)

Herman Ridder flings Japan at us. . . . What does he think now of Turkey? How can he reconcile the Kaiser's ostentatious appeal to the Children of Christ and his pretentious partnership with God—"Meinself und Gott"—with his calling the hordes of Mahomet to his aid? . . . May heaven protect the Vaterland from contamination and give the German people a chance! To Hell with the Hohenzollerns and the Hapsburgs!

"Profanity"

(February 19, 1918)

The profanity of the *Courier-Journal* is abhorrent.—Christian Churchman.

"Those vehicles of disjointed thought," as Dr. Rush called them—the newspapers—were never more "disjointed," and, for the matter of that, as far as light and leading go, less "vehicular," than they seem just now. To say truth there is much to perplex the average space-writer doing his daily grind. Turn whichever way he will he encounters dragons; she-dragons and he-dragons; the wild geese of Woman Suffrage and the wet hens of Prohibition; not to mention the War. "He was a bold man," the Dean of St. Patrick's tells us, "who first ate an oyster." But he who tackles a reformer is a hero.

Yet, nevertheless and notwithstanding, the dissonance of the press may after all prove a good thing. Out of a multiplicity of counsels, we are assured, wisdom comes. The one essential point of agreement—that we are going to lick the Huns—that we are on the way to Berlin in Prussia and Vienna in Austria, not to mention Kalamazoo in the Black Forest and Kickapoo on the Rhine!—will be nowhere disputed. It is our desire to be explicit and we hope we make ourselves reasonably clear, when we say "to Hell with the Hohenzollerns and the Hapsburgs."

Is that the kind of profanity the *Christian Churchman* abhors? If it is we'll be hornswaggled if we don't repeat it six days in the week and twice on Sundays! There!

WHERE IS CHRISTIANITY?

As the war wore on, the editor shared the depression of civilized beings over the trend of modern warfare and the diabolical enginery of destruction. It was in this mood that, in November, 1914, he wrote the third of the appended articles, inquiring whether Christendom were really Christian. This article reveals the simple devotion of his nature to the religion of Christ, but is also notable as an example of his metrical style. The final strophes—they are hardly prose—are bars of solemn music. It is likely that this ability to make his prose scan is one secret of the editor's influence upon the reading masses. It is a Celtic attribute, effective in journalism.

Is Christendom—Or Has It Ever Been—a Christian?

(November 26, 1914)

"It has been vouchsafed to us to remain at peace, with honor, and in some part to succor the suffering and supply the needs of those who are in want. We have been privileged by our own peace and self-control in some degree to steady the counsels and shape the hopes and purposes of a day of fear and distress. Our people have looked upon their own life as a nation with a deeper comprehension, a fuller realization of their responsibilities as well as of their blessings, and a keener sense of the moral and practical significance of what their part among the nations of the world may come to be.

"The hurtful effects of foreign war in their own industrial and commercial affairs have made them feel the more fully and see the more clearly their mutual interdependence upon one another and has stirred them to a helpful co-operation such as they have seldom practiced before. They have been quickened by a great moral stimulation. Their unmistakable ardor for peace, their earnest pity and disinterested sympathy for those who are suffering, their readiness to help and to think of the needs of others have revealed them to themselves as well as to the world.

"Our crops will feed all who need food; the self-possession of our people amidst the most serious anxieties and difficulties and the steadiness and resourcefulness of our business men will serve other nations as well as our own.

"The business of the country has been supplied with new

instrumentalities and the commerce of the world with new channels of trade and intercourse. The Panama canal has been opened to the commerce of the nations. The two continents of America have been bound in closer ties of friendship. New instrumentalities of international trade have been created which will be also new instrumentalities of acquaintance, intercourse and mutual service. Never before have the people of the United States been so situated for their own advantage or the advantage of their neighbors or so equipped to serve themselves and mankind."—The President's Thanksgiving Proclamation.

I

It would not be possible to find words more impressive and fit, and at the same time more all-embracing, than those chosen by the President of the United States in meeting "the honored custom of our people to turn in the fruitful autumn of the year in praise and thanksgiving to Almighty God for His many blessings and mercies to us as a Nation."

During a day of "fear and distress," there has been with us "a self-control," steadying our counsels and shaping our hopes. We do, in a larger and yet in a personal sense, realize our responsibilities as we begin more fully and clearly to conceive the part we are destined to play in the momentous readjustments of a world rent by war, nor able without our help to live, move and have its being. Thank God, our flocks and fields will suffice to clothe the naked everywhere, whilst "our crops will feed all who need food."

Thus the spiritual grace reflected from Heaven, brought home to us by the words of a devout Chief Magistrate, and vitalized in our hearts by the sense of pity for the stricken and the joy of giving to the starving, brings us, each and every one, face to face with God, with God the Father, God the Son and God the Holy Ghost, except we be foresworn as Christian men and women, false to all we have held sacred and dear, the babe in the cradle, the beloved in the grave, the Religion of Jesus the Redeemer come down to us through the ages—even of blood and terror—from the Star of Bethlehem and the Cross on Calvary.

The time is ripe, and it is meet that we stand uncovered whilst we ask ourselves whether the Jew of Jews was a mere pretender, whether for nineteen hundred years the world we miscall civilized has pursued a living lie, and, in short, whether Christendom is, or ever has been, a Christian.

II

The inquiry furnishes food for deepest thought, occasion for most prayerful consideration. The theologic Jew, who holds to the old Dispensation, believing Jesus of Nazareth an impostor, and looking still to the coming of a Messiah, is certainly supported by the history of these nineteen hundred years, for how many professed Christians, stigmatizing the Jew, yet follow the teachings of the Christ? When and where has Christendom shown itself a Christian? Yet we must not forget that more than a thousand of these nearly two thousand years of our Christian Era were years of darkness; the Bible unknown to the people; the Christ but a germ of belief, hardly other than a flower of faith. In self-defense we must keep this in mind.

Mortal, or angel, Son of God or prophet of an epoch, the Child that was born in a manger, lived for the good of man. He labored for the lowly and the poor. His ministrations were for the afflicted. He was the Prince of Peace. They have violated His precepts to their undoing. Has wealth brought happiness? Has glory justified itself? Is strife the natural state of man? Take the helplessness of the mighty—the skeletons in the closets of the great— for answer; and yet behold war elevated on the one hand into an exact science and on the other hand degenerated into wholesale destruction; the merciless sacrifice of unoffending millions to the insanity of Nations set on by the rapacity of Rulers, they of the tribes of Judea not more bloody-minded and brutal. If this be Christian, what is pagan? Unless we take from it a lesson of universal and perpetual peace, it were better that we confess a delusion and join the Jews in their adoration of a Christ that is yet to come.

To what end? Why should the King of Kings wait so long to send this Christ? Is not the fault with man? Has not Heaven fulfilled the promise? Who shall say that the message was so mysterious and complex that it required theology to expound and theologians to explain it?

Religion has not primarily to do with the concrete things of life. If not spiritual it is nothing. Delusion lies not in Christianity, but in dogma, and dogma was the invention of the devil appealing to the diabolic in man, so often abroad after power and pelf.

The groves were God's first temples. But, as organization made for strength, a Church was set up within very narrow earthly lines, and then cathedrals were built, enriched, adorned. Next came dignities and benefices, prelates and prelacy, with their gross material assumptions. The very priests were warriors, the wars for worldly dominion and glory. And when they were not fighting for pillage, they were fighting for creeds. They fought over baptism, infant damnation and the immaculate conception. They drew nice distinctions between orthodoxy and heterodoxy, between the tweedle-dums and tweedle-dees of doctrine, and he who believed not—though sure of hell-fire in the world to come—must be burnt at the stake in this world; and great were the winners in the battle; the very Kings of Men; forebears of the Hapsburgs and the Hohenzollerns plying the trade of war up and down Bitter Creek, all the way between Hell and the Iron Works; the one in Flanders the other in Krupp's murder mills at Essen on the Rhine.

III

Of the fraternal conflict between the two Sections of the American Union, said Abraham Lincoln—"Both read the same Bible and pray to the same God and each invokes His aid against the other—the prayers of both could not be answered." Napoleon declared that God is on the side of the heaviest battalions. Gladstone, according to Labouchere, not only had always a card up his sleeve, but believed religiously that the Almighty put it there. All this corresponds exactly with the self-proclaimed partnership between the Kaiser and God, as of the contention of each combatant that the Lord is with him and his murderous devices.

The call to battle has ever and everywhere been the same. Strike for your altars and your fires—"he wields the deadliest blade of all who lightest holds his life"—the foeman's heel is on thy breast—the arm that drives him thence "might brain a tyrant with a rose, or stab him with a thorn"—

> "Not man nor monarch half so proud
> As he whose flag becomes his shroud."

—and all the other martial gibberish indicating the valor and the disregard of life of the poets the further they get away from danger and the likelier they are to find an audience of admiring fools.

But the awakening! Here is a verse from a Southern war song of the gentle Henry Timrod. It was delivered in 1861—

> "The despot roves your fairest lands,
> And till he flies or fears,
> Your fields must grow but armed bands,
> Your sheaves be sheaves of spears;
> Give up to mildew and to rust,
> The useless tools of gain,
> And feed your country's sacred dust
> With floods of crimson rain."

So, too, the gentle Whittier sang to the North. And then four long years of dreadful slaughter in the name of the Lord of Hosts. But at the close—mark the difference—the day of Christmas, 1863, the same Henry Timrod cried:

"How grace this hallowed day?
Shall happy bells, from yonder ancient spire,
Send their glad greetings to each Christmas fire
    Round which the children play?

"Alas! for many a moon,
That tongueless tower hath cleaved the Sabbath air,
Mute as an obelisk of ice, aglare
    Beneath an Arctic noon.

"Shame to the foes that drown
Our psalms of worship with their impious drum,
The sweetest chimes in all the land lie dumb
    In some far rustic town.

"There, let us think, they keep,
Of the dead Yules which here beside the sea
They've ushered in with old-world, English glee,
    Some echoes in their sleep.

"How shall we grace the day?
With feast and song and dance, and antique sports,
And shout of happy children in the courts,
    And tales of ghost and fay?

"Is there indeed a door,
Where the old pastimes, with their lawful noise,
And all the merry round of Christmas joys,
    Could enter as of yore?

"Would not some pallid face
Look in upon the banquet, calling up
Dread shapes of battles in the wassail cup,
    And trouble all the place?

"How could we bear the mirth,
While some loved reveler of a year ago
Keeps his mute Christmas now beneath the snow,
    In cold Virginian earth?

"How shall we grace the day?
Ah! let the thought that on this holy morn
The Prince of Peace—the Prince of Peace was born,
    Employ us, while we pray!

"Pray for the peace which long
Hath left this tortured land, and haply now
Holds its white court on some far mountain's brow,
    There hardly safe from wrong!

"Let every sacred fane
Call its sad votaries to the shrine of God,
And, with the cloister and the tented sod,
    Join in one solemn strain!

"With pomp of Roman form,
With the grave ritual brought from England's shore,
And with the simple faith which asks no more
    Than that the heart be warm!

"He, who till time shall cease,
Will watch that earth, where once, not all in vain,
He died to give us peace, may not disdain
A prayer whose theme is—peace."

Words, only words! Though beautiful, how poor they seem, and some of them, how false they ring! What is the good of writing, of preaching? "All war is bad," said Franklin, "there will never be a good war." Did ever man fight his way to an end that might not have been better reached through fair and kindly agencies? Does not each man's reason tell him that this is true? We have not only abolished the code of honor and the duello in the South—as they did long ago at the North and in England— but we have made an appeal to them ridiculous. If gentlemen have ceased to fight, why should nations continue to fight? Why should the arbitraments of friendship not be substituted for the litigation of courts of law? The lion and the lamb we are told shall lie down together. Why not the human beasts that make the world hideous by their strife?

IV

Peace talk has rarely been popular. War talk always is, or seems to be. The saber-rattlers and the armor-plate makers form a noisy claque, Bellona the star upon the stage. When there is not an organized interest to drain the treasury, there is a party to play for advantage, or some demagogue to exploit himself. Lo, Senator Lodge with his haste to jump all over President Wilson anent Turkey, and Representative Gardiner with his inquiry into "the state of the National defense."

Where are we menaced? From what quarter may be look for invasion? With the great Nations all engaged and presently to be exhausted, who shall invent a "war scare" that will hold water? And, with the implements of murder changing from time to time, what guarantee that those we buy to-day may not be obsolete and valueless to-morrow?

Says the eminent David Starr Jordan:

"War is not a spontaneous thing. It requires long preparation and carefully hatched plans. It is brought about
largely through the influence in the national councils of representatives of the saber-rattlers and war traders.

"During my recent tour of Europe I found no one who
wanted war except these professional war mongers. The
Kaiser did not want it; that I know. It was the ill advice
of the ring with which he was surrounded. Germany's business men did not want it. Most certainly big business of
Europe counseled against it.

"But the armament manufacturers—in England and France, as well as in Germany—get fabulously rich and pay dividends on war. They spend a hundred times more for bribery to bring on a clash than it takes to build a Peace Palace."

Dr. Jordan shows that the United States yearly spends from seventy-one to seventy-three per cent. of her annual revenue for wars that have been and wars that may be. England yearly expends for her army and navy $350,000,000. The war debt of France is $6,000,000,000. All countries of the world could be run on the money the United States and Great Britain waste on their armaments. "The gigantic national debt for defense," he tells us, "involves an 'invisible empire' which directs and controls credit. The debt of Europe is thus controlled by a 'consortium' of bankers, comprising some eighteen families with the Rothschilds at their head. They constitute the 'Unseen Empire.' The war scares, with secret diplomacy and the overlordship of this 'unseen empire' are all necessary stages in the development of war. It is these men who work on the passions and fears of the people in order that behind a misguided patriotism they may reap their millions out of the blood of men." And then, the great president of Leland Stanford, quoting the German Chancellor who declared that "parchment is parchment, but that steel is force," finely says:

"The rape of Belgium made scrap-paper of the parchment of International Law. The sowing of mines in the fairways of commerce made scrap-paper of the rights of neutral nations. The torture of the Belgian people made scrap-paper of the rights of noncombatants.

"War may be never righteous, but it is sometimes honorable. In honorable war armies fight armies; armies do not fight private citizens. If armies give no needless provocation, they will receive none. The sacking of Malines, Aerschot, Dinant, is no act of honorable war. The wreck of Louvain, historic Louvain, five hundred years the venerated center of Catholic erudition, at the hands of blood-drunk soldiers, was an act of dishonorable war. It marks a stain on the record of Germany which the years will not efface. 'A needed example,' says the apologists for crime. The Duke of Alva gave the same 'needed example' to these same people in his day. For centuries the words 'Spanish blood' struck terror into people's hearts throughout the Netherlands. For centuries to come the word 'Prussian' will take its hated place.

"The good people of Germany do not burn universities. They are helpless in the hands of a monster of their own creation. The Germany of to-day is an anachronism. Her ideals in science are of the Twentieth century; her ideals in politics are of the Sixteenth. Her rulers have made her the most superb fighting machine in a world soul-weary of fighting. For victors in shining armor the modern world has no place. It will not worship them, it will not obey them. It will not respect those who either worship or obey. It finds no men good enough to rule over other men against their will.

"A great nation which its own people do not control is a nation without a Government. It is a derelict on the international sea. It is a danger to its neighbors, a greater danger to itself. Of all the many issues, good or bad, which may come from this war, none is more important than this, that the German people should take possession of Germany."

The case against war as made by Dr. Jordan embraces a series of convincing arguments addressed to the interest and reason of man. But we shall never get rid of the war lords and the saber-rattlers, the corrupt armor-plate syndicates and the self-exploiting patriots, until we put an end to the system of which they make themselves the leaders, each nation a bully with a chip on its shoulder, each people a flock of sheep to be driven to slaughter. The Christendom that pretends to be a Christian is not a follower of the Christ, but a vainglorious egotist, deluding itself with virtuous homilies and displays of fashionable piety. It is a pharisee and a hypocrite. It is not, and it never has been, a Christian.

* * *

Tramp, tramp, tramp, the boys are marching; marching and fighting; food for powder; brave lads from Severn and from Clyde, from the Rhine and the Rhone; little red-legged French boys out of the sweet Provence country, and beardless, oval-faced German boys from Bingen and Stuttgart; wood-choppers from the Black Forest and sail-makers from Belfast and Brittany— what's imperial Hecuba to them that they should fight for her, bleed for her, die for her? They, these noble youngsters, buried deep under Russian snows and lost in the trenches of Flanders, who is to father the coming generations? Our civilization has crumbled beneath our very feet, before our very eyes. There is nothing left but Christianity, if that be left. If it be not, what hope for humankind? Has this blight come as a curse, or as a revelation? It was not till Israel was crushed that Israel hoped. The land had run rivers of blood. When the people were not worshiping Moloch in the vale of Gehenna they were following Yahweh on the march of invasion and conquest. Then vanquishment, deso-

lation, despair, and, rising above the wreckage of the living and
the ashes of the dead, the dream of a golden time; the vision of the
Shepherd-prophet "when the mountains shall drop sweet wine
and all the hills shall melt, the plowman shall overtake the reaper
and the treader of grapes him that soweth seed." May not these
appalling cataclysms be the precursor of the realization forecast
by the men of old? May not Europe suffer and see, even as
Judea, and come forth in rags, to know at last that in strife there
is neither glory nor gain; in war only the wrath of God and
the ruin of the world? Yet, how long, oh Lord, how long?
When shall the lesson end, the travail cease? Hear Thou, dear
God, this day this prayer; make the nations sane again; drive out
the devils from the hearts of men; give us the eyes to see the
light, the minds to know the truth; give us the grace that passeth
understanding—peace on earth as it is in Heaven—peace—

> Peace in the quiet dales,
> Made rankly fertile by the blood of men,
> Peace in the woodland, and the lonely glen,
> Peace in the peopled vales!
>
> Peace in the crowded town,
> Peace in a thousand fields of waving grain,
> Peace in the highway and the flowery lane,
> Peace on the wind-swept down!
>
> Peace on the farthest seas,
> Peace in our sheltered bays and ample streams,
> Peace wheresoe'er our starry garland gleams,
> And Peace in every breeze!
>
> Peace in the whirling marts,
> Peace where the scholar thinks, the hunter roams,
> Peace, God of Peace! peace, peace, in all our homes,
> And peace in all our hearts!

ON THE LUSITANIA MURDERS

A day elapsed after the sinking of the *Lusitania* before Mr.
Watterson published the celebrated article which is number 4
in this group. The crime, while it filled his heart with horror,
fit closely into what he had been proclaiming as the natural
programme of the Kaisers. Now he warmed to his task of
persuading the American people that neutrality was impossible, that civilization and free institutions were menaced by
the desperate war lords of the Central Powers. "Nothing
in the annals of piracy can in wanton and cruel ferocity
equal this," he wrote; and he voiced the inquiry, soon to
become insistent and international, as to the meaning of the

phrase, "strict accountability." It was in this writing that he set out to divide, on a basis of responsibility for crime, the castes of the German people: a distinction which the President was later to adopt. This editorial, despite the passions of the moment in which it was written, is not jingoistic or a call to arms: it merely points to the inevitable.

Two days later, May 11, 1915, Mr. Watterson had formulated a sort of plan of action as a protest against the *Lusitania* murders. He urged the declaration of a "state of war" and the casting out of Germany from recognition as a civilized nation; but he did not propose the dispatch of fleets and armies. Throughout the article is discernible his feeling that the Germans could not be gotten at, with their fleet boxed up in the Kiel canal and their armies beset by the Allies.

Groping his way toward the best course for America to pursue, Mr. Watterson, nine days later, demanded the summoning of a disarmament congress of all the nations, including the Central Powers, at which the United States should demand the elimination of the aeroplane and the submarine from warfare. This is the one time he proposed such a council in the height of the war, it shortly becoming obvious that the plan was impracticable. He was well content with the representations made by Mr. Wilson, and thereafter devoted himself to arming the souls of his readers for the harsh action that was certain to come.

The Heart of Christ—The Sword of the Lord and Gideon

(May 9, 1915)

I

That which the *Courier-Journal* has feared—which it has been for weeks forecasting as likely to happen—has come to pass. A great ocean liner, passing peacefully to and from an American port—carrying a harmless ship's company of noncombatant men, women and children, many of them American citizens—has, without chance of escape, or time for prayer, been ruthlessly sent to the bottom of the deep and some thousand, or more, gone to their death, drowned and mangled by the murderous onset of a German submarine. Truly, the Nation of the black hand and the bloody heart has got in its work. It has got in its work not upon armed antagonists in fair fight on battle front, but upon the unoffending and the helpless, sailing what has always been and should ever remain to the peaceful and the peace-loving God's free and open sea.

Nothing in the annals of piracy can in wanton and cruel ferocity equal the destruction of the *Lusitania.*

It seems but yesterday that the *Titanic* went down. Dire tragedy!—it might have acted even upon the madmen of Berlin as a deterrent—served as an object lesson in pity—made the occasion of some reflection and relenting. But Berlin has lost all the perspectives of civilization. The General Staff knows not the laws of Heaven or earth. The Hohenzollern, infuriate, fears only the loss of his throne and his crown. The Highbrow professors and philosophers of the Prussian Universities, putting Christianity beneath their feet, have taught only the gospel of brutality and hate. With them might alone is right. Woe to him that gets in the way. And, in answer to the wail that went up from the ashes of Louvain—from the stricken of Antwerp and Rheims—to the cry of horror from human nature everywhere, came this answer, not in defense, but in reassertion:

"We have made one fundamental principle clear: for the fault of the individual the community to which he belonged must suffer. The village in which our troops had been shot at by the civilian population was burnt down. If the culprit was not discovered, a few representatives were taken out of the general population and shot, women and children not being touched, except when they were found with weapons in their hands.

"This principle may seem hard and cruel—it has been developed from the customs of modern and ancient war history, and as far as it can be spoken of at all is recognized. It is also justified by the theory of setting an awful example ('abschrecken'). The innocent must suffer with the guilty; and, when the latter cannot be found, they must suffer for the guilty, not because misdeeds have been done, but in order that they may be attempted no longer.

"Every burning down of a village, every shooting of hostages, every decimation of the population of a district whose inhabitants had taken up arms against the approaching troops is far less an act of vengeance than a signal of warning for the country which has not yet been occupied. And about this there can be no doubt; the burning of Battice, Herve, Louvain and Dinant were effective as warning signals.

"Does anybody in the world imagine that the population of Brussels would have allowed us to act as though we were in our own land if they had not trembled for our revenge, and were not trembling still?

"War is no drawing-room game; war is hell-fire. He who sticks his finger into it will burn his hand, his soul and his life. The poor, confused, misled Belgian Nation has been sacrificed to this fate."

As it was in Belgium and France so shall it be in Britain. As it was on the land so shall it be upon the ocean. The earth shall be made terrible and they that go down to the sea in ships shall know the fires of perdition and feel the wrath of Satan.

The decree of Satan went forth from Berlin. The instruments of Satan were forged at Essen. There was but a single Satanic abatement. Satan's Ambassador at Washington—shameless in his infamy, under the Sign Manual of Satan's Embassy, insolent in its disregard of law, or consequences—gave warning that the deed was hatched, that the tools were ready and that those who went upon this English boat, trusting to her convoy and her speed, took their lives in their hands, not recking the Devil's hatred, nor his devices. This was done not to save, but to intimidate; not to warn, but to terrorize.

Shall any just man say that the Count von Bernstorff is not guilty of murder and that his colleague in crime, Dernburg, is not accessory to murder, and that each and every German, or pretended German-American, applauding this fearful butchery is not a murderer at heart?

II

But, comes the query, what are we going to do about it? Are we at the mercy of the insane Hohenzollern, not only through his emissaries sending his odious system of government and debasing theories of castism affecting superiority to our doors, and proclaiming them, but bringing his war of conquest and murder across the line of our transit and travel over the high seas, which are ours to sail as we list without let or hindrance from man, or monarch, from him or from anyone on land or water? Must we as a people sit down like dogs and see our laws defied, our flag flouted and our protests whistled down the wind of this lordling's majestic disdain? Must we as a Nation emulate at once the impotence and the docility of China, and before such proof of the contempt in which we are held by him and his, throw up our hands in entreaty and despair, saying to the insistence of autocracy, to the insolence of vanity, "thy will is law!"?

What could the President have meant when he declared that the Government of the United States would hold the Government of Germany to "a strict accountability" in the event that its war zone pronunciamento resulted in the loss of the life of a single American? How did he intend that his countrymen should understand him when he put forth his supplementary protests? Are we a sovereign, or are we a vassal?

Please God, as all men on earth shall behold, we are a Nation; please God, as Europe and all the world shall know, we are Americans.

Too long already have we submitted to the free hand of the foreigner at home and abroad. Months ago should the Pan-German propaganda, issuing from the German Embassy—led by the German Ambassador—erecting in the heart of our country a treasonable organization to support the German foray upon Belgium and France, and control our own domestic politics—have been ended. Bernstorff should have been severely rebuked and warned to proceed at his peril. For less Genet, the Frenchman, and Crampton, the Englishman, had been ordered away. Dernburg should never have got beyond Ellis Island. Harvard should have sent Münsterburg packing. Ridder should have been put under bond. The followers of these among the German-Americans should have been given the option of repeating their oaths of allegiance, with fresh guarantees for good behavior, or of returning to the Fatherland they had fled to escape military service, to fight for their blessed Kaiser directly under his imperial eye and eagles. Bartholdt should have been promptly expelled from Congress and driven back to Hesse, where he came from and belongs. The poor and honest Germans of the United States—those who came here to better their fortunes and escape despotism and castism—those who when they took out their naturalization papers, confessing Republicanism and Democracy, meant it—those who have no interest, part or lot with Kaiserism, who ceased to be Germans and became Americans—should be rescued alike from the teaching and contamination of the newly rich of Germans whose dearest hope is to go "home" and build castles on the Rhine, and from the Highbrow writers and Herr Doctors who worship at the shrine of the Hohenzollern, having learned their lesson from the Highbrows of Heidelberg, Göttingen and Bonn.

Each of these latter is a German, not an American, and, in the event of war, or a state of war, would become a German spy. They have from the first relied upon the "German vote" to see them through. They were even bold enough to try it prematurely at Chicago. In all their newspapers they threaten us. In spite of the President's patience, his equal and exact neutrality, they are already abusing him and saying what they are going to do to him in 1916.

It is of the first importance that they be made to know that they are aliens and do not own the country yet, nor dominate its politics. They must be brought to understand that their enmity, not their friendship, is to be courted. As long as the German-

American Alliance pretended to charity and aspired to music it was, where not wholly approved, yet amiably tolerated, but, as a German Colony, planting imperial ideas, as a Know-Nothing Lodge, blacklisting Americans, we will none of it; and the sooner its leaders are made to realize this the better for them and for us.

The *Courier-Journal* will not go the length of saying that the President should convene the Congress and advise it to declare against these barbarians a State of War. This may yet become necessary. Whilst actual war is not possible—Germany having no fleet we can sweep off the briny deep, nor army near enough to be met face to face and exterminated—yet are we not wholly without reprisal for the murder of our citizens and the destruction of their property. There are many German ships—at least two German men-of-war—in the aggregate worth many millions of dollars, within our reach to make our losses—repudiated by Germany—good, and their owners—robbed by Germany—whole again.

We must not act either in haste or passion. This catastrophe is too real—the flashlight it throws upon the methods and purposes of Germany is too appalling—to leave us in any doubt what awaits us as the bloody and brutal work goes on. Civilization should abjure its neutrality. It should rise as one mighty, God-like force, and, as far as its moral influence and physical appliance can be made to prevail, forbid the riot of hate and debauch of blood that, like a madman, is running amuck among the innocent and the unprotected.

This holy Sabbath every pulpit in America should send a prayer to God in protest; every patriotic Minister of the Gospel of Christ should lift his voice in protest, and, more than all—the Christian President of the United States, a cool and brave man, sprung from a line of heroes and saints—ceasing longer to protest, should act, leaving no doubt in the minds and hearts of any that he is not merely a leader in Christ, but a leader of men and nations, and that he holds aloft the Sword of the Lord and Gideon!

It Is Up to the President

(May 11, 1915)

I

Upon the threshold of this the most momentous moral crisis since the crucifixion of Christ—which gave the world a system of religion dominating its civilization for nineteen hundred years—Christian men should pause and ask whether that civilization laid in that system of religion is to be turned backward and downward, a conceded failure, whilst they look on amazed, dazed and helpless.

Let there be no mistake; the immediate cause of disturbance is not merely an incident of war. It is a parting of the ways upon the broad Highroad of Life, one of the cross-ways leading to Heaven and the other to Hell. The most thoughtful and prayerful must stand appalled before the magnitude and complexity of the issue. But the good, the true and the brave will not quail before it.

Much is being said, mainly by those who have nothing else to say, about the wisdom of patience and the virtue of silence. The Chief Magistrate, and his official family, charged with supreme responsibility and the final word, should indeed do nothing rash, say nothing imprudent. Nor will they. But upon the press of the country is placed the double function of reflecting the popular volition and, according to its intelligence and conscience, of translating this into counsels just, expedient and efficacious.

At such a moment the *Courier-Journal* wishes to talk to its readers like an American, like an American journalist, having long and large experience with the affairs alike of peace and war, and at all times unafraid to utter its opinions, supported by profound conviction and the highest sense of right and duty. It desires to address the President as a citizen duly impressed by the dignity of his office, yet with the candor which one friend may adopt in conferring with another friend. We are not only unable to see good reason for reticence in such an emergency, but, in failure to speak out in meeting, a positive neglect of patriotic requirement. We would speak plainly but calmly of matters commonly held in reserve for discussion more or less private and personal.

Before whom and for what, let us ask, shall Truth blush and hang her head? It was "Secret Diplomacy" that began it. Are there any "secrets" now, is there any "diplomacy" still, forbidding an unfettered people to say their say and express their will in the hearing of all mankind, the world listening the while, to learn whether we are a race of honest Republicans and self-respecting freemen, or merely a huddle of political hucksters, seeking mostly office and the Almighty Dollar?

II

It is clear that the United States as a Democratic Nation—that humanity as a system of Christian ethics—has nothing to hope from the organized Empire of Germany.

In the ordinary concerns of life Castism takes no account of the commonalty. The people possess no rights the patrician is bound to respect. But Aristocracy enfuriate and at bay—Absolutism driven wounded and bellowing, like lion to its lair—strikes blindly, ruthlessly, remorselessly at all comers; but most savagely at those who contest the principle of its being, who oppose equally its capacity and its right to rule.

Thus our attitude of neutrality, arousing at the outset disappointment, and as it progressed awakening resentment, has deepened into actual hatred. Continued disregard of our several protests indicates likewise contempt. Part of this has been of our own doing. The license allowed the Count von Bernstorff and the Herr Doctor Dernburg, the support given them by the German-American press, the treasonable utterances of certain naturalized colonials calling themselves German-Americans resident among us, would probably have misled Berlin had Berlin been in a normal state of mind. But from the first Berlin has been abnormal. The precipitation of the war based upon similar misimpressions—especially with respect to England and Belgium—was a species of paranoia which the circumstances succeeding soon developed into emotional insanity, losing all distinction of moral values, of national character and standing, and of international relations and obligations.

Justification of the awful deeds done in France and Flanders could be looked for alone from madmen. The war zone decree was maniacal; an outburst of frenzy; at once the opportunity and a plea for murder. What can we expect from a Government putting such engineries at work? But shall its agents be permitted to defend them in our presence; to roam at will this Christian land with ill-concealed joy over a tragedy unexampled in the annals of crime; to gloat over the grief and horror of the living and to insult the dead lying yonder at the bottom of the sea, sent thither by their hands, the Count von Bernstorff, the German Ambassador, sneering at whatever the American people may choose to think touching what has happened, or of him and his Government; and the Herr Doctor Dernburg, his semi-official colleague, declaring the destruction of an ocean liner loaded with unoffending noncombatants, men, women and children, a triumph of German sea-power, claiming it justified by a war zone disputed by every civilized Nation, and making an actual merit of a "warning" on the part of the German Embassy which proves simply that the German Ambassador was fully apprised of impending murder and a willing party to it?

Has not the time come not only to put an end to all this but to exclude the German Empire from recognition by the family of Nations?

What have we, as a people, to lose by this? But, as a Christian people, why should we consider the cost at all? We are nowise interested in the physical triumph of any of the forces engaged on the other side of the ocean. Ultimately we may have to fight the winner. But we are very much concerned for the future of the world. If we submit to the proposed revolution in human nature— to the calling of murder by the name of war—if neither neutrals nor noncombatants are to be held safe against attack by armed men, what may we gain by holding aloof? It would in the end be better and cheaper that we put forth a power we still believe we possess than by our acquiescence give aid and comfort to the authors of innovations repugnant to the arts, principles and practices of war and abhorrent to responsible Government and righteous civilization. Assuredly, if we do nothing but mouth, we shall show ourselves objects of world-wide contempt, unworthy even of our own self-respect.

Alone, the President can do nothing, or next to nothing. With all his power he is but master of himself and the language. He can send the Count von Bernstorff away as Washington sent Genet and as Pierce sent Crampton and as Cleveland sent Sackville-West. The Ambassador is doubtless expecting this and in consequence is not only trimming his sails but his actions and utterances for Berlin. The Herr Doctor Dernburg we might frighten away by threatening to put him in jail. But to what real practical end and purpose? Neither of them amounts to a hill of beans.

Our people have been slain. Their property has been destroyed. We cannot hope for adequate indemnity at the hands of Germany. Shall there be no reprisal? But, if Congress be convened and a state of war be declared, we have within our reach some millions of dollars worth of German ships which we may confiscate and thence apply the proceeds to those who have suffered. The German Government we may be sure will respect nothing, feel nothing except the pressure of force. Having legitimized piracy and glorified murder, the Empire can be brought to some kind of proportion, some realizing sense—if at all short of the subjugation which awaits its armies—only by the assertion of the ruthless power it has invoked, and we owe it to ourselves as a Nation, and to our principles as Christians and Republicans, to assert it with a majesty which will illuminate whilst it crushes, leaving not a line or word to conjecture.

Nothing else, or less, seems at all to meet a situation unexampled, whichever way we take it, replete with horror and peril.

It is not for the *Courier-Journal* to look into the President's heart, or undertake to fathom his understanding. For his great abilities and genuine strength of character, as well as his rectitude of purpose, we entertain the very sincerest respect. We have no quarrel with any man's pacificism, whilst for the jingo we have alternating distrust and aversion. There is a half-way point between eager belligerency and sheer passivism—between let us say the Roosevelts and the Carnegies—which the Wilsons might consider with advantage.

That the country has been with the President thus far in his policies both as to Mexico and the European war—not ourselves agreeing with that as to Mexico—we have not doubted. The people do not want war anywhere, and therein they are right enough. But he who thinks that there will be no more war—that established arbitration will lead to universal brotherhood—that we can maintain our power and prestige without an army and a navy, and may not be compelled to fight whether we wish to or not—will waken soon or late to find himself mistaken.

The President should, and doubtless he does, bethink him of this. Assuredly he cannot afford a fluke in an emergency so pregnant. The least misstep may cost him dear if it does not involve the loss of much of the public confidence achieved by his fine record of useful and successful service, his rare tenacity and extraordinary poise. He may not pass this awful business by hoping to slick it over with a few diplomatic pen strokes. Even watchful waiting must have an end. And, it being up to the President to "do" something—to rise above the complacency and cowardice of the professional politicians who surround him—the *Courier-Journal*, his friend, and his party's friend, would have him above all else resolute—the Book of Books in one hand, the Sword of the Lord and of Gideon in the other—making precedents where none exist—stamping the acts of the German Empire as piracy and murder hateful to mankind—arraying us, as a Republican Nation and a Christian people not on the side of either belligerent, but against crime unspeakable and far-reaching wrong, which, if it go unpunished of the disinterested, may wreck both the religion and the civilization of the universe.

Nor were this bad policy from the partisan point of view. Already the plea of the Opposition is that the Democrats are incapable of handling great National affairs and owe the chance power they possess through a minority vote to division among Republicans. The failure of the Administration in this crisis will go far to unite them. It is most vulnerable in the Department of State. That the President fully realizes the gravity of the situation goes without the saying. Upon his decision we set great faith. These are meant as the merest suggestions to the fact that sometimes the highest prudence is disregard of consequences, and that, as he has before now violated usage with good results, he need not bind himself to any other rule, or object, than the Nation's dignity and honor, sure that he will find the people behind him.

Shall Murder Be the Last Word of Science?

(May 20, 1915)

"When Camillus, the Roman General, was besieging Falerii an opportunity was offered to secure a victory by murdering a number of children of the Falerians who had been treacherously placed in his power.

"The proposal was so shocking to Camillus that he said to those who were by:

" 'War at best is a savage thing and wades through a sea of blood and wrong; yet even war has its laws, which men of honor will not depart from; nor do they so pursue victory as to avail themselves by acts of villainy and baseness.' "—Plutarch's Lives.

I

Sitting as a Court of Inquiry into the State of Peace and War and calling to the stand Mr. Andrew Carnegie, the World's Chief Promoter of International Arbitration and foremost organizer of the Brotherhood of Man, and his ablest and most eloquent Apostle, Dr. David Starr Jordan, President of the Leland Stanford University, with President Emeritus Charles W. Eliot, of Harvard, and ex-President Woodrow Wilson, of Princeton, for Judges Advocate General, the *Courier-Journal* proposes to submit some questions in ordinary touching the most momentous moral crisis mortal kind has been given to meet since the Crucifixion of Christ.

In view of all that has happened, notwithstanding the noble hopes and excellent promise of The Hague Tribunal—the Russo-Japanese War, the War of the Balkans and this, the greatest and direst of all wars—leaving out of account the side-shows in South Africa, Tripoli and Mexico—does it not occur to the leaders of Pacificism at any price that they have allowed the horns to get ahead of the hounds, and that, if they would make real progress, they must retrace their steps, and, instead of rendering copy-book maxims about the glory of peace and the horror of War, they must address themselves to the practical work of ameliorating the conditions of actual war, its elimination beyond the power of prayers, or counsels?

The cause of reform has been in all ages beset and imperiled by the muddling of unreflecting extremism and the meddling of self-glorifying personal exploitation.

The recent hegira of women to The Hague—some of them foolishly obsessed and some of them filled with conceit—some seeking peace and some the limelight—all of them doubtless sincere—brought a kind of discredit through their magpie chatter alike upon themselves and their movement. That any of them believed it possible to penetrate the powder-cloud—to be heard above the din—revealed their lack of judgment and self-control. It excited contempt, which their claims as good women could not wholly repress. Their plan and scheme was absurdly impracticable. As well might a flock of geese invade a den of lions.

The brotherhood of man is nowhere remotely in sight. The unification of the world is therefore yet a chimera. Optimists may cry "Peace! Peace!" but there is no peace. The passions of men, unsubdued by the religion of Christ and untaught by the lights of civilized experience, are still so vital that a single nation may arouse them in all nations, and the showing is that science, instead of making for justice, truth and humanity, is making for cruel destruction and indiscriminate murder.

Said the patriotic, peace-loving Dr. Lyman Abbott at the Naval banquet in New York the other night:

"I am sorry to say that recent events have shown myself and a great many others that the era of the appeal to reason is a great deal further off than we thought. The first fundamental of government is protection of persons and property. If it does not protect it has no right to be called a Government. I respect the men of the peace societies, but I do not respect their opinion. They are not preaching peace, but anarchy. If there is no navy to protect neutrality on the high seas, then every ship must go armed, and that would mean international piracy. I am not for war, but we do want to be prepared to meet war if it comes to us. One thing is certain, this nation must have an army and navy adequate to fulfill its duty to itself and the world."

Each day is bringing the wisdom and the force of this directly home to us. Certainly we must have an army and a navy. Assuredly we must be at all times and in every way "prepared." No matter how devoted the President as a Christian and a philosopher may be to the gospel laid down by the Prince of Peace, as the capable head of a Government and a loyal leader of men, liable to be called at any moment, he may have, when he least expects it, to unsheath the sword and take the field. If such a time should come shall he command an army of murderers, a navy of assassins —committed to wholesale and unmanly butchery—or shall we now, whilst we have the chance and the power, put foot upon the ingenuity of modern science and outlaw the submarine, the aeroplane and the torpedo?

II

A soldier believed by many in South Carolina and Georgia to be bloody-minded to the point of ferocity told the world that "War is Hell." A soldier, who, whilst he was winning battles in Mississippi and Virginia, stood accused of the reckless and unconcerned sacrifice of life, declared that there had never been a war "that might not have been avoided." Those who personally knew General Sherman and General Grant will attest that two men less hard of heart, more generous and tender in nature, never lived.

But, they were men-at-arms; educated in the military service; and, though each of them spoke of war as he knew it to be, they used the weapons that came to their hands, the more destructive the more effective, just as their successors, the contemporary leaders of the Army and the Navy, are doing, no fault or blame to be found with them.

Again, the plate-armor people—the fabricators of the engineries of death—ever on the alert for new inventions in the machinery for killing—keeping a constant weather-eye upon the expansion of their business and the increase of their profits—have been these fifty years unwearying in their enterprise of encouraging war and popularizing its appliances.

Never a shopkeeper in the Rue de la Paix vainer, or more voluble, in displaying his newest "creation" before the delighted gaze of the fine ladies of swelldom, than the armorers of Essen in pressing upon the saber-rattlers of the Wilhelmstrasse the latest designs and devices in murder. Krupp, on the Rhine, has vied with Redfern, on the Seine, Worth, at Paris, has had no advantage over Zeppelin, at Zurich, in fashionable exploitation. The modern woman has been made over again into a miracle of artifice; the modern soldier into a miracle of destructiveness. All the Alchemists of Firenzi and Padua, with the sum-total of their poisons, were tyros and dabblers in the science of invisible destruction by comparison with the producers of the submarine and the airship, the one crawling assassin-like under the sea, the other robbing God of His thunderbolt to deal murder, cruel and cowardly, from the skies; both unworthy of soldiers, disgraceful to men.

The *Courier-Journal* is entreating the President to seize the opportunity afforded by the official interrogation between the Government of the United States and the Government of Germany, to call a Congress of the Neutral Powers to lay the fiat down to the belligerent Powers; that there shall be no more murder from under the ocean or out of the clouds; that the rules of war shall not be altered to suit the Zeppelins and the Krupps; that the last word of Science shall not be murder, unsparing and pitiless murder; in short, that the submarine is a pirate and the airship a brigand, and that both shall lie under the penalty that no Nation setting itself against the interdict shall ever again, either in commercial or political intercourse, be recognized by the thus reorganized family of Nations as one of its members.

We have the power to enforce it. There is nothing visionary in it. It is timely and practical. But, if we mean to preserve our civilization, it is indispensable. For, unless these inhuman and infamous agencies are put down—made contraband of war—they will become the universal and accepted usage of war; we must adopt them with the rest; and, as surely as we do, we set out on a journey toward something worse than barbarism, the brutalizing of the army and the navy, the sure precurser of degradation and savagery among the people.

We speak not less for the integrity of the soldier and the sailor than for the decencies of life; not less for honorable warfare in the field of arms than for the public morality at large and en masse. With Mr. Carnegie we would establish universal peace and with the President, Dr. Jordan and Dr. Abbott eliminate strife, but, if neither be possible, let us, as far as we can, moderate the passions and humanize the methods of war. If we cannot abolish war, let us restore its chivalry; give it back some of its sporting spirit; relax the grip of the Black Hand and the Bloody Heart, which now possess it, and inspire it with the refined courage and nobleness of soul of which in days gone by heroes were made.

In a recent book, "From the Trenches," Mr. Geoffrey Winthrop Young, an English writer, paints this sad picture: "War—the war of Ilium, of Agincourt, of Waterloo—used to be a brilliant affair. Death harnessed to a glittering car of Juggernaut. Men went under the wheels in the rush and flame of colors, and to the sound of bands and the applause of multitudes. The car is now hidden in a gray, deadly rolling cloud. We can only hear the rumble of the hidden wheels. Our sons and friends move into the darkness. Of many of them all we shall ever know is that they have not returned."

No more honors now. No more glory. Only a continuous performance of sickening endurance and paralyzing horror, which, instead of inspiring the mind and awakening the heart, strikes them with a dull thud into mute insensibility.

Why should we accept the submarine and the aeroplane unchallenged as legitimate implements of war—because they are the fashion and Europe has adopted them—much as equally without question a woman takes a new gown, however unsightly, because it is the latest "style." Under such hand and rule war becomes simply a contest in diabolism. It is no longer Nation to Nation, Army to Army, ship to ship and man to man, but a system of personal enmity and organized revenge laid upon the scientific process which can be most brutal and deadly.

We had in our own country four years of what is called Civil War. It was fought on both sides bravely, sincerely and to a finish. And, when it was over, and the fighters cooled off, they had no accusations of unmanly deeds or private malice to lay one against another, and have been fraternizing ever since to the limit as neighbors and Christians, so that it may be said the children of the second generation cannot distinguish the grandsire who wore the gray from the grandsire who wore the blue, or clearly understand just what they went to war about.

Even such wars set the clocks of civilization back; but here we have a world-war originating in trade rivalry and racial vanity, conducted with the spirit of cannibals and the weapons of demons.

Preachments are idle. But we are not helpless. Science, which long ago rejected God, has made the issue between war as the normal state of man and the canons of modern civilization; between a series of fiendish discoveries and devices for perpetuating war by planting broadcast the seeds of hatred, and the Christian effort to regenerate human life by enlarging the area of peace on earth, good will to men; between wholesale and indiscriminate murder as the expression of national prowess, and the limitations which natural feeling and personal honor have in all ages set to distinguish the man from the beast; in short, between the infernal machine, represented by the submarine, and the aeroplane and the torpedo, and the Christian religion. It is a straight issue. It is a world issue, and, if it be not up to the President of the United States to put forth the full power of this mighty Nation and this Christian people; put it forth now, decisively—that the opportunity illustrated by a horrible example has come to him—then farewell to the teaching of Christ, all hail the advent of Satan!

But, if he does he will win, and then the advocates of arbitration, the friends of universal brotherhood, may proceed with their holy work, having good hope of the ultimate disarmament of nations, when in every land, of every people and every army, it may be truly written:

> "The bravest are the tenderest,
> The loving are the daring."

EDITH CAVELL

"The insanity which has possession of the Teutonic mind" was the editor's explanation of the German defense of the execution of Edith Cavell. This article, which is seven in the appended group, bitterly reproved the New York *Sun* for opening its columns to technical justifications of the measures taken by Bissing, and is one of the few examples in this volume of many thunderbolts launched against other newspapers by Mr. Watterson.

From Haynau to Bissing

(November 2, 1915)

"Evil, be thou my God."—Satan.

"Pity is opposed to the tonic passions which enhance energy and the feelings of life. Its action is depressing. A man loses power when he pities. On the whole, sympathy thwarts the law of development, which is the law of selection." —Nietzsche.

I

Edith Cavell was an English nurse, long a resident of Brussels. She was the matron of a school of nurses and the head of a nursing home, where, since the present war began, she had ministered to the wounded of all armies. She was not young nor yet beautiful, but a woman whom everybody respected, honored and loved as one whose life had been dedicated to the alleviation of suffering.

The facts of the case may be summarized as follows: On the fifth of August she was arrested and placed in a military prison. For some reason several weeks passed before Brand Whitlock, the Minister of the United States, was requested by the British Government to inquire into her case and do what he could to insure just treatment for her. By persistent effort, he learned, on September 12, that she was accused of having assisted British and French soldiers whom she had nursed, and Belgians of military age, to get away from the country.

German military law allowed her a counsel, but forbade him to confer with her. Thus she faced a court-martial, on October 7 and 8, without legal representation. The deprivation was not of great consequence, however, because she frankly admitted the truth of the charges as well as full knowledge of the significance of her acts.

Thus is it that the legality of the verdict may not be gainsaid. The death penalty resided in the discretion of the court. She had knowingly violated the laws framed by the military government, and was subject to its judgment. But the circumstances which revolt every humane instinct are that the extreme penalty for treason and spying was exacted for a lesser offense; that the ruthless sentence was carried out in brutal haste in order to prevent a commutation and that the authorities lied to circumvent efforts in her behalf.

Two full days after sentence had been decreed the Governor-General assured Minister Whitlock that the case was still undetermined and that he would be kept advised of developments. This pledge was given at 6:20 o'clock in the evening of October 11. Two hours later, alarmed by reports they had heard, the Secretary of the American legation and the Spanish Minister sought out the Governor General again. He repeated his assurance; but, when they insisted that he make further inquiry, he did so, and he reported that what they had heard was true—Miss Cavell was to die before daylight.

Until midnight they continued to entreat him—not for pardon, which was beyond his power, but for delay. Nothing could move the military authorities. At 2 o'clock in the morning Miss Cavell was led to a secret place in the prison, a file of soldiers was lined up before her and she was shot.

These are the simple facts of a tragedy which has awakened the pity of the world and aroused all human kind to the deep damnation of her taking off.

II

Nothing could more signally disclose the insanity which has possession of the Teutonic mind than the defense of the execution of Miss Cavell, set up by the German Chancellor and echoed by the Germans in America. Since the same persons defended the massacres in the Irish Sea and approve the murderous operations of the Zeppelins, what else was to be expected? Yet we recall that before Bissing, Haynau—who only whipped women—stood before the world as the monster of modern history, and in this affair might have served both as a horrid example and a deterrent.

We may dismiss the German Government as confessedly barbaric and these German-Americans as equally diseased and disloyal. The halter were too good for them. But, what shall we think of those pervert Americans, few indeed but wantonly defiant, who rush into print to excuse and even to extol the crime of the butcher of Brussels? Surely of desert and of right they ought to be burned at the stake.

The New York *Sun* lowers its standard of patriotic duty if not its professional credit by giving in a recent issue space for a number of these reptiles—one, we regret to observe, writing from Louisville—to deface its columns and disgrace the human species by such screeds as the following:

"Miss Cavell said that she was guilty of aiding prisoners of war to escape, and she was executed for so doing.

"Fifty years ago Mrs. Surratt was executed for a crime that she said she had no knowledge of whatever. The Secretary of War, who was unscrupulous enough at the time to hang any one who labored under the slightest suspicion, allowed her to die.

"Shall Germany be adjudged guilty of a greater error than the United States? The pro-English sentiment, so strong in this country, cannot afford to cast odium on Germany, or on the much despised Turk, for that matter, when they consider the work of the United States soldiers in the Philippine Islands."

This insensate brute is equally disloyal to his country and his kind—assuming him to be a man and not an animal—and at the same time he is as ignorant as he is treasonable.

The proof against Mrs. Surratt was conclusive. The crime was murder. There was no escape from a verdict of guilty. Yet, because she was a woman, the Military Court which tried her recommended her to clemency. Save for some mystery never clearly explained she would not have been put to death. Her execution is a conceded blot upon our historic 'scutcheon. The Secretary of War had not the power of clemency. That lay with the President.

Just what this hound may think he means by his reference to "the work of United States soldiers in the Philippine Islands," it would probably be difficult even for such a degenerate to tell.

Says another one of the *Sun's* perverts:

"There isn't any shame for anybody involved in the facts of the Cavell case. For Miss Cavell there is the exact reverse.

"As for sending women spies out to do mischief and then contending that they are too dovelike to be dealt with, it must be admitted that such an exercise of unreason is permissible to people in the straits in which the belligerents find themselves.

"But what can be said for Americans, three thousand sea miles removed from the war, yet related by blood to all the contending parties, having a form of neutrality but denying the substance thereof? Absolutely nothing."

To the weak and flabby understanding of a creature like this, "absolutely nothing." The mind that could approve such a murder is a vile and crooked mind. The heart unappalled by it is a wicked, cowardly and vicious heart. A man who could write and confess himself possessed of such a mind and such a heart can only be a shameless villain. He should be whipped like a dog through the streets and then driven from the sight of decent people.

Finally, here is a third perversion of reason, truth and humanity, which we regret to see signed by the name of a woman, who, presumably a German, at least ought to be ashamed of herself:

"It does seem strange that the English are making so much fuss over the justified execution of Miss Cavell. Have they forgotten Joan of Arc so soon? And how about the German women put to death in France for helping Germany? What do people expect in time of war, a pink tea?"

The whole German contention, where it does not rest on brutality, rests on lying. No German woman has been "executed" in France, or elsewhere. Neither the case of Joan of Arc nor of Mrs. Surratt is illustrative in this connection except as the writers we have quoted may seek to justify the killing of both.

What, however, shall we say of the New York *Sun* for opening its columns to such cattle instead of sending out a deadly gas tank or a gigantic hose carriage to scald and drown them in a flood of boiling oil or molten lead?

THE IRISH AND THE "PIG-HEADED ENGLISH"

Mr. Watterson was always a partisan of the Irish cause. Sometimes he was confident that his County Down ancestry prevailed in his makeup. Whenever a question arose which suggested the slightest possibility of British blunders or oppression in Ireland, the editor was wont to fly to the defense of the Hibernian race. He made peace with the English during the Great War, but he bitterly attacked the extreme punitive measures taken against Sir Roger Casement, and in 1921 he sent a fiery anti-British telegram to an Irish Free State meeting in Louisville. Yet, as the following article reveals, he favored for Ireland only such measure of autonomy as was consistent with the integrity of the British Empire, the while adoring the genius of the Irish race with the passion of a poet.

The Irish at the Front

(July 9, 1916)

I

The Editor of the *Courier-Journal* has received from Mr. John E. Redmond a volume, bearing a friendly superscription and entitled "The Irish at the Front," by Michael MacDonagh, to which the distinguished Parliamentary leader of the Home Rule party has appended a striking foreword.

It is a little but an inspiring book, at once appealing and full of information. We have felt all along that the Irish, like the French, have been doing something more than their duty; the British something less. Here we learn for the first time the actual facts, either suppressed by the Censor, or left out of the Reports; how the Munsters saved the guns on the retreat from Mons; of the rally of the Irish Guards to the Green Flag at the Marne; of the fight for possession of the Channel Coast, the Leinsters, the Dublins and the Inniskillins along the Flanders front at Lille, Armentières and Ypres, leading every forward movement; and, finally, the immortal story of the landing of the Dublins at the Dardanelles, the carrying of "V" Beach, and the fall in action of Father Finn and Father Gwynn—"the place for a priest is by the side of the dying soldier," said they both—from one end to the other of the Irish line, daytime and nighttime, laughing, chaffing and singing—Chivalry not dead yet—the spirit of Fontenoy, of Albuera and of Waterloo alive in every daredevil bosom as the refrain rang out—

> "For Ireland, boys, hurrah; for Ireland, boys, hurrah;
> Here's dear old Ireland, fond old Ireland,
> Ireland, boys, hurrah!"

What a country England would be except for the English. The unseeing English! The pig-headed English! What wonder that there are Irishmen who hate England with a holy hate! Yet there are more who fight for her. "It is these soldiers of ours," says John Redmond in his introductory chapter, "with their astonishing courage and their beautiful faith, with their natural military genius, with their tenderness as well as their strength; carrying with them their green flags and their war-pipes; advancing to the charge, their fearless officers at their head, and followed by their beloved chaplains as great-hearted as themselves; bringing with them a quality all their own to the sordid modern battlefield; exhibiting the character of the Irishman at its noblest and greatest—it is these soldiers of ours to whose keeping the Cause of Ireland has passed." Yea, verily, and not to the Hohenzollerns and the Hapsburgs, to Hell with them!

Blessed they that have no history, the Cynic tells us. "God loves the Irish," a current cartoon puts it, "but He helps the Scotch," depicting Andrew Carnegie in a lordly motor car, Pat digging pipe lines on the side. "What can I do for you?" asked Dundas at the height of his power in England of an Irish lad who had rescued his daughter from drowning. "Make me a Scotchman," said the witty Celt, and, as quick as thought, and with equal wit the great Scotch peer replied, "I canna gi'e ye the prudence." That in truth tells the whole story. Since when was ever an Irishman prudent?

Is it better to have loved and lost? The tragedy of Ireland baffles inquiry. It is a mystery. Wherefore? Why the Phœnix Park murders? Why the collapse of Parnell? And, Home Rule's very foot in the stirrup, why Ulster, why Sir Edward Carson? One feels likewise like saying "To Hell with them!"

We are told that the English are angry with the Americans because we have not, with the Irish, rushed to the front. America will never be at one with England until England renders justice to Ireland. John Bull may put that in his pipe and smoke it.

The trouble has been mainly the religion. What religion? Whose religion? After these murders and this wholesale massacre will there be any religion left anywhere in Europe? Or shall the good and the true fling theology to the winds, and, the temples crushed to earth, the altars steeped in blood, kneel upon God's footstool under the canopy of Heaven, as the apostles did, to proclaim the brotherhood of man through the Gospel of Christ and Him crucified? Must Ulster stand out forever against justice in England and peace in Ireland? When shall Church and State part company; religion cease to be political, religionaries learn to practice humility and contrition; the prelate and the party leader, scorning subterfuge and cant, come to realize the futility of dogma?

II

Greater love hath no man than that a man lay down his life for his friends. Their is neither cant nor humbug, and mighty little if any politics on the battlefield, as we may learn from the glowing pages of Michael MacDonagh's book, but no end of genuine and practical religion; deeds of mercy equally with deeds of daring; the fearless rescue of disabled comrades; Drummer William Kenny carrying messages of relief across fire-swept ground; Corporal Joseph Toombs, "who of his own initiative crawled out repeatedly under a heavy shell and machine gun fire to bring in wounded men lying one hundred yards in front of our trenches."

We learn that this brave fellow rescued four men, "one of whom," the story tells, "he dragged back by means of a rifle-sling placed round his own neck and the body of the man, who was so badly hurt that unless immediately attended to he must have died."

Private Robert Morrow was another of the Irish heroes. He, as the rest, received the Victoria Cross, "for conspicuous bravery near Messines," when, on his own initiative, he rescued and carried to places of safety several men who had been buried under the débris of trenches, "knocked spachless" by shot and shell. Said one of the men thus rescued: "The enemy opened fire unexpectedly. A shell fell in the trench, burying over a dozen men, of whom I was one, in the wreckage. Those who were able ran to shelter; for that first shell was followed by many more; and, the trench being laid bare, the enemy opened a hot rifle and machine gun fire upon it. At the same time he was making a direct attack in force. It was a risky thing to be there. But Morrow didn't mind. He rushed up to where we were pinned under the remains of the parapet. He dragged me out and carried me on his back to safety. Then he returned to look for others. He made the journey six times, bringing away all that were alive."

Alas for glory! On the very day that notice was published of the award of the Victoria Cross to this noble soul he fell in battle, "while in the act," says the report, "of succoring the wounded." His widowed mother received the cross, instead, with an autograph letter from the King.

* * *

It is a debatable question how far the quality of emotion, with its attendant gift of expression, unfits a man for serious affairs and a people for self-government.

Men of letters we know have been rarely men of business; nor have artists often been; the exceptions, as the saying hath it, tending to prove the rule.

The Irish movements of '98 and '48 were inspired by oratory and poetry. They were led by dreamers: for what else were Lord Edward Fitzgerald and Robert Emmet, were John Mitchel and Thomas Francis Meagher? We may dismiss Sir Roger Casement as a hopeless lunatic. Help from Germany was sheer madness. The Sinn Fein uprising was insanity. The English Government could have afforded to treat it as such. A separate Irish Republic, save only after the dissolution of the British Empire, is the mirage of a disordered brain. But Home Rule is not, nor a Dublin Parliament, albeit the permanency of that scheme of settlement, the efficacy of that form of redress, can only be determined after it has been tried. With such a man as Redmond to head the movement and lead the people, the best results seem possible. Anything, however, were better than the system which has prevailed, and anyhow there ought to be a future for Ireland when England awakes, as England must, to the debt the Empire owes the Irish soldiers.

Away off here in the land of the free—let us believe also the home of the brave and the true—our debt to the Irish admitting of no dispute, our love for them spontaneous and eternal—we read this record of "The Irish at the Front" with beating hearts and we join in the singing of the song—

"We've seen the wedding and the wake, the pattern and the fair,
The well-knit frames at the grand old games in the kindly Irish air;
The loud 'Hurroo' we've heard it, too, and the thundering 'clear the way!'
Ah, dear old Ireland, gay old Ireland, Ireland, boys, hurray!"

NO TIME FOR PEACE TALK

Mr. Watterson, at the beginning of 1917, was impatient of the peace efforts which Washington and Rome variously attempted, and the next editorial in the war group shows him in that mood. He had long been certain that it was the obligation as well as the destiny of the United States to put the final weight in the scale against Kaiserism; and in this review of the case he again exclaims, "to Hell with the Hohenzollern and the Hapsburg."

The Case Is Made Up

(January 19, 1917)

At the outset of the murder-war begun by the Emperor of Austria to wreak vengeance upon Serbia for the Sarajevo assassinations and seized by the Emperor of Germany as his opportunity to launch a long-planned and fully-prepared thunderbolt, the *Courier-Journal* sought, in the kindest and most neighborly way, to warn the German-Americans of Louisville, and, for the matter of that, the country at large, against a train of dangers that menaced them.

The paper had always been their friend. By that token it spoke freely and frankly. It spoke truly. Instead of being met in that spirit, the newspapers printed in the German language here and elsewhere turned upon it savagely and the organized body calling itself the German-American Alliance threatened it with destruction.

Later along we learned why. The propaganda which five and forty years ago set out to educate the Teuton mind in the mysteries of "Kultur," an improved philosophy, which was to establish a new civilization throughout the world, Germany in the lead of arts and arms, did not limit itself to home work. It saw, or fancied it saw, a promising field in the United States. The '48 men, who to escape despotism and find freedom had fled hither, were most of them dead. Whilst they lived they had worn the brand of renegades and refugees. Their progeny, however, had prospered greatly. They might be worth while. The Kaiser scheme of universal conquest might need them in its business. The Kaiser began to tolerate certain rich Americans—especially in Kiel waters during the yacht racing season.

Prince Henry was sent over. The German-American Alliance, a body of Kaiser Reservists, was created. The German-American Press was subsidized. Thus the Hyphenates who fell under the spell so artfully contrived became literally and emphatically "another breed o' dogs."

They not only refused the friendly hand the *Courier-Journal* had offered them. They bit it. Then they threatened. They held the balance of voting power, they thought, and woe to the politicians that dare to say them nay. In the event of an armed conflict between the United States and Germany their organs shamelessly declared it would not be a foreign but a civil war. The native American knew nothing about the European situation. The German-American knew it all.

Two years of unutterable brutality followed. Horror succeeded horror. Slaughter was piled on slaughter. Yet from the first there had been but a single issue, Kaiserism and the right divine of kings versus Constitutionalism and the right divine of the people. The Feudal World ripe and ready had in the persons of old Franz Josef of Hapsburg and Wilhelm of Hohenzollern thrown down the gage of battle to the Modern World, represented by England and France, wholly unprepared and but for the fortuitous interposition of little David, of Belgium, all but the shouting in Vienna and Berlin would have been quickly over. Verily the *Courier-Journal* understood what it was talking about when it cried "To Hell with the Hohenzollern and the Hapsburg."

Now we are being told by these implacable Hyphenates that we are pulling England's chestnuts out of the fire. Readers of the *Courier-Journal* know very well where it stands and has always stood touching such English politics and policies as it has considered and discussed. It has consistently and earnestly urged the wisdom and the justice of Home Rule for Ireland. It believes no more in King-Craft than in Kaiser-Craft, holding the Tory and the Junker in equal aversion. But, with Lloyd George Prime Minister, hope for Ireland in sight, it is ready to stand by England, our historic enemy, even as it stands by France, our historic friend.

The slobbering flabbergast about peace which we hear from nymcompoops and mollycoddles deceives no one with a spoonful of sense. England, like her Allies, wants peace. She has refused no peace terms, because England was offered none. She was offered a trap, baited with fine words. "We all desire peace," says Lloyd George, "but it must be a real peace." And then—to quote his latest Guildhall speech—he finally continues:

"I have just returned from a council of war of the four great allied countries upon whose shoulders the burden of this terrible war falls. I can not give the conclusions reached there, but there were no delusions as to the magnitude of our task. Neither were there any doubts about the results. We looked all difficulties in the face, probed them, and made arrangements to deal with them.

"We separated with the feeling that if victory is difficult, defeat is impossible. There was no flinching, wavering, faintheartedness, or infirmity of purpose. There was grim resolution that at all costs we must achieve the high aims with which we accepted the challenge of the Prussian military caste and rid the world forever of its menace and save Europe from unspeakable despotism.

* * *

"After the war the world will be able to attend to its business in peace and in the future the best security for peace will be found when the nations of the world band themselves together to punish the first peace-breaker."

Nothing could be clearer than this. If the Hohenzollern and the Hapsburg could win the murder-war which for their own dynastic interests they precipitated upon mankind, or, as we said the other day, make a dog-fall of it, the world would not be fit to live in. Those German-Americans who wish to win it unfit themselves to be American citizens. Those Americans who wish it write themselves mongrels and traitors.

Germany will be better off without autocracy. Neither of the Kaisers is needful to the welfare of the German people upon whom to make for themselves a Roman holiday the two have inflicted ruthless slaughter. Nobody purposes wrong to the nations or the commonalty of Germany. Truly speaks the answer of the Allies to the note of the American President.

"It goes without saying that the Allies wish to liberate Europe from the brutal covetousness of Prussian militarism. It never has been their design, as has been alleged, to encompass the extermination of the German peoples and their political disappearance. That which they desire above all is to insure a peace upon the principles of liberty and justice, upon the invincible fidelity to international obligation with which the Government of the United States has never ceased to be inspired."

Now, let the President possess his soul in patience, because his latest obtrusion, as the *Courier-Journal* pointed out on the instant, was but to meddle and muddle.

HUSTLING BRYAN TO THE REAR

With the President and Congress only two days from a declaration of war against the Central Powers, Mr. Watterson
leveled his musket against the memorial which Mr. Bryan
sent to the national legislature in an effort to avert a declaration of war. Technically this article—the tenth in the war
group—would be classified under Personalities, and subheaded
Bryan, but the real topic of the editorial was the war. "A
plea for the Kaiser, a stab at the President and a sidestep
from national honor" was Mr. Watterson's summing up of
Mr. Bryan's final peace move.

On the Rampage Again

(April 4, 1917)

Mr. William Jennings Bryan addresses a memorial to Congress pleading that it do not issue a declaration of war against
Germany, nor proclaim "a state of war" between Germany and
the United States.

He is opposed to war. He would expunge the word from
the dictionary. He would expel the letters that spell it from the
alphabet. He recalls the old Georgia farmer who, in the wild-cat
banking days, came to Milledgeville and said to Robert Toombs,
at the time a State bank director, "Robert, the folks down our
way wants more money." To which Toombs, as was his wont, replied profanely, "How in the Hell are they going to get it?"
"Stomp it," says the farmer. "Well," answered Toombs, "if we
stamp it, how are we going to redeem it?" And, says the farmer,
emulating the Bryan logic, "Why, Robert, the folks down our way
is a'gin redemption."

Mr. Bryan would have a referendum. He would parley. He
believes in the talkee-talkee process of adjusting international
complications without regard to lingual, racial and political differences. He takes no account of conditions. "They can't put
you in jail for this," observed the lawyer in the Joe Miller story
to his incarcerated client. "But," replied the rueful client, "they
have put me in jail."

Mr. Bryan dwells upon the havoc of war. But he tells us
nothing new. Nor does he increase our horror, either by the
originality or the force of his statement. He does not touch
the actual situation at all. Did the Nobel prize obscure his
vision, or was it only the Chautauqua dates? What else could

have lured him from the walks and ways of a private citizen into the limelight of a Congressional memorialist?

That Mr. Bryan has been thrice a competing candidate for President of the United States gives to his utterances their only claim to public attention, for, in themselves, they are as a rule neither weighty nor striking. That he was thrice defeated for that great office constitutes, among many discouragements, a hope of the Republic. Such a man in the Chief Magistracy of a great Nation were in critical times like these a perpetual menace.

Conceding him sincerity, which it is not always easy to do in the face of systematic personal exploitation obviously aimed to advertise and promote his business as a peripatetic lecturer, his point of view is that of the copy-book moralist and his appeal to the rustic order of intelligence.

Sometimes—as in his free silver crusade—he has addressed himself to the baser motives of those who through the agency of cheap money would cheat their creditors of honest payment. To his teaching in this regard indeed we may ascribe many of the commercial immoralities of the time; the short turns of trade and barter; the prevailing disposition to obtain something for nothing and to get rich quick. Then as now his pretext was and is Wall Street. Wall Street had robbed the "peepul" by demonetizing silver—"let us flood the country with silver at the ratio of 16 to 1." Wall Street is robbing the country through foreign war profits and would rob it further by getting the country into the foreign war—"let us back the Germans and circumvent Wall Street."

Of course Mr. Bryan thinks, or says he thinks, that "the great newspapers" are whooping up the war sentiment and hurrying us into war. Why? The "great newspapers" have as much at stake as anybody. The patriotism of "the great newspapers" is as disinterested as the rest. The offense of "the great newspapers" is that they have refused to take Mr. Bryan at his own valuation; to accept his nostrums; to believe him other than a half-educated, commonplace person with a voice, a talking machine without a thinking apparatus.

Every paragraph of his petition to Congress embraces aid and comfort to Germany; contains a plea for the Kaiser and a stab at the President; suggests a sidestep from national honor and duty. He puts forward treaties that came to naught and forgets efforts made over and over again in the interest of peace. "The dispute with Germany has passed beyond the domain of diplomacy and some advise settlement by the sword," says he, and adds, "the metropolitan press, which tried to prevent the re-election of the President and failed, undismayed by a popular verdict of more than one-half million, now seeks to lash the country into a fury and urges the Government to take part in the European conflict," assuming that the re-election of Mr. Wilson was a declaration of peace at any price and that the friends of national safety, dignity and manhood are only those who opposed that re-election, a rank, false assumption.

From start to finish we have little other than this sort of thing. The following is a sample:

"Before you take this blood upon your hands consider, I pray you, first, that the wrongs which you would punish, cruel and unjustifiable as they are, are not intended primarily against this country, but are acts of desperation directed against other nations with which the defenders are at war. Second, that our land is not threatened with invasion, but that we are asked to go 3,000 miles for a chance to fight. Third, that we have not the excuse for going to war that the European nations had. They had no machinery for peace; we have a peace plan offered by this nation to the world and now embodied in thirty treaties with three-quarters of the population of the globe. The plan has the indorsement of the President, the commendation of the Senate, and the approval of the people at the polls. It provides for investigation of all disputes by an international tribunal before resort to war."

Here we have the language and the logic of the schoolboy. The acts of outlawry on land and sea, the murder of our citizens and the destruction of our industries, were merely "accidents" not meant for us, but because we got in the way, we got hurt. Most of them were "unfortunate casualties." The German propaganda with its organization of Kaiser reservists threatening us with civil war if we should resent it was the merest "incident." The *Lusitania* and other such happenings simply "served us right." They were "fair warnings." The Zimmermann scheme to array Mexico and Japan against us was "a diplomatic pleasantry." Finally, the "peace plan" which he parades was rejected by Germany and has since been torn to shreds by actual unquenchable and resistless war.

Forgetting all this, Mr. Bryan proceeds as if nothing had happened. He deals in pure chatter having no relation to actual conditions or speculative possibilities. Thus:

"Fortunately, these treaties compel us to employ the plan with Great Britain, France, Italy and Russia before going to war with them. Germany formally approved the plan, although no treaty has yet been concluded with her. Shall we repudiate our own plan the first time we have an opportunity to employ it? If, as the President recently declared, the American people do not want war, is it not worth while to try the peace plan before bringing upon the people the horrors of war? Until an attempt is made and fails, no one is able to say that it would be impossible to secure the suspension of 'ruthless' submarine warfare during the investigation for which the plan provides. Shall we deny to ourselves the credit of trying to settle the dispute with the treaty plan?

"And is it not worth while to do our part in trying to avoid injury? Would it not be better, as well as cheaper, for the Government to carry on its own vessels such Americans as must go to Europe rather than engage in war to vindicate the rights of citizens to disregard all risks and ride upon belligerent ships?

"Is it not worth while to separate passengers from contraband cargoes, so that the captains of passenger ships can give their entire attention to the safety of the passengers? Our nation is the world's foremost advocate of peace. If we go to war it should be for a cause which history will justify.

"If you reach the conclusion that nothing but war will satisfy the nation's honor, is it too much to ask that by a referendum you consult the wishes of those who must, in case of war, defend the nation's honor with their lives?"

In the midst of a great conflagration this visionary—to apply no worse name to him—would take out insurance papers, not to say discuss the original architectural plans. He may be answered in a sentence; we are invaded; not only is our country, but our political existence is menaced; and, except we help to put the Hohenzollerns and the Hapsburgs out of business—to Hell with them—we are lost. There is no alternative.

THE PULITZER PRIZE EDITORIALS

The next two articles were written to signalize the entrance of the United States into the war, a conclusion of which Mr. Watterson had never had any doubt since August, 1914, although for a long period he had not been quite clear as to how the war was to be entered. "Vae Victis" was introduced by a curious old backwoods invocational song, "The Hunters of Kentucky," and both articles confidently assumed that Berlin would be the goal of the doughboys. Those were the days when the vision of an armistice, with Germany uninvaded, would have been regarded as a craven dream.

For these two articles Mr. Watterson was solemnly invested by Columbia University with the Pulitzer Prize for 1917, a recognition which astonished and pleased him. "The gander-legged boys in the City Editor's room will find out that the old man is a promising journalist," he said, and sent the prize money to a war fund.

"Vae Victis"

(April 7, 1917)

"Rally round the flag, boys"—Uncle Sam's Battle song;
"Sound the bold anthem! War dogs are howling;
Proud bird of Liberty screams through the air!"
—The Hunters of Kentucky.

It is with solemnity, and a touch of sadness, that we write the familiar words of the old refrain beneath the invocation to the starry banner, the breezy call of hero-breeding bombast quite gone out of them; the glad shout of battle; the clarion note of defiance; because to us, not as to Nick of the Woods and his homely co-mates of the forest, the rather as to the men of '61, comes this present call to arms.

We may feel with the woman's heart of Rankin, of Montana, yet repudiate with manly disdain the sentimental scruples of Kitchin, of North Carolina.

There are times when feeling must be sent to the rear; when duty must toe the line; when the aversion brave men have for fighting must yield to the adjuration, "Give me liberty, or give me death!" That time is now upon us.

Unless Patrick Henry was wrong—unless Washington and the men of the Revolution were wrong, that time is upon us. It is a lie to pretend that the world is better than it was; that men are truer, wiser; that war is escapable; that peace may be had for the planning and the asking. The situation which without any act of ours rises before us is as exigent as that which rose before the Colonists in America when a mad English King, claiming to rule without accountability, asserted the right divine of Kings and sent an army to enforce it. A mad German Emperor, claiming partnership with God, again elevates the standard of right divine and bids the world to worship, or die.

From the beginning the issue was not less ours than of the countries first engaged. Each may have had ends of its own to serve. Nor were these ends precisely alike. At least France—to whom we owe all that we have of sovereignty and freedom—and

Belgium, the little David of Nations—fought to resist invasion; wanton, cruel invasion; to avert slavery, savage, pitiless slavery. Yet, whatever the animating purpose—whatever the selfish interests of England and Russia and Italy—the Kaiser scheme of world conquest justified it.

In us it sanctifies it. Why should any American split hairs over the European rights and wrongs involved when he sees before him grim and ghastly the mailed figure of Absolutism with hand uplifted to strike Columbia where these three years she has stood pleading for justice, peace and mercy? God of the free heart's hope and home forbid!

Each of these three years the German Kaiser was making war upon us. He was making war secretly, through his emissaries in destruction of our industries, secretly through his diplomats plotting not merely foreign but civil war against us, and, as we now know, seeking to foment servile and racial insurrection; then openly upon the high seas levying murder upon our people and visiting all our rights and claims with scorn and insult—with scorn and insult unspeakable—at this moment pretending to flout us with ignominy and contempt. Where would the honest pacifist draw the line?

Surely the time has arrived—many of us think it was long since overdue—for calling the braves to the colors. Nations must e'en take stock on occasion and manhood come to a showdown. It is but a truism to say so.

Fifty years the country has enjoyed surpassing prosperity. This has overcommercialized the character and habits of the people. Twenty-five years the gospel of passivism, with "business is business" for its text, has not only been preached—indiscriminately—oracularly—without let or hindrance, but has been richly financed and potentially organized. It has established a party. It has made a cult, justifying itself in a fad it has called Humanity—in many ways a most spurious humanity—and has set this above and against patriotic inclination and duty.

Like a bolt out of the blue flashed the war signal from the very heart of Europe. Across the Atlantic its reverberations rolled to find us divided, neutral and unprepared. For fifteen years a body of German reservists disguised as citizens have been marching and counter-marching. They grew at length bold enough to rally to the support of a pan-German scheme of conquest and a pro-German propaganda of "kultur," basing its effrontery in the German-American vote, which began its agitation by threatening us with civil war if we dared to go to war with Germany. There followed the assassin sea monsters and the airship campaign of murder.

All the while we looked on with either simpering idiocy, or

dazed apathy. Serbia? It was no affair of ours. Belgium? Why should we worry? Foodstuffs soaring—war stuffs roaring —everybody making money—the mercenary, the poor of heart, the mean of spirit, the bleak and barren of soul, could still plead the Hypocrisy of Uplift and chortle: "I did not raise my boy to be a soldier." Even the *Lusitania* did not awaken us to a sense of danger and arouse us from the stupefaction of ignorant and ignoble self-complacency.

First of all on bended knee we should pray God to forgive us. Then erect as men, Christian men, soldierly men, to the flag and the fray—wherever they lead us—over the ocean— through France to Flanders—across the Low Countries to Koln, Bonn and Koblens—tumbling the fortress of Ehrenbreitstein into the Rhine as we pass and damming the mouth of the Moselle with the débris of the ruin we make of it—then on, on to Berlin, the Black Horse Cavalry sweeping the Wilhelmstrasse like lava down the mountainside, the Junker and the saber rattler flying before us, the tunes being "Dixie" and "Yankee Doodle," the cry being, "Hail the French Republic—Hail the Republic of Russia —welcome the Commonwealth of the Vaterland—no peace with the Kaiser—no parley with Autocracy, Absolutism and the divine right of Kings—to Hell with the Hapsburg and the Hohenzollern!"

War Has Its Compensations

(April 10, 1917)

I

The man who is for peace at any price—who will fight on no provocation—for no cause—is apt to be either what men call "a poor creature," or an impostor set on by ulterior considerations. He may have an unworthy motive, or a selfish interest, or he may be a victim of the coward's fear of battle, or be obsessed by the doctrinaire's theory of universal brotherhood. But, craven or crank, or scheming rogue, he dishonors the noble heritage of manhood which, being common to us all, is only prized and extolled in conspicuous cases of sacrifice or prowess.

Pacifism, as it has shown itself in these times of emergency, has been compounded of each of these ingredients. But it would not have shown itself so strong if it had not been definitely organized, nor definitely organized if it had not been sufficiently financed. The Hague Arbitration movement, backed in this country by the Carnegie Foundation—actually started by the dethroned Czar of Russia—proposed a benefaction to humankind which few if any were disposed to question. It built itself upon a generally accepted truth. The gospel of "peace on earth, good-will to men," was preached as never before. Professional warriors arrayed themselves in its behalf. Civilized nations flocked to the new religion and raised the benign standard. Many treaties embodying its aims were negotiated. One, and one alone, of the great Powers held out. That was Germany. Why, we now see clearly what we then did not see at all.

How much, if any, of the Carnegie Foundation money has been applied to the recent agitations against war with Germany, we know not. The activities of Mr. Bryan and of Dr. Jordan would lead to the conclusion that it has not been idle, or grudging, since neither of them works for nothing. But it is quite certain that it has been cunningly supplemented and enormously increased by money sent from Berlin to maintain a propaganda to divide our people and paralyze our Government. The prosecution of this now becomes treason and the pacifist who adheres to it is a traitor.

The conspirator who, claiming to be a pacifist, engaged in the nefarious business will be at no loss to save his skin. If he be a German emissary sent over for the purpose he has only to slip away. If he be a Kaiser reservist masquerading as an American citizen he can shift his foot and change his coat. If he be a selfish politician of the Stone-La Follette variety, with an eye on the Hyphenated Vote, he can wink his other eye, hoist the flag and sing "The Star-Spangled Banner" as lustily as the rest.

Those who are most in danger and only in danger are the honest simpletons who stick to it that war is crime; that we have no case against Germany, but, if we have, that it will keep; who go around mouthing socialistic and infidelistic platitudes about a paradisaic dreamland which exists nowhere outside their muddled brains. They cannot see that we have pursued peace to the limit and that peace longer pursued will prove more costly than war. Perverse and egotistical, prompted by the half truths of defective education, uninspired by ideals having any relation to the state of the country, or the spiritual needs of existence, they will not stop their vain chatter until, obstructing enlistments, or menacing public works, they land in jail.

It is grievous that this should be so. Yet it were not occasion for serious comment except that there is a middle class of nondescripts who are more numerous than an earnest and luminous patriotism would have them; men, who were born without enthusiasm and have lived to make money; men, with whom "business is business"; men who are indifferent to what happens so it does not happen to them; in short, men who recall the citation from "The Cricket on the Hearth," put into the mouth of Caleb Plummer:

> "There was a jolly miller and he lived upon the Dee.
> He sang to himself, 'I care for nobody and nobody cares for me.'"

"a most equivocal jollity," as Dickens does not fail to remark.

These people have sprung from the over-commercialism of fifty years of a kind of uncanny prosperity. Their example has affected injuriously the nation's reputation and has trenched perilously upon the character and habits of the people. It needs to be checked. They need a lesson. Nothing short of the dire exigencies which have come upon us would reach a mass so dense and stoic, so paltry and sordid, so unworthy of the blessings which the heroism of the fathers has secured them. That check and lesson they are about to receive. War is not wholly without its compensations.

II

The woman who is for peace at any price—whose imagination is filled with the horror of war—who, true to her nature, shrinks from bloodshed—is not as the man who skulks from the line and lowers alike the flag of his country and his manhood. Ah, no! Peace is the glory of woman. Not upon the soul-stirring field of battle—the rather in the dread field hospital after the battle—are her trophies to be found.

Well may she stand out against the strife of nations—yet equally with brave men she has her place in the orbit of duty and valor—and, when there is no peace, when war has come, the woman who whines "I did not raise my boy to be a soldier" forfeits her right and claim to be considered only a little lower than the angels, dishonors the genius of Womanhood and removes herself from the company and category of the heroic mothers of the world.

War, horrible as war is—"Hell," as a great warrior said it was—is not without its compensations. No man has more than one time to die. In bringing the realization of death nearer to us war throws a new light upon life. The soldier is a picked man. Whether he be a soldier in arms or a soldier of the cross, his courage, his loyalty, his love and faith challenge the confidence of men and the adoration of women. If he falls he has paid his mortal debt with honor. If he survives, though crippled, he is not disabled. His crutch tells its own story and carries its mute appeal, and there is an eloquence, though silent, resistless, in the empty sleeve.

Christendom stands face to face with the dispersion of some

of its cherished ideals. There is much in its Bible that must needs be retranslated and readjusted. Although this will arouse the theologians, they will have to meet it.

Where this present cataclysm will leave us no man can foresee. Our world is, and will still remain, a world of sin, disease and death. This no man can deny. Science is minimizing disease. Death being certain, can creeds or statutes extirpate sin? Can they change the nature of man?

Before all else they must chasten it. For two thousand years theologic controversy has not only kept the world at war, but has driven its inhabitants further apart. It may be that this world war has come to cleanse the earth and to bring all tribes and races to a better understanding of what Christendom is, since there is no reason to doubt that the essential principles of Christianity will continue to dominate the universe.

'Tis a long way, we are told, to the Tipperary of Hibernia, but yet a longer to the Millennial Tipperary of Scriptural mythology. The Christ-child must be born again in the heart of man. At this moment it is not the star of Bethlehem that shines. It is the luminary of the war god. The drums beat as for the men of old. "To your tents, O Israel," comes the word out of the deeps of the far away, and from highway and byway, as if in answer, the refrain "Tramp, tramp, tramp, the boys are marching."

Yet the Associated Press dispatches carry the following:

"Washington, April 7.—Continuation of the pacifist fight on President Wilson's war programme was forecast to-day when the fifty Representatives who voted against the war resolution received the following identic telegram from Lelia Fay Secor, secretary of the Emergency Peace Federation:

"'On behalf of the Emergency Peace Federation I thank you for your patriotic stand in opposition to war. May I request that you communicate at once with Representative Kitchin, to whom I have written a letter suggesting co-operation between ourselves and the pacifists in congress.'

"Mr. Kitchin is at his home in North Carolina and details of the scheme outlined in the letter to him could not be learned. He announced before leaving Washington that his opposition to the War programme would end with his vote against the resolution.

"'Scissors!' shrieks Lelia Fay.

"'Scissors!' cries good Mrs. Garrison Villard."

And away off yonder from the limb of a tree the Dickey Bird, impersonated by Claude Kitchin, responds, "Not on your life, ladies!"

THE KAISER MUST NOT BE DEALT WITH

In the first flush of the war-days in the United States, "no peace with Potsdam," the Wattersonian slogan in the thirteenth article of this group, could not even have started an argument. Nobody then dreamed of the armistice in the wood of Compiègne, with Germany uninvaded and the German armies intact. The nation was in a war of undoubted long duration and there must be an overwhelming victory, no matter how long it required.

In this article, the editor paid his final respects to those German-Americans who, prior to 1917, had openly attacked him. The counsel that there must be no further negotiation with the Hohenzollern—"to Hell with him"—was identically pursued by the President nineteen months later when the German government sued for an armistice.

No Peace with Potsdam

(April 24, 1917)

The Romanoffs are gone—to Hell with the Hohenzollerns and the Hapsburgs—but, first and foremost the Hohenzollerns; the vilest of the vile; the rottenest of the rotten; no peace with them; no peace with Germany until they are exterminated.

First out of the box, the President should urge this upon Balfour and Viviani. The decisive word should go forth from the White House. America should proclaim to the world that Freedom will never be safe, peace secure, until an end is put to the obsession that the Kaiser is God with which the Hohenzollern has inoculated the German mind.

Let us recall two shocking examples. They will suffice to show the impious character of the man and the gullible character of the people. In his speech to the recruits on parade at Potsdam the Kaiser said:

"Only one is Master in the Empire, and I am that one; I will tolerate no other.

"I represent Monarchy by the grace of God.

"You must all have one will, and that is My will; there is only one law, and that is My law.

"If I order you to shoot down your relatives, brothers—yes, even your parents—you must obey Me without murmuring."

This reads like a travesty. Yet word for word it is what the Kaiser actually said. It underlies his whole case. In his "Proclamation" of the 13th of September, 1914, he profanely shouted:

"The spirit of God has descended upon Me because I am German Emperor. I am the instrument of the Most High. I am His sword. His representative on earth. Woe and Death to those who oppose My will. Death to the infidel who denies My mission! Let all the enemies of the German nation perish! God demands their destruction—God, who by My mouth summons you to carry out His decrees."

Coming down to brass tacks and boot heels, taking account of the situation and stock of the record, especially the Kaiser's recent promise of reform, our esteemed contemporary, the Indianapolis *News,* says:

"The plain truth is—and it might as well be spoken—that the present war is one between the so-called common people everywhere and the Hohenzollern and Hapsburg families. the *Courier-Journal* has not always been parliamentary in its discussion of the war and the problems growing out of it, but it has come nearer the truth than those cowards who have tried to carry water on both shoulders. . . . The point for us to remember is that we are at war, not with a few submarine commanders who are willing to commit murder, under orders, but with a system that must be destroyed. We and the Entente Allies have a common enemy and we should act together against him. There would be no submarine murders were there no Hohenzollern government."

It is strange that the honest American Germans have not seen the truth long ago that it is this Kaiser, who has posed so long as a superman, who by the assertion of his imperial absolutism, has plunged the world into the direst cataclysm of destruction and slaughter since time began.

It is he, and he alone, who whether exploited by tyrannous, unreflecting militarism or exploiting it, has wrecked the Great German Empire. He has lost every rood of its colonies, annihilated all its splendid commerce, desolated the land in ruin, crushed its people in poverty and famine, filled the muck of the trenches, the reek of the prisons, the maws of the buzzards, with the millions of its best manhood and made Kaiser imperialism abhorred and despised of all humankind.

Yet whether they saw it or not, this Kaiser sees it. He sees that the hour of reckoning is near; that the people whom he can deceive no longer will turn from his victims into his judges; that unless he concedes them part of the rights so long denied them, they will take all their rights? So, this self-elected partner of Jehovah pretends to be willing to become a partner of the people, whom he has trampled as mire under his feet, in the hope that by thus surrendering his claims to infallibility and omnipotence he may save his throne to himself and his long-necked, receding-chinned progeny?

Be sure that it is all pretense. He does not mean it. His kind of reform is not to come till after the war. Meanwhile let it be remembered that no Hohenzollern was ever known to keep a promise.

No peace is with the Hohenzollern. Wilhelm must walk the plank. There is no hope for Germany till he is out and down, dead and done for. We must destroy him if we have to fight for years. The blood of innumerable brave men will have been shed in vain if this ridiculous and archaic lunatic is permitted to retain one vestige of power. He tries to impose his will upon the world. By the world he must be judged and not by his besotted subjects. When he sought world-dominion he ceased to possess the right to have his fate decided solely by his own people. He must be dealt with by the nations he sought to ruin and enslave, by the peoples he is enslaving today; and there must be no paltering with any foolish sentimentalists who fear to see him treated as he deserves.

They are wide of the mark who think that if left to themselves the Germans will overcome the Imperial will and democratize their own institutions.

Politically the Germans are sheep, and even in their excesses they are merely artificially maddened sheep. There is not the smallest prospect of an internal movement in Germany against Kaiserism until the German armies have been finally routed in the field. When that day dawns anything may happen; but those who know German domestic politics best declare that Socialist outbursts in the Reichstag are humbug. The only sincere opponents of the existing order of things in Germany are the handful of Minority Socialists who are mostly under lock and key. The Majority Socialists who pretend to attack the Government hold the funds of the party and are subservient tools of the authorities. They are permitted to talk freely to deceive the Russian extremists.

There is not a breath of liberty stirring over the stagnant and miasmatic waters of Prussian absolutism. There never has been liberty in Germany, and it is not at all clear that the Germans want liberty or would know what to do with it if they had it. Politically they seem to like to be kicked and driven in herds.

Germany may in the end be regenerated from within, but never spontaneously. The pressure must come from without. Refusal to treat with the Hohenzollerns will be no empty threat. It will represent the considered verdict of the world, and it will sink into the German mind. The sheep will realize its meaning when the German armies are overthrown and when they see the ruin to which their leaders have brought them. To Hell, therefore, with the Hohenzollerns and the Hapsburgs!

FROM THE MAN WHO STARTED IT

When the news of the Kaiser's abdication was received, the *Courier-Journal* sought an interview with him, who, as early as September 3, 1914, proclaimed as the future slogan of the war "To Hell with the Hohenzollerns and the Hapsburgs!" Although the war was strictly in Europe and only thirty days old when this great exclamation appeared in the editorial columns of the *Courier-Journal*, Henry Watterson, then its Editor, foresaw that the Kaisers must go and that the United States must intervene to accomplish it.

From that date forward, in the face of attack, abuse and deprecation from people, press and pulpit, Mr. Watterson stuck to his task of educating the whole world. He knew that the military ideals and the conception of Kultur as personified in the Hohenzollern and the Hapsburg dynasties could not exist on the same planet with the American conception of liberty, that one or the other must be crushed, and he set out to show why. Events, as he knew they would, came to his aid, and the sinking of the *Lusitania* awakened the United States to the fact that it could not stay out of the conflict. Pounding away at his great principle, Mr. Watterson lived to see his country take it up through the President and to witness the return to his subscribers' fold of many readers who had opposed him and had then discovered how true was his inspiration.

Mr. Watterson was at his home, Mansfield, near Jeffersontown, on the afternoon of Nov. 11, 1918, when the *Courier-Journal* telephoned the news to him.

"You started it," he was told. "The Hohenzollern has now followed the Hapsburg into the hell of abdication on the *Courier-Journal's* fiftieth anniversary. Will you make some comment upon it? He replied:

"The *Courier-Journal's* abjuration touching the Hohenzollerns and the Hapsburgs has been answered sooner than I expected. Its prophecy that in thirty-five years there will not be a crowned head in Europe will also come true. It has been for a long time obvious that autocracy was on the down grade. This is a poor era for Kings, Kaisers and other figure-heads. The world is moving toward self-government. Each man thinks himself to wear the purple. Let us put upon the Kaiser's tomb Ben Jonson's inscription over the grave of a dead pig:

> " 'Whilst he lived he lived in clover;
> When he died he died all over.' "

THE LEAGUE—AND FINIS

August 7, 1918, his stock and enough more to transfer control of the *Courier-Journal* and the *Louisville Times* having been purchased by Judge Robert Worth Bingham, of Louisville, Mr. Watterson became, by his own selection of title, the Editor Emeritus. The American press "chattered," as he expressed it, about that designation, but Mr. Watterson said that the *Courier-Journal* was as much an institution as Harvard College and had a right to an Emeritus if it wanted one. For a little less than two years—or until April 2, 1919—the Editor Emeritus wrote for the *Courier-Journal* a number of articles on what pleased or interested him. But as the League of Nations came more into the foreground of fact, and as he totally disagreed with the *Courier-Journal's* espousal of the plan, he determined to take down his name from the mast-head where it had been for nearly fifty-one years and to relinquish his title and his very comfortable salary. In the subjoined group are a typical writing upon the subject of the League; and the notice of the final severance (by Mr. Watterson's express request) of all bonds between the Editor Emeritus and the *Courier-Journal*.

From that date until his death at Jacksonville, December 21, 1921, Mr. Watterson busied himself with such work against the League as he found strength to do, and he honestly rejoiced in its defeat by the Senate. It was the last great American issue which attracted his efforts, for, although he wrote a line or two in 1920 in favor of "Cox the Unbeatable" and for a few weeks thrilled at the prospect of another Democratic victory, he gave up hope in July that Mr. Harding could be defeated.

During the year and month he lived after November, 1920, the phantasmagoria of the world passed like a mist before his eyes, and he surveyed with languor the fevered concerns of mankind. No emotion stirred his pulses, except that intense

love of wife and family which had long since balanced the
sorrows of life and had brought him joys far more substantial than the applause of his countrymen.

League of Nations

(March 5, 1919)

I

The League of Nations, so-called, is one of those pretty conceits which, after the manner of the copybook maxims, are easier
recited than followed, or applied. Unlike the wedding gown of
the bride of the Vicar of Wakefield, such sayings are current in
the popular speech because of a fine, glossy exterior and
a melodious sound—not that they will bear analysis or wear
well. We know that honesty is the best policy, but no better
motive is repugnant to honest men, whilst thieves cannot see
it at all.

Inevitably Woodrow Wilson would be caught by such a
whimsy as the League of Nations. We must do the President no
wrong. He is our file leader. He possesses a fruitful, speculative mind. He is unafraid. What a journalist he would have
made! I wonder that, instead of the schoolroom, when groping
for a livelihood, he did not take to the newspaper. In France
the statesmen usually begin with journalism.

But the League of Nations! It is a fad. Politics, like society
and letters, has its fads. In society they call it fashion and in
literature originality. Politics gives the name of "issues" to its
fads. A taking issue is as a stunning gown, or "a best seller."
The President's mind wears a coat of many colors, and he can
change it at will, his mood being the objective point, not always
too far ahead, or clear of vision. Carl Schurz was wont to speak
of Gratz Brown as "a man of thoughts rather than of ideas."
I wonder if that can be justly said of the President. "Gentlemen
will please not shoot at the pianiste," adjured the superscription
over the music stand in the Dakota dive; "she is doing the best
that she knows how."

Already it is being proclaimed that Woodrow Wilson can have
a third nomination for the Presidency if he wants it—does a boy
want a pair of boots or a girl a new bonnet?—and nobody seems
shocked by it, which proves that the people grow degenerate and
foreshadows that one of these nights some fool with a spyglass
will break into Mars and let loose the myriads of warlike gyas-
cutes who inhabit that freak luminary, thence to slide down the
willing moonbeam and swallow us every one!

II

In a sense the Monroe Doctrine was a fad. Oblivious to Canada and British Columbia and the Spanish provinces, it warned the despots of Europe off the grass in America. We actually went to war with Mexico, having enjoyed two wars with England, and again and again we threatened to annex the Dominion. Everything betwixt hell and Halifax was Yankee preempted.

Truth to say, your Uncle Samuel was ever a jingo. But your Cousin Woodrow, enlarging on the original plan, would stretch our spiritual boundaries to the ends of the earth and make of us the moral custodian of the universe. This much, no less, he got of the school of sweetness and light in which he grew up.

I am a jingo myself. But a wicked, material jingo, who wants facts, not theories. If I thought it possible and that it would pay, I would annex the North Pole and colonize the Equator. It is, after the manner of the lady in the play, that the President "doth protest too much," which displeases me and where, in point of fact, I "get off the reservation."

That, being a politician and maybe a candidate, he is keenly alive to votes goes without saying. On the surface this League of Nations nonsense, having the word "peace" in big letters emblazoned both upon its forehead and the seat of its trousers—or, should I say, woven into the hem of its petticoat?—seems an appeal for votes. I do not believe it will bear discussion. In a way, it is tricky, tickling the ear without arresting or convincing the sense. There is nothing sentimental about the actualities of Government, much as public men seek to profit by arousing the passions of the people. Government is a hard and fast and dry reality. At best statesmanship can only half do the things it would. Its aims are most assured when tending a little leeward; its footing safest on its native heath. We have plenty to do on our own continent without seeking to right things on other continents. Too many of us—the President among the rest, I fear —miscalculate the distance between contingency and desire.

> "We figure to ourselves
> The thing we like; and then we build it up,
> As chance will have it on the rock or sand—
> When thought grows tired of wandering o'er the world,
> And homebound Fancy runs her bark ashore."

III

I am sorry to see the New York *World* fly off at a tangent about this latest of the Wilsonian hobbies. Frank Irving Cobb,

the editor of the *World,* is, as I have often said, the strongest
writer on the New York press since Horace Greeley. But he
can hardly be called a sentimentalist, as Greeley was, and there
is nothing but sentiment—gush and gammon—in the proposed
League of Nations.

It may be all right for England. There are certainly no flies
on it for France. But we don't need it. Its effects can only be
to tie our hands, not keep the dogs away, and even at the worst,
in stress of weather, we are strong enough to keep the dogs away
ourselves.

We should say to Europe: "Shinny on your own side of the
water and we will shinny on our side." It may be that Napoleon's
opinion will come true that ultimately Europe will be "all Cos-
sack or all republican." Part of it has come true already. Meanwhile it looks as though the United States, having exhausted the
reasonable possibilities of democracy, is beginning to turn crank.
Look at woman suffrage by Federal edict; look at prohibition by
act of Congress and constitutional amendment; tobacco next to
walk the plank; and then——! Lord, how glad I feel that I
am nearly a hundred years old and shall not live to see it!

Yet I love my country. Nor do I hate the hook-nosed tee-
totalers and short-haired angels—Carrie Catt and Anna Shaw.
And Rosalie Jones! But why tell tales out of school?

Under a Swiss dateline I read:

"German officers interned celebrated the birthday of the former Emperor at Lucerne, all of them drinking to his health, his
early return to Germany and his restoration to his former power."

Much as I think them mistaken, I take off my hat to their
fidelity. After all, what a pretty, if not a glorious, thing is
loyalty—love for one's native land—pride in its government and
institutions and emblems—the undiscerning, uncritical sense we
call patriotism. The late—the recent because still living—Kaiser
was not a thing of beauty, nor a joy forever. Yet they drink
to him. No more were the Stuarts; but they drank to them. I
know what it is. I have gone down to the seashore and, looking
westward, yearned—positively yearned—for the land across the
billows!

It is this sense that keeps me at the grindstone of the daily
newspaper. I need not work if I don't care to. I have a crust
of bread and a roof to cover me. I want to warn the people
against mischief. I would give them the benefit of long and varied
experience. I do not flatter them. I tell them plainly that they
are not much for beauty—that they have never been "nowhars
and don't know nothin'," as I am wont to say to the children—
but all in the way of affection, seeking nothing for myself. If
they don't like it they know what they can do and where they

may go. But, heavens! there is the dinner bell and the sound of a voice I never have ceased to heed!

Editorial in the *Courier-Journal*, April 2, 1919

Mr. Watterson retires as Editor Emeritus of the *Courier-Journal* with this issue. From 1868 until 1918 its editor, his brilliant, forceful and individual writings on public questions brought fame both for himself and this journal. Desiring to retire last August when control of the newspaper changed hands, he yet was persuaded to remain in the capacity of Editor Emeritus, through which connection he might continue to address the readers of the *Courier-Journal* while relieved of the active responsibilities of the editorship. He now requests his retirement, finding in conflict his views, opposing the League of Nations, and those of the *Courier-Journal*, favoring the proposal. His personality will continue to be an inspiration to *Courier-Journal* workers; his accomplishments, a standard of achievement; his name, one to be praised and loved. He has passed his seventy-ninth birthday. May he pass many another milestone before the world loses him as a companion or letters are deprived of the magic of his pen!

THE END